MEWAR RULERS AND THE BRITISH

MEWAR RULERS AND THE BRITISH

Edited by

S.R. BAKSHI

and

S.K. SHARMA

DEEP & DEEP PUBLICATIONS PVT. LTD.
F-159, Rajouri Garden, New Delhi-110027

MEWAR RULERS AND THE BRITISH

(THE GREAT RAJPUTS—6)

ISBN 81-7629-225-7

© 2000   S.R. BAKSHI
         S.K. SHARMA

All rights reserved with the Publisher, including the right to translate or to reproduce this book or parts thereof except for brief quotations in critical articles or reviews.

Typeset by PRINT INDIA, A-38/2, Phase I, Mayapuri, New Delhi-110064.

Printed in India at ELEGANT PRINTERS, A-38/2, Phase I, Mayapuri, New Delhi-110064.

Published by DEEP & DEEP PUBLICATIONS PVT. LTD., F-159, Rajouri Garden, New Delhi-110027. Phones: 5435369, 5440916.

Contents

    Preface   ix

1. **Antecedents**   1
   Hammir's Occupation of Chittor; Maharana Kshetrasimha (Kheta) (1364-1382 A.D.); Maharana Lakshasimha (Lakha) (1382-1397 A.D.); Lakha's Marriage with Rathor Rao Chunda's Daughter; Maharana Mokul; Relations with the Rathors of Mandor; Murder of Mokul.

2. **Throne Comes to Kumbha**   27
   Age of Kumbha at his Accession; So-called Battle of Sarangpur; Internal Troubles in Mewar.

3. **Relations with Malwa, Gujarat-Nagor**   44
   Relations with Malwa; Loss of Gagraun; Loss of Ajmer; Loss of Mandalgarh; Relations with Gujarat-Nagor.

4. **Relations with Rajput Chiefs**   70
   Settlement with Jodha Rathor; Relations with the Hadas of Bundi; Relations with Deora Chauhans of Sirohi and Abu; Relations with other Rajput Chiefs.

5. **Cultural Achievements**   85
   Literary Activity; Works of other Scholars; Scholars Associated with Court; Contribution of the Jains; Tapagachha Group; Painting; Architecture; Forts; Kumbhalgarh; Achalgarh; Chittorgarh; Temples; Ranpur Jain Temple; Ekalingji; Kumbhswami Temple; Shringar Chauri; Sculpture; Music; Religion; Vaishnavism; Jainism.

6. **Administrative and Economic Aspects**   118
   Fiscal Organisation; Other Taxes; Panchakula; Mandapika; Panchayats; Mewar Feudalism.

7. **Mewar and the British**   139

8. **Rising of 1857 and Mewar**   153
Situation in Mewar; Maharana Supports the Cause of the British; Mutinies at Nasirabad and Neemuch; Udaipur Troops Rescue British Refugees at Dungla; Rajput Chivalry Displayed at Kesunda; Pursuit of the Neemuch Mutineers; Stir in Udaipur Troops at Neemuch; Salumbar Chief Threat to the Maharana; British Reverses at Auwa and Kota; Maharana's Counsel to other Rajput Rulers; Occupation of Nimbahera by Mewar Troops; Attack of Neemuch; Tantia Tope in Mewar; Queen's Proclamation; Maharana's Congratulations; Khillat to Maharana; Nimbahera taken back from the Maharana; Recalcitrant Chiefs of Mewar; Towards a New Awakening.

9. **Resistance to the British**   190
Accession of Rana Shambhu Singh; *Sati* Affair on the Death of Maharana Swaroop Singh; Appointment of the Council of Regency; Measures to Suppress the *Sati* Custom; Maharana's Attendants and Relations Expelled from Udaipur; Direct Interference in the Internal Affairs; Thakur of Badnore Sentenced; Dismissal of Kothari Kesari Singh; British Government Approved Eden's Policy; Mehta Ajeet Singh's Case; Dismissal of Regency Council; Political Agent's Government (August 1863 to Nov. 1865); Unrest in Udaipur; Reforms by the Political Agent; Strike and Disturbance in Udaipur City; Punishment of Begun Chief; Resistance Calms Down.

10. **Beginning of Reforms**   214
Re-appointment of Kothari Singh; Maharana and the Chiefs; Reconciliation with the Salumbar Chief; The Succession Case of Amet Reopened; Reopaheli-Lamba Case; Deogarh Chief's Succession Fee Case; The Maharana Asserts his Suzerain Rights over Shahpura; Trial of Mehta Ajeet Singh; Extradition Treaty, 1868; Bhil Disturbances in the Hilly Tract; Illegal Detention of the British Prisoners; Maharana's Severe Measures against *Sati*; Cases of Witch-hunting; Ajmer *Durbar* of 1870; Establishment of Opium Scales at Udaipur; Administrative Reforms; Administration of Justices; Revenue Settlement; Changes in District Administration; Maharana Awarded with the Title of G.C.S.I.; Maharana's Serious Illness an Arrest of Mehta Pannalal and others; Personalty of Shambhu Singh.

11. **Maharana Sajjan Singh: Interference and Reforms**   248
    Attempt to Commit *Sati* by the Palace Ladies; Succession Dispute; Action against Sohan Singh; Regency Council's Government (Oct. 1874–Oct. 1876); Arrangements for Maharana's Education; Maharana attends Prince of Wales' Reception at Bombay; Viceroy's Visit to Udaipur; Gosain of Nathdwara; Expulsion of Maharana's Favourites from Udaipur; The Governor-General Disapprove's Col. Herberts Dealings; Maharana Invested with Ruling Powers; Maharana attends Delhi *Durbar* of 1877; Re-organisation to the State Council; Oppression of the Bhils in the Hilly Tract; Settlement Operations and Stir in the Peasants; Agreement Regarding Railway Line; Slavery, Traffic in Women and Cases of Infanticide; Salt Agreement; Bhil Disturbances in Hilly Districts; The Case of Mewar Portion of Merwara; Kalambandi with the Chiefs; Title of C.I.E. Conferred on Bakhta Singh; Banera Chief's Effort to be Independent of Mewar; Succession Dispute of Bohera Jagir; Administrative Changes; Various Measures of Reforms; History Department; Title of G.C.S.I Conferred on the Maharana; Personality of Sajjan Singh.

12. **Maharana Fateh Singh: Struggle for Internal Independence**   298
    Accession of Fateh Singh; Temporary Restrictions Placed upon the Maharana's Powers; Queen Victoria's Jubilee Celebrations; Visits of the Duke of Cannaught and Prince Albert; Completion of Revenue Settlement; Case of the 'Spurious' son of Sakat Singh; Maharana's Efforts to Gain Control of the Administration; Postponement of the Railway Project; Question of maintaining Imperial Service Troops; Seth's Affairs; Disagreement between the Resident and the A.G.G.; Wingate and Thompson Retire from Udaipur; Dismissal of Mehta Pannalal; Construction of Railway line from Chittor to Udaipur; Progress of Reforms.

13. **Setback for the Interference**   319
    Maharana Refuses to have a Dewan; Shyamji Krishna Verma and Harbhamji in Udaipur Service; Victoria's Diamond Jubilee Celebration; Famine Relief Measures; British Government Presses for Reforms; Withdrawal of Prohibitory Orders on Export of Cotton from Mewar; The Maharana asserts his Sovereignty over his Chiefs; Jawas Succession Case; Delhi *Durbar* of 1903; Visits of various Viceroys to

Udaipur; H.R.H. Prince of Wales Visit; Imperial Assemblage of 1911.

14. **Political Unrest: Fateh Singh's Abdication** 348
Anti-British Stir in Rajputana; Mewar: A Source of Trouble for the British Government; Imperial Interests and Mewar; Imperial Service Troops Raised in Mewar; Maharana's Cooperation in the Great War; Restriction on Poppy Cultivation in Mewar; Mica Mining Work Started in Mewar; Depreciation of the Value of British Rupee in Mewar; Question of Police Reforms in Mewar; Peasant Unrest; Delegation of Ruling Powers to the Maharaj Kumar; British Supremacy Restored in the Internal Affairs; Personality of Fateh Singh.

15. **The Assessment** 375

Index 386

Preface

An attempt has been made regarding Mewar rulers' relationship with the British Government. Their administrative, economic and cultural achievements have been highlighted. Beside the policy of the region regarding the Mutiny has been explained in chapter eight. The era of reforms and the problems faced by Maharana Sajjan Singh and Maharana Fateh Singh have been explained along with the political unrest and abdication of Maharana Fateh Singh.

The theme has been covered in fifteen chapters including an assessment. It mainly deals with the socio-economic, political and administrative developments in Mewar. It deals with its relations with Malwa and Gujarat, cultural achievements, Mewar and its relations with the British, commencements of the reforms, Maharana Sajjan Singh and Fateh Singh, political unrest and other problems for the rulers.

We have collected the material from several research institutions and libraries. These are Delhi University Library, Sapru House Library, Indian Council of Historical Research Library, Central Secretariat Library, Nehru Memorial Museum and Library and Jawaharlal Nehru University Library. We are grateful to these institutions for their academic support as well as to scholars whose writings were an asset to us to build up this theme.

S.R. BAKSHI
SRI KANT SHARMA

1

Antecedents

The medieval period of Indian history has acquired the character of one long narrative of the victory of Muslim arms over the Indian rulers, commonly called the Rajputs, who fell before the might of Islam like a motley crowd. The only resistance they offered was to bare their chest to receive the arrows and the spears of the Turkish invaders. The Muslim court chroniclers—the recognised sources of medieval Indian History—have exaggerated and have jubilently expressed the victories as meritorious achievements of their religion which according to them was invincible. Whatever set-backs or defeats they suffered are not to be found in their narratives. In this chain of defeats the stray cases of resistance offered by some of the Rajput chiefs naturally acquired a mythical form and the medieval bards found in such deeds, themes for weaving stories and reciting them in courts of the chiefs who successfully resisted the Turks and kept them out of their territories. One may admire the bravery with which the Rajputs sacrificed their lives but it would hardly be sober history to call them the traditional fighters in the defence of their home, hearth, religion and culture. The Rajputs hardly had any concept of country nor were they at any stage inspired by feelings of defending their religion. Correctly assessed, to the Rajput fighting was an important part of his life. He fought desperately in the battlefield, was more concerned with the display of valour and making the supreme sacrifice than winning the battle. Every battle was loss of so many flowers of Rajput manhood. Fighting for him was a part of a highly valued tradition irrespective of consequences. It is in this sequence that Mewar played an important role and occupied special place which deserve full consideration.

From the tenth century to the twelfth century we find a motley host of Rajput chiefs or Rajput groups (also called clans) constantly fighting each other. Their deeds of daring courage though admirable in appearance, hardly give any indication of their understanding of the political situation they were placed in. The powerful Pratihara Empire of northern India disintegrated to give rise to such groups as the Chahamanas (Chauhans), the Chandelas, the Paramars, the Chalukyas of Gujarat, the Kalachuris of Tripuri and the Gahadvalas of Kanauj. Bengal passed from the Palas to the Senas and the north-west came under the Shahis of Kabul. In the region of Mewar, the Guhilputras or Guhilots established themselves, but were too insignificant at early stages to play any positive role. These major groups in their turn were again sub-divided and remained fighting constantly amongst themselves. This neither gave peace to the country nor political stability to any of the powers. When the Arabs and the Turks came to the Rajput it was nothing more than entering a few more contestants in the "battle tournament."

The Chahamanas succeeded the Pratiharas as powerful ruling line, but they too were divided into various branches such as those of Ajmer, Ranthambhor, Nadol, Jalor, Sanchor, Devada, Lata and Madpat (Mewar). This wide distribution of the Chahamanas instead of making them a strong power only divided them resulting in their constant mutual wars. In the Marusthala the Guhilputras had established themselves. The geographical situation of the region and nature's bounty in bestowing the hill-fort of Chittor provided the Guhilputras with a shelter, which they fully exploited to maintain their position. However, for about two centuries, *i.e.* end of 10th to the last quarter of 12th century, they had to face the onslaught of the Paramars of Malwa, Chalukyas of Gujarat and the Chahamanas of Ajmer but managed to maintain their existence though precariously, always owing allegiance either to one or the other of the powerful neighbours. The centuries of hardship made the people of Marusthala or Medpat or Mewar hardy and desperate, ever ready to leave their homes for the wilderness whenever adversity so demanded.

The rise of Ghazanavides had resulted in the destruction of the Shahiya dynasty of Kabul and establishment of Turkish rule in the Punjab. The raids of Mahmud Ghazni had given a foretaste of the Turkish invasion but the Rajputs were incapable of learning any lesson from adversity. When Muhammad Ghori Muizuddin Muhammad bin Sam occupied the Punjab in 1186, it was hardly taken as a warning by the Chahamanas, the then dominating power in northern India. The defeat of Prithvi Raj Chauhan III in 1192 A.D. in the second battle of Tarain resulted in the establishment of Turkish rule in northern India. The Turks had a religion and ethos quite different from that of the Rajputs. Their religion, Islam, gave them an impelling force to conquer and spread their faith. To them victory in the battlefield was more important irrespective of the means through which it was achieved. While the Rajputs believed only in fighting, the Turks always strengthened their valour and courage with the use of ruse in the battlefield. While the Turks were establishing themselves in places like Delhi, Ajmer and Nagaur and were gradually spreading in the Doba the Guhilots of Guhilputras occupied the regions of Bagad, Chittor and Sisoda.

Chittor under Maharawal Jaitrasimha (1213-1251 A.D.) began to prosper and started playing a dominating role in Rajasthan. This was the result of the ability of Jaitrasimha and the contemporary political situation. The exit of the Chahamanas of Ajmer dislocated the Chahamana power and kept the Sultans of Delhi busy in establishing and consolidating their hold over the plains of northern India for almost the whole of the thirteenth century. Of the other powers, the Chalukyas of Gujarat and the Paramars of Malwa the traditional enemies of Mewar for two centuries were called upon to face the new rising power of the Yadavas of Devagiri which kept them busy in direction other than Mewar. These factors led to the rise of Mewar (Chittor) as a power and there are sufficient number of inscriptions of the period indicating the position enjoyed by the rulers of Mewar.

However, the rulers of Mewar completely failed to understand the political implications of the Turks gradually emerging as an imperial power. Various inscriptions in Mewar record the unsuccessful invasion by Turks of the regions of Mewar and Rajasthan; but the Guhils of Chittor and the Chauhans of Jalor instead of reading the signs on the wall and patching up their petty differences and offering a solid resistance to the spreading Turkish power of Delhi, continued to fight each other for possession of small tracts of arid land.

The ascendancy of Mewar as mentioned earlier began with the accession of Guhilaputra Jaitrasimha as Maharawal on the throne of Mewar. He ruled from 1213 to 1251 A.D. and during this period Mewar achieved a position she had never enjoyed before.[1] Such titles and epithets as *Maharajahdhiraja, Samastarajavali-Samalankrita; Maharajadhiraja-Bhagawan-narayana-dakshina-uttaradhisamana-mardana* used for him in some of the contemporary literature indicate that Mewar had come to occupy a respectable position in the 'State system' of northern India of the thirteenth century. He also successfully checked the Turkish incursions into Mewar. Jaitrasimha shifted his capital from Nagarhrda (Nagda) to Aghata and fortified Chitrakuta (Chittor) giving it new dimensions as a place of strategic importance and capable of playing important role in the future.

Jaitrasimha was succeeded as Maharawal by his son Tejsimha in 1251 A.D. who continued to rule most probably up to 1270 A.D., the earliest date known of his son and successor Samarsimha. Samarsimha ruled as Maharawal up to 1302 A.D. The thirty-two years of his rule over Mewar mark the most fateful years of the Guhilputras. His contemporaries, Hammir of Ranthambhor and Kanhadadeva of Jalor, were also powerful chiefs. But the three rulers could never think of combining and ousting the Turks from Delhi during the weak successor of Balban and confusion following the accession of Jalaluddin Khalji. Instead they wasted their energies in mutual warfare. In the meantime the character and policy of the Delhi Sultanate with the accession of Alauddin Khalji underwent a tremendous change. It acquired a new vigour and found on the throne of Delhi a monarch full of imperialistic zeal. Alauddin Khalji wanted to establish an empire embracing the entire length and the breadth of Hindustan. In his scheme the existence of independent Rajput States within striking distance of Delhi did not fit in. Naturally, Mewar could not avoid facing the Khalji arms for long. But Alauddin wanted to reduce them piecemeal.

Thus when he sent his army to Gujarat he asked for passage through Jalor which Kanhadadeva, the Sonegra chief, refused.[2] But when the same demand was made of Samarasimha, he obliged the Sultan. Maybe he was annoyed with the Gujarat chief for the loss of Abu, or may be he thought that by obliging the Sultan he would save his kingdom. Ojha and some other scholars have tried to prove that it is wrong to assume that Samarsimha granted passage through his country, but in the final analysis if we take into consideration all the evidence we find that Samarsimha did concede the passage to Ulugh Khan and his army through his Kingdom.[3] If Samarsimha expected that by following such a policy he would save his kingdom, he was wrong. Fate did not permit him to live to see his mistake. He died in 1302 A.D. leaving Mewar to his son Ratnasimha (1302-1303 A.D.) to face the brunt of the Khalji attack.

Alauddin Khalji captured Chittor on Monday, 26th August, 1303 after a prolonged seige extending for a period of more than six months. The usual practice of *Jauhar* was performed, and Muslim rule was established in Chittor with Prince Khizr Khan, the eldest son of the Sultan as its Governor and the city was given the name of Khizrabad.[4]

The Barwa Bhats and the Khyat writers have weaved in another story with this heroic defence of Chittor. According to them after Maharawal Ratna Simha was killed Rana Lakshamansimha of Sisoda took over the charge. While defending the fort Lakshmansimha had a dream in which he saw '*Van Mata*,' the protecting deity of Mewar, demanding that "I am hungry for the blood of kings. Let me drink the blood of seven of those who have won the diadem and only then the city may be saved." In accordance with the wishes of the goddess the sons of the Rana were successively raised to the throne and every one of them sallied forth each day at the head of a little band of brave followers and laid down his life in the defence of Chittor. But when the turn of the last of his sons came the Rana's courage failed him. He was afraid that it would be the extinction of his line. Substituting himself for his son, he ordered the latter to escape to Kailwara forests. The entire story is the outcome of confusion in the mind of the bards caused by various stories which came into circulation. The *Vam Mata's* demand for the blood of the crowned kings of the house is only a concoction to glorify the house. If she was a protecting deity of the house, she should have protected the house and demanded the blood of the enemy and not of those whom she was supposed to protect. However, the currency of such a story at least indicates credulity of the Rajputs and the part superstition played in their life.

Mewar remained under the direct control of Alauddin Khalji with Khizr Khan as the Governor with Chittor as his administrative headquarters. There is sufficient evidence to indicate that Khizr Khan remained at Chittor as Governor for about ten years and during this period he ordered construction of a bridge over the river Gambhiri and a *maqbara* outside Chittor bearing an inscription dated 11th May, 1312.[5] Firishta also conveys the impression that Malik Kafur intended to meet the crown prince at Chittor in AH 711/1311-12 A.D. while he was marching to the south.[6] Mehta Nainsi has at this stage interpolated the story of Sonegra Chauhan's occupation of Chittor. He writes that on the eve of the fall of Jalor (v.s. 1368/1311 A.D.), Kanhadadeva sent out of the fort his brother Maldeva (*Muchhalo*) along with his sons to preserve the line. Maldeva began to plunder the territories occupied by the Sultan. However, his differences were patched up when he saved the life of Sultan Alauddin and the latter in turn granted the fort of Chittor to Maldeva where he ruled for seven years before his death.[7] Mehta Nainsi writing much later after the incident seems to have been misled and slightly confused. We have epigraphic evidence at Chittor indicating that it continued in the possession of the Sultans of Delhi. It is a fragmentary inscription in Persian at Chittor and praises Sultan Tughlaq Shah and his nephew Asat-ud-din,[8] who was the Governor of Chittor and continued in the same capacity after the accession of Muhammad bin Tughlaq Shah. It was Sultan Muhammad bin Tughlaq Shah who appointed Maldeva, the Sonegra chief as Governor of Chittor. Dr. K.S. Lal seems to have followed Mehta Nainsi in assigning the governorship of Chittor to Maldeva in the reign of Alauddin Khalji whereas in reality it came to Maldeva during the reign of Muhammad bin Tughlaq Shah.

The statement of Firishta[9] that the people of Chittor (here it may refer to the country and not to the fort) in course of time towards the close of Alauddin's reign became so daring that they threw away the Mussalmans from the battlement of the fortress

Antecedents ✦ 7

after tying their hands and necks, truly speaking, refers to the attack of Maharana Bhawansimha, one of the brothers of Maharawal Ratan Singh and belonging to the group of the family members sent out of the fort by Ratna Singh before its final fall in 1303 A.D. The Ranpur Jain temple inscription mentions Maharana Bhawansimha as victor of Alauddin Khalji.[10] Ever since the occupation of Chittor by Alauddin Khalji the Sisodias had been trying to recover it and in the process nine princes had already laid down their lives before Bhawansimha. Bhawansimha achieved temporary success. He seems to have entered the fortress at a period when it was not probably defended, but could not retain it though he succeeded in causing some damage to the garrison. The attempt of the Sisodias to capture the fort continued during the reign of Tughlaq Shah and Muhammad Tughlaq. According to Kaviraj Shyamal Dass, Muhammad Tughlaq wanted to crush the Sisodias and in the battles that were fought Lakshmansimha and his son Arisimha were killed but the younger son Ajaysimha escaped to the Kailwara region of the Aravali hills where he died soon after. In the meantime the region of Chittor had been assigned to Maldeva Sonegra of Jalor. By this assignment it was expected that a Rajput was best suited to keep in order the other Rajputs. But the Sonegras could never remain in peace at Chittor because of the depredation of the Sisodias.[11]

Hammir's Occupation of Chittor

During the exile from Chittor Arisimha, son of Lakshman-simha had married secretly in the Chandana family of Unua village and Hammir was born of this union. After the death of Arisimha, Ajaysimha had taken shelter in Kailwara and was nursing the injuries sustained in the Chittor engagement. During this period Munja Balecha began to give him trouble. Ajaysimha's two sons Sajansimha and Khemsimha failed to check Munja. Just then some followers of Arisimha brought Hammir from the Unua village, a lad of thirteen or fourteen years. Hammir promised to his uncle that he would capture Munja Balecha. Hammir received news that Munja Balecha was attending some festival in the village Semori in District of Godwar. He at once started for the place and in a sudden attack severed his head and brought it to his uncle. A difficult task so easily performed impressed the dying Ajaysimha so much that he at once put the *Tika* on the forehead of Hammir with the blood of Munja Balecha. Ajaysimha died soon after and thus at the age of thirteen or fourteen Hammir became the Maharana. This was not, of course, his final accession rather it was more or less a family function which had become a tradition in the Sisodia family ever since the fall of Chittor in 1303 A.D.

Maharana Hammir though young in age, started depredation of the region of Chittor then under Maldeo. The tradition has it that after making several unsuccessful attempts to capture Chittor, Hammir lost all hopes and started with a few of his faithful followers towards Dwarka. While he was staying in Khorgaon in Gujarat he heard about Barbari, daughter of Chakhra Charan, who was credited with powers of prophesy. Maharana Hammir went to pay his respects to Barbari who advised him to return to Kailwara where he would soon be able to recover Chittor. She also told him to accept any marriage offer that may come to him and also promised to supply him with horse through her son Baru who used to trade in horses. Hammir was impressed with the advice and returned to Kailwara where he very soon received five hundred horses brought by Baru. Hammir's position thus considerably improved and Maldeo to pacify Hammir offered his daughter in marriage to him. Hammir readily accepted the proposal. In this marriage Maldeo gave the following eight hilly districts to Hammir: Magra, Sernala, Girwa, Godwar, Barath, Shyalpatti, Merwara and Ghateka Chaukhala. Maldeo also gave Mehta Maujiram as *Kamdar* to look after these districts as well as the financial affairs of Maharana Hammir. Kaviraj Shyamal Dass places the occupation of Chittor by Hammir during the life time of Maldeo through the stratagem of Mehta Maujiram.[12] Tod's date of Hammir's occupation of Chittor is vague and his narrative is in many forms similar to the one already noticed by Kaviraj Shyamal Dass of course with slight variations.[13] Ojha mentions that Hammir started attacking the territories of Maldeo after his death and finally succeeded in capturing the fort from his son Jaisa round about the year v.s. 1383/1326 A.D. which is not correct.[14] Maldeo seems to have continued to rule upto the end of 1335 A.D. as can be noted from an inscription in a Jain temple of Kareda dated *Pus sudi 7*, *Samvat* 1392 (Sunday, September 23,

1335) which mentions Banbir as officer-in-charge of Chitrakut (Chittor) son of Maharajadhiraj Maldeo, and of his silahdars Muhammad and Suhadsimha got erected a *gommata* (dome).[15] Thus Banbir should have succeeded sometimes towards the end of 1335 A.D. and Hammir's capture of the fort should have taken place in 1336 A.D. for as mentioned by Raghubir Singh it is unlikely that Hammir captured the historic fort within a week of the period Banbir is reported to have been on the throne.

Thus Hammir took possession of Chittor from Banbir possibly in early 1336 A.D. after defeating him in a battle at Sojat which finds mention in *Udaipur-ri-khyat*.[16] The bards of Rajasthan have weaved in many stories about Hammir but in a nutshell we can say that through consolidation of his position and with the help of Mehta Maujiram he occupied Chittor early in 1336 A.D. and from that time the Guhilputra Sisodias began to prosper. The political situation and problems of Muhammad bin Tughlaq kept him busy elsewhere and this gave Maharana Hammir a free hand to increase his power at Chittor. To gain support and loyalty of Banbir, Maharana Hammir granted to him Nimuch, Ratnapur and Khairar in *jagir* for his maintenance. Banbir later captured Bhaisrod and added it to Mewar.

After establishing himself at Chittor Maharana Hammir gradually started extending his supremacy over other Rajput chiefs weakened by constant onslaught of Turkish arms. They were just like petty zamindars with a fort and jurisdiction extending over a small area round the fort. Such chiefs could easily see the rising power of Hammir and preferred to remain on friendly terms with him. The weak administration of Firuzshah further encouraged the Rajput chiefs to organise themselves in Marwar, Dhusharh, Hadauti and Khichiwara.[17] These Rajput chiefs found in Maharana Hammir a capable leader, which enhanced the prestige of Mewar and with Mewar, Chittor became once more a prominent centre of Rajputs from the second half of the fourteenth century.

Vanshprakash the history of Bundi indicates that Maharana Hammir interfered in the internal feuds of the Rajputs. It is said that when Halu, the chief of Bambawada was attacked by Jait Singh Pawar and Bharat Khichi, Maharana Hammir sent a force with Vijayaraj, Sundardas and Kunwar Kheta to strengthen their forces. Hamma, the ruler of Bundi came to the assistance of

Halu. In the first encounter Vijayraj was killed and Kunwar Kheta was injured. This insensed the Maharana who personally marched upon Halu. At this Hamma of Bundi came to the Maharana and conciliated him by offering as blood price the hand of his grand-daughter (daughter of his son Lal Singh) in marriage to Kunwar Kheta.[18] Maharana Hammir seems to have been reconciled with this offer, obviously because he could foresee in this arrangement winning of a group of Rajputs on his side.

Maharana Hammir in his prosperity did not forget the assistance rendered to him by Barbari and brought her with honour from Koregaon and settled her in Chittor. After her death he erected a temple at the place of her residence which was called the *Arnapurna Mandir.*

Hammir had a fairly long reign of about twenty-nine years (if we take 1336 A.D. as the year of his occupation of Chittor) and during this period he restored Chittor, Mewar and the Sisodias once more to the same prominent position they enjoyed in 1303 A.D. By the time of his death in 1364 A.D. Sisodias were well established in Mewar. Of his four sons, Kheta, Luna, Khanga and Vairishal, the eldest Khetra succeeded him on the *gaddi* of Chittor in 1364 A.D.

Maharana Kshetrasimha (Kheta) (1364-1382 A.D.)

The process of territorial expansion started by Maharana Hammir was continued by his son and successor, Maharana Khetra (Kshetrasimha) who ruled over Mewar from 1364-1382 A.D. This brought him more into clash with the Rajputs than with the Turkish power of Delhi or the Turkish governors in the provinces. The Sultanate of Delhi had already shrunk in size. The Bahamani kingdom was prospering in the South of Tapti; Raja Ali Khan Faruqi was practically independent in Khandesh; the Governors of Gujarat and Malwa owed only a formal allegiance to Firuz Shah and were holding the provinces on terms of revenue farming. Under such a political situation the Rajput chiefs of Idar, Sirohi, Dungarpur, Khichiwara, Hadauti and Merwara were also trying to assert their independence and increase their territories. Thus when Maharana Kheta started claiming overlordship he came in clash only with the neighbouring Rajput chiefs. The inscriptions of the times of Maharana

Mokul, Kumbha and Raimal mention that Maharana Kheta defeated and imprisoned Ranmal, the king of Gujarat along with another hundred Rajas. This Ranmal of the inscriptions is obviously not the king of Gujarat because during that period there was no such Rajput king ruling over Gujarat. This Ranmal was the first independent chief of Idar. According to the inscription of Eklingji temple, Maharana Kheta imprisoned Ranmal and placed his son on the *gaddi*.[19] Ranmal of Eklingji inscription is the same Ranmal mentioned elsewhere as ruler of Gujarat. The hundred Rajas mentioned, are the chiefs or the Samantas of Ranmal of Idar and not independent rulers.

The aggression of Kheta on Idar certainly could not have won for him the loyalty of the Rajputs of Idar. Though the house was not deposed as a son was placed on the *gaddi* the rulers of Idar could not forget the humiliation suffered at the hands of the rulers of Chittor. Maharana Khetra had extended his territory up to village Panwar which later became a part of Jaipur.

The above mentioned inscription also mentions that Maharana Kheta defeated and imprisoned Ami Shah. There is no doubt that Ami Shah of the inscription is none other than Dilawar Khan Ghuri or Amid Shah Daud, the founder of the independent kingdom of Malwa. Dilawar Khan *alias* Ami Shah figures in history from 1387 A.D. onwards. Before this date he was an ordinary customs officer in Malwa on the high road of Delhi.[20] At that time when Maharana Khetra captured and imprisoned Ami Shah he was a very petty officer not even worth mentioning. But the inscriptions are of the period of Mokul, Kumbha and Raimal when the independent kingdom of Malwa had already been founded and Ami Shah happened to be the founder of this kingdom. Thus those inscriptions take pride in mentioning that the Maharana of Mewar had once defeated and captured the founder king of his neighbouring kingdom of Malwa. Maharana Kheta also extended his sway in the region of Bagad where the Guhilputra Maharawals—a collateral of Sisodias—had already established themselves with Dungarpur as their centre.

The circumstances that brought about the end of Maharana Kheta are not very clear, though it is very significant and is of far reaching consequences for the history of Mewar. Kheta's marriage with Hada Lal Simha's daughter had been agreed upon and engagement ceremony performed during the life-time of Hammir. Hammir died in 1364 A.D. and Kheta died in 1382 A.D. i.e. he ruled for eighteen years before he died. Thus he could not have been killed in a broil with the Hadas at the time of his marriage, because the marriage certainly could not have been postponed for eighteen long years. The story of his death as it is found in the stories of the bards runs thus: Once Baru *barhat* had accompanied Maharana Kheta to the court of Lal Simha where in the *durbar* Baru declared that he could see no Rajput besides Maharana Kheta and therefore he could accept gifts only from him. Hada Lal Simha felt rather humiliated but remained silent. Later he invited Baru on the pretext of seeking his advice on certain matters. When Baru reached Bundi he was confined in the house by Lal Simha who insisted that Baru must accept some gift from him. Finding himself helpless Baru struck a bargain with Lal Simha that the Hada Chief must first accept what Baru would give him and in return Baru would accept whatever gift was given to him by Lal Simha. Lal Simha could not guess the game of Baru and accepted his condition.[21] Baru in the meantime connived with one Bhat boy that he would carry the severed head of Baru to Hada Lal Simha and then relate the story to Maharana Kheta who would amply reward him for this service. According to the plan Baru severed his head which was then presented to Hada Lal Simha wrapped in cloth by the Bhat boy. Hada Lal Simha realised the injury caused by this rash act of Baru and could foresee that it was bound to lead to war between Chittor and Bundi or in other words a Sisodia and Hada conflict was sure to take place. According to Mehta Nainsi, the enmity between the two as a result of this act of Baru lasted for quite some time. According to Kaviraj Shyamal Dass[22] when the Bhat boy told the entire story to Maharana Kheta, the Sisodia chief was incensed and attacked Bundi. The siege continued for quite some time. Finding that it was difficult to capture the fort of Bundi, Maharana Kheta in order to encourage his soldiers personally scaled the walls of the fort but in the skirmish inside the fort he was killed. Hada Lal Simha was also killed though his brother Bar Singh and his son Jaitrasimha and Naubrahama with a large number of other Hadas escaped from the fort before it fell to the Sisodias. The incidents are given in this form but the greater probability is that dispute arose between the Sisodias and Hadas on the question of handing over some of the villages which Hada Lal Simha had agreed to cede while offering his daughter as a bridge to prince Kheta during the reign of Rana Hammir. For some time Bundi remained in the possession of Sisodias. Thus came the end of Maharana Kheta in 1382 A.D.

Maharana Kheta left a fairly large progeny. His eldest son was Lakha or Lakshasimha who succeeded him as Maharana. His other sons were Bhakhar whose descendents came to be known as Bhakhrot Sisodia; Mahap; Bhawansimha; Bhuchan whose descendents are known as Bhuchrot; Salkha, whose descendents are known as Sakhrawat. Besides these children from his wives, he had two sons "Chacha" and "Mera" born of a concubine. Maharana Kheta seems to have left the State of Mewar in a quite prosperous condition or in other words he gave good start for the ascendency of Mewar which was to play a prominent role for about a century and a half.

Maharana Lakshasimha (Lakha) (1382-1397 A.D.)

The suggestion of Dr. S. Dutta[23] that Maharana Kheta died in 1405 A.D. demands scrutiny before it is accepted particularly when we find G.S. Ojha and Kaviraj Shyamal Dass placing the accession of Lakha in 1382 A.D. The date 1382 A.D. as given by Kaviraj Shyamal Dass[24] and G.S. Ojha[25] seems to be correct because none of the Jain works *Som Sobhagya Kavya*[26] it is mentioned that in v.s. 1450/1393 A.D. when Som Sundar Sur visited Dilwara, Maharana Lakha, the ruler of Mewar, Kunwar Chunda and minister Ram Deva visited him. From the trend of the narrative it is clear that Maharana Lakha had been ruling in Mewar in v.s. 1450/1393 A.D. for quite some time. This indicates that Maharana Kheta had died earlier. According to Nainsi the enmity between the Sisodias and the Hadas continued for some time and it was only when the Hadas realised that they would not be able to stand the enmity for long that they came forward and patched up the differences. It is stated that Hadas Bar Singh, Jaitrasimha and Naubrahma approached Maharana Lakha and explained that the entire incident took place because of Baru's rashness and that they were not responsible for it. They also pleaded that they were prepared to serve as vassals of Chittor. Maharana Lakha then restored Bundi to them. To further appease the Maharana, Bar Singh, Jaitrasimha and Naubrahma gave in marriage twelve daughters of their own and their brothers to the brothers and Samants of Maharana Lakha and in dowry gave six villages Jilgari (Jalandhari), Khined, Dharwara, Bajna, Bhilrio and Banko to the Sisodias.[27] It is obvious that Rana Lakha too was anxious to patch up the differences and accepted the offer of the Hadas. The feud between the Sisodias and the Hadas was patched up but the Hadas could not forget the humiliation they had to undergo. No doubt they continued to put up a show of friendliness with the Maharanas of Chittor but never hesitated to help their enemies whenever circumstances provided them with an opportunity. Maharana Lakha's reign (1382-97 A.D.) witnessed great upheavals in the Sultanate of Delhi. The death of Firuzshah Tughlaq in 1388 A.D. was followed by dynastic trouble in which temporarily the crown fell to the lot of Ghiyas-ud-din Tughlaq II and remained with him till August, 1389 A.D. when he was killed. The crown then passed to Abu-Bakr Shah who retained it till September, 1390 when he was killed. He was followed by Nasiruddin Muhammad Shah who remained on the throne till January 1398 A.D. when death claimed him. These domestic troubles in the Delhi Sultanate provided a good opportunity to Maharana Lakha to consolidate his position and extended his suzerainty over petty chiefs neighbouring the region of Chittor.

Maharana Lakha seems to have strengthened considerably the position of Mewar, which alarmed the neighbouring Muslim rulers. Zafar Khan who was building up his position in Gujarat considered the rise of Mewar as detrimental to his interest and to check this rising power he invaded Mandalgarh, a tributary of Mewar, in 1396 A.D. The fort of Mandalgarh, however, proved too strong and Zafar had to return without achieving success.[28] From Mandalgarh, Zafar Khan proceeded to Ajmer to pay homage to the Shrine of Sheikh Mainuddin Chisti. While returning from Ajmer he plundered the townships of Sambhar and Didwana causing damage to the population of these places.

Maharana Lakha won over the Dodias of Sardulgarh who rendered valuable services to him. Rao Singh Dodia with his sons Kalu and Dhawal helped the Mewar contingent accompanying Maharana Lakha's mother on her pilgrimage to Dwarkanath. Rao Singh was killed in a battle with the highway robbers, but Kalu and Dhawal succeeded in bringing safely the entire entourage upto the border of Mewar. In recognition of his service Maharana Lakha invited Dhawal Dodia to his court in 1387 A.D. and by granting him a *jagir* worth five lakhs, consisting of Ratangarh, Nandrai Masauda, made him a Samant at his court. It is recorded in the Khyats that Sultan Ghiyasuddin Tughlaq II invaded Mewar but was defeated by Maharana Lakha in the battle of Badnor. This incident we can place between January 1388 A.D. and August 1389 A.D. In a history of Sardargarh it is recorded that in the battle against Ghiyasuddin, Dhawal Dodia and his son Haru were killed.[29] During this period Maharana Lakha also defeated the Sankhla Rajputs near Amer (Ambar).

Lakha's Marriage with Rathor Rao Chunda's Daughter

The *Khyats* have different versions regarding the marriage of Lakha in his old age. Mehta Nainsi's narrative should have been most reliable because in it the Rathors were involved, but it has certain points which become difficult to reconcile. According to Nainsi, Rao Chunda of Mandor, being infatuated with his Mohili wife exiled his eldest son Ranmal and nominated Mohili's son Kanha as his successor. Ranmal in exile first took up his residence along with his followers in village Nadol over which the Sonegara Rao ruled. After staying there for some time Ranmal came to Chittor where the thirty-six branches of the Rajputs served the Maharana and therefore Ranmal had no hesitation in taking up service in the Chittor Rajya. The question that need consideration is whether he came to Chittor after the marriage of his sister Hansabai with Maharana Lakha or before the marriage. Nainsi's narrative would have us believe that he came to Chittor before the marriage, *i.e.* when he was exiled from Mandor by his father he had with him his sister who shared his wanderings. This seems rather incredible. Even about the marriage, according to Nainsi, once Rana Lakha seeing a bridegroom took a deep sigh indicating that he had become too old though he would like to marry again. Kunwar Chunda who was with Rana Lakha felt the lonliness of his father and started searching a bride for him. In the search he learnt about the sister of Ranmal then in the employ of the Mewar State. The proposal, however, was not acceptable to Ranmal on the ground that according to Rajput custom the eldest son succeeded the *gaddi* and the younger brothers served him, the son of his sister will have to serve Chunda who was the eldest and was to succeed as the Maharana. He also expressed his wish that he would be only too glad to marry his sister to Kunwar Chunda. But Chunda gave his word on oath that if Ranmal's sister would give birth to a son he would renounce his claim and serve the younger brother.[30] Another version which seems to be more logical and normal is that Rao Chunda of Mandor sent through his son Ranmal the 'coconut' to offer his daughter Hansabai to Kunwar Chunda, the eldest son of Rana Lakha. When the messengers arrived in the court Rana Lakha courteously received them and informed that Kunwar Chunda would soon return and take the gage. However, in a jest he remarked while drawing his fingers over his moustaches that none would send such things for an old greybeard like him. "This little sally was, of course, applauded and repeated, but Chunda offended at delicacy being sacrificed to wit, declined accepting the symbol which his father had even in jest supposed might be intended for him."[31] Rana Lakha tried to persuade his son to accept the offer since the rejection was considered as a gross insult, but Chunda remained firm and asked his father to accept the offer for himself. On the other hand, Ranmal was not prepared to marry his sister to the old Rana, because the children born of his sister would only be servant to the throne. When Kunwar Chunda discovered that objection was not because of the old age of his father but because of the right of the succession, he declared on oath that a son born to sister of Ranmal would ascend the *gaddi* of Chittor and he would serve him.

Of these two versions, the second one seems more probable and also that when this incident took place Ranmal still was living in his father's territories. The anxiety on the part of the Rana and Kunwar Chunda could only have meaning when read in the context that the offer had come from Rathor ruler of Mandor and not from Ranmal when he was a servant of the Rana. Therefore, it seems more probable that it was some time after the marriage of Rana Lakha with Hansabai, the sister of Ranmal, that the latter left Mandor and came to Chittor where he was granted a *jagir* by Rana Lakha. It is said that thirteen months after the marriage, Hansabai gave birth to a son who was named Mokul.

Maharana Lakha died in v.s. 1454/1397 A.D. and left behind a large progeny and a prosperous State of Mewar the income of which was further augmented by the discovery of silver and lead mine at Jawar in district Magra. This mine yielded sufficient quantity of silver and lead which not only increased the State revenue but also developed Jawar into a prosperous *qasba*, Maharana Lakha also extended his sway in the hilly regions of Marwar and also habitated Badnor.

The sons of Maharana Lakha were Chunda, Raghavadeva, Ajja, Dulha, Dungar Singh Gaj Singh, Luna, Mokul and Bagh Singh.[32]

Maharana Mokul

The date of birth of Maharana Mokul as well as that of his accession has been variously given, but a more accurate date of his birth can be arrived at from Hoshangshah's conquest of Gagraun. According to Charan Shivadas the siege was started on 8th *Shukla Aswin* and lasted up to 8th Kartik of v.s. 1480.[33] (September 13 to September 27, 1423 A.D.). According to Nizamuddin and Firishta, Hoshangshah started in 826/1423 for the conquest of Gagraun and after a short siege conquered it.[34] Both these authors are silent about the name of the ruler of Gagraun but Shihab Hakim mentions Achaldas Khichi as ruler from whom Hoshangshah conquered Gagraun.[35] Achaldas Khichi of Gagraun was son-in-law of Maharana Mokul. Charan Shivadas informs us that Maharana Mokul's daughter Lali Mewari was the senior queen of Achaldas and the administrative affairs of the State were looked after by her, while Uma Sankhli, daughter of Khiwsi Sankhla of Janglu, was his second queen. Achaldas had sought help from Maharana Mokul but it could not come in time. Finding that holding fort for long was not possible, Achaldas decided to come out of the fort and fight to the last. On 8th Kartik of 1480 v.s./September 27, 1423 A.D. the women led by the queens Lali Mewari and Uma Sankhli entered the fire lit inside the fort so as to relieve their men of their worries before last battle. While the women burnt themselves the men fought till their last breath. Thus in 1423 Lali Mewari should have been quite mature and must have been at least sixteen years of age if not more, and by allowing all possible margin Mokul could not have been less than thirty-two years of age, the greater possibility being that he might have been older. According to this calculation Mokul should have been born not later than v.s. 1448/1391 A.D. Thus at the time of the death of Maharana Lakha in v.s. 1454/1397 A.D. Mokul was about six years of age and ascended the throne rather at a tender age. Scrutiny of the date of birth of Mokul becomes necessary because the dates given by some of the prominent historians of Rajasthan differ in a wide range. Harbilas Sarda[36] in his monograph *Maharana Kumbha* puts the date of Lakha's death in between 1419 and 1421 A.D., when according to him Mokul was very young. Bisheshwarnath Rau[37] gives v.s. 1466-67/1409-10 A.D. as the approximate year of birth of Mokul. All these dates in view of Mokul having a daughter of about sixteen years in 1423 becomes an obvious error. The present writer noticed these discrepancies after his book was published and he takes this opportunity to correct himself and wishes to point out that the dates given by him in this connection earlier are wrong.[38]

According to the *Khyats* of Mewar when Maharana Lakha died in v.s. 1454/1397 A.D.[39] Hansabai, the mother of Mokul expressed her wish to perform the *rite* of *sati* and enquired from Chunda the *jagir* that he wanted to give to her son Mokul. But Chunda reminded her of his former vow and informed her that Mokul was to succeed his father on the throne and that he and his brothers would serve Maharana Mokul. In return for this sacrifice Hansabai, the queen-mother declared that thenceforth the sign of the spear-head which used to be drawn by the Maharana would be done by Chunda. After this final settlement Chunda led the boy Mokul to the *gaddi* and declaring him as Maharana paid his homage and offerings which was followed by offerings of his younger brothers. Thus Mokul ascended the throne of Mewar superseding all his elder brothers. But Mokul being young the entire work of the State was carried out by Chunda and on all State orders Chunda used to draw the spearhead below which Maharana Mokul wrote his name as a mark of his approval of the document.[40] One may, however, question that in renouncing his personal claim to the throne to what extent Chunda was competent to renounce the claims of all his brothers who was elder to Mokul. The probability, therefore, seems to be that Maharana Lakha had nominated Mokul as his successor and had taken concurrence of all other possible claimants to the throne with Chunda as guarantee to carry out his wishes.

For some time matters within Mewar seem to have moved smoothly, but the court was not free from intrigues. Ranmal Rathor was the eldest son of Rao Chunda Rathor of Mandor but for some reason Rao Chunda nominated his younger son Kanha as his successor. Ranmal was annoyed at the action of his father and came to Chittor seeking service with the Maharana.[41] He being the brother of Hansabai, Maharana Lakha took him into service and granted the village of Dhanla as his maintenance *Jagir*. According to the *Khyats of Mewar* this incident took place sometimes in v.s. 1450/1393 A.D., *i.e.* he came to the court of Lakha a few years after the marriage of his sister and the birth of his nephew Mokul. After having stayed in Mewar for some time Ranmal had slowly collected a number of Rathors around him, and also won over a number of nobles on his side. After having thus strengthened his position he started intriguing against Chunda and instigated his sister to such an extent that ultimately Hansabai, the queen-mother, asked Chunda that if he considered himself a servant of the Maharana he should leave Mewar and go elsewhere otherwise he should ascend the throne of Mewar and[42] allot a *jagir* to her son Mokul where she would retire with her son. This was too much for Chunda and as Tod has put it "knowing the purity of his own motives, made liberal allowance for maternal solicitude; but upbraiding the queen (mother) with the injustice of her suspicions, and advising a vigilant care to the rights of the Sisodias, he retired to the court of Mandu..." According to Kaviraj Shyamal Dass, Chunda left Mewar along with his brothers but left Raghava Deva in Mewar to protect Maharana Mokul from falling entirely into the clutches of Ranmal.[43] However, the real intention was to protect the interests of the Sisodias as against that of the Rathors. Chunda had foreseen that in manipulating the matters in such a way Ranmal aimed at establishing Rathor ascendancy in the court of Mewar.

Chunda seems to have left Mewar sometimes between 1401 and 1406 A.D. This assumption is based on the information contained in the *Khyats of Mewar* which narrate that Chunda left Mewar and took shelter in the court of Dilawar Khan.[44] Though Chunda remained away from Mewar, he never became indifferent towards the course of events taking place there. In Mewar most of the administrative work now fell into the hands of Ranmal and Mokul as youngman of about 15 years seems to have started leading a life of comfortable ease. Ranmal no doubt served the Maharana loyally and rendered valuable service in protecting the kingdom from the invasions of the rising power of the neighbouring Muslim Kingdoms. Within the State of Mewar, however, jealousy between the Rathors and Sisodias kept on brewing below the surface. Ranmal on his part while serving Mewar did not overlook to utilise the resources of Mewar for the promotion of his personal interests. He collected a large number of Rathor followers around him much to the displeasure of the Sisodias.

During the reign of Maharana Mokul partly due to party faction and partly due to his own character and irresolute nature, Mewar lost much of the strength acquired during the reigns of Kheta and Lakha. The Rajput chiefs who had been subjugated by Lakha started hostility against Mewar. The Rao of Sirohi started encroaching into the regions of Godwar. The Hadas of Bundi who had been always hostile to the Sisodias, occupied regions up to Mandalgarh and started helping the enemies of Mewar. Ranmal during this period kept himself busy in subduing the various uprisings in different parts of the kingdom, but his main motive was to strengthen himself at the expense of Mewar so as to get his ancestral territory of Mandor, therefore, his efforts could not prevent Mewar from becoming weak.

Among the neighbouring Muslim kingdoms the greatest threat was from the rising powers of Malwa and Gujarat. In the north-west the principality of Nagor was also a menace. Nagor had been assigned by Muzaffar Shah I of Gujarat to his brother Shams Khan Dandani. He was succeeded by his son Firuz Khan who was a contemporary of Maharana Mokul as well as Maharana Kumbha. Maharana Mokul and Firuz Khan were not on friendly terms and often came into conflict with each other though neither side could ever achieve a decisive success.[45] According to *Kyamkhan Rasa*, Muhammad Kyamkhan fought from the side of Firuz Khan in one of the engagements and changed the victory of Maharana Mokul into a defeat.[46] The conflict with Nagor was handed over by Mokul as a legacy to his son Kumbha.

Relations with the Rathors of Mandor

Maharana Mokul wanted to maintain good relations with Mandor and was not willing to interfere in the internal affairs of Mandor. Rao Chunda of Mandor was killed in a battle with Salim Khan of Multan in v.s. 1480/1423 A.D.[47] He was succeeded by his younger son Kanha according to his own nomination by passing Ranmal who was his eldest son. Kanha died after a rule of one year which was followed by a combined resistance to Ranmal by his two brothers Satta and Randhir and Ranmal had to return to Chittor disappointed. Maharana Mokul at this time did not help Ranmal to wrest Mandor from his brothers. Subsequently, however, the sons of Satta and Randhir quarrelled and Narbad the son of Satta made matters difficult for Randhir who fled to Chittor and instigated Ranmal to oust Satta and occupy Mandor which rightfully belonged to him. This internal dissension encouraged Maharana Mokul to help Ranmal and with Mewari forces he marched upon Mandor and occupied it.[48] Satta and Narbad accompanied Maharana Mokul to Chittor. After some time Maharana Mokul granted to Narbad the *Jagir* of Kaylana yielding an income of one lakh rupees. Ranmal started ruling at Mandor and also kept a close watch over the affairs of Mewar.

Maharana Mokul lacked in political farsight and military vigour. He could hardly foresee the rising clouds around Mewar. So far Ranmal was concerned, he kept himself busy in extending the territories of Mandor. In 1423 A.D. when Hoshang Shah invaded Gagraun and Achaldas Khichi its ruler sought help from Chittor, the necessary help could not be sent with the consequence that Gagraun passed into the hands of the ruler of Malwa and thus weakened the eastern boundary of Mewar. The weakness of Mewar during this period is also evident from the stand of the Rajput chiefs who had taken the side of Hoshang Shah. From *Achaldas Khichi ri-Vachanika* we learn that Hadas of Bundi, Shivabhan Dewra and Devi Singh all joined the camp of Hoshang Shah. The statement of Mehta Nainsi that Ranmal was proceeding for the help of Achaldas, but on receiving the news of the murder of Maharana Mokul returned to Mewar is not correct. Mokul died much later near about 1433 A.D.

Murder of Mokul

The weakness of Mewar encouraged her neighbours to encroach upon her territories. While the eastern boundary was gradually getting exposed to the inroads of Sultan Hoshang Shah of Malwa, the southern and western territories became regions of activity of Sultan Ahmad Shah of Gujarat who had reached the pinnacle of his power by 1432 A.D. In February 1433 A.D. Ahmad Shah marched upon Mewar reducing on his way to Dungarpur which kept him engaged for sometime and avoiding Chittor he ravaged the country of Kilwara and Dilwara. The news of Ahmad Shah's movements alarmed Maharana Mokul and he marched out to meet Ahmad Shah. While he was halting in Bagad he was murdered in his camp. Mokul was murdered by his uncles Chacha and Mera born of a low caste maid-servant of Maharana Kheta. The incidents connected with the murder have been differently given by different writers. Mehta Nainsi who was associated with the Rathors puts the matter in such a way as to elevate the personality of Ranmal Rathor. It is not very unlikely that when he was writing he followed the story as it was in circulation in the court of Jodhpur. According to Nainsi,[49] Maharana Mokul hated Chacha and Mera because of their mother belonging to a low-caste (carpenter). Mahapa Pawar of Ajmer, who was not on good terms with Mokul and Ranmal also sided with Chacha and Mera and helped them in organising a sizeable opposition to the Maharana. Nainsi also records that Maharana Mokul was repeatedly warned against the conspiracy that was being hatched up by Chacha and Mera but he never took any notice of the warning. The attempt to glorify Ranmal is obvious in the narrative of Nainsi. If Ranmal knew about the conspiracy one wonders, why did he not take any positive steps to break it when it is claimed that Ranmal was ever vigilant in protecting the interest of Mewar. In *Mewar Khyats* the incident, however, is mentioned differently. Here an attempt has been made to ascribe the incident as an outcome of sudden provocation caused by an uncalled for remark of Maharana Mokul, while camping in Bagor, at the instigation of Maldeo Hada in the service of the Maharana.[50] The murder of Maharana Mokul took place in 1433 A.D. He had one daughter who had been married to Achaldas Khichi, and seven sons. The seven sons were: (1) Kumbha Karan (Kumbha), (2) Khem Karan, (3) Shiva,

(4) Satta, (5) Nath Simha, (6) Virandeo, and (7) Rajdhar.[51]

Notes and References

1. "*India, Historical Quarterly,*" 1951, p. 52; D. Sharma, "*Rajasthan through the Ages*", p. 658.
2. "*Kanhada-de-Prabandh*" (Padmanabha, ed. K.B. Vyas, Jaipur 1953) i, pp. 32, 33.
3. "*Vividhatirtha-Kalpa,*" Jinaprabha Suri, p. 30 (*Singhi Jaina Granthamala*, vol. x, 1934): *Kanhada-de-Prabandha*, i, p. 50.
4. Amir Khusrau, "*Khazain-ul-Futuh,*" pp. 64-69.
5. Ojha, *History of Udaipur*, p. 193, fn. 1.
6. Briggs, i, pp. 378-79.
7. *Mehta Nainsi Ri Khyat* (Jodhpur), p. 205.
8. "*Epigraphie Indo Maslamica*" 1955-56, pp. 67-70; *Vir Vinod*, i, pp. 425-26.
9. *Firishta*, i, p. 115.
10. *Ranpur Inscription*.
11. *Vir Vinod*, i, p. 293.
12. *Vir Vinod*, i, pp. 295-296. Kaviraj Shyamal Dass has included an interesting story in this connection which relates that Maldeo's daughter after her marriage with Hammir told him that henceforth as his wife her first loyalty was to him. She advised Hammir that if he intended to take possession of Chittor he should ask for the services of Mehta Maujiram. Hammir on her advice asked Maldeo to put Mehta Maujiram in his service so that he may look after the places given to him. Maldeo transferred the services of Mehta Maujiram and asked him to look to the interests of Hammir as onwards he would be in his service. Hammir also took Mehta Maujiram into his confidence according to the advice of his wife. On the pretext of hunting Hammir started from his camp and on the second night reached Chittor where Mehta Maujiram declared his identity and asked the keepers to open the fort. Mehta Maujiram used to visit the fort to distribute the salary of the men posted in the fort and, therefore, they opened the gates without any suspicion which gave an opportunity to Hammir to enter the fort without resistance. Once inside the fort Hammir's men fell upon the inmates of the fort many of whom were killed and others were expelled. Hammir posted his own men inside the fort, Learning Hammir's occupation of Chittor, Maldeo at once attacked with his five sons Jaisa, Kirtipal, Banbir, Randhir and Kelan. In the engagement that took place Maldeo was defeated and was forced to return to his home. Maldeo made one or two more attempts on Chittor but could succeed in his venture. Maldeo then appealed to

Muhammad bin Tughlaq who personality marched upon Chittor and while camping at Singolia he was attacked by Maharana Hammir who by then had collected a strong force. In the sudden attack Muhammad bin Tughlaq was taken as captive and Maldeo's grandson Haridas was killed. After remaining in captivity for three months the Sultan purchased his release by ceding Ajmer, Ranthambhor and Shivpur and a cash of 50 lakhs of rupees and 100 elephants. Shyamal Dass also observes that this incident is not mentioned in Persian chronicles because they seldom mention the defeat of the Muslims. However the entire story of Shyamal Dass is typically a Rajasthani version based on the narratives the *Barwa Bhats.*

13. Tod, *Annals etc.,* i, pp. 219-220.
14. Ojha, *Rajputane ka Itihas,* ii, 546, Hammir captured Chittor from Banbir and not from Jaisa.
15. *Jain Lekh Sangraha,* i, p. 242. See also D. Sharma, *Lectures on Rajput History and Culture,* p. 46, and fn. 1.
16. *Indian Historical Quarterly,* 1951, pp 68-69, fn. 27.
17. Firuzshah Tughlaq wanted to capture the fort of Gagraun in Khichiwara and for this purpose had sent an expedition under Malik Sar-dawatdar and Malikzada Firuz Khan, but with all their efforts the two generals failed to reduce the fort.—Day, *Medieval Malwa,* p. 49.
18. *Vir Vinod,* i, p. 300; Ojha, *Rajputane ka Itihas,* ii, pp. 561-2. The objection of Ojha—that Lal Singh's daughter could not have been married to Kheta, because he takes Debi Singh as contemporary of Hammir and Lal Singh his fifth descendant—can be easily resolved if we re-examine the chronology of the Hadas. Hada Hammir or Hamma was certainly a contemporary of Maharana Hammir, and therefore there is nothing unusual in the marriage so as to be rejected.
19. *Vir Vinod,* i, p. 418; *Ekalinji Prashasti,* verse 30.
20. U.N. Day, *Medieval Malwa,* pp. 9-14.
21. *Vir Vinod,* i, p. 303.
22. *Vir Vinod,* i, p. 303. The Bhat boy was granted the village of Chikalvas according to the wishes of Baru by Maharana Kheta and when *Vir Vinod* was being compiled the descendants of this Bhat boy were living in the village of Chikalvas near Udaipur.
23. *Delhi Sultanate* (Bharatiya Vidya Bhawan), p. 328.
24. *Vir Vinod,* i, p. 305.
25. *Udaipur Rajya ka Itihas,* i, p. 259.
26. Somani, *Maharana Kumbha,* pp. 26-27 and fn. 84.
27. *Mehta Nainsi Ki Khyat,* i, p. 59, fn. 12A and p. 60; *Vir Vinod,* i, p. 305. These villages might have been the cause of dispute

between the two referred earlier.
28. *Tabaqat-i-Akbari*, iii, p. 86, S.C. Misra, *The Rise of Muslim Power in Gujarat*, pp. 148-149.
29. *Vir Vinod*, i, p. 306.
30. Mehta Nainsi, *Khyat*, ii, pp. 331-332.
31. Tod—*Annals*, i, p. 223.
32. Various branches of the Sisodias sprung from these sons of Lakha,
    1. Chunda: *Chundawat*, their thikanes are Salumber, Deogarh, Begu, Amet, Meja, Bhainsrod, Kurabar, Asind, Chawand, Bhadesar, Bemali, Lunda, Bambora, Bhawanpura, Lasani and Samgramgarh.
    2. Ajja: *Sarangdevot* through Ajja's son Sarangdeva; thikanes, Kanor, and Batharara.
    3. Dulha: *Dulhawat*, thikanes, Bhanpur, Saimrada.
    4. Dungar Singh: *Bhandawat*.
    5. Gaj Singh: *Gajsinghhot*.
    6. Luna: *Lunawat*, thikanes, Malpur, Kathara, Kheda.
33. *Achaldas Khichiri Vachanika*, p. 24.
34. *Tabaqat-i-Akbari*, iii, p. 293, *Firishta*, ii, p. 469.
35. *Maasir-i-Mahmudshasi*, Fol. 134.
36. Harbilas Sarda, *Maharana Kumbha*, p. 22. See also Muni Jinvijaya, *Prachin Lekh Sangraha*, II, p. 221.
37. Bisheshwarnath Reu, *Marwar Ka Itihas*, i, p. 75 and notes.
38. U.N. Day, *Medieval Malwa*, p. 64 and notes 2, 3.
39. D. Sharma, *Lectures on Rajput History and Culture*, p. 47. Prof. Sharma states that Mokul must have come to the throne between the years 1418 and 1421 A.D., and perhaps at an age when he could not have independently handled the affairs of the State. Prof. Sharma obviously has reproduced the dates as given by Harbilas Sarda without caring to examine them. In view of Mokul's date of birth as discussed above, the date of Lakha's death and Mokul's accession as given in *Mewar Khyats* and mentioned by Kaviraj Shyamal Dass (*Vir Vinod*, i, p. 311) seem to be correct and hence accepted here.
40. Tod, *Annals etc.*, i, p. 224; *Vir Vinod*, I, p. 310. According to Kaviraj Shyamal Dass, the practice of drawing the spearhead and writing the name continued till Maharana Sanga replaced it by writing *Sahi* after the fashion of Muslim Sultans.
41. Reu, I, p. 70; Mehta Nainsi, *Khyat*, ii, p. 329, *Vigat*, i, p. 26; Ojha, *Udaipur Rajya ka Itihas*, i, p. 265.
42. *Vir Vinod*, i, p. 311, Tod, i, p. 224.
43. *Vir Vinod*, i, p. 311.
44. *Medieval Malwa*, p. 64 note 3 stands corrected here. The statement was based on the wrong reckoning of the date of birth of Mokul.

45. *Mirat-i-Sikandari*, p. 40, mentions Shams Khan Dandani which implies earlier years of the reign of Mokul. *Vir Vinod*, i, pp. 314-15, has Firuz Khan of Nagor. Firuz Khan was certainly the ruler of Nagor in 1428 A.D. as can be found from the Sammidheswar Mahadeva Temple Prashasti of the time of Mokul dated v.s 1486/1428 A.D. vide, *Vir Vinod*, p. 406.
46. *Kyamkhan Rasa*, pp. 29-30, verses 343 to 352.
47. Ramkaran Asopa, *Marwar ka Sankshipt Itihas*, p. 107.
48. *Vir Vinod*, i, p. 312; Ojha, *Rajputane Ka Itihas*, iv, pt. i, p. 213; Asopa *op. cit.*, pp. 11, 131, 132.
49. Nainsi, *Khyat*, ii pp. 115-116.
50. *Vir Vinod*, i, p. 315; Ojha, *Udaipur Rajya Ka Itihas*, i, pp. 277-278.
51. *Vir Vinod*, i, p. 316; Nainsi has Adu and Garhu in place of Nath Simha and Rajdhar. It is quite likely that Nainsi has given the pet names of these two sons.

2

Throne Comes to Kumbha

The assassination of Maharana Mokul in v.s. 1490/1433 A.D. created confusion in the camp but before the assassins could gain an upper hand, Kumbha, who was also in the camp, escaped. The version of Nainsi that immediately after the assassination Chacha declared himself as Maharana with Mahapa Pawar or Mahipal as his chief minister seems to be correct.[1] It becomes difficult to accept that Chacha after having murdered Mokul would declare Kumbha as the new Maharana. We are further informed that Kumbha fled from the camp and after taking a horse from the house of a *patel* headed for Chittor where the chiefs declared him as the new Maharana. Thus the accession of Kumbha took place in v.s. 1490/1433 A.D. Chacha and his group subsequently set up a separate camp hostile to Kumbha and occupied the hilly tract of Pai-Kotra where they erected improvised defences to their shelter. Maharana Kumbha could not take action against them immediately after his accession. He had to weigh the strength of his supporters who had rallied round him. Ranmal, too, who had been serving Chittor was busy at Mandor where his own position was seriously exposed because of the activities of Sultan Ahmad Shah Gujarati who was marching to Nagor through the regions of Marwar.[2] It was only after the return of Ahmad Shah from Nagor to his own country that Ranmal at Mandor and Kumbha at Chittor could take a sigh of relief and could plan actions that were to be taken against the conspirators and other enemies of Chittor. Thus for some months Chacha and his group remained undisturbed in their hilly refuge.

Age of Kumbha at his Accession

In the absence of information regarding the exact date of birth of Kumbha it became a matter of speculation for historians to fix his age at his accession. Bisheshwarnath Reu fixes his age at about eight or nine years[3], while Harbilas Sarda and Ojha both maintain that Kumbha was young at the time of his accession[4] and, therefore, Ranmal Rathor looked after the affairs of the State. The assumption that Kumbha was young at the time of his accession is based on the erroneous reckoning of the age of Mokul as well as that of his accession. According to our present calculation as noted earlier Mokul was born not later than 1391 A.D. and ascended the throne in 1397 A.D. In 1423 A.D. his eldest child, a daughter, was about 16 years. Kumbha was younger to this daughter. The incidents that took place immediately after Mokul's murder indicate that Kumbha could not have been that young as mentioned by Shri Reu. According to Nainsi, Kumbha fled from the camp and after taking a horse from the house of a *patel* reached Chittor. Allowing all extraordinary courage to a Rajput youth, performance of such a task still remains beyond comprehension by a lad of nine. Nainsi has also mentioned that Kumbha took active part in bringing about the end of Ranmal Rathor in 1438 A.D. which again for a lad of thirteen or fourteen to perform would not have been possible. Last of all, we find that Kumbha was murdered by his eldest son Uda or Udaisimha in v.s. 1525/1468 A.D. after having ruled for about 35 years. At the time of Kumbha's murder Uda had two grown up sons, Sahasmal and Surajmal and also a marriageable daughter. This could have been possible only if Kumbha was seventeen or eighteen years of age at the time of his accession. Thus we can conclude that Kumbha was born not later than 1415 A.D. and was quite grown up to look after the affairs of the State at his accession. Kumbha has been deliberately assigned a young age to glorify Ranmal Rathor and to give him all the credit for all earlier achievements of Maharana Kumbha. In reality, Ranmal served Maharana Kumbha as one of his *samantas* and during the course of service worked hard to augment his own position and power.

During the first three or four years of his reign Maharana Kumbha was not disturbed by the two powerful Muslim States of Gujarat and Malwa and he could devote this time to consolidate his position within the State and also to deal with such Rajput chiefs as were hostile to Mewar. Ahmad Shah after his return from Nagor remained busy on the southern border of his kingdom against the activities of Ahmad Shah Bahmani (1422-1436 A.D.) in the regions of Sultanpur and Nandurbar. During this period Ahmad Shah also had to look after the activities of the Rajput chiefs of Idar, Jhalawar, Champaner, Nandod and other petty Rajput chiefs living within the kingdom of Gujarat. Thus he could hardly get time to move into Mewar. Hoshang Shah of Malwa too remained busy from 1433 A.D. till his death in 1435 A.D. over the affairs of Kalpi and Kherla. Besides, Hoshang Shah had never adopted a policy of direct offensive against Mewar. He had preferred to befriend the Rajput enemies of the rulers of Mewar and also provide asylum to Rajput exiles of Mewar. Chunda and Ajja were already in Malwa where the Sultan had granted to them *jagirs*. The Hadas of Bundi were also on friendly terms with him and had rendered him assistance in the conquest of Gagraun, a stronghold of the Khichi Chauhans who were on friendly terms with the rulers of Mewar.

Taking full advantage of the political situation outside, Kumbha adopted the policy of crushing the enemies of Mewar. His first step, of course, was to avenge the murder of his father.[5] For this purpose he summoned all the *samantas* and also sent a message to Ranmal Rathor at Mandor. These measures certainly were taken only after the return of Ahmad Shah from Nagor. Rathor forces under Ranmal and Sisodia forces under Raghavadeva encircled the hilly region of Pai-Kotra but siege lasted for more than six months and the final success could be achieved only through the help of a *Mer* chief and the sons of Gameti *Bhil*.[6] Chacha and Mewar were killed but Mahapa and Chacha's son Ekka escaped and after wandering here and there finally they entered the kingdom of Malwa where Chunda and Ajja were living. The camp of Chacha was plundered and the five hundred girls of Mewar who were rescued from the camp were brought to Dilwara by Ranmal where he ordered them to be married to Rathor soldiers. Raghava Deva who was present in the camp resented such a plan and brought all the girls to Chittor where they were married to the Sisodias. Ranmal did not dare to oppose Raghavadeva but felt insulted and started conspiring against him. This resulted in a clear division of the court in two groups, that of the Sisodias and the Rathors. Harbilas Sarda has mentioned that Ranmal took Chacha's daughter to wife making Chacha's body serve as *bajot* to sit on at the ceremony.[7] If there is any truth in the story it indicates the callousness of Ranmal's character and also the insult that he inflicted on the Sisodias under the garb of avenging the murder of Mokul.

In the resources and fertile land of Mewar, Ranmal could see the prospects of building up his own power. As an astute politician, he refrained from showing open hostility to Raghavadeva who was looked upon by the Sisodias as their leader, instead he started slowly to post as many of his men to key-posts in Chittor as he could. In his work he made full use of the position and respect enjoyed by his sister Hansabai, the grand-mother of Maharana Kumbha. He gave the post of *Kiledar* of Chittor to Shatrashal Bhati who was one of his trusted men.[8] This was a key-post as he could easily check people coming in or going out of the fort. Even then Ranmal rendered valuable assistance to Maharana Kumbha in the early years of his reign. No doubt his personal motive in helping the Maharana was there, but the value of his services cannot be ignored. He adopted the policy of reducing the Rajput enemies of Mewar before proceeding against the rulers of Gujarat and Malwa. The first to attract his attention was Rao Sahasmal (1424-1451 A.D.), the Dewra Chauhan ruler of Sirohi. The Dewra Chauhans had been always hostile to the Guhils of Mewar and the Rathors of Mandor. Besides, Sirohi also occupied a strategic position. The commercial routes to Gujarat and the Deccan from the Punjab passed through the regions of Sirohi, and the fertile soil of Sirohi provided the Dewra Chauhans with substantial resources. Being close to Gujarat they were always exposed to the might of the Gujarati Sultan and always tried to keep them in good humour by pretending allegiance to them. Rao Sahasmal was both ambitious and opportunist. Taking full advantage of the disorder in Chittor following the murder of Mokul he occupied a number of villages belonging to Mewar.[9] In 1434 A.D. Kumbha sent a force under Dodia Narsingh and in the battle Rao Sahasmal was defeated and was forced to cede Abu, Basantgarh, Bhula and some areas of eastern Sirohi to Maharana Kumbha.[10] To protect the boundary of the Sirohi side, at the instance of Ranmal, Maharana Kumbha ordered for the construction of the fort of Achalgarh on the Aravali peaks of Abu.[11]

Kumbha next turned his attention towards Hadauti where the Hadas were quite powerful. They had been in alliance with the Sultan of Malwa but during the years 1433 and 1434 A.D. Hoshang Shah was busy in reducing Kherla and after his return from Kherla he died on 5th July, 1435/8th Zilhijja 838.[12] His death was followed by internal problems and some disturbance. This provided a good opportunity to Maharana Kumbha to reduce the Hadas of Bundi who had been hostile towards Mewar from the time of Maharana Lakha. Sometimes between 1435 and 1436 A.D. Maharana Kumbha asked Ranmal to attack Bundi. Bairisal (1413-1459 A.D.), the ruler of Bundi who had helped Hoshang Shah in the conquest of Gagraun could now hardly expect any help from that quarter and when attacked by Ranmal he sued for peace and ceded Mandalgarh to the ruler of Mewar and quite likely also acknowledged his suzerainty. The Hadas had submitted to Ranmal as a matter of expediency but they could not reconcile to their being subordinate to the ruler of Mewar and thus internal bickering remained. So far Mewar was concerned the possession of Mandalgarh provided her with a strong buttress on her eastern side.

In Malwa a new political situation was created by the murder of Sultan Muhammad Ghuri in *Shawwal*/839/ April-May 1436 A.D.[13] The rule passed into the hands of Mahmud Khalji who had to face organised opposition by the members and supporters of the Ghuri dynasty. Prince Umar Khan, son of Hoshang Shah, had escaped from Malwa during the turmoil following the accession of Mahmud Khalji. After a brief stay in Gujarat, Umar Khan arrived in the court of Maharana Kumbha where he was well received. Maharana Kumbha also promised to give him military assistance. No doubt this was a good opportunity for Kumbha to interfere in the affairs of Malwa, but he seems to have been hesitant in taking immediate action. We find Umar Khan moving in Malwa with a small following in 1438 A.D. at a time when Ahmad Shah Gujarati was also invading Malwa.

So-called Battle of Sarangpur

The *Bards* of Mewar and Jodhpur in their attempt to eulogize Maharana Kumbha and Ranmal Rathor vied with each other and tried to glorify their respective heroes by crediting them with conquests and victories which fail to stand the test of historical evidence. One such incident is the so-called battle of Sarangpur in which the credit of victory is given to Ranmal. The date of this battle is not to be found in any contemporary literature—Rajasthani or Persian. But modern writers depending on the bardic literature have given dates which they found convenient to fit in their narrations.

The historians of Rajasthan maintains that on Mahmud Khalji's refusal to hand over Ekka and Mahapa, Rana Kumbha with his maternal uncle Rana Ranmal of Mandor invaded Malwa. Mahmud Khalji was first defeated at Sarangpur and then he was besieged in Mandu. Mahmud Khalji could not hold his position long and capitulated, whereupon he was imprisoned and taken as captive to Chittor. After being imprisoned for six months he was released by Rana Kumbha without paying any tribute.[14] While the tale of Mahmud's captivity has been dilated upon by the historians of Rajputana, we do not find the incident mentioned even indirectly by the Muslim historians. It becomes, therefore, necessary to examine, whether the Muslim historians have suppressed a fact or the Rajputana historians have been misled by some bardic recitation.

According to Kaviraj Shyamal Das this battle of Sarangpur was fought in v.s. 1496[15]/1439 A.D. Ojha, however, rejects this date and assigns v.s. 1494[16]/1437 A.D. as the date of this battle of Sarangpur. According to Ojha, Ranmal who was then looking after the affairs of Chittor was present in the battle. Ranmal was killed in v.s. 1495, and Mahmud Khalji had ascended the throne in v.s. 1493/A.D. 1436, therefore, this battle must have been fought between these two dates[17] *i.e.,* sometimes in v.s. 1494/ 1437 A.D.

Tod's version of the event is extremely confused and defective. Tod says, "In the midst of his (Kumbha's) prosperity these two States (Malwa and Gujarat) formed a league against him, and in v.s. 1496/1440 A.D. both kings, at the head of powerful armies, invaded Mewar. Koombho (Kumbha) met them on the plains of Malwa bordering on his own State, and at the head of one hundred thousand horse and foot and fourteen hundred elephants, gave them an entire defeat, carrying captive to Cheetore (Chittor) Mahmood, the Ghilji sovereign of Malwa, Abul Fazl relates this victory, and dilates on Koombho's greatness of soul in setting his enemy at liberty, not only without ransom but with gifts".[18]

The league of the two States as mentioned by Tod did not take place in 1440 A.D., but much later in 1451 A.D. during the reign of Qutbuddin. Regarding Abul Fazl's[19] praise of Kumbha's conduct we find him praising Rana Sanga and not Rana Kumbha.

Sarda in his monograph on Maharana Kumbha has accepted the version as found in *Vir Vinod* without caring to examine it thoroughly. Sarda says, "As Mahapa Panwar was given shelter by the Sultan of Mandu, a demand for his person was made by the Maharana. Sultan Mahmud, however, declined to surrender the refugee, pleading that it was against all notion of dignity and sovereignty to do so. The Maharana thereupon prepared for hostilities and left Chittor to attack Mandu. The Sultan advanced with a powerful army to meet the Maharana".[20]

"Mahmud Khalji now asked Chonda to lead the Mandu army against Ranmal, the commander of Mewar forces, and take revenge for the murder of Raghavadeva. The patriotic Chonda replied that he would gladly have led the army against Ranmal Rathor but then it was against his *dharma* to take up arms against the Maharana. Rather than stay at Mandu he retired to his *jagirs*".[21]

"The two armies met in A.D. 1437 near Sarangpur. After a severe engagement the Sultan's army was utterly routed. The Sultan fled and shut himself up in the fort of Mandu. Kumbha stormed and took the fort. Ranmal captured Sultan Mahmud Khalji. The Maharana returned to Chittor bringing the Sultan captive with him".[22]

"To commemorate this great victory, the Maharana built the great *Jaya Stambha* in the fortress of Chittor, which still adorns that far-famed stronghold".

"Mahmud Khalji remained a prisoner in Chittor for a period of six months after which he was liberated without ransom by the magnanimous Maharana Kumbha".[23]

Sarda is so much obsessed with the idea of Mahmud Khalji's imprisonment that he takes it for granted that Mahmud's subsequent attacks on Mewar were simply to wipe out this disgrace and to avenge his defeat. Sarda says, "In A.D. 1443 Maharana Kumbha had to go to Haravati to punish some rebels. Finding Mewar unprotected, Sultan Mahmud Khalji of Mandu, who had been smarting under the shame of having been kept a prisoner in Chittor by Maharana Kumbha, and burning with a desire to take revenge and wipe off his disgrace of A.D. 1437, invaded Mewar".[24]

At another place Sarda says, "Altogether five attempts were made by the Sultan (Mahmud Khalji) to wipe out his disgrace of A.D. 1437, but every time he was defeated by the Maharana".[25]

This story of Mahmud Khalji's imprisonment had found so much currency in Mewar that Erskine[26] while compiling the *Gazetteer of Rajputana* unhesitatingly included it in his narrative of the historical events.

According to these versions Mahmud Khalji was defeated and imprisoned some times between 1437 and 1439 A.D. To examine the validity of this statement we may examine the activities of Mahmud Khalji during this period.

Mahmud's accession took place[27] on 29th Shawwal 839/14th May, 1436 A.D. It was followed by a conspiracy for his life in July-August 1436 A.D./840 A.H.[28] After the failure of the conspiracy Mahmud, on the advice of his father A'zam Humayun gave some *jagirs* to some of the prominent conspirators who represented the previous regime of the Ghuris. The distribution of *jagirs*, however, did not quell the opposition at once. The new incumbents soon raised the standard of rebellion in their respective *jagirs*. Amongst these rebels there was also *Shahzada* Ahmad Khan, son of Sultan Hoshang Shah. A'zam Humayun who was sent to quell these rebellions is found near Bhilsa on 17th Ramazan 840 A.H.[29]/25-3-1437 A.D. While this process of subjugation was going on, Ahmad Shah Gujarati took up the cause of *Shahzada* Mas'ud Khan, son of Sultan Muhammad Ghuri, and invaded Malwa[30] in Rajab, 841 A.H./Jan. 1438 A.D. For a few months he remained engaged in besieging the fort, and after fighting some indecisive skirmishes he shifted his camp to Ujjain. Mahmud Khalji had also come out of Shadiabad Mandu and had moved towards Sarangpur, from where he marched against 'Umar Khan, another son of Hoshang Shah who had brought some aid from the Rana of Chittor, in the direction of Bhilsa. During this encounter 'Umar Khan was killed and very soon Sultan Ahmad Shah also returned to Gujarat[31] in 842 A.H./1439-39 A.D., promising Mas'ud Khan to come again with him next year. After the departure of Ahmad Shah Gujarati, Mahmud Khalji had gone for the final subjugation of Chanderi and remained there engaged for quite some time in reducing the fort. After the final subjugation of Chanderi, Mahmud had gone towards Gwalior for the relief of Shahar Nau (Narwar) in response to the appeal of Bahar Khan, the *muqta* of the place. We are informed by the contemporary historian that Shahar Nau and its vicinities were being ravaged by Dungar Sen of Gwalior and Kumbha of Chittor.[32] Mahmud's attack on Gwalior had at once diverted the attention of Dungar Sen who immediately returned towards his own capital. Mahmud avoiding all possible encounter with Dungar Sen arrived at Shahar Nau from where he returned to Shadiabad and started completion of the mausoleum of Hoshang Shah.

From a record of these events we find that Mahmud was present in Malwa during the years 1437, 1438, 1439 and 1440 A.D., i.e., the period when it is claimed that he had been imprisoned in Chittor. During this period he was engaged in subjugation of rebellion as well as facing the invasion of Sultan Ahmad Shah Gujarati. Mahmud had ascended the throne by removing the successors of the house of the Ghuris and, therefore, earlier years of his reign were devoted in liquidating the opposition organised by the supporters of the Ghuris and also of those who were jealous of his rise. Even if we place Mahmud's imprisonment after the death of *Shahzadas* Ahmad Khan and 'Umar Khan, *Shahzada* Mas'ud Khan was still living and Ahmad Shah Gujarati was certainly not the person to miss such an opportunity offered by the absence of Mahmud Khalji and that too in disgrace as a prisoner in the hands of the Rajputs at Chittor.

For an usurper, because Mahmud had no other claim than usurpation, to be absent and to be imprisoned in another kingdom in the very beginning of his reign would have led the legitimists to set up a new king at once. But we do not find anything of the kind happening in Malwa during these years.

Thus taking all the evidence into consideration we find that Mahmud was neither imprisoned by Rana Kumbha nor was he defeated during the years mentioned. In fact during this period Mahmud Khalji avoided all possible encounter with the Rajputs. It is also significant that none of the contemporary Rajput epigraphs mentions the imprisonment of Mahmud Khalji at the hands of Rana Kumbha. The prevalence of such a story in Rajputana may have been due to the mistake of the bards who might have confused the imprisonment of Mahmud Khalji II in the hands of Rana Sanga with the name of Mahmud Khalji I; the two names being identical such a mistake is not very unlikely. Thus the claim that Mahmud Khalji was imprisoned by Rana Kumbha is only a cooked up story. From the various evidences it is also certain that no battle took place at Sarangpur between Maharana Kumbha and Mahmud Khalji I during the years 1437 A.D. to 1440 A.D. The *Kirtistambha* of Chittor was erected not to commemorate victory, it is only a structure dedicated to Vishnu.

Internal Troubles in Mewar

The subjugation of the Hadas marked the zenith of Ranmal's power. He found himself master of Mewar all but in name. To consolidate his power he decided to remove his rival Raghavadeva whose presence in Mewar he found was the greatest obstacle in his way. Besides, Ranmal had not forgotten that Raghvadeva had foiled his play of marrying the Sisodia girls to the Rathor soldiers. In 1437 A.D. he started instigating Maharana Kumbha against Raghavadeva by insinuating all kinds of false allegations. Nainsi who was a court historian of the Rathors puts the blame on Raghavadeva that he was creating trouble in the territories of the Maharana who decided to get rid of him.[33] The fact, however, is that Kumbha was not yet mature enough to form his own judgment and easily lent his years to the machinations of Ranmal who hatched up a conspiracy in collusion with the Maharana and brought about the assassination of Raghavadeva in 1437 A.D.[34] The murder of Raghavadeva apparently removed the obstacle from the path of Ranmal, but ultimately it proved detrimental to his own interest. It not only resulted in his own murder but also brought about a rupture in the Sisodia-Rathor relations. It divided the two into hostile camps and proved detrimental to the interest of both of them particularly when their united effort was much required to meet growing hostility of Gujarat and Malwa.

The ascendancy of the Rathors and the ever increasing power of Ranmal after the murder of Raghavadeva scared Kumbha who could then see through the game of Ranmal and started suspecting his motives. To counter-balance the strength of Ranmal, Kumbha gradually started building up a group who were opposed to the Rathors. As a preliminary step Kumbha pardoned Mahapa and Ekka who were allowed to return to Chittor where they were taken into service by Kumbha. This should have served as a warning to Ranmal and his men, but they seem to have been too complacent. Mahapa and Ekka both were avowed enemies of Ranmal. Ekka was burning with the Rajput vendatta of avenging his father's death. They took advantage of all possible occasions to instigate Kumbha. After the murder of Raghavadeva the Sisodia group also seems to have been determined to oust the Rathors, as they were apprehensive of their own safety in the continued ascendancy of the Rathors. According to Nainsi, Ekka while massaging the leg of Maharana Kumbha started weeping and on being questioned by the Maharana Kumbha about the cause of his sorrow, he expressed that he was distressed because the land of the Sisodias had passed over to the Rathors.[35] According to Kaviraj Shyamal Dass, Mahapa (Mahipal) informed the Maharana that the Rathors were determined to occupy the *Mewar Raj* by force.[36]

Maharana Kumbha, who was himself suspicious of the motives of Ranmal listened to Ekka and Mahapa but did not take any step immediately. But very soon certain incidents happened which conceived Kumbha about the foul intentions of Ranmal. Being alarmed at the possible danger he decided to take quick action to get rid of Ranmal. The story runs that one night under the influence of intoxication Ranmal told Bharmali, the maid servant of Kumbha's mother that very soon she would not be servant of anybody, rather those who lived in Chittor would have to serve her. Though a mistress of Ranmal, she was true to her salt and did not relish the intentions of Ranmal. She related the entire incident to Saubhagya Devi. The queen mother was alarmed at the information and discussed the situation with her son. At her instance Maharana Kumbha decided to recall Chunda from Malwa and for this purpose sent a fast messenger with his summons. Ranmal on getting information of the recall of Chunda protested with the queen mother that Chunda in his old age might be tempted to get the throne for himself. But she silenced him with the simple argument that if Chunda, who had renounced his claim to the throne of Mewar, was prevented from entering Chittor people would denounce the State policy. Ranmal could not press the matter further but started taking precautions for the safety of his family. He increased the guards of the fort and also posted his sons with them with instructions not to come inside the fort even if called by him personally.[37]

Ranmal's addiction to wine and his attachment to the maid servant Bharmali ultimately brought about his end. The story as it runs is that Bharmali was taken into confidence and on the fixed night she plied Ranmal with wine and in his state of unconsciousness tied him to the cot with his turban. It was in this condition that Mahapa and other attacked him. Tod on the basis of Marwar stories mentions that,"In stature he (Ranmal) was almost gigantic and was the most athletic of all athletes of his nation". "With no arms but a brass vessel of ablution he levelled to the earth several of his assailants. . .".[38] But ultimately done to death.

According to *Vir Vinod* Ranmal was murdered in v.s. 1500/1443 A.D. which, in view of the Ranpur Jain temple inscription of v.s. 1496/1439 A.D. mentioning Kumbha's occupation of Mandor was occupied by the Sisodias prior to the date of the inscription. According to Reu[39], the murder took place on *Kartik Badi* 30, 1495/2nd November, 1438 A.D. The date given by Reu seems to be correct as it stands the test of the chronology of subsequent events.[40]

Death of Ranmal was a signal for the fall of the Rathors from their position in Mewar. Sisodias who had been rankling under the domination of Ranmal now started with full vigour under the leadership of Chunda to crush the Rathors. The first to bear the onslaught were the sons of Ranmal who under Jodha were posted at the foot of the fort. The *khyats* and bards who were fond of narrating events with some dramatic touch inform that Jodha was informed about the incidents and the death of

Ranmal on the music which used to be playing at the *naubat khana*. Jodha was alarmed and realizing the weakness of his own position immediately fled from the place with his followers and thus saved himself from the attack of Chunda. Here after Jodha had to lead a life in exile moving from place to place and making efforts to organise the Rathors to fight the Sisodias.

After the murder of Ranmal, Sisodias under the leadership of Chunda pursued Jodha and his companions. In the first encounter a number of Rathors were killed. Among the killed mention may be made of Chandrawat, Shivaraj, Puna Bhati, Bhima, Barishal, Barjang Bhimawat, and Ranmal's brother Bhim. Jodha and his brother Kandhal, however, managed to escape. Chunda continued his pursuit and another skirmish took place near the Aravali Hills which caused heavy casualty among the followers of Jodha. Chunda finally reached Mandor and occupied it. Mandor was annexed to Mewar and for its protection and administration Chunda left his sons Kuntal, Manja and Suwa and to assist them Jhala Vikramaditya and Hinglu Ahra were also posted in the region.[41] To further strengthen the position military outposts were set up in Chaukari and Kosna where Banbir Bhati, Rana Bisaldeva, Rawal Duda and other daring Rajputs were posted.[42]

At this stage it may be pointed out that Maharana Kumbha and Chunda did not follow a policy of complete annihilation of the Rathors which certainly would have been impossible. The enmity seems to have been against Ranmal and his supporters and not with the entire Rathor Rajputs. We find Kumbha at this stage following a policy of winning over a section of the Rathors on his side who could serve as a balance to the activities of Jodha and his brothers. With this aim in view he granted Sojat to Raghavadeva Chundawat, son of Hansmal. Raghavadeva Chundawat further extended his sway over Kaprada, Bagri, etc. Narbad already with the Maharana and to assuage his apprehensions he was confirmed in his *jagir* of Kaylana.

Exit of Ranmal and the days of adversity of Jodha and his brothers no doubt strengthened the position of the Sisodias, but Kumbha could not built an unified house. The family dissensions which was a bane of the Rajputs appeared in the ruling house because of hostile attitude of Kumbha and Khem Karan, the two brothers, towards each other. Of the two brothers

Kumbha being elder had ascended the throne, but he did not bear good feelings towards Khem Karan as he was his step brother.

According to general practice Khem Karan expected to be provided with a suitable *jagir*. But Kumbha was not willing to provide him suitably and only after persuasion and hesitation allotted him some *jagir* which was not liked by Khem Karan. Khem Karan instead of going to the allotted *jagir*, moved out with his followers and forcibly occupied Bari Sadri.[43] Kaviraj Shyamal Dass and G.S. Ojha both express the view that Kumbha was young at the time of his accession and, therefore, Khem Karan was still younger. But we have noticed earlier that Kumbha was quite grown up when he ascended the throne. Though we cannot definitely state the difference in the age of the two brothers, yet the incidents as mentioned indicate that Khem Karan was not much younger to Kumbha. We are informed that Kumbha could not tolerate Khem Karan's occupation of Bari Sadri and ousted him from there by force whereupon Khem Karan retired to Malwa[44] where he was welcomed by Mahmud Khalji as the Malwa Sultan expected to get valuable information and help from him.[45] Our difficulty is in fixing the possible date of ousting Khem Karan from Bari Sadri and his taking shelter in Malwa. In the absence of a definite statement we can at best only deduce from circumstantial evidence. Till his death in 1437 A.D. Ranmal is credited with almost all the territorial extension and campaigns of Kumbha, but it is not mentioned that he drove away Khem Karan from Bari Sadri which leads to the conclusion that the incident did not take place in his life time. It is also probable that Khem Karan might have occupied Bari Sadri after 1438 A.D. perhaps in 1439 A.D. at the earliest,[46] a period when Chunda was busy against Jodha and his brothers. Our next problem is to determine the date when Khem Karan was ousted from Bari Sadri and took refuge in Malwa. For this we may look into the history of Malwa during the period.

By 1439 A.D. Maharana Kumbha had subjugated portions of Kanthal and Hadauti over which Hoshang Shah had established his suzerainty. Mahmud Khalji was deeply concerned over the growing power of Mewar but could not take any step because of internal difficulties. By 1441 A.D. he had considerably strengthened himself by subduing Khandwa

Sarguja and had even ventured to march towards Delhi. On his way he even subdued some petty chiefs of Hadauti, but even then he did not attempt to test his strength against Mewar. Shihab Hakim's statement that Mahamud did not consider it desirable to leave Malwa and march into Mewar as his absence would provide an opportunity to Ahmad Shah Gujarati to invade Malwa[47] is only an indirect form of expressing that Mahmud Khalji could not think himself strong enough to march into Mewar. Because it is during this period that he did leave Malwa and even marched northwards towards Delhi. After his return from Delhi he marched into Mewar. This brings in the question as to what circumstances suddenly encouraged him to move into the direction of Mewar. This changed situation was the outcome of Khem Karan's arrival to his court. Thus it seems quite probable that Khem Karan was ousted from Bari Sadri sometimes between 1441 A.D. and 1442 A.D. Mahmud Khalji welcomed Khem Karan, because in his person he found a scion of the house of the Sisodias, and he could easily pretend that he was marching into Mewar only to restore the claims of Khem Karan. Besides, he could get many informations and also support of a group of Rajputs who were on the side of Khem Karan. Khem Karan was an enemy of Kumbha and was willing to take up arms against his brother. Throughout his life Khem Karan remained an enemy of Mewar and with the help of Malwa Sultan brought about considerable harm to Mewar.[48]

Thus we find that while Maharana Kumbha extended the territories of Mewar, strengthened his position, and reduced the Hadas, the Rathors of Mandor, but the policy of expansion was not liked by the Rajputs and they not only became hostile towards him, but by either extended assistance to the rulers of Gujarat and Malwa, and creating internal troubles within Mewar they created problems for Maharana Kumbha who had to meet external as well as internal enemies and it must be said to the credit of Maharana Kumbha that with so many odds against him he still managed not only to keep intact his kingdom, but also conquered fresh territories and brought about prosperity within his kingdom.

Notes and References

1. Nainsi, *Khyat*, ii, p. 116, *Vir Vinod*, i, p. 315.
2. *Tabaqat-i-Akbari*, iii (Tr.) pp. 220-221.
3. Bisheshwarnath Reu, *Marwar Ka Itihas*, i, p. 75.
4. H.B. Sarda, *Maharana Kumbha*, p. 41; *Udaipur Rajya ka Itihas*.
5. Kirtistambha *Prashasti*, Verse 150.
6. Nainsi, *Khyat*, i, pp. 27-28, ii, p. 117; *Vir Vinod*, i, pp. 318-319; H.B. Sarda, *Maharana Kumbha*, p. 37.
7. H.B. Sarda, *Maharana Kumbha*, pp. 39-40.
8. Reu, *Marwar ka Itihas*, i, p. 86.
9. Ojha, *Sirohi Rajya ka Itihas*, p. 115.
10. The inscription of Nandia (in Sirohi) of v.s. 1494 (1435 A.D.); Ojha, *Sirohi Rajya ka Itihas*, p. 194; Abu proper was not conquered at this stage. Only some tracts belonging to Abu were ceased. Abu proper was conquered later sometime near about 1449 A.D. or a little earlier.
11. Harbilas Sarda, *Maharana Kumbha*, p. 81.
12. *Massir-i-Mahmudshashi* (MS.), fol. 52b; Day, *Medieval Malwa*, p. 60.
13. *Ibid.*, fol. 57a; Day, *Medieval Malwa*, p. 82.
14. *Vir Vinod*, i, p. 320.
15. *Ibid.*, i. p. 319.
16. Ojha, *Udaipur Rajya ka Itihas*, i, p. 598.
17. *Ibid.*, i, p. 593, fn. 2.
18. Tod, i, p. 231.
19. *Ain*, ii (Tr. Jarrett and Sarkar), p. 230.
20. Sarda, *Maharana Kumbha*, p. 49.
21. *Ibid.*, p. 50.
22. *Ibid.*, p. 51; *Archaeological Survey Reports*, XXIII, p. 112.
23. Sarda, *Maharana Kumbha*, p. 52.
24. *Ibid.*, p. 85.
25. *Ibid.*, p. 93.
26. *Rajputana Gazetteer*, ii-A, Mewar Residency, P. Erskine writes, "He (Kumbha) defeated Mahmud Khalji of Malwa, kept him prisoner at Chittor for six months and, in commemoration of this and other victories, erected the triumphal pillar (*Jai Stambha*) at the place last mentioned".
27. *Ma'a Tir-i-Mahmudshahi*, fol. 276 b.
28. *Ibid.*, fol. 66 a.
29. *Ibid.*, fol. 68 a.
30. *Ibid.*, fol. 73 b.
31. *Ibid.*, fol. 77 a.
32. *Ibid.*, fol. 93 b.

33. Nainsi, *Khyat*, i, p. 30.
34. *Vir Vinod*, p. 319.
35. Nainsi, *Khyat*, i, pp. 28-29.
36. *Vir Vinod*, i, pp. 320-321; Ojha, *Udaipur Rajya ka Itihas*, i, p. 288; Sarda, *Maharana Kumbha*, p. 288.
37. *Vir Vinod*, i, p. 322, Nainsi, *Khyat*, i, pp. 28-9, ii, pp. 341-42; Ojha, *Udaipur Rajya ka Itihas*, i, p. 289.
    Shyamal Dass has taken the story from Nainsi.
38. Tod, *Annals etc.*, ii, p. 12, i, p. 226.
39. Reu, *Marwar ka Itihas*, i, p. 78.
40. See: Sarda, *Maharana Kumbha*, p. 64; Ojha, *Jodhpur Rajya ka Itihas*, i, p. 227; Nainsi, *Khyat*, i, p. 17, ii, p. 342; *Vigat*, i, p. 30.
41. Nainsi, *Vigat*, i, p. 32; *Vir Vinod*, i, p. 322. According to Nainsi's *Vigat*, Aka Sisodia was made overall in charge of Mandor. Renayar Mehta is also mentioned among the officers posted there.
42. Reu—*Marwar ka Itihas*, i, p. 85, Sarda—*Maharana Kumbha*, p. 68. Nainsi, *Vigat*, i, p. 32.
43. *Vir Vinod*, ii, p. 1053.
44. *Ibid.*, p. 1054.
45. Day, *Medieval Malwa*, fn. 4.
46. Ghalot, *Rajputana ka Itihas*, p. 516. According to Ghalot, Khem Karan occupied Bari Sadri in v.s. 1494/1437 A.D. but he gives neither reason nor source for accepting this date.
47. *Ma'asir-i-Mahmudshahi*, fol. 114 b. Shihab Hakim mentions that Mahmud Khalji return from Delhi, reached Mandu on first of Muharram 846/May 12, 1442 A.D.; Day, *Medieval Malwa*, p. 170.
48. Day, *Medieval Malwa*, pp. 171-172.

3

Relations with Malwa, Gujarat-Nagor

A. RELATIONS WITH MALWA

Maharana Kumbha of Mewar and Mahmud Khalji I of Malwa were contemporaries. Throughout their reigns they devoted themselves to convert their respective territories into strong and powerful kingdoms. The boundaries of their kingdoms marched together with the result that conflict and clash between the two kingdoms became inevitable. The relations of Mewar with Malwa and Gujarat also throw some light on the inter-State relations in India of the fifteenth century. It is during the course of this study that one finds that the Muslim rulers of the fifteenth century had evolved a kind of treaty of law based on mutual consent by which they could resolve their differences, could specify the areas where each could attempt territorial expansion, and could agree that the treaty signed was binding and was to be honoured by the respective monarchs. The source of the treaty law was derived from the *shariat* and was intended to offer a united front to the rising Hindu powers. In contrast with the Muslim rulers the Rajputs had become conspicuous by the absence of such an understanding. Family feud, clan rivalry and personal vanity had taken a firm hold on their minds and had so much blurred their vision that they could never locate a common enemy.

Mewar started feeling the pressure of Malwa forces from 1442 A.D. onwards. It is quite probable that the presence of Khem Karan, Kumbha's younger brother, as refugee in Malwa added to the strength of Mahmud Khalji who could pretend taking up the cause of the dispossessed prince to his ancestral possessions and could expect to get both information and assistance from the Sisodia prince and his Rajput followers. Besides, death of Ahmad Shah Gujarati removed the danger of Gujarati invasion of Malwa and he could feel himself free to move against Mewar. However, Mahmud was yet not sure of his strength and, therefore, instead of directly invading Chittor, the capital of Maharana Kumbha, he followed the policy of attacking the outlying strongholds of Mewar. Mahmud Khalji started for Mewar on Rajab 26, 846/A.H. 30th, November, 1442 A.D. and after reviewing his army at Sarangpur he marched towards the region of Kelwara which contained the strong fort of Machhindarpur.[1]

Machhindarpur was the earlier name of the fort which after some additions and strengthening of the fortifications was renamed as Kumbhalgarh by Maharana Kumbha.[2] The fort even as it stood prior to renovations was invincible and had stood the attack of Ahmad Shah Gujarati. Mahmud Khalji also realised the futility of attempting to storm the fort. However, he could discover that the temple of *Banmata* situated near the fort and protected by fortifications was a major source of strength to the main fort. He, therefore, decided to destroy the temple. The fortifications were under Dip Singh who defended it for seven days after which he fell fighting. With his death the temple was occupied and destroyed by Mahmud Khalji.[3] Maharana Kumbha could not send any help to Dip Singh as he himself had gone towards Hadauti to reduce the recalcitrant elements there. However, while Mahmud was still in the vicinity of Machhindarpur and halting at Pankarah, he received information of Maharana Kumbha's return to Chittor. For Mahmud the situation was becoming difficult and he divided his army into two sections. One was sent in advance towards Chittor obviously with the intention of checking Maharana Kumbha in case he marched against him. The other he kept under his personal command. He had also realised the possibility of cutting his routes through *Kanthal* where the Rajputs under Kalba had already started disturbance. To meet the situation he had summoned his father Azam Humayun to subjugate these chiefs around Mandsor. In the course of subjugation of these chiefs of *Kanthal*, Azam Humayun fell ill and died.[4] Mahmud returned to Mandsor in haste and made arrangements for sending the body to Shadiabad Mandu. He then appointed Taj Khan as incharge of Mandsor with instructions to reduce the surrounding regions in *Kanthal*.

From Mandsor, Mahmud marched towards Chittor, but finding his position not very safe he retraced his steps and encamped at an elevated place under the pretext of approaching rainy season. Maharana Kumbha made a night attack.[5] The result of the engagement remained indecisive. Mahmud certainly did not find his position strong and returned to his capital declaring that he would invade Chittor the following year. Historians of Rajputana claim that Maharana Kumbha gained victory[6] which is as much an exaggeration as the claim of Muslim historians that Mahmud gained a victory. Neither side gained any decisive victory though the edge seems to have been with Kumbha for otherwise, Mahmud certainly would have pressed further his advantage instead of returning to the capital. However, one fails to understand the reasons that kept Maharana Kumbha inactive against Mahmud of Malwa and instead of taking an offensive he preferred to remain on the defensive.

Mahmud Khalji recognised the strength of Maharana Kumbha and realised that it was necessary to subjugate petty Rajput principalities situated in Khichiwara and Hadauti before undertaking a direct attack on Chittor. It may be pointed out that Mahmud's aim was to curtail the influence of the Maharana. While the Malwa Sultan could undertake the reduction of these places, Maharana Kumbha did not take adequate steps for the protection of these outskirts. It is quite likely that Kumbha was not sure of the loyalty of these chiefs and possibly also the constant Rathor menace prevented him from personally marching against the Malwa Sultan. The obvious outcome, therefore, was that the Malwa Sultan extended his sway at the expense of Mewar.

Loss of Gagraun

Gagraun was the headquarters of the Khichi Chauhans after whom the region was called Khichiwara. The Khichis were in close alliance with the Ranas of Mewar. With the rise of Mewar into prominence Khichis served as a strong buttress on the eastern side of the kingdom. Achaldas Khichi, the ruler of Gagraun was son-in-law of Maharana Mokul. When he fell fighting against Hoshang Shah of Malwa the fort passed into the hands of the Malwa Sultan. Hoshang Shah placed Gagraun under Ghazni Khan who further strengthened its fortifications. Sultan Mahmud had placed the fort under Badar Khan and on his death in a battle against Ahmad Shah Gujarati, the fort was placed under Dilshad. When Sultan Mahmud was busy in quelling interal disturbances Palhan Singh, son of Achaldas[7] had reconquered the fort, may be with the assistance of Mewar forces. Mahmud Khalji being too much involved within his own kingdom had to defer its reconquest.

After his return from the expedition into Mewar region he decided to attack Gagraun. After several marches he pitched his tents on the bank of the river Ahuti on 3rd February, 1444.[8] From the bank of the Ahuti Mahmud moved upto the river Sind and at once besieged the fort and tried to close all access to it. Palhan Singh had in the meantime sought the help from Maharana Kumbha and received from him reinforcements under the command of Dahir. For seven days fighting continued but on the seventh day Dahir was killed. The death of Dahir unnerved Palhan Singh who tried to save himself by escaping out of the fort but outside the fort he was killed by a group of Bhils, who never liked the domination of the Khichis over them. The news of the death of Palhan Singh decided the fate of the fort. The Rajputs performed the *jauhar*. Sultan Mahmud ordered for the restoration of the fortifications and renamed it as Mustafabad.[9] Gagraun was not a part of Mewar and its loss did not mean loss of any territory of Mewar, but it was a strong fort, almost a dependency of Mewar and with its passing into the hands of Malwa Sultan it became a Malwi outpost on the border of Mewar and in the heart of Khichiwara. It resulted in subjugation of petty Khichi chiefs and also served as a base for Mahmud Khalji to send expeditions further north into Hadauti and the eastern borders of Mewar.

Mahmud's main aim was to acquire Mandalgarh which served as a strong buttress on the eastern frontier of Mewar. Mandalgarh had been acquired by Maharana Kumbha from the Hadas, sometime between 1435 A.D. and 1436 A.D. Bairi Sal Hada, the ruler of Bundi, outwardly owed allegiance to Chittor but never relished his position and does not seem to have offered any resistance to Mahmud Khalji.

The success achieved by Mahmud Khalji at Gagraun emboldened him and instead of returning to his capital he proceeded towards Mandalgarh. Mandalgarh had been well protected by Maharana Kumbha and when Mahmud reached the bank of the Banas river and was still two *karoh* away from Mandalgarh, fighting started with the soldiers of Maharana Kumbha. For the details of the attack we have to depend on the account of Shihab Hakim who compiled the history of the reign of Mahmud Khalji. According to Shihab Hakim after the fighting had lasted for three days some negotiations for settlement of a peace took place. From the side of Maharana Kumbha, Jeetarmal, Teja Purhot and a few other courtiers were sent and from the side of Sultan Mahmud, Mansur-ul-Mulk, Ariz Chashm Mansur and Malik Ilias were deputed to discuss the terms of peace. Precise nature of the terms discussed is not known though Shihab Hakim says that Maharana Kumbha's deputies agreed to pay one lakh tankas on condition of Sultan Mahmud's withdrawal from the place.[10] However, the manner in which Shihab Hakim has summed up the narrative creates doubt if such an offer was made. Like the usual manner of Persian chroniclers Shihab Hakim says that the Sultan ordered that "as the summer has set in and the rainy season is fast approaching and though this return Kumbha may boast as his victory, God willing I shall return next year and give him proper punishment."[11] From the above statement it is difficult to believe that an offer for payment was made which was rejected by the Sultan though he quitely returned to the capital on the plea of approaching rainy season. It is obvious that all was not well for Mahmud Khalji and odds were against him. It is also possible that he might have suffered some reverses. However, if we accept that Kumbha defeated him, we will also have to accept lack of forsight on the part of the Maharana, who knowing the danger from the Malwa Sultan did not press hard his gains to inflict a crushing defeat. It is, therefore, more likely that Kumbha did not gain any decisive victory and remained satisfied with the withdrawal of the Sultan.

Sultan Mahmud started for second time to conquer Mandalgarh on 11th October, 1446 A.D./Rajab 20, 850 A.H.[12] He went directly to Ranthambhor as he felt that fresh arrangements for its protection was of prime necessity. Bahar Khan, the commandant of the fort, he felt, was not competent enough to protect the fort in case of a direct attack by Dungar Sen of Gwalior. At Ranthambhor he placed Bhar Khan by Malik Saifuddin and ordered him to strengthen the fortifications and to keep himself ready to defend the fort in case of attack. It seems that Dungar Sen being on friendly terms with Maharana Kumbha, Mahmud thought it prudent to take these steps so that he might not be attacked just when he would be engaged with the forces of the Maharana. However, no such move was made by Dungar Sen. He also ordered Taj Khan, Ikhtiyar Khan and Ghalib Khan to march towards Alhanpur in Hadauti and to collect *khidmati* from the *muqadams* of Boli and Panchwara and to reduce the surrounding areas.

So far the actual attack of Mandalgarh is concerned the account of Shihab Hakim is extremely coloured but one can discern facts out of it. According to Shihab Hakim when Mahmud reached the vicinity of Mandalgarh, he found the fort situated on a hill surrounded by hilly regions and dense forests, and, therefore, pitched his tents on the bank of the Banas river.[13] From this statement it is obvious that on the first occasion he had not even reached the vicinity of the fort. Shihab Hakim writes further that for the first two days the battle remained indecisive. On the third day the Sultan appointed Ghazi Khan to attack the enemy. When Maharana Kumbha found that the battle may result in his defeat, he sent a large sum of money for army expenses and sued for peace. Sultan's men also represented that it was very hot, and therefore, he should accept the money and return, and the Sultan did likewise.[14] A close scrutiny of the statement of Shihab Hakim brings out that Mahmud was not victorious. The statement that Kumbha sent a large sum of money because he was sure of his defeat is a typical expression of Medieval Muslim court chronicler for whom it was difficult to write the defeat of a Muslim ruler against a Hindu ruler.

Mahmud's aim was conquest of Mandalgarh and if victory was sure where was the need for the Sultan's men to request him to accept money and return. It is obvious from the statement of Shihab Hakim that Mahmud could gain no advantage. However, from the point of view of Mewar one will have to accept that Maharana Kumbha, a great soldier that he was, once again failed to press home whatever initial advantage he had gained. From the behaviour of Maharana Kumbha it appears that he was not sure of his military strength and loyalty of the Rajput chiefs to pursue Mahmud Khalji and inflict upon him a crushing defeat. The accounts of the historians of Rajputana are equally misleading.[15] They have only tried to glorify Maharana Kumbha without analysing the problems that he was called upon to face.

In 1448 A.D. Sultan Mahmud again moved northwards but could not gain any success at Gwalior and Agra. Subsequently he moved towards Bayana. Bayana once had been a stronghold of the Rajputs, but the Sultan of Delhi had occupied it and converted it into a strong outpost against the Rajputs. Situated in Karauli it occupied a strategic position commanding the route to Delhi, the Doab and Mewar. For Mahmud the political situation was favourable. Muhammad Khan of Bayana and Yusuf Khan of Hindaun were not on good terms with each other, and, though governors on behalf of the Sayyid Sultan of Delhi, they found themselves in a precarious position, with the rise of the Rajput power of Mewar on the one hand and decline of the power of the Sultan of Delhi on the other. Thus both Muhammad Khan of Bayana and Yusuf Khan of Hindaun offered their allegiance to Mahmud Khalji of Malwa, who was quite powerful and from whom they could expect succour. Maharana Kumbha should have reduced these principalities, but then he was too busy in looking after his own territories. The importance of these places was recognised later by his grandson, Maharana Sanga.

Loss of Ajmer

Ajmer occupied a position of great strategic importance; situated at the highest elevation in the plains, it was considered as the vantage point from where Rajput powers of Rajasthan could be checked. Ever since the occupation of Delhi by the Turks, Ajmer was considered as the most important place. From the religious point of view it had a sanctity for both the Hindus and the Muslims. The close proximity of Pushkar made it important for the Hindus, and the tomb of *Shaikh* Muin-ud-din Chishti, endeared it to Muslim sentiments. During the disturbances following the invasion of Timur and because of the involvement of the Sayyid Sultans in settling their affairs in the capital and also those of their recalcitrant chiefs, Rao Ranmal Rathor of Mandor, the maternal uncle of Rana Mokal, had seized it and restored it to the ruler of Mewar.[16]

Sometime in 1455 A.D. when Mahmud was at Mandor he received a petition from the Muslim residents of Ajmer against the Hindu Governor of Ajmer who was holding it for Mewar. To Mahmud who was always ready to utilize any opportunity offered to him to enhance his political prestige, it was an offer by the dissatisfied Muslim population which was very tempting because it could make its conquest easier. From Mandsor, Mahmud marched directly to Ajmer and encamped opposite the tomb of Khawaja Muin-ud-din Chishti and prayed for the blessings of the saint.

The fort of Ajmer was under the charge of Gajadhar Singh who protected the fort for four days but on the fifth day he was killed in a battle with the besiegers. On his death confusion prevailed in the Rajput army and with the pandemonium of the retreating forces Malwi soldiers got mixed up with them and succeeded in entering the fort. The Malwi soldiers who had thus entered the fort opened the gates and the fort was captured by Mahmud Khalji without further difficulty. On this success Mahmud Khalji performed the *rites* of offering thanks to god and attained to the honour of circumambulating the grave of Shaikh Muin-ud-din Chishti. He also made arrangements for the preservation of the fort by appointing Khwaja Naimullah entitled Saif Khan as its commandant. After ordering for the construction of a mosque, and bestowing rewards and stipends upon the attendants of the holy place he returned towards Mandalgarh.[17]

Ajmer was thus lost to Mewar for the time being, but from the subsequent events one can infer that Mahmud did not intend to hold the place permanently. Maybe he was aware of the difficulties of protecting the place from his capital at Mandu. The conquest of Ajmer from the non-believers was an act of piety in the eyes of the Muslims and Mahmud by restoring it to the

Muslims enhanced his prestige. The subsequent silence about Ajmer in the history of the remaining years of Mahmud's reign suggests that sometimes later the place was reconquered by Maharana Kumbha, may be, during the years when Mahmud was busy with the Bahmani rulers in the Deccan. The Ajmer affair also indicates that in all likelihood Maharana Kumbha had by then adopted the policy of avoiding direct clash of arms with these rulers, instead he found it more convenient to attack them when they were retreating or to ambush them and harass them and after their departure to reoccupy the places by driving out whatever small contingents were left behind to look after the occupied places.

Loss of Mandalgarh

Emboldened by his success at Ajmer and strengthened with the blessings at the Dargah of the Saint, Mahmud turned towards Mandalgarh and reached the Banas river sometimes in 860/1456 A.D. where he pitched his tents on the southern banks of the river. Mahmud then divided his army into several detachments and ordered them to attack the fort from various directions. Maharana Kumbha who was then present in the fort also divided his army into three groups which attacked simultaneously the Malwi forces. In the battle that ensued Malwi forces under Taj Khan and Ali Khan suffered heavy losses and towards the end of the day the armies on both sides retired to their respective camps. Nizamuddin Ahmad and Firishta both have given a very coloured account to conceal the real position. According to them, after the reverses suffered by the forces of Taj Khan and Ali Khan the next morning the *amirs* advised Mahmud to return to his capital to re-equip the army and also to avoid the hazards of the approaching season. Mahmud accepted the proposal and returned to his capital.[18] The account of Shihab Hakim, however, indicates that Mahmud was not in a happy position.[19] From these accounts we can easily deduce that Mahmud, if not actually defeated, was sure of his defeat if the battle was prolonged and returned to his capital on the plea of approaching rainy season. Maharana Kumbha thus saved Mandalgarh again on this occasion, but what intrigues most is Maharana's abstinence from pursuing the retreating forces of the Malwi Sultan. Certainly it would be wrong to ascribe such a course to the Rajput sense of chivalry, simply because such a sense, if it had prevailed in earlier centuries, had disappeared in the course of changing circumstances. If we examine the chronology, the years 1456 A.D. and 1457 A.D. were difficult years for Maharana Kumbha because of Gujarati activity in the south-west and Rathor hostility in the north-west of his kingdom. Therefore, it seems reasonable to deduce that Maharana Kumbha did not consider it prudent to expose his forces to any damage which could have been an outcome of a clash with the retreating forces. In 860 A.H./1456 A.D. Maharana Kumbha, after return of Mahmud Khalji, rushed to Kumbhalgarh on which side Sultan Qutbuddin Gujarati was advancing and had already moved to Abu and Sirohi.

After return of Mahmud Khalji, Maharana Kumbha moved westwards to settle his score with Sultan Qutbuddin of Gujarat and Rathors of Mandor. This pre-occupation of Kumbha offered an opportunity to Mahmud Khalji to make yet another attempt on Mandalgarh. On 26th of Muharram 861 A.H./24th December, 1456 A.D. Mahmud started for the conquest of the fort of Mandalgarh.[20] Nizamuddin Ahmad mentions that armies of Nagor, Ajmer and Hadauti joined Mahmud. But Nagor was not a part of Mahmud's territory and by itself was not in a position to render any assistance. Similarly, there was hardly any army at Ajmer to assist Mahmud. It is, however, not unlikely that the Hadas of Bundi might have joined Mahmud to avenge their defeat and loss of Mandalgarh to Maharana Kumbha. Shihab Hakim does not speak of any army from these places joining Mahmud, but simply says that Mahmud had already reduced Nagor, Ajmer, Toda Ghiyasgir, Chatsu, Ranthambhor and Hadauti before he marched for the conquest of Mandalgarh. Nagor, however, was never reduced by Mahmud Khalji.

Mahmud had already acquired a full knowledge of the topography of Mandalgarh through his repeated unsuccessful attempts on the fort. The fort was situated on a hill and was surrounded by rugged stony land and dense vegetation. He, therefore, pitched his tents at a distance of one *karoh* on its eastern side. From this base he ordered for clearing of the foliage, cutting through the rocks and to prepare a passage to the top of the hill on the western side of the fort so as to enable him to mount the siege engines for battering the fortifications.

During this process the Rajputs from within the fort constantly sallied out to prevent the proceedings, but Mahmud had employed enough soldiers to keep them engaged so that the construction work could continue undisturbed. After the construction was completed he fixed his tents at the hill-top and arranged for a complete blockade of the fort. *Manjaniks* were used from both the sides, but in the process of the siege the best of the *manjaniks* inside the fort were damaged. But the strength of the fort stood them well and in the earlier stages of the siege the Rajputs put up a determined resistance and kept on repairing whatever minor damages could be effected by the besieging army. The constant battering, however, finally brought about a wide breach in the outer fortifications which created confusion inside the fort as a large number of the inmates started searching for safer shelters in the inner fort.[21] Mahmud then cut off the source of water supply and also got filled up a portion of the ditch surrounding the outer wall so as to enable the army to enter the fort. Finding their cause lost the Rajputs sallied out of the fort and gave a stiff battle in their traditional manner. Though most of them perished fighting, a few submitted. Mahmud allowed them to evacuate the fort which was occupied by the Malwi forces on 1st Zilhijjah, 861 A.H./20th October, 1457 A.D.[22] As a mark of the fulfilment of his long cherished desire Mahmud ordered for the conversion of a temple within the fort into a mosque and also appointed a *qazi,* a *mufti,* a *khatib* and a *muazzin* and also fixed their stipends.

The siege and conquest of Mandalgarh had taken more than ten months and during this period we do not find Maharana Kumbha making any attempt to send relief to the fort. This certainly was not an outcome of pusillanimity of the Maharana, but was the result of his involvement elsewhere in the western Rajasthan. Attack of Qutbuddin Gujarati, the Nagor tangle and the confrontation with Jodha kept Kumbha pre-occupied and prevented him from sending relief to Mandalgarh. Mahmud Khalji on the other hand was assisted by the Hadas and Khem Karan, the younger brother of Kumbha. Khem Karan's motive in assisting Mahmud was to oust Kumbha and secure the throne of Chittor for himself. The motive of the Hadas in assisting Mahmud is rather complicated. Mahmud had at an earlier stage ousted Sanda from Kotah and had given it to his younger brother Bhonk or Bhanda and it was Hadas under Bhanda who assisted Mahmud, may be, he expected that Mahmud might hand over Mandalgarh also to him.[23]

While returning from Mandalgarh, Mahmud made another raid into Mewar territory and after plundering some place in Kelwara and Delwara he returned to his capital. In 863 A.H./1458-9 A.D. Mahmud made another attempt on Kumbhalgarh but finding the fort too strong he returned and plundered some areas in Chhappan and returned to his capital. Mahmud made yet another raid into Mewar in 1467 A.D. but the war tactics of Maharana Kumbha completely baffled him and after suffering heavy losses he returned to his capital. After this he did not come to Mewar any more. Thus Maharana Kumbha and Mahmud Khalji remained enemies throughout their lives. Though Mewar retained its honour and never suffered defeat from Malwa yet much of the energy of the State was wasted in resisting the repeated attacks of Mahmud Khalji and more so because Maharana Kumbha could never inflict a crushing defeat which was the result of his defensive policy. Had he taken the offensive and invaded the territory of Malwa he could have put pressure on Mahmud Khalji and could prevent him from marching into Mewar whenever he so liked. By invading Malwa Kumbha could have caused similar damage to the people of Malwa as Mahmud was bringing upon the people inhabiting the regions of Kelwara, Delwara, Chhappan, etc. In the final analysis we find that Maharana Kumbha and Mahmud Khalji left as a legacy to their successors the contest for supremacy between these two States.

B. RELATIONS WITH GUJARAT-NAGOR

Maharana Kumbha inherited as a legacy the hostility with Gujarat. It was during the raid of Sultan Ahmed Shah in 1433 A.D. while Maharana Mokul was marching to oppose him that he was murdered. In 1433 A.D. Sultan Ahmed Shah had not tarried long in Marwar but had moved to Nagor where he received homage from his uncle Firuz Khan son of Shams Khan *Dandani*,[24] and after confirming him at Nagor he had returned to Ahmadabad. After his return he remained busy elsewhere in his kingdom till his death on 4th Rabi II, 846 A.H./2nd August,

1442 A.D. Ahmad Shah was succeeded by his son Muhammad Shah II who ruled upto the beginning of 855 A.H./February 1451 A.D. during his rule Gujarat remained engaged in quelling internal disturbances and subduing the Rajput States adjacent to Gujarat, with the result that Mewar, during his reign, remained free from confrontation with Gujarat. Maharana Kumbha made full use of the situation in consolidating his position in Mewar. Muhammad Shah II was succeeded Qutbuddin Ahmad Shah who ruled over Gujarat till Rajab 23, 863 A.H./26th May, 1459 A.D. On his death his uncle Daud Shah ascended the throne but his reign lasted for even less than a month when the *amirs* deposed him and raised to the throne Shahzada Fateh Khan, son of Muhammad Shah II on Shaban 1863 A.H./3rd June, 1459 A.D. with the regnal title of Mahmud Shah popularly known as Mahmud Begada. Mahmud Bagada ruled over Gujarat till his death on 23rd November, 1511 A.D. Thus Maharana Kumbha was contemporary to five rulers of Gujarat and it must be put to his credit that he kept the territory of Mewar intact against Gujarati aggression and also maintained the honour of Mewari forces by his timely moves. However, it seems that Maharana Kumbha wanted to avoid entanglement with the ruler of Gujarat, if it could be possible and that is why we find that in 849 A.H./1445-46 A.D. When Sultan Muhammad Shah raided and subdued Hari Rai, son of Punja, the ruler of Idar, and Raja Ganesh, the ruler of Dungarpur, he remained aloof and did not send any assistance to them.

But Maharana Kumbha could not avoid the conflict for long. His involvement in the affairs of Nagor brought him in direct clash with Sultan Qutbuddin Gujarati. Nagor being the cause of conflict the details of the affairs deserve closer examination.

The year 857 A.H./1451-2 A.D. proved to be of importance for Maharana Kumbha. In the beginning of the year Sultan Qutbuddin Ahmad ascended to the throne of Gujarat[25] and by the end of the same year he concluded a treaty with Sultan Mahmud Khalji of Malwa.[26] Kaviraj Shymal Dass and Harbilas Sarda have erroneously placed the treaty in 1456 A.D. and arrive at the conclusion that the two Sultans having failed in their attempts to defeat Maharana Kumbha concluded the treaty.[27] In reality, however, Maharana Kumbha had to face the combined efforts of the two Sultans from the year 1452 A.D. and not after 1456 A.D. In the same year, *i.e.* 855 A.H./1451-2 Firuz Khan, son of Shams Khan *Dandani* died which led to a dispute between his brother Mujahid Khan and his son Shams Khan,[28] Mujahid Khan proved stronger and occupied Nagor. Shams Khan for fear of his life sought the protection of Maharana Kumbha and asked for his help to recover Nagor from Mujahid Khan. For Maharana Kumbha there hardly could have been a better opportunity to establish his suzerainty over Nagor with its ruler as his protege. Maharana Kumbha was also conscious of the prolonged struggle between his father Maharana Mokul and Firuz Khan in which neither had succeeded in reducing the other. Thus he might have thought that by assisting Shams Khan he would be closing the struggle and at the same time establish his supremacy over that region. By restoring Nagor to Shams Khan he could also expect to have a useful ally to check the growing menace of the Rathors under Jodha.

As a practical man Maharana Kumbha laid down a condition for rendering assistance. The condition he imposed was that Shams Khan after getting occupation of Nagor would have to demolish three turrets of the fort of Nagor. According to Nizamuddin Ahmad such a condition was imposed by Maharana Kumbha to prove to the world that although Maharana Mokul had been defeated and driven away from the battlefield by Firuz Khan yet he (Kumbha) having acquired power over the fort had his revenge. Nizamuddin, however, feels shy of mentioning the occasion when Firuz Khan too had been defeated and driven away from the battlefield by Maharana Mokul which finds mention without reservations in *Kayam Khan Rasa*.[29] Truth of the matter is that demolition of a part of fortification was considered in medieval India as recognition of overlordship of the person at whose command such a demolition was carried out. Ranakpur Inscription[30] of v.s. 1496/1439 A.D. mentioning the conquest of Nagor by Maharana Kumbha can only refer to some punitive expedition led by Ranmal Rathor who was then serving Mewar, because Firuz Khan bin Shams Khan *Dandani* continued in the possession of Nagor till his death.

Shams Khan who was hardly in a position to bargain, accepted the terms dictated by Maharana Kumbha. On his acceptance of the terms Maharana Kumbha accompanied Shams

Khan and marched towards Nagor. The news of Maharana Kumbha's march alarmed Mujahid Khan who could not feel himself strong enough to face the forces of Mewar and retired to the court of Sultan Mahmud Khalji of Malwa thus leaving Nagor open to be occupied by Shams Khan. Shams Khan occupied Nagor without any battle being fought between the forces of Mewar and that of Nagor. According to Nizamuddin Ahmad after Shams Khan's occupation of the fort of Nagor, Maharana Kumbha sent him a message that he should carry out his promise.[31] Sikandar simply says that Shams Khan taking assistance from the Rana reached Nagor and occupied it.[32] It, therefore, seems that at this stage Maharana Kumbha stayed back and did not personally go as far as Nagor or else he could have caused the turrets to be pulled down in his own presence. Shams Khan on his part was in no mood to comply with the terms of agreement he had entered into earlier and on receiving the demand of Maharana Kumbha summoned the *amirs* and heads of the clans and placed the matter before them for their opinion. In the meeting some of them tauntingly remarked that "It was a matter of pity, Firuz Khan had not begotten a daughter so that she might have saved the honour of the family."[33] Harbilas Sarda writes, "On this, Shams Khan humbly prayed to the Maharana to spare the fort just then, for otherwise his nobles would kill him after the Maharana was gone. He promised to demolish the battlements himself later on. The Maharana granted this prayer and returned to Mewar."[34] Sikandar gives still another version. According to him after Shams Khan's occupation of Nagor, Rana Kumbha wanted to destroy certain buildings which was not allowed by Shams Khan whereupon fighting took place in which many persons were killed. The Rana felt sore about it and returned to his country to collect more force to invade it and returned to his country to collect more force to invade Nagor.[35] Harbilas Sarda and Sikandar both convey the sense that Kumbha was present in Nagor at the time of its occupation by Shams Khan and according to the former Maharana Kumbha returned on the request of Shams Khan while according to the latter Maharana Kumbha returned finding himself not strong enough to enforce his will. It becomes difficult to accept either of the versions, because Maharana Kumbha was not so indifferent that he would know nothing about the meeting had he been personally present in Nagor and would allow himself to fall into the ruse of Shams Khan so easily, nor was he so weak as to find himself in difficulty against Shams Khan when he had moved well prepared to drive out Mujahid Khan from Nagor. The truth of the matter was that Kumbha had not gone as far as Nagor because Mujahid Khan had already vacated the place on getting information of his movement in that direction. Nizamuddin Ahmad's version seems to be nearer the truth, when he says that in reply to the demand of the Rana, Shams Khan informed that 'it was not possible that any part should be demolished till many heads should have been cut off.'

After sending the reply Shams Khan ordered for the repair of the ruined parts and also for further strengthening of the fortifications anticipating that non-compliance of the agreement on his part would not be tolerated by Maharana Kumbha who certainly would not hesitate to invade Nagor. The anticipation of Shams Khan turned out to be correct, because on receiving the reply and subsequently the information that instead of demolition, Shams Khan was actually strengthening the fortifications, Maharana Kumbha did invade Nagor to punish him. However, Shams Khan could get sufficient time to repair and strengthen the fortifications before Rana Kumbha could reach Nagor.

On getting information that Rana Kumba was marching against Nagor, Shams Khan lost courage and instead of meeting him or resisting him he left his army and his officers for the defence of the fort while personally he proceeded to the court of Gujarat to seek the help of Sultan Qutbuddin Ahmad Shah. Shams Khan was welcomed by the Gujarati Sultan who was further pleased when Shams Khan offered his daughter in marriage to him. Qutbuddin promised to help him in recovering Nagor. Thus Shams Khan's taking shelter in the court of Sultan Qutbuddin brought about a conflict between Gujarat and Mewar.

After the marriage festivities were over Sultan Qutbuddin sent Rai Ram Chandra Naik and Malik Gadai and some other *amirs* to reinforce the men at Nagor while he kept Shams Khan as a guest in his court. The reinforcement sent by the Sultan according to Sikandar reached Nagor in time and gave battle to

Rana Kumbha.[36] In the battle that followed the entire army consisted of the Gujarati reinforcement and local men of Nagor were defeated and a large number of their men were slain. Rana Kumha also devastated the territory of Nagor destroying cultivation and slaughtering people residing outside the fort.[37] However, after this victory, Rana Kumbha did not annex Nagor because we do not find establishment of Mewari *thanas* or appointment of officials by Rana Kumbha in Nagor. He seems to have been satisfied by devastating the country and punishing the people almost in the same manner in which Mahmud Khalji was behaving in his raids in Mewar. It is quite likely that the activities of Rao Jodha Rathor who had occupied Mandor by v.s. 1510/1453/857 and was constantly attacking various places in Mewar, prevented Rana Kumbha from devoting sufficient time to make necessary arrangements for its incorporation in the State of Mewar.[38]

The news of the sack of Nagor and the defeat of the army sent under Ram Chandra and Malik Gadai was a serious blow to the prestige of Sultan Qutbuddin Gujarati and to retrieve it he marched out in person with a well equipped army in 860/1456 A.D.[39] On the basis of this date we can calculate that Rana Kumbha should have sacked Nagor sometimes in 859/1454-55 A.D., this date, however, in the absence of any concrete evidence, is at best hypothetical and subject to alteration on the availability of further information.

Nizamuddin Ahmad says that Sultan Qutbuddin proceeded towards Kumbhalgarh[40] but we should not forget that the real aim was the recovery of Nagor and, therefore, the route followed by the Gujarati Sultan may have been through the vicinity of Kumbhalgarh and because the Sultan could not go beyond this place the chronicler mentions this place as the aim of the march of the Sultan. When the Sultan was in the vicinity of Abu, the Deora Chief who had been dispossessed of it by Rana Kumbha came as a suppliant to the Sultan for restoration of Abu to him. Sultan Qutbuddin expected the restored Deora Chief at Abu would be a useful vassal against Kumbha and, therefore, agreed to provide assistance for his restoration. Sultan Qutbuddin appointed Malik Shaban Imadul Mulk to proceed against Abu to reconquer it and himself proceeded towards Sirohi. While the Sultan was still on his way to Sirohi Malik Shaban Imadul Mulk fought a battle with the Mewari forces posted at Abu and was defeated suffering heavy losses. This was another set back to the Gujarati Sultan and he recalled Imadul Mulk to join immediately. The ruler of Sirohi, who during this period was having cordial relations with Rana Kumbha, tried to block the passage of Sultan Qutbuddin long enough to allow Rana Kumbha to drive away Mahmud Khalji from Mandalgarh and personally reach Kumbhalgarh before the arrival of Sultan Qutbuddin.

It is claimed that on reaching the environs of Kumbhalgarh, Sultan Qutbuddin ordered for the devastation of the country side. However, it may be remembered that the topography of the region is such that there could be hardly anything to be devastated or destroyed in the country side. According to Nizamuddin Ahmad and Sikandar, Maharana Kumbha came out of the fort, fought an engagement in which he was defeated and here entered the fort. From inside the fort he started sending parties everyday to give battle, but each time they were defeated. Ultimately Maharana came forward in distress and humility and offered suitable tribute, whereupon the Sultan returned to Ahmedabad.[41] Sikandar even goes to length of stating that Kumbha even promised that in future he would not invade Nagor or any other Islamic territory which pleased the Sultan and he returned to his capital. Such statements, however, are hardly credible. Sultan Qutbuddin had moved with the intention of restoring Nagor to Shams Khan and if he had succeeded in defeating Maharana Kumbha what prevented him from proceeding to Nagor and restoring it to Shams Khan. The real position, therefore, seems to be that either Sultan Qutbuddin was defeated or being harassed by the military tactics adopted by Maharana Kumbha, he found himself in a difficult situation and preferred to return to his capital without achieving any success in his objective, and Shams Khan had to remain at Ahmedabad nursing the hope of recovering Nagor in near future.

In 861/1456-57 A.D. Sultan Qutbuddin again moved into the territory of Mewar and marched in the direction of Kumbhalgarh. On getting information about the movements of the Gujarati Sultan, Maharana Kumbha who was then at Chittor started for Kumbhalgarh and by forced marches reached the fort before the arrival of Qutbuddin. Maharana Kumbha had already seen the effectiveness of his evasive battle tactics in the previous engagement and, therefore, instead of fighting a pitched battle he adopted the old tactics taking advantage of the defiles and uneven land. As to the outcome of this attack the Persian chroniclers state that Kumbha being defeated sued for peace and offered handsome tribute besides pledging that in future he would not cause any injury to the country of Nagor. Sultan Qutbuddin was satisfied and returned with triumph and victory to Ahmedabad. Such, however, was not the outcome of the attack which will be understandable from the contradictory remarks found in these sources. Sikandar mentions that Kumbha returned to Chittor which was besieged by the Sultan and Kumbha asked for pardon and negotiated for peace from Chittor. But as mentioned earlier the attack was on Kumbhalgarh and the skirmishes took place round that centre. We may also remember that during the whole year Kumbha remained away from Chittor which allowed a comparatively free hand to Mahmud Khalji of Malwa to capture the fort of Mandalgarh. In this attack, like the previous one, Sultan Qutbuddin did not achieve any success. Nagor remained just in the same condition as it was earlier, and the only damage that he could inflict on Maharana Kumbha was that he kept the Rana busy and engaged with himself which brought about the loss of Mandalgarh. The tribute mentioned by the chroniclers might have been the plunder collected during the Gujarati Sultan's activity in the territory of Mewar which has been conveniently put as the tribute paid by the ruler of Mewar.

Nizamuddin Ahmad and Sikandar both mention that hardly three months had elapsed since the return of Sultan Qutbuddin when news arrived that Maharana Kumbha was again attempting, with an army of fifty thousand horsemen, to devastate Nagor. The Sultan on getting this news came out of Ahmedabad and halted for about a month for the purpose of mustering the troops. Maharana Kumbha hearing the news of the Sultan's preparations retired to his own place, and the Sultan on getting the news of Rana Kumbha's return, re-entered Ahmedabad.[42]

This event as narrated is misleading. The information that Maharana Kumbha had moved out of Chittor and was marching in the direction of Nagor, no doubt, was correct. But Maharana

Kumbha was actually marching against Rao Jodha and on this occasion had not moved out to attack Nagor. It was in this engagement that a treaty was concluded with Jodha, which ended the long feud between Jodha and Kumbha started from the time when Rao Ranmal was killed in Chittor.[43] It was after the conclusion of the treaty and settlement with Jodha that Maharana Kumbha returned to Chittor, and not because he was afraid of Sultan Qutbuddin who had stationed himself outside Ahmedabad and mustering soldiers.

According to Persian chronicles Sultan Qutbuddin again marched against Rana Kumbha in 862/1457-58 A.D. (19-11-1457 to 7-11-1458) and on his way again plundered and revaged Sirohi for the third time. Nizamuddin says that while the Sultan personally proceeded towards Kumbhalgarh, he sent detachment to ravage the dominions of Rana Kumbha. He finally besieged the Rana in the fort of Kumbhalgarh with a firm determination; but as considerable time lapsed, and he knew that it would be difficult to seize it, he gave up the siege and advanced towards the fortress of Chittor; and after plundering and ravaging the country around it, went back to Ahmedabad. Nizamuddin Ahmad further says that to every one of the soldiers whose horses had become disabled during the campaigns, the Sultan gave the price of one from the treasury. Nizamuddin Ahmad also says that Rana Kumbha sent envoys after the Sultan and in great humility and distress prayed to be excused for his offences; and the Sultan again drew the pen of forgiveness across his guilt and sent back the envoys pleased and happy.[44] From the same source we learn that in 863/1458-59 A.D. the Sultan again wanted to march against Rana Kumbha but he fell ill and died within the year.

This account is an extremely distorted version of the actual incidents. First of all we find that it mentions of the Maharana being besieged in the fort of Kumbhalgarh then the Sultan finding it difficult to capture it raised the siege and raided some place in region of Chittor and after his return he had to pay to the soldiers for re-equipping themselves. If the Sultan had not suffered loss from where the necessity of payment for re-equipment arose. After the return of the Sultan why should the Maharana sent envoys seeking for his forgiveness. It is Sultan Qutbuddin who had invaded and not the Maharana. Then again if the Sultan had drawn the pen of forgiveness why did he intend to march against the Maharana again in the following year. The answer to these questions can be found in the incidents that took place at Nagor. After the settlement with Rao Jodha Rathor, Maharana Kumbha had raided Nagor sometime in 1458 A.D. and brought about complete devastation to the city and the country round it. The reference of the sack and devastation of Nagor as given in the *Eklinga Mahatmya* and Chittorgarh *Kirtistambha Prashasti* and quoted by Harbilas Sarda actually refers to the last raid carried out by Rana Kumbha in which it is said that he defeated the king of the Shah (Muslims), slew the heroes of Nagpur (Nagor), destroyed the fort, captured elephants, imprisoned large number of Muslim women and massacred large number of Muslims. He gained victory over the king of Gujarat, burnt the city of Nagor and destroyed all the mosques therein.[45] If such was the devastation caused by Rana Kumbha, Sultan Qutbuddin certainly could feel humiliated and insulted and to avenge the wrong he led the subsequent invasion and besieged Kumbha in the fort of Kumbhalgarh, but to his chagrin had to return without achieving any success. To conceal the repeated failures of the Gujarati Sultan the court historians of Gujarat interpolated for each occasion that Rana Kumbha sought pardon and the Sultan drew the pen of forgiveness across the guilt of Rana Kumbha. So far Shams Khan was concerned, he failed to assess the situation correctly and could never return to Nagor. In seeking shelter with Sultan Qutbuddin he only chose a *wrong* refuge and after the death of the Sultan, the nobles of Gujarat put him to death and also killed his daughter who suspected of administering poison to the Sultan at the instigation of Shams Khan. To the people of Nagor, Shams Khan only brought ruin and carnage by incurring the wrath of Rana Kumbha. The suspicion of administering poison by Shams Khan is a clear pointer to the failure of Qutbuddin to restore Shams Khan to Nagor which could have been thought by the nobles as sufficient provocation for him to take recourse to such a *heinous* act.

By entangling himself in the Nagor affair Rana Kumbha also could not achieve his object. He had expected that Shams Khan would be obliged to him for reinstatement at Nagor. But Shams Khan betrayed his expectations. His involvement in

Nagor resulted in a direct conflict with Gujarat which otherwise could have been avoided. Though Rana Kumbha vindicated his position as a commander and a soldier/warrior but this conflict prevented him from devoting his full resources against Sultan Mahmud of Malwa and Rao Jodha Rathor. He could not even protect Sirohi from being sacked thrice by the Gujarati Sultan during the course of his raids on Mewar. It is also doubtful if Rana Kumbha retained his hold over Nagor for long.

Viewed historically Rana Kumbha's sack of Nagor, however, illustrates that in Medieval India it was a common practice to carry out destruction and pillage in the territory of an enemy and in the process of devastation no consideration was shown either towards the civil population or towards the places of religious worship. It indicates that the Rajputs were no exception to the general practice of the age, and that they too had adopted the same retaliatory methods which are generally associated with Muslim monarchs of Medieval India.

Internal condition of Gujarat following the death of Sultan Qutbuddin put to a halt the Gujarati aggression on Mewar. After the death of Sultan Qutbuddin in 1459 the nobles and important officers of the State raised his uncle Daud, son of Sultan Ahmad Shah to the throne. But he could not retain the favour of his *amirs* who deposed him within the month of his accession and raised to the throne Fath Khan bin Muhmmad Shah with the title of Mahmud Shah who became famous in the history of the Gujarat by his epithet of Begda. At the time of his accession Mahmud was a young boy of about fourteen years, and for about five years he remained under the care of Imad-ul-mulk, the *wazir*. By the year 1463 Mahmud Begda started taking decisions independently. Such a political situation in Gujarat left Rana Kumbha undisturbed and he too on his part avoided all direct conflict. In the absence of any positive evidence, no doubt, it is difficult to say if the two kingdoms of Mewar and Gujarat ever came into direct conflict after 1458 but in the incidents of Girnar we have some indirect hints to suggest that Rana Kumbha was not altogether oblivious of whatever was happening outside his kingdom. Girnar in Saurashtra was a fairly prosperous territory and Mahmud Begda wanted to annex it to his kingdom. He invaded Girnar in 1464, 1466 and 1467 and on each occasion

Mahmud Begda returned after extracting tribute. The Raja of Girnar, Mandalik Chudasama was the son-in-law of Rana Kumbha and it is quite likely that he was receiving assistance from the Rana. Mahmud Begda also seems to have been unwilling to pick up unnecessary quarrel with Mewar and, therefore, remained contented with the tribute on these occasions. Such a conclusion, of course, is based on subsequent events. Mahmud Begda again invaded Girnar in 1469 after the assassination of Rana Kumbha and during the period of uneasiness in Mewar after the accession of Udai Singh and not only conquered the place by 1470 but forced the Mandalik Raja to embrace Islam. That Mahud Begda did not or could not oust the Mandalik Raja during his raids of 1464, 1466 and 1467 but succeeded in achieving his object in 1469-70 hints that probably the Mandalik Raja was getting some kind of help from Rana Kumbha and Mahmud Begda was in no mood to come in direct conflict with the Rana. The assassination of Kumbha in 1468 followed by internal trouble in Mewar allowed Mahmud Begda a free hand to annex Girnar. That the Mandalik embraced Islam also indicates that after the exit of Rana Kumbha he did not expect any help or even a shelter in Mewar and, therefore, remained in Gujarat though as a Muslim.[46]

Poet Udairaj who composed *Raj Vinod Mahakavya* sometimes between 1462 and 1469 under the patronage of Mahmud Begda mentions Rana Kumbha in humiliating terms.[47] This mention of Rana Kumbha, though not relevant to his narrative indicates the Mahmud Begda had some ill-feeling towards Kumbha which may have been due to his help to Mandalik Raja, and Udairaj though it prudent to show indignation towards Rana Kumbha and belittle him so as to gain the favour of Sultan Mahmud Begda.

In his relations with Malwa and Gujarat we have seen that Rana Kumbha always followed a defensive policy. Instead of invading the territories of these two kingdoms, he allowed them to march into Mewar and preferred to meet them within his own territory. One would not be wrong to deduce that in reality Rana Kumbha tried his best to avoid conflict, and whenever he had to meet them he did it not by his own choice but as sometime forced upon him. However such a policy was not an outcome of any personal weakness or because of absence of personal valour.

It was the internal condition of Mewar and the attitude of the various *samantas* and the *thikanas* that demanded Rana Kumbha's constant vigilance and personal presence in Mewar which did not permit him to move out of Mewar.

NOTES AND REFERENCES

1. *Ma'asir-i-Mahmudshahi*, fol. 129a.
2. Day, *Medieval Malwa*, pp. 173-74; Sarda, *Maharana Kumbha*, p. 128. According to Sardar, reconstruction of Kumbhalgarh was started in 1443 A.D. and completed in 1458 A.D. *Kirtistambh Prashasti*, Verse 185 gives 1515 v.s. as the date of completion.
3. Day, *Medieval Malwa*, p. 174, fn. 3.
4. *Ma'asir-i-Mahmudshahi*, fols. 130 a.b.
5. *Ibid.*, fol. 132a. Shihab Hakim reckons Kumbha's force at ten thousand horse and twenty three thousand infantry; Firishta ii, p. 488 puts the figures at ten thousand cavalry and six thousand infantry. The figures mentioned by these chroniclers are doubtful.
6. *Vir Vinod*, i, p. 325.
7. Balhan of *Mathir-i-Mahmudshahi* is same as Palhan. Palhan Singh had left the fort before the final *Jauhar* after which it was captured by Hoshang Shah. See *Achaldas Khichi-ri-Vachanika*, p. 34 et. seqi. *Zafar-ul-walih*, p. 199.
8. Ahuti or Ahoo river is a tributary of the Sindh and Gagraun is situated almost on the confluence of these two rivers. See Day, *Medieval Malwa*, p. 177.
9. *Ibid.*, p. 178.
10. *Ma'asir-i-Mahmudshahi*, fol. 139 b.
11. *Ibid.*, fol. 140a.
12. *Ibid.*, fol. 156a: Mahmud Khalji had already captured Ranthambhor and had posted his own commandant of the fort.
13. *Ibid.*, fol. 158a; *Firishta*, ii, p. 491.
14. *Ibid.*, fol. 159a; *Firishta*, ii, p. 491.
15. See *Vir Vinod*, i, p. 325; Sarda, *Maharana Kumbha*, pp. 87-88.
16. Sarda, *Maharana Kumbha*, p. 90; *Ajmer, Historical and Descriptive*, p. 149.
17. Day, *Medieval Malwa*, p. 185 and fn. 1, 2, 3.
18. *Tabaqat-i-Akbari*, III, p. 339; *Firishta*, ii, p. 496.
19. *Ma'asir-i-Mahmudshahi*, fol. 159a.
20. *Ibid.*, fol. 210b; *Tabaqat-i-Akbari*, iii, p. 339; *Firishta*, ii, p. 496; *Zafar-ul-walih*, p. 203.
21. Day, *Medieval Malwa*, p. 188.
22. *Ma'asir-i-Mahmudshahi*, fol. 209a; *Vir Vinod*, i, p. 331. The date of

the conquest of Mandalgarh given in *Vir Vinod* as 860 A.H./1456 A.D./1513 v.s. is not correct.
23. See Chapter on Relations with the Rajputs.
24. S.C. Misra, *The Rise of Muslim Power in Gujarat*, pp. 202-3; Misra mentions Shams Khan Dandani as the ruler of Nagor against whom Sultan Ahmad Shah marched in 1433 A.D., and he refers to *Tabaqat-i-Akbari*, iii, p. 123. But the text as well as the transition of *Tabaqat-i-Akbari* mentions Firuz Khan, son of Shams Khan *Dandani* as the ruler who submitted to Ahmad Shah in 1433 A.D. The reference as well as the statement of Prof. S.C. Misra is not correct. Shams Khan *Dandani* had died earlier at Nagor and his son Firuz Khan had succeeded him. Firuz Khan fought a number of engagements with Maharana Mokul. The earliest reference is found in the *Prashasti* of Sammidheshwar Mahadeva Temple dated v.s. 1458/1428 A.D. The battle between Firuz Khan and Maharana Mokul is also mentioned in the *Prashasti* of Ekalinga Mahadeva and also finds mention in the *Prashasti* of Kumbhalgarh. Ekalinga Mahadeva *Prashasti*, verse 44.
The incident is also mentioned in *Kayamkhand Rasa*, p. 29. From these references it is clear that Shams Khan *Dandani* had died long ago. Firuz Khan was contemporary of Maharana Mokul and it was against him that Ahmad Shah had marched in 1433 A.D. Firuz Khan of Nagor was also a contemporary of Maharana Kumbha.
25. Accession of Qutbuddin Ahmad took place on Muharram 11-855 A.H./13th, Feb. 1451 A.D.
26. *Ma'asir-i-Mahmudshahi*, fol., 183b; Year 855 A.H. ended on Jan. 22, 1452; Day, *Medieval Malwa*, p. 135.
27. *Vir Vinod*, i, p. 328; Sarda, *Maharana Kumbha*, (1932), p. 100.
28. *Tabaqat-i-Akbari*, iii, p. 129; *Mirat-i-Sikandari*, p. 82.
29. *Kayam Khan Rasa*, p. 29, verses 344-45.
30. Ranakpur Inscription, *Vir Vinod*, i, p. 409.
31. *Tabaqat-i-Akbari*, iii, p. 129.
32. *Mirat-i-Sikandari*, p. 82.
33. *Tabaqat-i-Akbari*, iii, 130.
34. Sarda, *Maharana Kumbha*, p. 96.
35. *Mirat-i-Sikandari*, p. 83.
36. *Ibid.*, p. 83.
37. *Tabaqat-i-Akbari*, iii, p. 130.
38. Ojha, *Rajputana ka Itihas*, iv, p. 239; *Reu, Marwar ka Itihas*, i, p. 87; *Bankidas ri Khyat*, p. 7.
39. A.H. 860 started on December 11, 1455 and ended on November, 28, 1456.
40. *Tabaqat-i-Akbari*, iii, p. 130; *Mirat-i-Sikandari*, p. 83. Sikandar

wrongly states Gita Deora as the Chief of Sirohi.
41. *Tabaqat-i-Akbari*, iii, p. 131; *Mirat-i-Sikandari*, p. 84.
42. *Tabaqat-i-Akbari*, iii, p. 132; *Mirat-i-Sikandari*, p. 85. Sikandar's version is slightly more coloured but on main points it agrees with that of Nizamuddin.
43. The treaty with Jodha was concluded in 1457 A.D., after which his coronation took place in 1515/1458 A.D.
44. *Tabaqat-i-Akbari*, iii, pp. 132-33; *Mirat-i-Sikandari*, p. 85. Sikandar is very brief in his narration of this event.
45. *Kirtistambha Prashasti*, verses 19-23:
46. *Amar Kavya*, a later composition mentions of Kumbha's help to the Mandalik raja.
Mandalik Chudasama's wife Ramabai the daughter of Rana Kumbha returned to Mewar after the conversion of the Mandalik and stayed in Mewar in Jawar till her death sometimes after v.s. 1554. *Vide, Jawar Prashasti* q.v. Somani, *Maharana Kumbha* (Hindi) p. 43.
47. *Raj Vinod Mahakavya*, p. 10, verse 4.12.

4

Relations with Rajput Chiefs

A. SETTLEMENT WITH JODHA RATHOR

We have already noticed that after the murder of Ranmal Rathor in 1438 A.D. Jodha with his brothers escaped from Chittor which was followed by the occupation of Mandor and other places that once constituted the territory of Ranmal. Mandor had been placed under the control of Kuntal, Manja and Siwa, the sons of Chunda Sisodia, and for its security outposts were set up at Chaukadi and Kosana. Sojat, Kaparda, Bagri and Kailana were placed under such Rathors as were loyal to Maharana Kumbha. Thus from 1439 A.D. Jodha Rathor had to move from place to place without getting any respite because of continued expeditions sent against him. These operations were directed by Chunda Sisodia who seems to have been determined to destroy the house of Ranmal Rathor. During this plight Jodha took shelter in the arid (*jangal*) region of northern Marwar at Kahuni (situated about 32 kilometres from Bikaner). Even at Kahuni he could not remain in peace because of the attacks of Narbad, the son of Satta Rathor.[1] Narbad, who was in the service of Maharana Kumbha, bore special grudge against Jodha because his father Satta had been deprived of Mandor by Jodha's father, Ranmal. Narbad's attack on Jodha, therefore, might have been an outcome of his desire to avenge the wrong done to him. No doubt such operations of Maharana Kumbha must have reduced Jodha to great straits but he could not be crushed, instead the days of adversity intensified his determination, and the instinct of survival goaded him to keep up his perseverance.

Plight of Jodha continued for about fifteen years during which period he moved from pillar to post and contacted all possible favourable Rajput chiefs. He ultimately succeeded in securing the assistance and blessings of Harbhu Sankhla which somewhat improved his position. Encouraged by the assurance and assistance of Harbhu Sankhla, Jodha successfully managed to procure 140 horses from the stables of the Rao of Setrawa through the assistance of the wife of the Rao.[2] The acquisition of the horses considerably improved his position and he thereafter secured the alliance of Idas of Idawati, Sikhade Chauhans and Bhatis of Bikupur Pungal, etc. Thus by the end of the year 1453 A.D. Jodha was prepared to take action.

The Mewar version of these incidents has been put in a different form, according to which Hansabai, the grandmother of Maharana Kumbha appealed to the Maharana that it was because of her marriage into the house of Mewar that Jodha was made to suffer while the Rathors had done no harm to him, and, therefore, the Maharana should rethink of his policy towards Jodha. Upon this appeal the Maharana assured her that if Jodha occupied Mandor he would not take any action against him. It was on receipt of the message of Hansabai that Jodha was encouraged to make all these preparations and started attacking the territories of the Maharana. Dashrath Sharma has rightly doubted the veracity of the version on the ground that such considerations hardly could have any place in matters purely political, besides the constant fight of Mewar forces with Jodha indicates the real attitude.[3] The truth of the matter seems to be that the *Charans* in their attempt to eulogise Maharana Kumbha overlooked the problems that the Maharana was called upon to face, and also finally when the Maharana resolved his differences with Jodha after the latter had gained sufficient power, they found in such a story a reasonable explanation to glorify Maharana Kumbha and belittle Jodha.

In the process of strengthening his position Jodha turned to the Kyamkhanis for establishing friendly relations may be with a view to eliminate the possibilities of clash with them. He entered into a matrimonial alliance with them by marrying a Rathor girl (may be his daughter) to Shams Khan son of Muhammad Khan Kyamkhani of Jhunjhunu. The relationship is mentioned twice in the *Kymkhani Rasa* in two different contexts. First time it is mentioned that Jodha in order to strengthen his position thought of establishing friendly relations with the Kyamkhanis by offering in marriage a daughter. His first choice was for Fatah Khan of senior branch, but on his refusal he sent the *dola* to Shams Khan son of Muhammad Khan of Jhunjhunu belonging to the junior branch of the Kyamkhanis.[4] The relationship is again mentioned in the context of the differences between the brothers, Fatah Khan and Mubarak Shah of Jhunjhunu. According to the *Rasa* after the death of Shams Khan his son Fatah Khan, who was married in the family of Bahlol, did not care to share the produce of Jhunjhunu with his younger brother Mubarak Shah and his stepmother. Mubarak Shah in distress went to his grandfather Rao Jodha for help. Rao Jodha in his turn directed Mubarak Shah to contact his uncles Bika and Bida who being nearer to Jhunjhunu could be of greater help. But Mubarak Shah could get no help from his uncles Bika and Bida.[5] The mention of marriage acquires credibility by the indication of relationship with the progeny, and, therefore, the version of *Kyamkhani Rasa* need not be discarded as fiction. Through the matrimonial alliance Jodha secured the assistance of the Kyamkhanis who were Chauhans and who took pride in their being so though they had accepted Islam as their religion.

With all these preparations Jodha was set ready for action, but he waited for some favourable opportunity. It seems that during this period he had also managed to infiltrate some of his trusted men as spies into the fort of Mandor and other outposts. As already mentioned the treaty between the Sultans of Gujarat and Malwa concluded in 1451-52 A.D. resulted in their combined offensive against Mewar. The nature of these offensives became all the more dangerous because of the presence of Kumbha's younger brother Khem Karan in the camp of Mahmud Khalji of Malwa. In his attempt to protect Mewar from the aggression of Malwa and Gujarat, Maharana Kumbha had to take greater care of these boundaries and the northern side had to remain comparatively neglected. Maybe, Maharana Kumbha was conscious of the situation of the Marwar side, and to counter-balance the possible activities of Jodha, assisted Shams Khan of Nagor to regain his territories expecting that Shams Khan under obligation would prove a useful ally against Jodha. However, Maharana Kumbha's policy, whatever it might have been, did not turn favourable to him, and as already pointed out resulted only in his involvement with a series of conflicts with Gujarat. Jodha on his part made full use of the situation. He made a night attack on Mandor on receiving the signal from Kala Mangla who had mixed with the men in the fort and stayed there with his relative without being detected. Kala Mangla got the gates of the fort opened and sent the news that the men in the fort were down with slumber as an after effect of opium.[6] Jodha's attack on the fort thus caught the inmates absolutely unprepared and thereby made his task easy. In the melee Akka Sisodia, Heinglu Ahara, Muhta Rayanayar, Kandhal and Manja were killed. Mandor was lost to Mewar sometimes in 1454 A.D. Ojha[7] and Sarda[8] place the occupation of Mandor by Jodha after he had captured other outposts. But the version as given in Nainsi's *Vigat* seems more logical and in the absence of any other authentic contradictory evidence there seems to be no reason to give preference to the versions of modern writers. Mandor actually was the headquarters of Mewar's occupations in Marwar and once it was captured through a surprise attack the dependencies would be scared and would hardly get time to consolidate if they were attacked without loss of time, whereas an attack on some outpost would send alarm to Mandor which would provide an opportunity to the occupants to take necessary steps for security. Thus we find that Jodha adopted a wiser plan in capturing Mandor first of all. After the capture of the fort Jodha made some hasty arrangements for the security of Mandor.[9] He posted one of his brothers and one Bija at Mandor and himself attacked Chaukari where Bhati Banbir, Visaldeo and Rawal Duda fell fighting but Rathor Raghavdas escaped with some of his soldiers and fled towards Mewar. Chaukari passed into the possession of Jodha. Kosana was also occupied from where Jodha acquired some horses with equipments. After these series of successes Jodha sent one force under Kandhal towards Merta and with another force he marched on Sojat. Merta and Sojat both were conquered. Jodha liked the natural resources of

Sojat and stayed there for about 2 years after its occupation before finally moving to Mandor.[10] The reason for Jodha not to return to Mandor immediately after the conquest of Sojat seems to be more an outcome of political necessity than merely his liking of the environment. Jodha must have expected that Maharana Kumbha would certainly make attempts to reconquer Mandor and that he might be entrapped inside the fort, whereas if he was outside he could always attack the forces marching on Mandor or attack them from outside if they besieged the fort. Thus within a short period and almost with hurricane speed Jodha recovered a fair portion of Marwar which he considered as his patrimony. By 1456 A.D. Jodha had fully entrenched himself in Marwar. He even started occupying areas of Godwad. The gain of Jodha was thus the loss of Mewar.

Maharana Kumbha did not take things for granted nor did he acquiesce to Jodha's occupation of these places as the *Mewar Khyats* would have us believe by interpolation of the story of Hansabai. Several Mewari forces were sent from time to time against Jodha who, however, could not be dislodged from the territories he had occupied. During this period Maharana Kumbha was busy in other directions and he could afford to send only such forces as he could spare. Maybe exasperated by repeated failure of the Mewari forces Maharana Kumbha personally marched against Jodha. The two forces met at Pali. It is doubtful if any serious engagement took place between the two sides. Both sides seem to have hesitated in taking the initiative. It is also quite likely that both Jodha and Maharana Kumbha realised that the clash would only result in huge loss of manpower which was badly needed against the rulers of Gujarat and Malwa. They also realised the futility of continued hostility and once at least good sense seems to have prevailed upon them. After giving due discount to the narrations of the *Khyats*[11] we can deduce that some negotiations for the settlement of dispute took place. This settlement we may call treaty between the two. According to this treaty the two sides agreed to discontinue hostility against each other and agreed to a line of demarcation of the territories of Mewar and Marwar. It was agreed that the land which had *amla* trees would mark the land of Mewar while the land having *babool* trees would mark the beginning of Jodha's territory.[12] To mark the end of the feud in Rajput fashion Jodha gave his daughter Shringar Devi in marriage to Kanwar Raimal, the second son of Maharana Kumbha.[13] This treaty should have been concluded sometimes towards the close of the year 1557 A.D.[14] which gave a free hand to Rao Jodha Rathor to make arrangements in Marwar without any apprehension of attack from Mewar and enabled him to lay the foundation of the fort on the hill of Chiriatunk (the fort of Jodhpur) on Saturday the 11th Jaishta Sudi Samvat 1515 which Ojha has converted to 12 May, 1459 A.D.[15]

The policy of concluding peace with Jodha Rathor ending thereby the long feud which had started with the murder of Ranmal, was certainly a wise decision of Maharana Kumbha. The resources of Maharana Kumbha no doubt were greater than that of Jodha, but for Jodha it was a matter of survival and, therefore, he would have continued fighting till his last breath which in its turn would have only depleted the resources of Mewar and would have added further to the injury already caused to the State between 1453 and 1457 A.D.

B. RELATIONS WITH THE HADAS OF BUNDI

Hadauti, the land of the Hadas, situated between Mewar, Malwa and Delhi existed in precarious condition as it was subject to the pressure from all the three powers, the intensity of which depended on the relative strength of these powers. The Hadas inhabiting this region were brave warriors and kept themselves always ready to offer resistance to the attacking power in defence of this home and honour. But with meagre resources they were never in a position to endure the pressure for any considerable length of time. In the course of its history the Hadas had learnt the value of expediency and, therefore, instead of fighting an annihilating war, they always paid some tribute to the power that reached the spot with a force, and after the departure of the force continued to behave independently. Thus none of the aggressors could exercise suzerainty over the people of this region for any considerable length of time.

We have noticed earlier that Bairisal (1413-1458 A.D.) the ruler of Bundi rendered assistance to Sultan Hoshang Shah of Malwa in his conquest of Gagraun, which to the Maharana of Mewar was like acceptance of Malwa suzerainty. During the earlier years of Maharana Kumbha's reign Ranmal Rathor invaded Bundi in 1436-7 A.D. and forced Bairisal to cede Mandalgarh and accept the Mewar suzerainty. Mahmud Khalji who ascended the throne of Malwa in 1436 A.D. could not at this time take any step to help or prevent the ruler of Bundi from going over to the side of Mewar as he had enough troubles within his own kingdom. But Sultan Mahmud Khalji could not afford to allow Bundi to remain on the side of Mewar for long. By 1442 A.D. he was well settled in Malwa and took steps to reduce the Bundi Chief by raiding the region of Hadauti. We do not know precisely the nature of relationship he established in Hadauti, but his venture there and his return to his capital Mandu (May 1442) after making an abortive attempt on Delhi through the region of Hadauti must have aroused the suspicion of Maharana Kumbha that Bairisal might have gone over to the side of Malwa. Maharana Kumbha, therefore, marched into Hadauti immediately after the return of Mahmud Khalji to reassert his own suzerainty and also to realise tribute. Thus we find Bairisal was facing a double pressure, one from Malwa and the other from Mewar and certainly he could not have been in a happy position. The region of Hadauti had specific importance for Mewar as it could serve as a strong buttress particularly when Mewar was being hard pressed by the Sultan of Malwa, and Maharana Kumbha should have taken some measures to keep the Hadas on his side instead of just marching into the region and extracting tribute from Hadauti. He could have won over the Hadas by adopting a policy of reconciling the brave warriors by granting them concessions.

The activities of Maharana Kumbha in Hadauti led Mahmud Khalji to send another expedition in 1446 A.D. into Hadauti.[16] Taj Khan, Ikhtiyar Khan and Ghalib Khan, the Malwi generals caused some damage to the country-side. However, this was nothing more than a punitive expedition sent with the intention of warning the Hada Chief of the consequences of his unfriendly attitude. The Hadas had to suffer just because they had submitted to Maharana Kumbha, but without receiving any succour from him when invaded by the forces of Malwa.

Mahmud Khalji was fully conscious that holding of Hadauti permanently was a difficult task. He, therefore, took to stratagem and thought of dividing the Hadas by causing internal dissension in the ruling house. Bairisal had granted Kotah to his younger son Sanda against the wishes of his elder son Bhanda or Bhandeo (Bhonk of Persian Chronicles). In his raids on Hadauti Mahmud Khalji had subjugated Kotah and Sanda had agreed to pay tribute to him, but the intelligence service of the Sultan informed him that Sanda was secretly in collusion with Maharana Kumbha. Mahmud Khalji thought of some alternative and around the year 1448-9 A.D., when he was subjugating Bayana and Hindaun he suddenly turned towards Kotah. This sudden move of Mahmud Khalji was to avail of the opportunity offered to him by the defection of Bhandeo who approached the Sultan to give him Kotah. Sanda did not offer any resistance to Mahmud Khalji and came to meet him with the tribute comprising of one lakh and twenty thousand tankas. Mahmud Khalji instead of accepting his submission removed him from Kotah and gave it to Bhandeo.[17] This move of Mahmud Khalji was certainly advantageous to him. Being separated from the main house which was under his father Bairisal, Bhandeo had to remain dependent on the support of Mahmud Khalji and at the same time the divided house of the Hadas made them comparatively weak. Thus Maharana Kumbha was outmanoeuvred by Mahmud Khalji. Maharana Kumbha did not take any positive steps to prevent Kotah from passing into the hands of a protege of the Malwa Sultan. He also did not take any measure to add to the strength of Bairisal who remained on his side.

Bairisal at Bundi became hostile to Mahmud Khalji and the Malwa Sultan had to send some punitive expeditions into Hadauti between 1455 and 1456 A.D. By the end of 1457 A.D. there was again trouble when Bairisal tried to drive out the officers posted in some of the outposts of Hadauti. Exasperated by these repeated troubles Mahmud Khalji sent a strong force under Fidan Khan and Taj Khan with instructions to ravage the country thoroughly and to punish the ruler of Bundi in such a manner that none would dare to raise their heads in future.[18] In the final encounter sometimes in 1458 A.D. Bairisal was killed. His two other sons were captured and subsequently converted to Islam and came to be known as Umarkandi and Samarkandi. This ended the prolonged resistance of Bundi to the Sultan of Malwa. Bhandeo at Kotah, already a dependent on the support of Mahmud Khalji was placed on the throne of Bundi. Rao

Bhandeo continued to rule at Bundi with the goodwill of Malwa Sultan and did not give him any trouble. He outlived both Maharana Kumbha and Mahmud Khalji and continued in Bundi upto 1503 A.D.

Thus in the final analysis we find that Maharana Kumbha's policy towards Hadauti was defective. He not only lost Mandalgarh but also lost the allegiance of the Hadas. As ruler of Mewar, Kumbha was very keen on asserting his suzerainty over Hadauti, but when it came to assisting the ruler of Hadauti against an aggressor the Mewar assistance was conspicuous by its absence. While Maharana Kumbha was busy in Mewar, Rao Bairisal was constantly resisting the Malwa Sultan, but he could not stand indefinitely against the forces of a larger State with greater resources. If Maharana Kumbha had rendered timely assistance to Bairisal or had prevented Bhandeo from going over to the side of the Sultan of Malwa or even simultaneously attacked Malwa when the Malwa Sultan was busy in Hadauti he could have earned the gratitude of a brave fighting community who would have continued their resistance and would have also helped Mewar.

C. RELATIONS WITH DEORA CHAUHANS OF SIROHI AND ABU

The Deora Chauhans under Maharao Lumbha had occupied the region of Arbudachala around v.s. 1368/1311 A.D. and on the slopes of the Sirnawa hills Maharao Shivabhan founded his capital in v.s. 1462/1405 A.D. and named it Shivapuri, which still exists two miles east of present Sirohi and is known as old Sirohi. He was succeeded by his son Maharao Sahasmal who founded the present Sirohi in v.s. 1482/1425 A.D. and continued to rule over it till v.s. 1508/1451 A.D. when he died and was succeeded by his son Maharao Lakha who in his turn ruled over Sirohi till his death in v.s. 1540/1483 A.D. After him his eldest son Jagmal succeeded as Maharao of Sirohi.[19] Thus Maharao Sahasmal and Maharao Lakha were contemporaries of Maharana Kumbha. As mentioned earlier Maharao had been defeated in 1434 A.D. and had been compelled to cede Basantgarh, Bhula, some areas of Abu and certain territories in eastern Sirohi to Maharana Kumbha. In earlier works in the list of territories acquired by Mewar at this stage, Abu has been wrongly included.[20] Abu was conquered later. Maharao Sahasmal who had to cede territories to Mewar could not reconcile to the loss, but he could never feel himself strong enough to take up arms against Maharana Kumbha. Under the circumstances he kept on encouraging his feudatories to harass and resist the officers of Mewar posted in the regions once forming a part of Sirohi. Abu was under the Deora collaterals of the main house of Sirohi and existed as feudatories of the Maharaos of Sirohi. In the line of the Deora chiefs of Abu we find mention of Bisa, Kumbha, Chunda and Dungar. The inscriptions of Deora Chunda dated v.s. 1494/1437 A.D. and v.s. 1497/1440 A.D. are available which indicate that Deora Chunda was in possession of Abu certainly to that date and may be a little longer. The earliest inscription of Maharana Kumbha at Abu is dated v.s. 1506/1449 A.D.[21] On the basis of these evidences we can infer that Maharana Kumbha occupied Abu after 1440 A.D. and prior to 1449 A.D. Somani suggests the date of Maharana Kumbha's occupation of Abu as v.s. 1500/1443 A.D. though he does not give any reason for advocating this date as the year of occupation.[22]

After 1434 A.D. when Maharao Sahasmal had to cede certain territories to Maharana Kumbha it is quite possible that Deora Chunda and his son Deora Dungar continued to harass and attack the outposts of Mewar in that region which ultimately led to their expulsion and occupation of Abu by Maharana Kumbha. After their expulsion the Deoras of Abu seem to have received shelter with Maharao Sahasmal. At Sirohi Deora Chunda and Deora Dungar might have been expecting some help to recover Abu but the death of Maharao Sahasmal in 1451 A.D. altered the situation. Maharao Lakha, the successor of Sahasmal realised the futility of continued hostility with Mewar and felt it prudent to establish friendly relation. Mewar had become quite powerful and he might have felt that friendship with the neighbouring powerful Rajput State could be of assistance particularly when the Sultan of Gujarat was gradually becoming more aggressive. No doubt, Lakha was a relation of Maharana Kumbha,[23] but relationship hardly played any part in establishing friendship among the Rajputs. The establishment of friendly relations with Mewar by Maharao Lakha was only an outcome of political consideration. This growing friendship between Maharao Lakha and Maharana Kumbha made it obvious to Deora Chunda and Deora Dungar that help from Maharao Lakha to recover Abu would never come and they started looking for succour in other direction. As the relations of Deora chief of Sirohi with Mewar began to improve and so the relations between the Deoras of Sirohi and Abu began to deteriorate. The Deoras of Abu now started inhabiting the defiles of the hilly region and started seeking assistance from the Sultan of Gujarat.

Thus the Deora Chief who sought the help of Sultan Qutbuddin of Gujarat when the latter marched against Maharana Kumbha in 1456 A.D. was Deora Chunda or his son Deora Dungar and not Maharao Lakha of Sirohi.[24] The two Deora chiefs of Abu and Sirohi have been confused by the Persian chroniclers with the result that we find contradictory statements in them. On the one hand it is stated that the Deora chief of Sirohi sought the help of the Gujarati Sultan to recover Abu from Kumbha and also that the Sultan did send some forces for the purpose and on its failure promised to recover the place in near future, on the other it is stated that Sultan Qutbuddin sacked Sirohi thrice during the course of his raids on Mewar.[25] So far Abu is concerned it remained with Maharana Kumbha till his end and it was only after his death that Deora Dungar, son of Deora Chunda, succeeded in recovering Abu, whose first available inscription is dated v.s. 1525/1468-9 A.D.[26] Thus we find that Sultan Qutbuddin who was getting apprehensive of the growing power of Mewar under Maharana Kumbha found in Deora Chunda and his son Dungar supplicants who could be useful to him and, therefore, tried to reinstal them at Abu, though in his efforts he could not achieve success. In his raids on Abu and Kumbhalgarh Sultan Qutbuddin met obstructions from Deora Maharao Lakha of Sirohi. To remove this obstruction two alternatives were open to him, either to reduce the Sirohi ruler to his obedience or to oust Maharao Lakha from Sirohi and to annex it and place it under the Deoras of Abu as feudatories of Gujarat. It was with this aim in view that Sultan Qutbuddin raided and plundered Sirohi thrice during the course of his raids on Mewar. Thus the Gujarati Sultan went for the assistance of one branch of the Deoras, *i.e.* of Abu and plundered the territories of the main branch of the Deoras, *i.e.* of Sirohi. Thus Sirohi was exposed to the depredations of Sultan Qutbuddin because Maharao Lakha had taken sides with Maharana Kumbha. However, he could get no help from Mewar and every time saved himself by taking shelter in the mountainous defiles of the Aravalis. Failure on the part of Maharana Kumbha to render assistance to Deora Lakha no doubt was the result of his own involvements in various directions but so far Deoras of Sirohi were concerned they must have learnt that it was futile for them to expect any assistance from Mewar. The alliance with Mewar at best could have been a booster of their morale. Under such conditions Maharana Kumbha could hardly get allies who would stand by him and he was left to meet his adversaries all by himself.

Relations with other Rajput Chiefs

Maharana Kumbha wanted to establish Mewar supremacy/ suzerainty over entire Rajasthan and to achieve this aim he adopted an aggressive policy against all Rajput Chiefs who refused to accept his overlordship. We can get some idea of his policy in this respect from the *Kumbhalgarh Prashasti* which mentions his conquests and victories besides his other achievements. Similarly, the *Kirtistambha Prashasti* also mentions his victories and throws light on his policy as a whole. These *Prashastis*, of course, are eulogistic in character and often minor incidents are narrated with a good deal of exaggeration and one would have to give due discount to the narrations in these *prashastis* in drawing conclusions. From the *Kumbhalgarh Prashasti* we find that Maharana Kumbha not only defeated the chief of Naradiyanagar but also brought a large number of women captives belonging to the household of the chief and employed them as slaves in his own household.[27] This Naradiyanagar, according to Dasharath Sharma, is situated on the route from Ranakpur to Someshwar pass.[28] The *Prashasti* also informs that Maharana Kumbha recaptured Yoginipura which can be identified as Jawar. He also defeated Rana Vikram of Hammirpur and carried away his girls.[29] From the same list we may mention of Maharana Kumbha's uprooting of Dhanyanagara, conquests of Yagpura (Jahazpur), Vardhmangiri (Badnor) and Janakachala; burning and destruction of Yavali, Sikhali, Karali Partali, Vrindavati (Bundi), Mallaranyapura and devastation of Bambawada. He also defeated Gayapala of Dungarpur. Thus we find that Maharana Kumbha's policy was based on force. He thought that by defeating the chiefs and by burning and devastating their territories he would strike terror in their hearts and would thus make them suppliant. But himself a Rajput and warrior, Maharana Kumbha failed to understand the spirit of the Rajputs who were ever ready to sacrifice their lives for their honour. We have already noticed the struggle of Jodha Rathor and also his ultimate success, a struggle which caused so much harm to Mewar. In the case of the Deoras of Sirohi and the Hadas of Bundi and Bambawada we have noticed Maharana Kumbha extracted tribute from them, cut away slices from their land and annexing them to his own territory but he could never help them when they were attacked by the Sultans of Malwa and Gujarat. The policy of extracting tribute and forcing the Rajput chiefs to accept the suzerainty of Marwar but failing to render assistance when they were subjected to aggression of the enemies certainly could not have infused confidence in those who accepted the suzerainty of Mewar. The *Prashastis* may glorify Maharana Kumbha but to his contemporary Rajputs he could not have been anything better than an oppressor. Taking away of women from Naradiyanagara and Hammirpur might have provided a subject for eulogising Maharana Kumbha but such actions certainly could not have been appreciated by those who were effected by it. It seems that Maharana Kumbha was following almost an identical policy as was followed by the Sultans regarding the womenfolk of the defeated. To his contemporary Rajput chiefs he could not have been any better than the Muslim Sultans who at least protected those who accepted their suzerainty. It is mentioned that he captured Muslim women from Nagor and Sarangpur but then in what way could it be different from his actions taken against Naradiyanagara and Hammirpur. The medieval political ethics seems to have a common standard irrespective of the religion. On the whole, the policy of Maharana Kumbha towards the Rajput chiefs was certainly not a wise one. Instead of following the policy of crushing ruthlessly, Maharana Kumbha would have done better had he followed a policy of appeasement. As such he only succeeded in creating a number of enemies. As a consequence, hegemony of Mewar over the Rajputs could not be achieved, though Mewar during his reign emerged as the most powerful State of Rajputana.

NOTES AND REFERENCES

1. *Dayaldas ri Khyat*, i, pp. 106-7; Nainsi, *Vigat*, i, p. 32.
2. Nainsi, *Vigat*, i, p. 34; *Khyat*, iii, p. 8; *Bankidas ri Khyat*, No. 159. Ojha, *Jodhpur Rajya ka Itihas*, i, p. 239. According to Ojha, Harbhu Sankhala's help was received after Jodha had acquired the horses from Setrawa, but there seems to be no reason to ignore the statement of Nainsi and Bankidas.
3. Dashrath Sharma, *Lecture on Rajput History and Culture*, p. 87.
4. *Kyamkhani Rasa*, p. 36 verses 432 to 436.
5. *Ibid.*, p. 39, verses 466-468. That Rao Jodha had no objections to such relationship is further corroborated by another such relationship. Jodha had assigned Nahadsar to his sons Karmsi and Rayapal who married their sister (*i.e.* Jodha's daughter) Bhaga to Salha Khan of Nagor and received from him in return the village of Asop and Kheewsar (vide, *Vigat*, i, p. 40).
6. Nainsi, *Vigat*, i, p. 34.
7. Ojha, *Jodhpur Rajya ka Itihas*, i, 239.
8. Sarda, H.B., *Maharana Kumbha*, p. 75.
9. Nainsi, *Vigat*, i, p. 34.
10. Nainsi, *Vigat*, i, p. 35.
11. Nainsi, *Khyat*, iii, pp. 9-12; *Dayal Das ri Khyat*, i, p. 109.
12. Nainsi, *Vigat*, i, p. 36. Asopa, *Marwar ka Sankshipt Itihas*, p. 179 and *Marwar ka Mool Itihas*, p. 108. Asopa mentions that Maharana Kumbha sent his eldest son Udai Singh to negotiate and settle the terms through which this boundary was agreed upon.
13. Sarda, *Maharana Kumbha*, p. 76; *J.A.S.B.*, Vol. 55; Pt. i, pp. 79-82. Ojha, *Jodhpur Rajya ka Itihas*, i, pp. 240-41, Sharma, D., *Lectures On Rajput History and Culture*, p. 81. Dashrath Sharma puts this marriage during the reign of Raimal. "He (Raimal) brought the war with the Rathors to an end by marrying Shringar Devi, a daughter of Jodha, the Rathors Chief of Jodhpur."
14. It was on 20th October, 1457 that Mandalgarh was lost to Malwa after a seige of about ten months, and this can be explained only on the basis of Maharana Kumbha's involvement with Jodha—Day, *Medieval Malwa*, pp. 189-193.
15. Nainsi, *Vigat*, i, p. 38; Ojha, *Jodhpur Rajya ka Itihas*, i, p. 241.
16. Day—*Medieval Malwa*, p. 179.
17. *Ibid.*, p. 200.
18. *Ibid.*, p. 194.

19. Ojha, *Sirohi Rajya ka Itihas*, pp. 200-201.
20. Sarda, *Maharana Kumbha*, p. 79; Ojha, *Sirohi Rajya ka Itihas*, p. 194.
21. Abu Inscription of v.s. 1506.
22. Somani, *Maharana Kumbha* (Hindi), 81.
23. *Tabaqat-i-Akbari*, iii (Tr.), p. 234. Nizamuddin mentions that Deora Chief of Sirohi was a relation of Maharana Kumbha though he does not spell out the exact nature of the relationship.
    Ojha, *Sirohi Rajya ka Itihas*, p. 200. There seems to have been a lot of inter-marriage between the two houses of the Deoras of Sirohi and the Sisodias of Chittor during the reign of Maharana Kumbha and Maharana Raimal. One of the wives of Maharao Lakha, Lakshmi Kuwar was a daughter of Maharana Kumbha. Maharao Lakha's daughter Champa Kuwar was married to Maharana Raimal and later Maharana Raimal's daughter, Anand Kuwar was married to Maharao Jagmal.
24. *Cambridge History of India*, iii, p. 302, has mentioned Sains Mal as the Chief of Sirohi. This Sains Mal is no other than Sahasmal who had died in 1451 A.D. and, therefore, his son Lakha was ruling over Sirohi as Maharao in 1456 A.D. when Qutbuddin Gujarati invaded and devastated Sirohi.
25. Ojha, *Sirohi Rajya ka Itihas*, pp. 197-8; The *Sirohi Khyats* have given a confused version of the attacks of Sultan Qutbuddin on Abu and Sirohi.
26. An inscription from Pitalhar temple.
27. *Kumbhalgarh Prashasti*, verse 246.
28. D. Sharma, *Lectures on Rajput History and Culture*, p. 70.
29. *Kumbhalgarh Prashasti*, verses, 250-251.

5

Cultural Achievements

The resurgence of Mewar under Hammir set in a process of allround development of the State, but it was under Kumbha that the achievements became pronounced. It was during his reign that the cultural achievements of Mewar reached such height which stand by itself unique in the history of Mewar. For the purpose of survey the cultural achievements have been divided under heads; Literary Activity; Painting; Architecture; Sculpture; Music and Religion.

A. LITERARY ACTIVITY

In the personality of Kumbha we find a rare combination of the qualities of a warrior, a scholar, a musician and a connoisseur of arts. Himself a scholar and author of several literary and critical works, he extended the royal patronage to scholars which gave impetus to literary activity and brought about literary efflorescence which stands as the greatest achievement of Mewar under Maharana Kumbha. According to the traditions of Mewar, Kumbha was a great scholar and is credited to have acquired mastery over various branches of learning then prevalent. It is mentioned that he acquired knowledge of the *Vedas*, the *Smritis*, *Mimansa*, *Naya Shastra*, the works Bharat Muni, *Rajaniti Shastra*, *Ganit*, *Vyakarana*, *Upanishads*, *Tarka Shastra*, *Siddhanta* and *Sahitya*.[1] The list as given in the *Ekalinga-Mahatmya* is really a formidable one and hardly leaves out anything. If we take into account the political career of Kumbha and his continuous involvement in various armed conflicts, the items mentioned create an impression of incredibility. However, if Kumbha had acquired even a fraction out of this list he certainly has to be accepted as an unusual personality. It may be that the list only indicates that he took interest in all the branches of learning then prevalent in India.

Maharana Kumbha is credited with the authorship of a large number of works, though we may safely infer that all these works might not have been written by him personally but by various scholars attached to his court. These works being assignments to scholars in the capacity of research assistants the authorship has been ascribed to the Maharana for whom they worked. The works for which Maharana Kumbha is credited with the authorship are *Sangitraj, Rasik Priya,* Commentary on *Chandi-Shatak, Suda Prabandh, Kamraj-Ratisar,* Commentary on *Gitagovinda* in Mewari language and *Natak-prabandha*. Of all these works *Sangit-raj* is the most erudite and a voluminous work consisting of 16,000 verses. The entire work is divided into five parts each under a separate title as *Pathyaratna Kosha, Geetratna Kosha, Vadyaratna Kosha, Nrityaratna Kosha* and *Rasaratna Kosha*. Though the majority of the manuscripts have Kumbhakarna as the author in the colophon as well as in the body of the text a few manuscripts have Kalasena in place of Kumbhakarna. This has led some to ascribe the authorship to Kalasena. Dr. Kunhan Raj, the editor of *Pathyaratna Kosha*, not being able to decide about the authorship writes in his edition of the work, "Although the author is Kumbhakarna, still I must respect the manuscript which formed the basis of this edition and I must accurately present the manuscript material. So I have given the work as by Kalasena and I have given the name of Kumbhakarna only in the title page and that within brackets."[2] Shri Rasiklal Chhotalal Parikh, the editor of *Nrityaratna Kosha* points out in his introduction that the majority of references gives to Kumbhakarna the title to authorship. "We have also consulted the other *Ratnakoshas*" writes Shri Parikh, "in the *Sangitraj* MS. belonging to the library of Oriental Institute of M.S. University, Baroda. They uniformly mention in their colophons Kumbhakarna as the author... In the light of the evidence ... it is reasonable to conclude that as between Kalasena and Kumbhakarna the authorship of *Nrityaratna Kosha* should be assigned to Kumbhakarna."[3] While composing *Sangitraj* earlier works like the *Natyashastra* of Bharat with its four *Bhashyas* and also *Sangitratnakara* of Sarangdeva as well as its commentary *Kalanidhi* of Kallinath, from which quotations are found in the text of *Nrityaratna Kosha*,[4] were consulted. Kumbha, however, preferred to retain the purer form as given by Bharat and avoided some of the confusions existing in the *Sangitratnakara*.

As a treatise *Sangitraj* has included all the aspects, associated with the art of Indian music. According to Indian traditions music included, vocal music with notations, musical instruments, recitation, poetical metres and figure of speech, dance, *tala* and *rasa* and *Sangitraj* deals with all these aspects quite exhaustively. However, it would not be doing injustice to Kumbha if we accept that various scholars including Kanha Vyas had been commissioned to work on the project of composing *Sangitraj* under the personal direction and supervision of Maharana Kumbha. A project of such magnitude by itself must have provided means of livelihood to a host of scholars and must have enhanced literary activity in Mewar.

Rasik-priya, another work of Kumbha is actually a commentary on the famous *Gitagovinda* of Jaideva, treating Radha and Krishna as the beloved and the lover and full of delicate feelings often bordering on erotics. Like the traditional writers the commentary starts with salutations to great servants like Bharat and Matanga. The commentary bears witness of Kumbha's wide knowledge as he quotes relevant portions from works like *Kumar-Sambhava* and *Nishadh-Charit*. *Rasikpriya* has a good treatment of various *rasas*. Besides, each *pad* bears an indication of the *raga* in which it is to be sung. The *ragas* and *talas* indicated in the *Rasikpriya* are quite distinct from those indicated in the *Gitagovinda*, and herein we find the originality and daring of Kumbha who could dare to break away from the old traditional rules and introduce new modes. This Kumbha could do only because he had acquired full command over music.

Chandi-Shatak: The commentary on *Chandi-Shatak* of Bana though credited to the authorship of Kumbha is in reality a product of some scholar attached to his court. The style of this work differs very much from that of *Rasikpriya*, and there is an obvious laboured effort to display scholarship in diction at the cost of poetical merit and spontaneity in flow.

Suda-prabandha: This work in reality should form a companion volume of *Rasikpriya*. It delineates the various couplets of *Gitagovinda* into their musical metres. The work was completed in v.s. 1505/1448 A.D. at Chittor. According to Dashrath Sharma the actual author of this work may not have been Kumbha himself. The manuscript mentions that "it was written according to the instructions of Shri Saranga Vyasa. So it is perhaps best to ascribe the authorship to the Vyasa."[5] However, the theme and inter-relation between *Rasikpriya* and *Suda-prabandha* suggests that whosoever might have done the actual writing had done so under the personal supervision of Kumbha.[6]

Kamraj-ratisar is in essence a book on erotics. It starts with salutations to Ganapati, Bageshwari and Kamdeva. It seems to have been divided into four sections and the entire work was completed on the Vijaya Dashami of v.s. 1518/1461 A.D. The author expresses acknowledgment of the assistance rendered by Hiranand, a Jain scholar.[7]

Maharana Kumbha is also credited with composing a Mewari commentary on *Gitagovinda*. But according to Dashrath Sharma this might not have been the work of a single author. He further states that the various copies of the manuscript of this work found in the libraries of Jodhpur, Bikaner and Udaipur differ widely from each other and were probably written by different *pandits* attached to Kumbha's court.[8]

Works of other Scholars

A scholar king like Kumbha attracted a host of scholars and created a formidable literary circle around himself. These scholars received full patronage of Kumbha and were encouraged from time to time by grant of various awards. The result of such an attitude on the part of Kumbha was that the State of Mewar during his reign achieved prominence through its activity. Not only the court but the entire State was illuminated with places of learning and scholars carried on their activities in different places. The contribution of Jain scholars too was not insignificant. The Jains belonging to the business community seem to have received special encouragement from Kumbha, who in their turn contributed towards the material prosperity of the State.

Scholars Associated with Court

Among the scholars associated with the court the name of Atri stands as most prominent. He came from a family of scholars. His father Keshava had received the grant of village Pipli during the reign of Maharana Lakha. Atri was in fairly advanced age in the time of Maharana Kumbha when he was entrusted with the task of composing the *Kirtistambha Prashasti*. He could not complete the *Prashasti* due to his death and left the work to be completed by his son Mahesh. Atri was a critic of poetry and had acquired mastery over *Mimansa, Nyaya* and *Vedanta*. Next to Atri his son Mahesh deserves mention who completed the unfinished *Kirtistambha Prashasti*. Mahesh was a scholar with a critical outlook and even when composing the *prashastis* which were intended for glorification, he tried to restrain himself as much as was possible. The *Kirtistambha Prashasti* contains the dates of the construction of *Kirtistambha*, Achalgarh and Kumbhalgarh besides many other minor ones. He received full recognition from Maharana Kumbha who presented to him two *chanwars* with gold handles, a white umbrella and two elephants.[9] Mahesh survived Kumbha and was alive during the reign of Raimal. It seems, however, that after the murder of Kumbha he left Mewar and returned after the deposition of Udai Singh and accession of Raimal. In Mewar he was recognised for his ability to compose *prashastis* as several of them have been found in different buildings. Maharana Raimal also honoured him and gave to him the village of Ratnakhetak as a *sasan* grant.

Kanha Vyas who speaks of himself as *arthadas*, was a poet in the employment of Maharana Kumbha. Kanha Vyas was not a poet endowed with poetic imagination but compensated this deficiency by his ability to put together matters collected from different sources. He is known for his work *Ekalinga Mahatmya*, but in preparing it he has freely borrowed verses from the *Kirtistambha Prashasti, Kumbhalgarh Prashasti*, the *Prashasti* of Mahavir temple of Chittor, *Gitagovinda* and *Sangitraj*. Ramballabh Somani has given a list comparing the borrowings and mentions that the work is divided into seven sections.[10] At one stage Kanha Vyas was credited with the composition of *Kumbhalgarh Prashasti*, because of certain common verses and certain similarities existing in the *Ekalinga Mahatmya* and

Kumbhalgarh Prashasti, but now it is accepted that the common factors are an outcome of the borrowing in the former from the latter. However, with all its limitations *Ekalinga Mahatmya* is a valuable contribution for which Kanha Vyas deserves credit even though as a compiler.

Kumbhalgarh Prashasti which is a valuable literary contribution of the reign of Maharana Kumbha unfortunately remains an anonymous work. Brijmohan Javalia's stand of assigning the authorship of Atri[11] has been rightly refuted by Ramballabh Somani on the ground of difference in the styles of the *prashastis* of Kumbhalgarh and Chittor.[12] Besides, *Kumbhalgarh Prashasti* was composed later whereas Atri had died earlier even before he could complete the *Kirtistambha Prashasti* was composed later where as Atri had died earlier even before he could complete the *Kirtistambha Prashasti*.

The name of the composer of *Kadia Prashasti* of v.s. 1500/1443 A.D. is mentioned in the text of the *prashasti* as Kalyan, son of Murari.[13] This *prashasti* includes a description of the family of Tilhabhatta from which came the spiritual guides (*gurus*) of the Maharanas of Mewar. The style of Kalyan is rather involved as he is fond of using metaphors too often.

Besides poetical works, Mewar also witnessed the composition of several manuals on architecture and iconography. This contribution came from Mandan and his family members which enriched considerably the literary achievements of Mewar during the reign of Kumbha.

The ancestors of Mandan originally belonged to Gujarat from where they had migrated to Mewar after the collapse of the Chalukyas of Gujarat. In Mewar Mandan was in the fourth generation as his great-grand-father had migrated to Mewar. Mandan was son of Kheta or Kshetra who has been mentioned as an architect.[14] Though Mandan was by caste a Brahmin belonging to the Bhangora group of Bharadwaj gotra, his family was called the family of *shilawats* because of their profession. Mandan was essentially a scholar and had acquired proficiency in astronomy and astrology. He has given the auspicious moments for starting structures on the basis of the zodiac signs and placement of different stars relevant to the scope and aspect of the work. He was also good at arithmetic and geometry and has discussed methods for calculating areas of different shapes and also methods for calculating proportion of various shapes of object of three dimensions. Of the various books written by Mandan only *Prasadmandan, Rajballabhmandan, Devtamurti-prakaran, Rupmandan* and *Vastumandan* are available.

Prasadmandan is a treatise on the lines of *Mansara* and *Samrangana* and discusses the types of temples classifying them into Nagara, Dravida, Bhumija, Latin, Sarvadhara, Vimana, Nagarvimana, Pushyak and Shringa. The text of *Prasadmandan* is divided into eight chapters. These chapters treat the types of temples and their origins, the characteristics of the land or what we may call consideration for the environment, auspicious planets, size of various pieces of stones to be used in different parts of the structure, the proportion of components in relation to the whole structure, placement of various icons, of details of *mandapas*, arrangement for water and defects to be carefully avoided.

Rajvallabhmandan discusses the rules and principles that should be observed in the construction of residential buildings, wells, water-reservoirs and tanks. Lay-out for towns, and the auspicious and inauspicious characteristics of the lay-out have been dealt with in details. Lay-out of forts and palaces with their component attachments have been also properly treated. He has also discussed the effects of the planets of zodiac signs of the builder which should be taken into consideration in planning the structures. The work is divided into fourteen chapters and is a valuable manual on the civil and military architecture of medieval Mewar.

Devta-murti-prakaran and *Rupmandan* discuss the rules to be observed by the sculptures when carving icons. He has discussed the proportions, symbols and placement of icons in relation to their comparative importance with the patron deity of the temple. The works are companion volumes, the former being divided into eight chapters and the latter into six.

Vastumandan is like a text book and discusses in general the rules that are to be observed by the architects and deals mostly with volume, weight and various calculations.

In the family of Mandan his younger brother Natha wrote a treatise known as *Vastumanjari*. Of the two sons of Mandan the elder Govinda wrote three books under the titles *Uddharghorni, Kalanidhi* and *Dwardipika*. His younger son Ishwar was the architect of the Vishnu temple constructed by Rama Bai, the daughter of Kumbha after the death of her father. The impact of Mandan has lasted in Rajasthan and the Sompura group of masons observe the rules laid down by Mandan even in modern times when constructing temples.

Contribution of the Jains

The contribution of the Jains to the literature of Mewar came mainly from those who had renounced the worldly life and had taken to the life of teaching and preaching to whom Maharana Kumbha extended full patronage. Of these teachers the bulk of contribution came from those belonging to Tapagachha and Kharataragachha groups. The contribution of the Jain scholars to the literature of Mewar is quite substantial both in quantity and in quality. They contributed towards the growth of Sanskrit as well as Mewari literature. Some of these works are in the nature of commentaries on texts as explanations for the common man. Jain *Shreshthis* also made substantial financial contributions to assist the scholars to devote themselves without worries to their studies and write books. The *Shreshthis* also rendered financial assistance to make copies of books written earlier. Some of them were fond of maintaining *bhandars* of books similar to our libraries. All these activities lent a great deal for educating the people and also for developing the local language.

Tapagachha Group

The Tapagachha group came into prominence from the time of *Acharya* Som Sundar who came to Delwara in 1393 A.D. and was appointed as a *vachak* (preacher) subsequently he was raised to the status of *Acharya* in 1400 A.D. and continued in that position till his death in 1442 A.D. He made a substantial contribution to the literature of Mewar. His works can be divided into two categories. In the first category would come such works which were intended to build the character and personality of young students who studied them. The second category would include treatises of advanced nature. In the first mention may be made of *Upadeshablavabodh Yogashastrabalavabod, Shadavashyakbalavabodh, Shashthishatakbalavabodh* and *Aradhanapatakabalavabodh*. In the second category comes works like *Bhashyatrayachurni*

Kalyanakaustava and *Ratnakosha*.[15]

The person to succeed Som Sundar to the position of *Acharya* in 1442 A.D. was Muni Sunder; initiated in 1386 A.D. he reached to this position in the 63rd year of his life. He was a scholar of Sanskrit and also a prolific writer who seems to have devoted his lifetime in writing books. His principal works are *Adhyatma Kalpadrum, Tridashatirangani, Upadesharatnakara, Stotraratnakosha Mitrachatushtaka, Shantikarastotra* and *Tapagachhapattavali*. Besides these he also wrote many other books.[16]

Muni Sundar was followed by Jaichandra who in his turn was succeeded by Ratnashekhar Suri as Acharya about the year 1446 A.D. Ratnashekhar Suri also wrote a few books of which more prominent are *Shradhapratikramanvriti, Shradhavidhisutravriti* and *Acharpradeep*. He died sometime in 1460 A.D. and was succeeded by Lakshmisagar Suri as *Acharya* who survived Maharana Kumbha. Under the guidance of these Acharyas the Tapagachha group prospered in Mewar.

Besides the *Acharyas* there were other scholarly disciples who also contributed to the literature of Mewar during the reign of Maharana Kumbha. Prominent among the disciples *Acharya* Som Sundar were Jaichandra Suri, Somadeva Suri, Bhuwan Sundar Suri, and Jinasundar Suri. Somadev Suri earned his reputation as a scholar because of his power of oratory with which he could hold his listeners spell-bound and his command of logic because of which seldom could anyone succeed in defeating him in debate. Maharana Kumbha in recognition of his scholarship honoured him[17] and conferred upon him the title of *kaviraj*.

Among other scholars, Jinavardhan composed *Gurvavali* of the Tapagachha, Jaishekhar Suri wrote *Gachhachar* in 1434 A.D. almost at the beginning of the reign of Maharana Kumbha. This work was undertaken at the instance of *Shreshthi* Sindha who personally financed its composition.[18] Pratistha Som, a monk composed *Somsaubhagya Kavya*. This versified work vividly describes the luxurious life led by the *Shreshthis* and also throws some light on the mode of life led by *sadhus* from the time of their initiation to the end of their life. Another monk Ratnamandirgani wrote *Upadeshtarangini*. Shubhasheel, a disciple of Muni Sundar was another scholar who also contributed to the literature of Mewar. Of his works mention may be made of

Vikramcharitra, Punyadhananripkatha, Bharateshwarbahubaliswadhyaya and *Shatrujayakalpa*. All these books were written during the reign of Maharana Kumbha.

The contribution of the Kharataragachha group to the literature of Mewar cannot be overlooked though in quantity they do not appear as formidable as that of the Tapagachha group. The most prominent *Acharya* of this group during the reign of Kumbha was Jinasagar Suri. In 1435 A.D. he composed the second volume of *Avashyakvrihadvriti* in Delwara at the instance of Sahanpal Nawlakha, a minister of Kumbha, who maintained a *bhandar* (library) in Delwara.[19] Among other scholars mention must be made of Hiranand Suri of Vrihadgachha and Hrishivardhan of Achalgachha both being scholars of outstanding merit.

Sakalkirti and Bhuwankirti were eminent Digambar Jain scholars during the reign of Maharana Kumbha. Sakalkirti was a scholar of Sanskrit, Prakrit, and Rajasthani languages. He is credited with the authorship of twenty-eight books in Sanskrit and six books in Rajasthani. Among his Sanskrit works most important ones are *Adipurana, Uttarapurana, Shantinathcharitra, Vardhamancharitra, Mallinathcharitra, Yashodharcharitra, Agamsar* and *Shripalcharitra*. Of the works in Rajasthani language mention may be made of *Aradhanapratibodhsar, Nemishwargeet,* and *Muktawaligeet*. Bhuwankirti was a disciple of Sakalkirti and like his *guru* he was also a scholar of Sanskrit, Prakrit and Rajasthani languages. Of his works in Rajasthani, *Nemirajulgeet, Jivandharrasa* and *Jambuswamirasa* are valuable contributions to the literature in Rajasthani language.

The account of literary activity of Mewar cannot be closed without mentioning Kumbha's recognition of Mewari as a language by itself. As already mentioned, he not only personally adopted this language in some of his own composition but also encouraged other scholars to write in Mewari language and extended royal patronage to them.

B. PAINTING

Art is something abstract and is latent in man surrounding him without his being conscious of it. A man emotionally moved at times feels an urge within him to create something beautiful.

His emotions urge him to translate in words, in lines, in colour or in solids his feelings and desires. It is an urge to give a definite form to the dimly felt or perceived experience and the form that he gives by translating into words or lines or colour or solids is his art and the creator, the artist. In giving form the mind of the artist undergoes simultaneously a double fold operation, *i.e.* translation of perceptual form and mental logical activity. The logical activity consists of the collection by piecemeal of observations and putting them together into one. It has, therefore, been aptly said that in art man reveals himself and not the object; thus man instinctively embodies its deepest thoughts and ideals in painting and sculpture and through it speaks to the world in a language which needs no translation. The art of any period, therefore, provides us with a very useful means of understanding the ideals and ideas of the age in which it is produced. It serves as a standard for measuring the cultural development of the society at any particular period.

The urge of the artist to express himself leads him to develop a technique which in its turn becomes an accepted vehicle, each successive generation adding to it and remain in vogue till new technique is evolved. In India the mural paintings of Ajanta and the Mughal-Rajput miniature paintings were considered till very recent past as the ideals of Indian painting and pervaded in the mind as a nostalgic haze. But in-between these two limits another technique evolved during the fourteenth and fifteenth century which with regional variations flourished in Gujarat, Mewar, and Marwar generally called Western India style and in Malwa designated as Central India style.

That the inspiration for painting was derived from the paintings of Ajanta is a debatable point, but the dominant role of local folk painting in giving shapes for further development can hardly be doubted. Western Rajasthan, Southern Rajasthan, Central Rajasthan and Gujarat during the centuries prior to Alauddin Khalji's occupation had a cultural unity and had so much in common in their life that the style developed in this region was quite similar irrespective of the place where it was executed. Thus the style of Gujarat, Marwar and Mewar have so much in common that one would not be able to distinguish them.

The Sultans of Delhi were called upon to devote their energies for more pressing needs of conquest and consolidation and, therefore, the only art that could claim their attention were those which tended to outward display of sovereignty rather than those arising out of intimate private enjoyment. It was during this period that the Jains in Western and Central India started illuminating their religious and folk-lore books with paintings which may be taken as the beginning of miniature painting in India. These miniature paintings though static and stereotyped continued to survive and kept awaiting for fresh inspirations to blossom into later Rajput paintings.

It was in the tradition of Western India miniature painting that the Jains of Mewar produced some specimens, of which the palm-leaf manuscript of *Sawagpadikaman Sutta Chunni* composed in 1260 A.D. and executed in Ahar in Mewar, preserved in the Bosten collection, deserves mention. Another illuminated work *Supasanahachariyam* was executed at Devakulapataka (Delwara) in 1423 A.D. during the reign of Maharana Mokul. This is a specimen of early paper manuscript, now in Jnana Bhandar of Patan, painted in Western India style. Its freedom and inventiveness, and the fact that full page illustrations appear for the first time, are not without significance and confirm that Mewar was an important and vital centre of the Western India style.[20] Though this work does not directly fall under the period under review but it gives a fair illustration of the style prevalent in Mewar which continued unchanged during the reign of Maharana Kumbha as can be discerned from the similarities found in later works. This work contains thirty-seven illustrations, some of them cover the entire page. In the rendering the artist has used his imagination in composition and use of colour. Gold has also been used though sparingly. Among the colours used red and yellow dominate, the colours which happen to be dominant tones used in the dress of the people of Rajasthan. The use of these tones can also be an indication that the painters remained nearer to the people instead of becoming artificially sophisticated.

In the Mewar painting the filling-in has been done through decorations and the bunches of trees and other motifs have been introduced with laboured intention but lack spontaneity. In these paintings the faces are not in pure profile; the nose drawn like parrot's beak is made to protrude beyond the other cheek which makes the face look rather queer. The chins are slightly small and out of proportion and line of the eye has been elongated with small pupils which stands quite in contrast with figures drawn in the *Mandu Kalpasutra* of 1439 A.D. The second eye in the semi-profile are drawn rather detached which was the conventional idiom of the paintings in the Jain manuscripts of Western India during the fifteenth century. In rendering the torso, the chest has been exaggerated with a comparatively narrower waist. The posture as a whole is stiff and lacks naturalness. The overall impression is that of crudeness.

The paintings of Mewar certainly fall under the category of miniature painting adopted for illuminating the manuscripts. Mewar paintings during the reign of Maharana Kumbha no doubt look rather crude, but they are not lacking in vitality and served as a base for the development of Rajput painting after him. Among the collections of Coomarswamy notice has been drawn towards the manuscripts of one *Kalpasutra* and *Kalikacharya*, though believed to have been written in 1447 A.D. but it is doubtful if they should be placed prior to 1500 A.D.

Mewar also bears evidence for the existence of mural paintings. In some of the residential buildings constructed by Maharana Kumbha one can discern even now remains of paintings on the walls, though very much diffused and not intelligible. We cannot precisely indicate the technique adopted for preparing the base, *i.e.* the *vajralep* for these paintings. These murals come under the category of *Bhitichitra* and have been used for decorating the walls. The text of the *Sangeetraja* contains instructions on the decorations for the interior of *Natyashala*. *Rajaballabhamandan* also contains instructions for decorating the interior of the palace walls with pleasing scenes and to avoid painting of such scenes as may scare the on looker and vitiate the atmosphere. We also learn from *Som Saubhagya Kavya* that the interiors of the house of the *Shreshthis* also used to be decorated with pleasing paintings.

Thus we find that the art of painting was quite popular in Mewar and to conclude we can say that Mewar during the reign of Maharana Kumbha witnessed the continuity of the past and handed over as a legacy to his successors to develop, improve upon and revitalise them to full blossom.

Architecture

Mewar has a rich legacy of architecture extending over centuries. This architecture was an outcome of building activity of the rulers and the merchants both Hindu and Jain. No doubt the remains of this architectural activity is to be found in the shape of temples, quite a few being repaired, renovated and reconstructed from time to time so that they cannot be considered as true representative of the period when they were actually built. While the religious monuments dominate in numbers it does not imply that civil and military architecture was absent. Architecture in India had acquired the stature of *shastra* even prior to the Gupta rulers. The term *Vastu* in the context of building includes *prasada, mandapa, sabha sala, prapa* and *oranga*. Sculpture being a part of a building was also included in *vastu*. The term *vastushastra* was used for the science dealing with the rules of construction of all kinds of buildings. In the *vastushastra,* buildings in broad sense have been divided on the basis of functional quality into two categories, *i.e.* private buildings and public buildings. The public buildings are for three purposes: defence, religion and security of the public.[21]

The region of Maharana Kumbha witnessed a period of all-round cultural development in which architecture, with others occupied an equally important position. Maharana Kumbha was very interested in building activity. Because of political situation he was primarily concerned with the construction of forts and is generally credited with the construction of thirty-two out of eighty-four forts in Mewar.[22] Side by side with the forts Maharana Kumbha took sufficient interest in the construction of temples and residential buildings as well. Thus the architectural monuments of his period can be grouped under military, civil and religious buildings. So far the building activity of the Maharana is concerned it was mainly in Kumbhalgarh, Achalgarh and Chittorgarh. Besides the Maharana, the rich Jain *shreshthis* also contributed their might in erecting temples dedicated to the *Tirthankaras*. They also constructed their residential buildings which have been in course of time altered beyond recognition.

Forts

Leaving aside the major forts we may mention first the

smaller ones. Kumbha erected the fort of Vasanti on the western border of Mewar to defend his boundary from the side of Sirohi and also fortified the defiles of the hilly region. To defend Sher Nalla and Devagarh against the Mers of Aravalli he built the fort of Machan. He also built the fort of Kolan near Amba Bhawani, and the fort of Vairat near Badnor and refortified the fort of Ahore and named it Kailashmeru. He built several forts to overawe the *Bhumia* Bhils of Jalore and Panora. In fact the whole of Mewar was dotted with fortresses and were located at various strategic places. These fortresses, however, were meant to serve as *chaukis* and belonged to different classes. Besides, at times cities were also fortified and they too have been mentioned as forts or *durga*.

As fortified cities, the forts are called *sibira, vahini-mukha, sthaniya, dronaka, samviddha, kolaka, nigama* and *skandhavara*.

For purely military purposes, they have been classified into various categories. *Giri-durga* or hill fort is one which is on the high level and is supplied with plenty of water. *Vana durga* (forest-fort) is one which is encircled by huge thorns and clusters of trees. *Salila-durga, i.e.* water-fort is that which is surrounded by great sheets of water. *Parikha* fort is that which is surrounded on all sides by great ditches (*parikha*). *Parikha* fort is known to be that which is protected by wall of bricks, stones and mud. *Panka-durga* is a fort made entirely of mud. *Dhanva-durga* is known to be that round about which there is no water. *Sahaya durga* or help fort is used both for the forts belonging to valorous friendly kinsfolk and for such forts as were complementary to the main fort. Another term *Sainya-durga* is also found which implies a troop-fort, *i.e.* one which is protected by heroes well up in *vyuhas* or military defence, and hence impregnable. However, the last named might have been more associated with battle array or at times of camping of armies rather than as a fort proper.

Some basic rules also have been laid down as the essentials of a fort. In shape the forts could be circular, square or rectangular. They are to be surrounded with *parikha* (moats), enclosure-walls, and ramparts, and are to be furnished with various entrances, exits and gateways (*partoli*). Circumambulating flights of steps and secret staircases are to be constructed in the walls. Towers are to be built on the enclosure walls and should be mounted with weapons of defence. In the interior, tanks, ponds or canals are to be constructed. In a fortified city roads are to be constructed and buildings for the people of different castes and professions should be provided in a suitable manner. Provision for a secret entrance and exit was to be provided in all categories of forts.

Kumbhalgarh

Among the major forts of Maharana Kumbha mention must be made first of Kumbhalgarh. This impregnable *giridurga* stands on a high peak of the most westerly range of the Aravali hills on the borders of Mewar and Marwar. It can be approached from Ranakpur Jain temple and Parashuram Shiva temple, more convenient approach is from the side of Kailwara, the side that was chosen by Mahmud Khalji in his attempts on this fort. According to tradition it was originally built by a Jain King Samprati centuries ago. But the old fort was almost ruined and the present one should be credited to Kumbha. The whole structure was reconstructed and fortifications erected and the necessary arrangements were made by Maharana Kumbha. According to *Kirtistambha Prashasti* the fort was completed in v.s. 1515/1458 A.D. though the work was started some two decades earlier that is it took about twenty years to complete this massive fort. In *Maasir-i-Mahmudshahi* this fort has been mentioned as Machhindarpur and is mentioned to have a complementary fort. This, however, refers to an earlier period of Kumbha's reign when the construction work was in progress and the new name had not still been given to it. It was originally named as Kumbhalmer but came to be known popularly as Kumbhalgarh.

The defence of the fort is well arranged with gates on all of its approaches. The first gate is Aretpol which serves as a barrier thrown across the first narrow ascent about a mile from Kailwara. Further on comes Hullapol and then Hanumanpol after which comes Vijaypol and Rampol. Beyond this starts the fort proper as the strong high walls start from Rampol. On the road leading from Rampol to the main wall there are five other gates, Bhairavapol, Neebupol, Chauganpol, Pakhadapol and Ganeshpol. Thus through the several gateways along a winding approach the fort is defended by a series of walls with battlements and bastions built on the slopes of the hill. The surrounding battlemented wall is so thick as to allow eight horsemen to ride abreast. The formidable bastions in the battlemented wall of the fortification are peculiar in shape and are so built that enemy cannot scale them by means of ladders.

Within the fort the residential buildings, simple in their construction, were provided with necessary accessories like store-houses and water reservoirs for the inmates of the fort and also for standing seige. Kumbhalgarh also contains quite a number of temples which will be discussed separately. Here in Kumbhalgarh one may really see the ingenuity of the architect in combining technique with environment without sacrificing the aesthetics.

The fort had remained proud possession of the Maharanas of Mewar who in their turn added many constructions according to their needs and also reconstructed many of the original structures adding a large number of residential quarters. The main structure, however, remains as it was built by Maharana Kumbha and stands as a true representative of the medieval Indian military architecture and an enduring contribution of the scholar king.

Achalgarh

On the peak of Mount Abu there existed a ruined fortress of the Paramara Kings which was reconstructed and renovated in 1452 A.D. by Maharana Kumbha and was named as Achalgarh. Actually, Achalgarh is the citadel of the fortifications surrounding the area and also falls under the category of *giridurga*. The fort of Achalgarh has remained neglected ever since the decline of Mewar after Maharana Sanga with result that it is now almost in ruins. Even in ruins it speaks of the grandeur that it possessed in the days of Maharana Kumbha. The ruined towers of the fort still exist. The first gate of the fort is called Hanumanpol which is composed of two towers built of huge blocks of grey granite. The top of the two towers had been connected by a series of rooms to serve as guard rooms. This gate serves as an entrance to the lower fort whose dilapidated walls can be traced up the irregular ascent. After some ascent there is another gate the Champapol, which serves as an entrance to the inner fort. Inside the inner fort stands a Jain temple. The upper fortress was only repaired, renovated and strengthened by Maharana Kumbha though it is attributed to him as his creation. Within this inner fort we find the existence of a granary coated with heavy and enduring plaster. There are ruins of residential buildings as well. The citadel also contains a small lake which is called *Sawan-Bhadon*, which seems to have some perennial source of water supply. On one of the elevated mounds of the eastern side the ruins of an alarm tower testifies to the steps taken for the defence purposes.

Chittorgarh

The fortified city of Chittor is a gift of nature. Situated on a plateau it has a natural defence which was further strengthened by human efforts. Chittor was captured by Alauddin Khalji in 1303 A.D. and it was after this victory of the Khalji Sultan that Chittor came to be associated with Rajput valour and their spirit to sacrifice their blood and life for the defence of their cloister and hearth. Alauddin after the conquest of the fort caused a bridge to be constructed over the Gambhiri river below the fortress. The gate that was constructed and the towers raised over the abutments have disappeared but ten massive arches of grey limestone still exist. After the resurgence of Mewar under the Guhilputra Sisodias the rulers remained vigilant to maintain the defences of the fort. Chittor, being the capital of Mewar, continued to receive the attention for proper upkeep by the Maharanas from the time of Hammir. Thus the fortifications, bastions, residential quarters and religious shrines do not represent the reign of one king but of severals. However, some of the remains of the time of Maharana Kumbha may be noticed. Of course, there is nothing much different purely from the point of view of architecture from what has already been observed for the forts of Kumbhalgarh and Achalgarh.

Maharana Kumbha strengthened the fortifications by repairing, reconstructing and remodelling the outer walls of the defence, and also repaired the existing gates adding some new ones. He is associated with seven gates. *Ramarathya* or Rampol was constructed with round bastions, which was partly demolished during the reign of Shahjahan. The plinth of these bastions still retain carved friezes which are indications of the ornamental style. *Hanumanagopura* or Hanumanpol, *Bhairavankavishikha* (commonly known as Bhairavpol after the name of Bhairavdas Solanki who fell fighting at this gate in 1535 A.D. while defending the fort against Bahadurshah Gujarati), *Mahalakshmirathya* or

Lakshmipol, *Chamundapratoli* or Chamundpol, *Tararathya* or Tarapol, *Rajapratoli* or Rajpol. Tarapol was provided with projected balcony.[23]

The use of terms *Ratha, Gopura, Vishikha* and *Pvatoli* is quite interesting. These terms are used for gates of different type and for different occasions. *Ratha* has several meanings of which the one standing for a gate represents the structure rising into greater heights in storeys and having the gate-way either through it or in-between two such structures raised on the two sides of the road together serving as a gate. The *Nagara* type *ratha* is square and those in Chittor come under this category. Thus Rampol, Lakshmipol and Tarapol were structures standing on the two sides and the space in-between serving as the entrance gate. The term *Gopura* was used for gate-houses of palaces and cities as well as for the temple but its use was to exclusively restricted for the temple. The *gopura* also has several storeys, hence Hanumanpol was a gate-house with several storeys which increased its height making it an imposing structure. *Pratoli* is used for a gateway sometimes provided with a flight of steps; *Vishikha* stands for the gate-way on the main street.[24]

Maharana Kumbha built a road to facilitate the heavy carriages to go up the hill up to the fort by paving and broadening the foot-path that was there before him.[25] During his time this was the only road access to the fort. He also built the *Rama Kunda* and a number of stepped wells and reservoirs for storing water. Among the residential quarters a few of the ruins of those built by Kumbha can still be seen. One can have some idea of the placements of various adjuncts of the building with some traces of paintings on some of the walls, but beyond this one is left guessing.

Chittorgarh has the famous *Kirtistambha* which does not form a part of the fortifications or defence, but deserves special notice both from architectural and iconographical point of view. The structure forms an example of the combination of religious and secular architecture. This magnificent piece of architecture was started sometime in v.s. 1496/1439 A.D. and its construction continued upto v.s. 1516/1459 A.D. as found from the various inscriptions bearing various dates placed in different storeys of the structure.[26] This *stambha* stands in conformity with the tradition of *stambhas* prevalent in India and Rajasthan. Such a view is supported by the existence of another Jain tower which stands in Chittor. This Jain tower is a *singularly* elegant specimen of its class about 75 ft. in height and adorned with sculptures and mouldings from the base to the summit. It stands on a basement 20 fit. square and 9 ft. high with a stair on the southern side leading to the doorway, which is 6 ft. 2 in. above the platform. The shaft of the tower is about 13 ft. square below, and is four storeys high to the open canopy of twelve pillars the floor of which is 64 ft. from the ground. This tower most probably belongs to the twelfth century as in its style it is quite consistent of the style of *stambhas* of that century. This Jain structure probably dedicated to Adinath the first of the Jain *Tirthankaras*, and nude figures of them are repeated some hundreds of time on the face of the tower, distinguishing it as Digambara monument.[27] "The upper portion of the tower had become shaken and one of the balconies had fallen, a fourth of it or 20 ft. has been taken down, and rebuilt with imitations of the old work to replace lost portions."[28]

Kirtistambha is not a Tower of Victory as has been mentioned by Sarda, to commemorate his victory over Mahmud Khalji of Malwa. It is more in the nature of a *Vishnustambha* than any thing else and is attached to Kumbhaswami temple. The placement of the statue of Vishnu (*Janardana*) at its entrance confirms it as a *Vaishnava* structure. The entire structure stands as evidence for the skill of the architects and sculptures of Rajasthan.

In the construction of *Kirtistambha* a number of *sutradhars* seem to have been associated, though it would be correct to deduce that it was primarily designed by *sutradhar* Jaita (Jaitra) and was taken over from him by his sons Napa and Punja. Another inscription mentions of *sutradhar* Poma. Yet another inscription mentions of Jita and his sons Napa, Bhumi and Chuthi.

The structure is about 122 ft. in height and 35 ft. broad at the base and at the summit immediately under the cupola it comes to 18 ft. It stands on a square basement with sides of 47 ft. and a height of 10 ft. The basement itself speaks of the prethinking in which the architect had calculated the weight of the mass that it was expected to carry. The entire height of the *stambha* is divided into nine storeys with openings at every face of each storey and all these doors have colonnaded porticos. The outside surface all along its height has been properly punctuated. Each of the nine divisions has been furnished with its windows, balustrades *chhajjas* (eaves) and emphasized by columns, pilasters and numberless horizontal bands and cornices. Each storey is lighted by trellis windows and the engles and recesses not intersected by steps are utilised for statues and ornaments. The entire structure is covered with architectural ornaments and sculptures of Hindu deities or personification of divinities according to the cannons mentioned by Mandan in his treatise *Rupamandana*. These ornaments, no doubt, have been so profusely used that hardly any space has been left plain, yet this mass of decoration has been kept subdued in a manner that it, in no way, interferes with the outline of the structure or reduces the grandeur of the *stambha*. A stair in the interior connects seven out of the nine storeys. The peculiarity of the staircase consists in its winding alternately through a central well and a gallary formed round it. The eighth and the ninth storeys are open in the manner of pavilion with pillars supporting the weight of the roofs. The ninth storeys actually is a reconstruction done by Maharana Swarup Singh in 1911 A.D., and the dome that now crowns the tower is not the original one of the time of Maharana Kumbha. The *Kirtistambha* is a contribution of Maharana Kumbha to Mewar which has stood the vagaries of time and even to-day stands as an evidence of Mewar that was once great.

Temples

The temple architecture of India had acquired a personality of its own. It had been laid down that:

> "Temples are constructed for the prosperity of the people and ornamentation of the cities; for the enjoyment of the people in this world leading to their salvation; for upholding truth; for permanence of religion in this world; for providing means of sport for Gods; and, to bring fame, longevity and welfare for the king."

Thus construction of temples by the kings and the people was considered an act of merit. The construction of a temple was governed by the principles laid down in the *Vastushastra*. The architect could not take liberties and was enjoined to carry out all the detailed instructions laid down in the manuals. These manuals, of which Mandan's *Prasadmandan* and *Rupmandan* are the principal ones for the period of Kumbha. They contain exhaustive treatment of every aspect of the temple, such as names of various types of temples, the selection of site, the time when the construction work should begin, the materials of which the temple should be made, the plan of the temple, laws of proportions, the nature of superstructure, the image to be sculpted for the temple, in short, every little thing from the laying of the foundation to the finish have been meticulously laid down. A temple would not be acceptable to society if it were not built according to the cannonical rules, and no one not versed in the *Vastushastra* was recognised to possess any right to engage himself in temple building.

As a result of such rules and influences of physical features as well as religious beliefs three distinct styles of temples architectures evolved in India. These three broad styles have in their turn again sub-divided into a number of smaller groups. The three broad divisions of the style are: Nagara Dravida and Vesara. The connotation *Bhumija* used by Mandan is only another name of Vesara.[29] The Vesara style is distinguished by a barrel roof, the Dravida by its octagonal or hexagonal and Nagara by its quadrangular shape. These distinguishing features are noticed at the upper part of the building. The best example of Vesara style in western India is to be found in the Telika Mandir in the fort of Gwalior. The Vesara style is rather rare. The Nagara and the Dravida styles are widely spread over India. The two styles vary considerably: pillars, capitals, mouldings differ in each but the most distinguishing feature is to be found in the *shikhara*. In the Nagara style the *shikhara* is curvilinear and conical in form and crowned by a coping stone (*amalaka*) resembling a flat fluted melon supporting an inverting picher. In the Dravida style the *shikhara* is pyramidical ascending in a series of horizontal terraces crowned by a conical cup which looks like a miniature stupa.

In Rajasthan temple architecture acquired a distinctive type with the Nagara style. The plinth of these temples stand on a high platform as those of the temples of Khajoraho, while the spires bear a striking resemblance to those of early Bhubaneswar temples. Another feature is that they usually consist of five buildings with the shrine house in the centre and belong to the type known as *panchayatana*. The reign of Maharana Kumbha witnessed a period of extraordinary religious liberalism in Mewar. Ekalinga, *i.e.* Shiva was the patron deity of the Maharanas according to which Kumbha should have been a follower of Shaivism, yet we find that the personal leanings of the Maharana was more towards Vaishnavism if the number of temples dedicated to Vishnu and Shiva constructed under the royal commands can be accepted as indication. Among the temples built under the royal command the number of Vishnu temples certainly exceed the number of Shiva temples. The statues and temples of *Matrikas* indicate that he had equal belief in *Shakti*. His liberal attitude towards the Jains encouraged them to construct temples dedicated to their *Tirthankaras*. Thus the total building activity in Mewar during the reign of Kumbha is remarkable. For the purpose of examination we may more conveniently follow the chronological order of the construction of these temples.

Ranpur Jain Temple

In the chronological order the Jain temple at Ranpur comes first. It was built in 1439 A.D. as is borne out by an inscription which states that the temple was built by a Jain *Shreshthi* named Dharanak in v.s. 1496. This temple is situated near Sadri in Godwar within the valley on the western slopes of the Aravali hills and below Kumbhalgarh. The spot selected for its natural beauty testifies the builder's consciousness of the environment.

The temple is built on a lofty basement almost square being 198 ft. by 205 ft. exclusive of the projections on each face. In the centre stands the main shrine open on four sides with the principal statue consisting of four figures placed on a pedestal back to back so as to face the four directions. This combined image is that of Adinath and made out of white marble. The temples comes under the *Chaumukha* style. Architecturally the temple has many qualities. The design itself is that of a complex of structures. The upper storey also contains a similar shrine accessible by four doors opening from the terraced roofs of the building. The lower and principal shrine has no door but only a small porch called *Mukhamandapa*. On a lower level is a *Sabha mandapa* on each side approached by a flight of steps. Near the four angles of the court are four smaller shrines and on each of them are 20 dome like structures (*mandaps*) supported by about 240 columns, four of these *mandaps, i.e.* the central one of each group, are three storeys in height and stands higher than others. The one facing the principal entrance has a second dome over the first supported by 16 columns and is 36 ft. in diameter the others being 24 ft. only in their diameter. Light is admitted to the building by four uncovered courts at the sides of these domes. The sides of the temple, between the subsidiary shrines and the entrance, are occupied by ranges of cells for images each with a pyramidal roof of its own but without any partitioning walls. The total dimension covering about 48,000 sq. ft. (forty-eight thousand) by itself speaks of the immensity of the entire structure.

Besides the twelve in the central *shikharas* there are eighty-six cells of very varied form and size surrounding the interior, and all their facades are adorned with sculptures. The internal effect of the cluster of columns is such that it is impossible to reproduce the variety of perspective and the play of light and shade which results from the disposition of the pillars and of the domes and from the mode in which the light is introduced. The immense number of parts in the building, their variety, their beauty of detail—no two pillars in the whole building being alike—the grace with which they are arranged, the tasteful admixture of domes of different height combined with *shikharas* and the mode in which the light is introduced combine to produce an excellent effect.[30]

Ekalingji

Ekalingji is the patron deity of the Maharanas of Mewar. The Maharanas even professed Ekalingji as the ruler of Mewar and claimed themselves only to be his *diwan*. "Early in the eighth century, the sage Harita conferred on Bappa Rawal the title of Regent of Ekalingji, and to this day the Maharanas of Mewar, as *diwans* or regents of Shiva, supersede the high priest in his duties and themselves perform the ceremonies when they visit the temple."[31]

The temple of Ekalingji is dedicated to Shiva. Bappa Rawal is credited with the construction of the original structure which was rebuilt by Maharana Mokul and renovated by Maharana Kumbha. The temple is situated in a defile 13 miles north of the present Udaipur. "The hills towering around it on all sides are of primitive formation, and their scrapped summits are clustered with honeycombs. There are abundant small springs of water, which keep verdant numerous shrubs, the flowers of which are acceptable to the deity; especially the *kiner* or oleander, which grows in great luxuriance on the Aravalli. Groves of bamboo and mango were formerly common . . . there are, however, still many trees sacred to the deity scattered around."[32]

To this sacred temple Maharana Kumbha added a large *mandap* (*kumbhamandap*) in front of the original temple and also erected a *torana* to serve as entrance to the *mandap* which leads to sanctuary containing the *girbhagriha*. The plan of the temple is composed of a sanctuary and an assembly hall (*mandap*) with a *vrisha-mandap*. The sanctuary consists of a double storeyed body over which stands the *shikhara* surmounted by a *kalasha* which was of gold. The *mandap* is also a double storeyed structure with a rather flattened roof the exterior of which is covered with innumerable circular kobs. This seems to have been the style prevalent during the reign of Kumbha as it can also be found over the *mandap* roof of Kumbhaswami temple at Chittor. The *vrisha-mandap* containing the statue of *Nandi* is rather an open pavilion with a pyramidal roof supported by columns and stands facing the deity in the main shrine.

Kumbhswami Temple

Maharana Kumbha is said to have built three Vishnu temples called Kumbhswami, one each at Chittor, Kumbhalgarh and Achalgarh. The Kumbhswami temple of Chittor was truly speaking not built by Kumbha though the *Kirtistambha Prashasti* records that he constructed the temple.[33] The structural and decorative motifs as found in the *Garbhagriha*, the *Pradakshinapatha* and the *Jangha* (wall parts)[34] clearly indicate them to belong to a period not later than tenth century. The contrast between the sculptural art found at the plinth level and the roof level are clear indications of the different dates of their construction.

The plan of the temple is quite elaborate and Maharana Kumbha repaired, renovated and added some structure to it. The *shikhara* of the main shrine containing the *garbhagriha* and the *pradakshinapatha* seems to have been reconstructed by Maharana Kumbha. The style of the *shikhara* bears a close resemblance with the earlier Orissan temples. It contains three *mandapas*, in succession one after the other, and, in certain respect it follows the Chalukyan style. Immediately in front of the shrine in the *kulya mandapa* or *sabha mandapa* next to it comes the *praggriva mandapa* then comes another *mandapa* which was meant for *kirtan* or dance or *rasa*.[35] All constructed on an elevated *jagati*.[36]

Viewed critically from pure architectural point the whole structure is rather a poor example. It lacks proportion and in composition the different parts have not been constructed in a manner to balance with the total mass. The structure also carries an impression of hasty construction.

Shringar Chauri

This is a Jain temple dedicated to Shantinath and probably built in the last quarter of the thirteenth century. During the reign of Maharana Kumbha when building activity received great impetus, this temple was repaired and renovated by Vela, son of Kela, in v.s. 1505/1448-49 A.D. Vela was a *bhandari* (treasurer) of Maharana Kumbha. The main building consists of a square hall with four wings projecting from four sides. Like the usual style of Mewar this building too stands on a raised *jagati* five feet in height. The central chamber is twenty feet square. The entrance to the main chamber seems to have been from all the four sides when it was built but subsequently the eastern and southern entrances were filled up by trellis windows. "In the centre of this building, and raised 4.1 "from its floor, is a forty-two sided and ornamental *vedi*, or altar, which supports four carved pillars each 7 feet high and bearing lintels 1.3 deep." The four pillars deserve our notice. They are octagonal from the base, which convert into twelve sides in the middle and end in round shape at the top over which the lintels are placed. The roof of the *mandapa* is octagonal and rests on *kirtimukha* brackets.

"The exterior walls are beautifully sculptured in horizontal bands containing numerous figures and floral scrods."[37] Architecturally the building presents a good example of distribution of weight and placement of the mass without losing balance. Much of what we find at present are later alterations and renovations.

Besides these major temples Mewar is full of temples in all its places, and in Chittor, Achalgarh and Kumbhalgarh their number is so great that one feels as if he is amidst a forest of temples. With so much building activity one wonders at the absence of any improvement or addition to the technique of architecture. The domination of the horizontal over the vertical is marked so much that the building appear squat and stunted. Maybe the rules laid down for religious structures hardly left any scope for the architect to use his imagination as he was required to reproduce according to the rules.

Sculpture

Mewar under Maharana Kumbha had two master *silpis* in Sutradhar Mandan and Sutradhar Jaita. Mandan influenced the western Mewar with Kumbhalgarh as centre while Jaita influenced the eastern Mewar with Chittor as centre. From iconographical point of view the contribution of Mewar during this period is remarkable both in variety and in number. The heroic age of Mewar witnessed many deeds of human valour and sacrifice and the soul of the artist was moved to immortalise them by carving out statues of human beings representing the heroes. The personification of the forces of nature as indicated in the Puranic stories provided the artist with an equally interesting subject for his sculpture. Thus in the sculptures of Mewar man and god have a fair representation.

Among the gods there is hardly any mythological figure that is not represented in the icons that decorate the walls, the jambs and the niches. The *Kirtistambha* alone contains a large number of them. Vishnu, Brahma, Shiva, Shakti, the Jain *Tirthankaras,* besides the various imaginary fairies. *Upsaras* can be found almost everywhere. Thus iconographically Mewar presents a rich harvest in quantity. Every form indicated in canons for various images of gods and goddesses are found here in the temples. It presents almost a panorama of mythology depicted in sculptured form.

But from sculptural point of view one feels rather sad about the manner of their execution. These sculptures are devoid of rhythm. They are static and expressionless. A comparison of the sculptures of Khajoraho or Vimalsh's temple of Abu would at once bring out the difference. The subject demands for an intensive and exhaustive study which the space at the disposal forbids to undertake. I would close it with the remark that the decline in the standard of sculpture is obvious for whatever reasons it may have been.

Music

Mewar under Maharana Kumbha contributed substantially to the music of India. With his mastery of Indian music and his proficiency as a *vina* player, the Maharana easily created a circle of musicians around himself. During his reign music, dance and drama gained status in social life. Musicians readily found in the Maharana a patron. As already mentioned Maharana Kumbha composed the *Sangitraja* which by itself is an index of the standard achieved in the field of music.

Maharana Kumbha had studied all the earlier authorities for his own musical compositions and his theories and concepts are traditional.[38] He had also carefully studied *Sangeet Ratnakara* or Sarangdeva with all its commentaries. He makes a special reference to *Kalanidhi* of Kallinath, which is a commentary on *Ratnakara*, in his *Nrityaratnakosha*.[39] Maharana Kumbha could not agree with Sarangdeva on every aspect of music. Such point where Kumbha had no disagreement with Sarangdeva he accepted, but he considered them only as material handed over to Sarangdeva by tradition and not as his original contribution. Throughout the text of *Sangitraja* Kumbha's unswerving devotion to Bharata is clearly pronounced. In providing a textbook for the guidance of music Kumbha has critically sifted all traditional material available in his time and has used them for recording important opinions of authorities. Although he has all respect for all earlier authorities, he has not blindly followed any opinion.[40] Kumbha evinces "a special partiality for more ancient authorities, who do not seem to possess the same degree of appeal for contemporary writers. His bias for the scriptures as the original source of musical science is unmistakable. The work (*Sangitraja*) stands to glowing monument to the versatile genius of its author and to his special concern for restoring and preserving what was best in Hindu musical culture and tradition."[41]

Religion

Religion played a dominant role in the lives of the people during the medieval age and even in modern age it has not completely lost its hold though it has rounded its sharp corners. Rajasthan during the fifteenth century presents a milieu of religious belief and superstition, the latter maintaining a strong grip over the minds of the people. During the fifteenth century one can find Shaivism with its ramifications, Vaishnivism, Shakti cult, Jainism with its division into Swaitamber and Digambar all existed side by side. In every form of ramification of the Hinduism the believers centred their faith on some patron deity which distinguished them from others.

Ekalingji (Shiva) continued to be regarded as the real lord even during the reign of Kumbha, but Shaivism did not maintain an exclusive hold over Mewar. The temple of Ekalingji was repaired by Maharana Kumbha who also granted the villages of Nagda, Kathdavan, Malakkheda and Bhimana to the temple for its maintenance and also to meet the expenses for the worship of the deity. In Chittor too an important temple of Shiva, renovated by Maharana Mokul, flourished during the reign of Maharana Kumbha. The idol of this temple has six hands, rather an unusual icon of Shiva.[42]

Lakuleesh sect of Shaivism worshipping the Pashupat Shiva form had entered Mewar quite early, may be in the ninth century and continued during the reign of Maharana Kumbha. According to the belief of the Lakuleesh sect the cause of the universe was Parameshwar, *Jiva* or life was the form of work this necessary rituals being besmearing the body with ash, repetition of the Name and circumambulation of the deity. Music, dance and uttering loud sounds from the navel and prostration before the deity were considered as essential rituals of worship. Menal in Mewar was an important centre of the Lakuleesh sect. The mode of worship and the ideas behind the forms were rather too intriguing to give popularity to this form of Shaivism. During the reign of Kumbha it had lost its hold over the people and remained confined to a group of *sadhus* only.

Side by side with Shaivism, Shakti cult also existed. Shakti, recognised as the source of power of the gods was actually a continuity of Mother Cult. Rajputs being warrior always offered their prayers to Shakti before going out to the battlefield. During the reign of Kumbha, Shakti worship prevailed and the various forms of Shakti like Chamunda, Durga, Bhawani, etc., continued to be worshipped in Mewar. *Navaratri* was specially observed.

In Mewar some minor sects existed most likely as sub-division of some major faiths. Of these the *Nathpanthi* monks and *siddas* seem to have held a strong position in the form of popular belief. This becomes evident when we find Maharana Kumbha mentioning the names of Gorakhnath, Meennath, and Siddhnath among the gods to be worshipped.[43] The villages of Lasadia and Titardi were prominent among the centres of *Nathpanthis*.

Vaishnavism

Maharana Kumbha was personally a devotee of Vishnu, though he continued to regard Ekalingji as the patron deity of the royal family. As already mentioned, during his reign old Vishnu temples were repaired and many new ones were constructed. His commentary on *Gitagovinda* is another testimony of his personal belief. During his reign it appears that Vaishnavism was gaining ground and was gradually becoming a popular religion.

Jainism

Jainism had flourished in Rajasthan and Gujarat from earlier times and remained in a flourishing condition in Mewar during the reign of Maharana Kumbha. During his reign the Swetamber sect of the Jains had a special hold in the regions of Delwara, Chittor, Kareda, and Kumbhalgarh while the Digambar sect held Bijolia and Hrishabhdev. In Delwara the temples of Adinath (1434 A.D.) and Parashvanath (1437 A.D.) were looked upon with veneration. It was in Delwara, that, a Oswal Shanpal Nawlakha on the advice of Jina Sagar Suri caused the second part of *Avashyakvrihadvriti* to be written. *Gachhachar* was also written here. The temple of Shantinath at Nagda was also constructed during this period. In 1438 A.D. the temple of Mahavirswami was constructed in Chittor. In Godwar too a number of Jain temples were constructed. The Kharatargachha and Tapagachha seem to have been enjoying a better position during the reign of Kumbha. Jina Sagar Suri and Jina Sundar Suri were most prominent monks of the Kharatargachha group. The religious function of Swetambar Jains were performed with a show of pomp and grandeur.

In Bijolia the Digamber Jains maintained their position and had a greater following than at other places. The temple of Keshariaji was an important place of their pilgrimage. Of the Digambar monks and preachers Sakalkirti and Bhuvankirti were most prominent during the reign of Kumbha. Maharana Kumbha was extremely tolerant towards all. To the Jains he extended unreserved honour and never hesitated in receiving them with honour in his court. In 1454 A.D. Jasvir, a prosperous Jain merchant of Malwa with his business set up at Mandu visited Mewar and also came to the court of Maharana Kumbha. In spite of the fact that the two States had no friendly relations Maharana Kumbha did not hesitate to honour Jasvir.[44] Jasvir visited many of the places of Jain pilgrimage and everywhere he distributed charity. He had set up fifty-two *Sanghapatis* and was himself honoured with the title of *Sangheshwar*.

Thus we find that Mewar during the reign of Maharana Kumbha witnessed a period of perfect religious harmony. The various sects existed side by side and all of them respected each other. Such a behaviour and attitude is certainly an index of a high standard of cultural development which inculcates a regard for the sentiments of others.

NOTES AND REFERENCES

1. *Ekalinga Mahatmya, Rajvarnan Adhyaya,* Slokas-172-173.
2. *Nrityaratna Kosha,* Part ii, Introduction, p. 3, fn. 1.
3. *Ibid.,* p. 4.
4. *Nrityaratna Kosha,* pp. 64, 74, 134.
   In one of the Introductory verses of *Sangitraja,* Kumbha declares that he was studied *Ratnakara* with all its commentaries. *Sangitraja,* verse 39.
5. D. Sharma, *Lectures on Rajput History and Culture,* p. 74.
6. Prashasti of *Suda-prabandha,* quoted by Somani, *Maharana Kumbha,* p. 238, fn. 46.
7. D. Sharma, *op. cit.,* p. 75.
8. *Ibid.,* p. 74.
9. D. Sharma, *op. cit.,* p. 76; *Kirtistambha Prashasti,* verses 190-192.
10. Ramballabh Somani, *op. cit.,* pp. 221-222.
11. *Rajasthan Bharati,* March, 1963, pp. 81-83.
12. Ramballabh Somani, *op. cit.,* p. 222, fn. 26.

13. *Prashasti*:

"आगात्रै मिषं पात्रपुजनगराकात्यायनीयाग्रणी, वाक्यतर्कंगता वहींद्र समतः साहित्य रत्नाकरः।
श्रौतस्मार्त यतेः कृत श्रीमन्मुरारैः सुतः श्री कल्याणकरोतनिष्टशिवदां कृष्णप्रशस्ति परां ।।"

14. According to *Rupmandan*:

"श्री मदेशे मेदपाययिधाने क्षेत्राख्योंऽभूत सुत्रधारो वरिष्ठः।
पुत्रो ज्येष्ठो मण्डनस्तस्य तेन प्रोक्तं शास्त्रं मण्डनं रूपपूर्वम् ।।"

15. Ramballabh Somani, *op. cit.*, pp. 211-212.
16. Motichand Girdharilal Kapadia, Introduction to *Adhyatma-kalpadrum*.
17. *Gurugunratnakar*, 2, 107.
18. *Journal, Bandarkar Oriental Research Institute*, XVII, pt. i, p. 332.
19. *Devakulpataka*, p. 35.
20. *Painting of India*, Douglas Barrett and Basil Gray, 1963, Lussanne.
21. P.K. Acharya, *A Dictionary of Hindu Architecture*, pp. 546 and 547. In Manasara buildings are divided into six classes, classified as *prasada, mandapa, sabha, sala, prapa* and *oranga*. Manasara III, 7-12. "Building is divided into two parts, the first regulates the general plan of walls of a city and its public buildings; the other relates to private buildings. Public buildings are for three purposes; defence, religion and the security of the public." The Hindu Vastushastra in relation to architecture trades special note of three things. (i) "Of things on which architecture depends," (ii) "Of the different branches of architecture", (iii) 'Of the choice of healthy situations."
22. *Vir Vinod*, i, p. 334.
23. For these terms see *Kirtistambha Prashasti*, verses 36, 38, 39, 40, 41, 42, 125, given in Appendix A.
24. P.K. Acharya, *A Dictionary of Hindu Architecture* (O.U.P.) 1927, pp. 74, 366.
25. *Kirtistambha Prashasti*, verse 34.
26. The first inscription is dated v.s. 1499/1442 A.D. and is in the first storey; the second is dated v.s. 1507/1450 A.D. and is in the second storey; the third is dated v.s. 1510/1403 A.D.; the fourth is of v.s. 1510/1403 A.D.; the fifth is dated v.s. 1515/1458 A.D.; the sixth bears the date v.s. 1516/1459 A.D. and after its completion the full *Prashasti* dated v.s. 1517-1460 A.D. was fixed to indicate its completion and other aspects of the structure as well as to proclaim the greatness of Maharana Kumbha.
27. James Fergusson, *History of Indian and Eastern Architecture*, ii, pp. 57-59.
28. *Ibid.*, ii, p. 59, fn. 2. (The period it refers is prior to 1910 A.D.)
29. P.K. Acharya, A *Dictionary of Hindu Architecture*, p. 314. "In one of

the epigraphical quotation (No.15) *Bhumija* is mentioned alongside *Dravida* and *Nagara*, and this *Bhumija* (lit., originated in the land before the document was written) is apparently same as Vesara."

30. *Archaeological Survey of India, Annual Report*, 1907-8, p. 211; Fergusson, *History of Indian and Eastern Architecture*, (Delhi) ii, pp. 45-47.
31. Sarda, *Maharana Kumbha*, p. 156.
32. Tod, *Annals etc.*, i, p. 410.
33. *Kirtistambha Prashasti*, verse 28.
34. *Jangha*, represents the wall parts of a temple in the northern usage, and corresponds to *pada* of the southern usage, *bada* of the eastern and Kalinga usage and *mandovar* of the western Gujarati usage. It stands for the *bhitti*, the term used in the earliest northern texts vide, Soundara Rajan, K.V., *Indian Temple Styles*, p. 85.
35. *Ardhamandapa*. The antechamber immediately adjoining the *garbhagriha*, essentially forming the entrance framework for the main shrine, known as *antarala* in the north; generally rectangular transversely and leading immediately to the *mahamandapa* in the southern temples. In the early forms, however, both in the north and in the south the temple unit contains only cella and *ardhamandapa*, which in such cases would be called *Mukhamandapa* (Ibid., p. 85); *Praggriva* represents an incipient *mudhamandapa* or *antarala* terminating the temple unit. (*Ibid.*, p. 92.)
36. *Jagati*, In northern temples *jagati* signifies a spacious structural terrace upon which the main temple is erected.
37. H.B. Sarda, *Maharana Kumbha*, p. 162.
38. Text, *Sangitraja*, p. 16.
39. Text, *Nrityaratnakosha*, pp. 74, 133, 134
40. Introduction to *Sangitraja*, p. 85.
41. *Ibid.*, p. 151.
42. Ojha, *Nibandha Sangraha*, Vol. i, pp. 220-21.
43. *Nrityaratnakosha*, p. 14, verses 153-157.
44. *Journal of Madhya Pradesh Itihas Parishad*, iv, p. 89.

6

Administrative and Economic Aspects

The State of Mewar emerged as an important power during the fifteenth century. For administrative purpose it adopted the system already in existence among the Rajputs of earlier centuries, such as the Pratharas, the Chalukyas, the Gahadwalas, etc. In form it was monarchical and the Maharana was considered as the deputy (*Diwan*) of Ekalingji who was recognised as the head of the State. As the deputy of the Ekalingji the Maharana was held responsible for the protection of the people and maintenance of law. Perhaps the Sisodias too believed that good people could not live in a State where the ruler acted arbitrarily just as the ancients had believed. In character, however, the State was only a politically organised clan of which the ruler was looked upon like the head of the family. Every member of the clan expected to enjoy a share of the State. As a consequence the kingdom was parcelled out into *thikanes* under *Thakurs* who looked after the administration of the *thikanes* placed under them. This feeling was very strong and the Sisodias considered it their right to share administration with the Maharana. Thus when Ranmal Rathor distributed positions among the Rathors he caused resistance to be organised by the Sisodias resulting in his assassination and persecution of Jodha Rathor. However, the Sisodias could not prevail in making Mewar an exclusive preserve of their own clan. Rajputs of other clans who wanted to serve the Maharana were retained and were allowed to enjoy the proceeds of the *thikanes* placed under them. In actual practice we find a good degree of decentralisation of authority though in theory the Maharana continued to be considered as the possessor of all authority.

The Maharana being the supreme authority could act independently and behave in autocratic manner, but in actual practice he could hardly afford to ignore the sentiments of his collaterals and followers on whose support and assistance depended his own existence. During the period under present discussion the position of the Maharana as head of the State has been compared with that of the chairman of a *sabha*. He was required to respect the sentiments of the members and honour the learned. He was expected to possess sufficient intelligence so as to be able to make distinction between good and bad persons. He personally was expected to be well read and benevolent. He was not to be niggardly in his habits. He was required to be ambitious and fond of display of grandeur. We know that Maharana Kumbha is credited with the possession of all these qualities.

The Maharana used to hold court with some grandeur. Seated on a throne made of precious metal embedded with precious stones he was surrounded by armed guards ready to sacrifice their lives to protect the Maharana. When on march the Maharana was accompanied by armed soldiers who could understand all the indications of the Maharana. Besides, there were royal umbrella bearers, fly-whisk bearers and other accessory bearers too. The body guards and personal attendants were provided with quarters on the right side of the palace. Such paraphernalia and precautions indicate that the Maharana was maintaining a grand court and that his personal life was not very different from those of the Sultans of Gujarat and Malwa. It also indicates that certain amount of danger to the personal life of the Maharana was there which necessitated these precautions. That the court was not free from intrigues can be illustrated from the murder of Raghvadeva and Ranmal and that the person of the Maharana was not free from danger is amply borne out by the assassination of Maharana Mokul and also the assassination of Maharana Kumbha. In the former case the murderers were the uncles and in the latter case the murderer was the son.

On policy matters the Maharana was aided by a council which was an important institution of the political set up of Mewar. The membership of this council varied from four to eight. The *Mukhya-mantri, Sachiva,* the Crown prince, *Rajguru, Purohit* who was also an astrologer and *Vaidya* were regular members of this council. In the time of Maharana Kumbha the office of *Mukhya-mantri* was entrusted to Shah Sahanpal, son of Shah Naulakha. We cannot precisely say if the *Mukhya-mantri* of Maharana Kumbha participated in battles as we find later in the time of Maharana Sanga and Maharana Pratap, but the application of Shah certainly indicates that Sahanpal belonged to a wealthy family and may be with his wealth he was assisting the Maharana in meeting sudden demands of expenditure required for military purposes.

The Royal seal was kept in the custody of *Mukhya-mantri* who was looked upon as overall in charge of the administrative machinery. The *Mukhya-mantri* was assisted by a number of *mantris* out of which one kept the account of income and was generally addressed as *Shrikarnadhikari* and another kept account of the expenditure addressed as *Vayaganana*. The *Mukhya-mantri* generally put his signature on charity grand deeds but we cannot definitely state the extent to which his signature was compulsory on such deeds. This doubt arises because we find that deeds executed by some of the samantas do not bear the signature of the *Mukhya-mantri*. The probability is that he used to put his signature on royal grants which certainly enjoyed a higher status than others. The *mantris* also at times addressed as *amatya* distributed various duties amongst themselves which included foreign affairs, home affairs. The *Sachiva* was one of the *mantris* but in all likelihood served as the personal secretary of the Maharana. The lower officers of State were directly recruited by the Maharana personally and remained attached to him. The system granting territories to the various collaterals hardly left much scope for greater administrative responsibilities at the Centre. Maharana Kumbha does not seem to have interfered in the management of the *thikanes* which were placed under the Thakurs which will be discussed under different types of grantees. One fact, however, remains clear that Mewar under Maharana Kumbha while made tremendous progress in all other aspects of life, in the field of administration it could not evolve a system which could generate energy to manage the State with the result that the strength and weakness of the State depended entirely on the personality of the Maharana. The privilege enjoyed by the Maharana for granting pardon to offenders against the State, and the persons who had conspired against Ranmal when pardoned, certainly set an example for indulging in intrigues and of setting the Maharana against any one whom they wanted to throw out. That the Maharana could send anybody into exile with whom he was displeased was also another source of weakness that existed in the body politic of the State.

Mewar and all other States of Rajputana professed to have inherited the ancient Hindu traditions and also that they administered the country according to the rules laid down by the earlier sages. However, in actual practice the departure is as wide as the time gap. The division of the kingdom into parts had existed prior to the rise of Mewar into prominence and terms like *bhukti* and *vishaya* which were common earlier we do not find them used in the inscriptions of Maharana Kumbha. The term *bhukti* was used for larger areas. They at times even indicate a region and Mewar not being so large in area probably could not think of using this term. *Bhuktis* were sub-divided into *Vishaya* but this term also does not find mention in the administrative divisions of Mewar. *Vishaya* was further sub-divided into *pratijagrahana* or *pratigana* which under the Turks during the thirteenth and fourteenth century became *pargana*. *Pargana* existed in the whole of Rajasthan and it was also there in Mewar. In Mewar during the reign of Maharana Kumbha elaborated divisions on some regular and systematic way do not seem to have existed.

For proper control and safety some kind of divisions of the kingdom was made keeping an important fort as the controlling centre of the division. Thus after occupation of Abu fort while it served as a powerful bastion in the region of Godwar including Pindwara, Basantgarh, Bhula, etc., it was controlled from Kumbhalgarh which we may say constituted the divisional headquarter. Similarly, Chittor controlled a certain area; forts of Mandor, Pali, Badnur, Mandalgarh (during the period these were under the possession of Maharana Kumbha) and subsequently Jahazpur looked after the regions around them, and if we may so desire, call them as administrative divisions. Critically viewed, however, these divisions were more for defence purposes than for administration and we can deduce that during the reign of Maharana Kumbha military considerations dominated in administrative matters over purely civil affairs.

Among the officers attached to the royal household, the court and administrative machinery we find mention of *Raj Bhandari* (treasurer), *Rasoiya* (Chief Cook), *panehari, kavi, dharmadhikarana, vamshakar* (keeper of the family genealogy), *dungarbhoj* and *selhath*. Of these *dungarbhoj* and *selhath* were concerned with revenue collection and were posted at different places. In some respect they were similar to the *amils* of the Sultanate administration, but they exercised greater powers and enjoyed certain privileges which were absent in the case of the *amils*

Fiscal Organisation

The sources of State income can be broadly classified under heads: land tax, market tax, octroi duty or custom duty. What exactly was the State share during the reign of Maharana Kumbha or his immediate successors is not known and therefore it is useless to make guesses which with maximum amount of approximation may yet remain far off from the reality. Some taxes were also paid in cash, particularly on perishable commodities which was called *Hiranya*. *Hiranya* also included taxes paid partly in cash and partly in kind. The share of the State collected in kind was called *Lata*. In case of *Lata* at the time of collection the village headman generally called *Patel*, the government collector and the cultivator; all the three heads to be present, and the share was collected with the agreement of all the three. This term also occurs in inscriptions referring to a portion out of *Lata* granted to temple as State contribution towards the maintenance of the temple. In all such cases the portion of the *Lata* is indicated in kind.

From a study of *Rajballabhamandana* we find existence of a system of measuring the fields and also of process of calculating its area. It refers to three different standards, the major, medium and the small. The major standard was used for measuring land both rural and urban, the medium standard was used for buildings like temples, houses, etc., and the small standard was applied to throne, canopy, weapons, etc. The standard was called yard (*gaz*) but it is difficult to determine the ratio of the three yards under major, medium and small.

Both agricultural land and waste land were properly demarcated and their boundaries defined and recorded. In the grant deeds or gifts recorded on copper plates the boundaries are always to be found properly defined. Such was the practice before Maharana Kumbha but in the absence of availability of grant deeds of the time of Maharana Kumbha, it is difficult to state categorically that such was the practice; but by correlating the statement found in *Rajballabhamandana* and continuity of many earlier systems of the past we may hypothetically assume that the practice continued under Maharana Kumbha. The existence of the system of measuring land, however, does not give any indication if it was used for determining the land revenue or it was simply used to define the holdings and to keep record of land under cultivation and the possibilities of extension of cultivation. The quantum of agricultural land was also indicated in terms of ploughs, *i.e.*, as much area as could be cultivated by employing one plough, thus holdings of two or three ploughs indicated an area that could be cultivated by means of two or three ploughs as the case may be.

Other Taxes

The inscription of Delwara of v.s. 1491/1443 A.D. mentions various taxes that were collected at Delwara and were prevalent during the reign of Maharana Kumbha. Some of these taxes certainly refer to taxes collected on the sale of commodities in the market. The inscription, however, does not throw light on the rate of the taxes, but only indicates the amount collected under the different heads. Thus 2 tankas were collected from the sale of salt, 1 tanka from cotton cloth, 5 tankas were collected under *mandavi* and 4 tankas from *mapa*, 2 tankas from *manhedavata*. Besides taxes on sale levied at market, there existed a regular system of levying custom duty or octroi duty on all commodities coming in or going out. We find mention of various posts for collection of such taxes. The custom house or better still the tent of the tax collector was known as *mandapika* and the income as *mandavi*. However, we find it difficult to state precisely the location of the *mandapikas*. Of course, it was there at all the religious places and also at important outposts, but could it be that a commodity passing a number of *mandapikas* had to *mandavi* at every post. The logic of the tax indicates that *mandavi* was to be paid at the *mandapika* only on commodities brought for sale with its jurisdiction or else if it had to be paid at every *mandapika* through which the commodity passed the burden of the tax would become too heavy. In case it was given a clearance to proceed to its destination what procedure was followed it is not known. However, this point is yet to be determined by more intensive study than what could be done at present.

The places of religious worship are many in Mewar and at these places some tax was collected from the pilgrims the proceeds of which were utilised towards the upkeep of the place. Maharana Kumbha abolished some of the taxes collected at Abu as we find from the Abu inscription of v.s. 1506/1449 A.D.

In the administrative set up of Mewar the Maharana had little to worry about the day-to-day life of his people. His main concern was confined to defence, collection of certain dues for the maintenance of his household and upkeep of the forts for the defence of the country. The daily life of the people was looked after by various types of local organisations which we may call as self-constituted tribunals. The entire State was loaded with these institutions which were of various types and flourished independently of the State and went to the Maharana only if they failed to resolve their differences and sought the arbitration of the Crown for final settlement. These local organisations existed at various levels of the society. They can be found in temples, in towns, in villages, in merchant guilds, in craft guilds; in other words, there was hardly an aspect of social life which was not covered by one or the other organisation.

In the towns there used to be an organisation generally known as *Mahajana Sabha*. This organisation looked after the civic life of the people residing in the towns, and for meeting its expenses it could levy taxes in the town. It looked after places of public utility such as temples, *baolis*, tanks, etc. In short, it performed the duties which in modern times are put under the care of municipality. However, their existence can be found only in some of the important towns. Besides, we are not in a position to ascertain exactly the relationship it had with the government of the Maharana.

Panchakula

Another civic body with a wide range of duties and powers was the *Panchakula*. As an institution the *panchakula* was partly social and partly political. The institution of *panchakula* was not new. It had come down as a legacy from very early ages down through the Pratihara and post-Pratihara period. In one of the works the five members of the *panchakula* are mentioned as *Adayak, Nibandhak, Pratibandhak, Nivigrahak* and *Rajadhakshya*. It is not possible to state what exactly were the functions of these posts, and also if such were the designations during the reign of Maharana Kumbha. The five members which constituted the *panchakula* were representatives of the religious organisations, caste panchayats, craft guilds on the one side and one from the side of the government. The government representative could be a *mantri*, or *amatya* or *selahatha*. Anong the functions of the *panchakula* mention may be made of its power to make grants to temples or religious and educational institutions. It also assisted the *thakurs* of the *thikanes* in the administration of justice. The *panchakula* also acted as arbitrator between disputing parties. It was authorised to issue certificates of sale. It could also grant concession to traders who could farm out villages. The *panchakula* enjoyed the privilege of taking cognisance not only of religious grants but also secular grants. It also collected the State share of the revenue assigned to it by the Maharana.

Mandapika

Mandapika was another semi-official and semi-civic body which was set up at various out-posts to collect octroi duty. According to Dasharath Sharma this name was given to the octroi post because the *sulkadhyaksha*, *i.e.*, customs officer set up his office in a *mandapika* (small tent or pavilion) near the main gate of the city. As already mentioned earlier it collected various dues under customs as well as various other miscellaneous cesses fixed by the State. The funds collected by the *mandapika* were utilised in a manner as directed by the State. Some of the officers were also paid out the funds collected by the *mandapika* which were called *mandavi*. It is also very likely that the *mandapika* functioned under the direct supervision of the *panchakula*.

Panchayats

In the rural areas a little remote from the cities there existed *panchayats* which looked after the interest of the villagers and settled their disputes regarding their holdings and other matters. The village *panchayat* had as its member only the resident of the village, outsiders were carefully kept out of them. The village *patwari* and the *patel* were like *ex-officio* members of the committee. The elders of the *panch* were elected by the residents. In the socio-economic life of the people the *panchayats* played a vital role and relieved the government of much of its burden and also lessened legal cases. The *panchayats* are more conspicuous in the caste *panchayats*. The caste *panchayats* settled disputes arising out of marriage relations and also looked after charges of moral lapses on the part of the members of the caste. It also imposed punishments on its members for violating caste norms. It was authorised to impose fines, receive petitions for pardon or deal with the matter in manner it thought fit for the occasion. The judgment of the *panchayat* was fully recognised by the State.

Mewar during the reign of Maharana Kumbha does not seem to have possessed an elaborate judiciary as a separate department. The cases were decided at the *panchayat* level and the *panchayats* enjoyed the sanction of the society as well as that of the Maharana. However, Maharana was considered as the highest authority to whom anybody could approach for redress, if not satisfied with the judgment of the *panchayat*. Of course, during our period the cases were not many because most of the personal disputes were settled by the sword and the administration hardly ever interfered in these matters. We may say that in this respect Mewar was still in a primitive stage. Theoretically Mewar as a Hindu State might have professed to follow the *Smriti* codes but in actual practice there was hardly any scope for its application.

The information about the economic life of Mewar during the reign of Maharana Kumbha is so meagre that no analysis on any aspect is possible. At best an attempt can be made at describing the items that were produced within the kingdom and the commodities that were exported outside the kingdom were procured from neighbouring territories, calling the information from various literary works of the period.

We may first take up the agricultural produce, where again

adequate data is lacking regarding the quantity produced. Agriculture, it seems, was not an exclusive engagement of the rural people. During the off season they seem to have engaged themselves in other professions as well. Besides, in Mewar men of all castes including the Brahmins had taken to the tilling of the soil. For the purpose of irrigation wells, tanks and reservoirs were used, water from which was drawn by means of Persian wheel (*rahat*). The land in Mewar is rather fertile as compared to the areas of other States of Rajasthan and therefore the reward from the labour of cultivation was not unremunerative. Certain tracts yielded even two crops in a year.

Among the chief agricultural produce we find mention of wheat, barley, milled (*jawar*) and sesame (*til*) and pulse like gram, *urad, masoor,* and *moong.* Sugarcane, poppy, hemp (*san*) and cotton were also produced which provided raw material for cottage industries. As for the peasants we find both peasant proprietors and tenant cultivators. Some prosperous peasants could afford to let on hire their ploughs which enabled the poorer ones who could pay for the hire but could not afford to possess their own to cultivate their fields. As for the condition of the peasants we can only infer that in a kingdom where people of all castes took to cultivation the profession could not have been considered socially as one of lower order. Besides the cultivators could not have been exploited to the extreme for the simple reason that economically Mewar had to depend much on them. In Mewar in times of difficulty the cultivators also participated in the defence of the country with their own arms. Yet the fact that big moneylenders, the *Shahs* and stockists of foodgrains flourished in Mewar suggests that the cultivators had two part away with substantial share of their produce. In fact to mutually contradictory positions seem to exist in Mewar which, with the present available information, it is difficult to resolve.

India during the fifteenth century was having cottage industry almost everywhere, and Mewar was no exception to it. Small scale or cottage industry was widespread and every village of Mewar had one or the other industry according to its needs and depending on the raw material produced with the village. Thus villages growing sugarcane engaged in producing jaggery which was consumed locally and also sold to other villages where sugarcane was not grown. Crushing of the oilseeds was a common industry. Spinning and weaving associated with textile or cotton fabric was almost universal and every village produced some quantity of cotton textile; along with textile its auxiliary dyeing industry also existed. Hemp was used for making strings and robes. Poppy provided the raw material for producing opium which was widely produced in Mewar and formed an article of internal consumption as well as of export. Some large establishments were also there which handled metals. We learn that Bhilwara was centre of iron industry where weapons were manufactured in large quantities. Gold and silver were used for ornaments and a village without a goldsmith would be too small and insignificant. Copper, brass and bronze were used for utensils. Some heavy metal icons of the period of Maharana Kumbha are also available which indicate the existence of larger furnaces and mouldings for smelting and casting them which also speaks of skill acquired by the artisans in this trade.

Commerce during the fifteenth century was carried by the merchants mostly Jains in Mewar, and they had a free access into all kingdoms irrespective of the political relations between them. Through them Mewar imported silken and dyed and printed cotton textile from Gujarat. Horses were regularly imported and there were regular horse traders in Mewar. Salt was also imported. From Sirohi, Mewar received a substantial quantity of swords. Mewar exported jaggery, opium, grains and cotton textile. The items of import are in excess over the item of export. The commerce certainly was not based on barter economy and the merchants used to pay in precious metals for the value of commodities purchased outside or purchased inside from traders coming from outside.

While on the face of it these aspects of economic life may suggest a prosperous condition with greater resources at the disposal of Maharana Kumbha and also an increase in the total wealth of the kingdom, but it is in no way an index of the real position of the people. The rich merchants controlled the market and enjoyed monopoly over commerce through which they amassed wealth but the villagers lived almost in a stage of self-sufficiency. There was considerable concentration of wealth in a few families the rest of the people lived a life of day-to-day existence.

Social life of Mewar does not present a picture in any way different from what is found in other Hindu States of the fifteenth century. The society was laden with caste system with all its ramifications. Apart from the division and sub-division of the regular four *varnas*, in Mewar as else where, castes appeared on the basis of professions. Thus, barber, *tamboli*, *gwala* (milk-man), dyers (*rangez*), goldsmith, potter, ironsmith, *teli* (oil-man), *mali*, *dhobi*, *weaver*, tailor, liquor vendor, all those formed separate caste groups and maintained their identity as such it is significant that in allocation of quarters in a city Mandan suggests separate arrangement for them clustered into different groups. He suggests that the sale of flowers, betel leaf, ivory works, incense and scents, pearls and precious metals should be arranged near the main gate or in front of the temple. Dyers, weavers and washermen should be settled in the north-east side of the city; iron smelters and metal workers should be provided with quarters in the south-east of the city; leather-workers and workers in hide, bamboo workers, liquor distillers should be settled in south of the city, and the south western side should house the prostitutes.

The same author suggests even a division of the idols to be worshipped by different groups. In his *Rupmandan* while describing the various icons of Vishnu he mentions that Narayana, Keshava, Madhava and Madhusudana should be worshipped by the Brahmins; Madhusudana and Vishnu should be worshipped by the Kshatriyas; Trivikrama and Vamana should be worshipped by the Vaish community; for leather workers and hide tanners, washermen, and acrobats (*nat*) the icon of Shridhar is best suited; Bhils, hunters, potters, *telis*, liquor distillers and prostitutes should worship Hrishikesh. Thus provision for separate quarters and separate forms of the same deity clearly indicates that while there was a socially integrated common society, yet segregated into distinct groups to maintain their separate identity.

Standard of civilisation can be judged best from the status enjoyed by women in the society. During the middle ages and certainly during the fifteenth century Hindu society maintained a double standard regarding the status of women. On the one hand great respect was shown to women and to sacrifice life for the protection and honour of women was looked upon as their first duty by men, on the other hand women were considered as object of pleasure, a property or a chattel by men. No doubt, women were accepted as an integral part of the society but they were considered inferior to men. Mewar was no exception to this kind of outlook.

From her birth till her death women remained dependent on men. As a young girl, she was dependent on her father or her brother for her existence who were deemed as her guardian, as a wife she was dependent on her husband, and as a widow she remained dependent on her sons. She had no voice in selecting her husband and was married to a person of the choice of her guardian. There is no dearth of instances to support this view. The case of Hansabai can be taken as a good example. Her marriage relationship was negotiated for Kunwar Chunda but on his refusal she was married to Maharana Lakha, father of Kunwar Chunda. Hadas of Bundi married their daughters to the Sisodias just to appease them in which the girls had no voice. The story of Narbad Rathor and Supardevi, the daughter of Sihad Sankhla of Roon is mentioned in all accounts. The callousness of the attitude of the Rajputs towards the sentiments of women is best illustrated in the account of Ranmall Rathor's case mentioned by Harbilas Sarda. "Ranmall took Chacha's daughter to wife making Chacha's body serve as *bajot* to sit on the ceremony". Human feelings certainly were thrown to dust when the daughter was forced to marry not only the slayer of her father but worse still the dead body of her father was used as a seat for the marriage ceremony. People capable of performing such atrocious deed might be proclaimed as heroes by their retained bards but such acts certainly indicate complete absence of human values in them, and the women had to bear all this simply because she was helpless. Giving of a daughter to settle disputes was a common practice though by such offerings they seldom succeeded in resolving their enmity on an enduring footing. In such cases a girl was treated in a manner no better than an ordinary commodity or a medium of exchange.

The practice of polygamy prevalent during medieval India was so common among the Rajputs that from the Maharana down to the common man there used to be number of wives, depending on the ability of the person to feed them. To have a large number of wives was looked upon as a mark of virility by men. No doubt in a society where fighting was inseparable part of life causing constant loss of manpower the institution of polygamy had its importance as it kept on replenishing the manpower at a higher rate. But from the point of view of women the multiple number of wives caused jealousy among them and hardly provided them with any mental peace. Being helpless, however, they had reconciled to this way of life.

Slave girls and prostitutes were usual features of the society. We have already mentioned that Maharana Kumbha captured women of the defeated chiefs and reduced them to the position of slaves. Slave girls were also given as part of presentation to bridegroom at time of departure with his bride. That prostitutes were considered as important limb of the society can be seen from the writings of Mandan who laid down direction of the city where the prostitutes were to be provided with their quarters. These prostitutes and dancing girls used to work as spies for the State and used to secure valuable information about the enemy.

Of course, the position of woman as a mother was different. The mother was granted the highest respect and the sons ever remained ready to carry out the orders of the mother. The history of Mewar is full of instances where the wishes of the mother were respected and fulfilled by the sons. But even in this she was dependent on the sons for her maintenance. Her's was a dignified position without any authority in the legal sense.

The overall picture presents a miserable condition of women and the only relief she had was in performance of *Sati*. The popularity of the custom to end their misery rather than to continue with an ignominious life.

Mewar Feudalism

The socio-political structure of Mewar was to a greater extent responsible for the form of government and administration. The system was equally important for military efficiency of the State. Though the Rajput form of kingship is generally designated as patriarchal based upon the conception that the whole kingdom was a family or a clan, but by the fourteenth century it did not remain an exclusive preserve of one single clan. The blood relationship no doubt was a strong binding force but it could no longer keep the Rajputs belonging to the same clan into a well knit body. To some extent the blood bond led to the growth of a system in which each important person of the clan, the sons of the ruling king and after him the brothers and uncles of the succeeding king—all had to be given some share which created chiefs and sub-chiefs. Such a position created two mutually contradictory positions. On the one hand it became the source of loyalty, on the other hand it also gave rise to jealousy and created enmity within the family. Whatever the old ideal might have been during fourteenth and the fifteenth centuries it was absent. During these centuries and certainly afterwards family feud was the most common feature. If we take the case of Maharana Kumbha we find that his younger brother Khem Karan disputed over the territory granted to him and left Mewar and thereafter remained an enemy of Mewar as long as he lived.

The system of making provision for the relatives resulted in the creation of chiefs who in their turn had their own children to whom they made grants out of their own holdings, and thus created sub-chiefs. We may not use the terms vassal and sub-vassal but the position of the chiefs and sub-chiefs was not very different from them. All these chiefs are given a common designation, that of *Samanta*. The chief was attached to the king and in his won turn he had his sub-chiefs attached to himself. The sub-chiefs were attached to their chief to the extent that they would sacrifice their lives for their own chief in case the chief came into conflict with the king. Thus the king could claim loyalty of the warriors through their chiefs. As a precautionary measure the Maharana also maintained warriors who were attached to him and were ever ready to sacrifice their lives for the cause of the Maharana. These also had to be provided for which further complicated the situation.

In Mewar the system in many respects resembled the structure which is commonly called the feudal system. No doubt, the system of Rajputs was not identical with the European feudalism nor did it arise out of a similar situation. The Rajput feudalism grew out of the patriarchal social structure in which all the children had to be provided for, which in course of time acquired distinct names and were indicated by the title attached as their lineage. They were all granted revenue assignments and in return of their personal service to the Maharana they also received adequate maintenance allowances.

Within the family of the Maharana we may easily trace these groups. Among the sons of Maharana Kheta, the eldest son Lakha succeeded as the Maharana and the descendants of his other sons acquired distinct names indicating the lineal descent from the son. Thus the descendants of Bhakhar are known as Bhakhrot Sisodia, Bhuchan's as Bhucharot, Salkha's as Salkhawat and Shankar's as Shakharawat. From the sons of Maharana Lakha, while Mokul became the Maharana the descendants of Chunda Sisodia became Chundawat, the descendants of other sons acquired the following names. Ajja's as Sarangdevot, Dulha's as Dulhawat, Dungar's as Mandawat, Gajsingh's as Gajsinghot and Luna's as Lunawat. Thus we find that during the reign of Maharana Kumbha the royal family itself was divided into so many sub-branches.

However, the comparison by Tod of the European feudalism with the system that he found in Rajasthan is somewhat over drawn. Its main defect lies in that he covers the whole of the Rajasthan and compares cases from different States and not exclusively from Mewar. Besides, he compared the situation as he found it which was more an outcome of the Mughal rule than the one that existed during the fifteenth century. Institutions like Relief, Fines of Allienation, Escheat, Aids, Wardship and Marriage are not to be found in their forms as described by Tod nor in the context and meaning in which he has taken them.

The Mewar feudalism during the fifteenth century constituted basically in the various types of grants made by the Maharanas prior to Maharana Kumbha and to which in his own turn he also added some. Maharana Kumbha throughout his reign was busy fighting his enemies and therefore could ill-afford to displease the various *samantas* who were enjoying various types of grants and to win over to his side he also made fresh grants. These grants were not confirmed to the Sisodias alone, but were extended to other Rajputs as well. Thus we find Raghavadeva Chundawat Rathor was given Sojat, Narbad Rathor was granted Kailana and was one of the most trusted and loyal *samanta* to the Maharana. We also find mention of Idas, Bhatis and Sankhalas as *samantas*. All these grants have been designated as *jagir* in the *khyats* but the *khyats* were written during the Mughal rule and the writers have borrowed the term from Mughal administrative terminology and have used it indiscriminately without caring for the implication of the term *jagir*. Thus *jagir* in the context of Maharana Kumbha should not be taken to imply the same meaning as it had in the Mughal administrative terminology.

Of the various types of grants the first and qualitatively the highest in merit was called *Bhumia*. *Bhumia* hold again was of two kinds. The first consisted of such territories which were already in the possession of some chief who accepted the Maharana as his lord and gave him his full support. The Maharana allowed him to continue in his ancestral possessions and it acquired the character of hereditary property. The second type of *Bhumia* hold consisted of grants made by the Maharana to such of his relatives or their descendants who sacrificed their lives for the Maharana and for the defence of the kingdom. Such holdings too were hereditary and the holders considered it their privilege to keep them and defend them with pride. The *Bhumia samantas* also had a place in the council of the Maharana. The *Bhumia samantas* managed their own holdings and the Maharana hardly ever interfered in the internal affairs unless special appeal was made to the Maharana. The *Bhumias* should not be confused with ordinary peasant proprietors; they were chiefs with their own cultivators as their tenants.

The second category of grants was called *Grasia* holding. This type of grant was made by the Maharana for the livelihood of his supporters or his favourites. These grants were made for the life time of the grantee but could be renewed by his successors through the permission of the Maharana and after paying a succession fee. The grants of Kayalana to Narbad and Sojat to Raghavadeva Rathor fall under this category.

The third type of grantees were known as *Bandhavas*. This type of grant was made to the brothers and very close relatives for their maintenance. The grantees were exempted from *Rekh*, *Chakri* and *Hukumnama* payments to the State treasury for three generations. After three generations they became just like other holders. However, in course of time some of them became *Bhumias*, some *Grasias* depending on the amount of confidence and loyalty and closeness they could maintain with the successors of the Maharana.

The government officials were also at time granted revenue assignments which also appeared like a grant. Since these were made in lieu of salary it was to be enjoyed by the grantee so long he remained in the service of the Maharana. However, the Maharana could made them hereditary if he was pleased with his service. Once it became hereditary it acquired the character of any of the three types of holdings mentioned above.

Another type of grant known as *Shasan* was very common in Mewar and was also prevalent during the reign of Maharana Kumbha. *Shasan* grants were made to *Bhats, Charans, Purohits,* Brahmins and also as religious endowments to temples. These grants were revenue free, *i.e.,* the grantee had not to pay anything to the State and maintained himself from the income of the village granted to him. These grants were generally executed on copper plates so as to enable them to stand the vagaries of time instances of *Shasan* grants are best illustrated in some of the cases known to us. There may be many more. In the first instance, Maharana before his occupation of Chittor made a grant to Baru, the son of Barbari through whom he received five hundred horses. For his services he was given the grant of several villages in the Kailwara region which are distinct from the other grants though mentioned in one sequence in *Vir Vinod*. Hammir appointed Baru as his *Barhat* and for this he granted him the village of Antri as a hereditary grant executing the grant deed on a copper plate. Kaviraj Shymal Dass observes that that remained with the descendants of Baru when he was composing *Vir Vinod*. Another instance is found in the case of the Bhat boy who conveys the message of Baru to Maharana and to whom Maharana Lakha granted the village of Chikalvas near modern Udaipur where his descendants were still in possession of lands during the nineteenth century. Similarly, Maharana Lakha granted the village Pipli to some Jhoting Brahmin at the time of Solar eclipse. He also granted to Dhaneshwar Bhatt, the village Panchdeola near Chittor. However the *Shasan* grants could be resumed by the Maharana at his pleasure. We learn that Maharana Kumbha had expelled all the *Charans* because some astrologers had prophesied that his death would come from the hands of a *Charan*. It is also recorded that before his assassination Maharana being pleased with a *Charan* at his request recalled all the expelled *Charans* and restored them to their grants.

All these types of grants and different types of holdings certainly created a structure which acquired a feudal character.

In the case of these grants the State abandoned all or a part of its rights to the grantee and the people inhabiting in these areas were left to the care of the grantee. However, one point may here be mentioned that in case of these grants wherever the cultivators were settled they were allowed to continue and were not dispossessed. But it cannot be started with certainty the extent to which it was because of the law which did not permit eviction of the cultivators and also under the circumstances of having lesser number of cultivators he could not afford to drive them out because in such a case the field would remain uncultivated and the grantee would be deprived of the income.

The forces of the *samantas* constituted the total military strength of the Maharana. Among the *samantas* because of forms in which the grants had been made the claim of blood and kinship no longer remained a binding force. The *samantas* because of their forces could prevail upon the Maharana to respect their opinion. Prior to Kumbha we have the case of Maharawal Samant Singh who in his attempt to crush the *samantas* resumed their grants but had to leave Mewar because of their pressure. After Kumbha, his son Udai Singh could not continue on the throne of Mewar, as being a patricide, he was hated by the majority of the *samantas*. Still later, though not concerned with our period, we may refer to case of Banbir, the natural son of Prithwiraj.

In spite of the fact that the *samantas* in Mewar exercised certain voice, the Maharana was never reduced to such a position as to allow the *samantas* to usurp all the powers associated with monarchy. In this respect we find a difference in the growth of European feudalism and the form that developed in Mewar. In Mewar the *samantas* received their authority from the Maharana. The other differences can be found in the category of peasants who were freemen and not serfs. The right of adoption was fully recognised by the State and at the same time the Maharana could not dictate the marriage of the minor *samantas* in any family according to his own desire. The Rajput society was free from such aspect of feudalism.

Along with other aspects the question of land ownership also deserves certain observations. To have a proper comprehension of this aspect one would have to bear in mind the historical background of the sub-continent of India. The history of India presents a panaroma of small kingdoms with different codes in different ages both area-wise and period-wise and at the same time the nature of these States also differed. Such forms of government as republics, kingships and monarchies came into existence which in their turn kept on changing their shapes; in some they stayed for longer periods and in some areas they retained some of the features almost permanently. During this long course of time empires sprang up and for some time incorporated a number of smaller principalities only to be again disintegrated giving birth to smaller kingdoms. During this course of history polity too kept on changing and many principles were advocated from time to time in which land was treated in different manners and on different basis. Regarding land the most important aspect which needs examination is to find out whether from the earliest time the land was located as the property of the ruler or of the tiller of the soil. In the case of the Rajputs this question becomes all the more important and, because of various types of grants made by the rulers, it is the most difficult one.

The grant of land by the king in various forms at the face of it suggests that the Rajput ruler claimed the entire land as his property and enjoyed the right to deal with it in any manner he liked. However, the situation is not so simple. In making the grants the principle involved was that the king transferred to the grantee only those rights over the land which the king enjoyed. This becomes clear from some of the grants in which the grantee had been clearly assigned some of the taxes which were due to the king. While discussing the aspect of ownership we should not look at it from the modern or post-capitalist concept of absolute proprietorship. In medieval India the land was considered as a free gift of nature and therefore over it many types of rights could exist without prejudice to any party. The concept of *dharma* or duty was a dominating social factor and it was considered as the *dharma* of the cultivator to till the soil and produce; it was his contribution to the society of which he was an important limb and without which the society could not survive.

In the land, thus, we can discern the existence of certain rights of three distinct parties, *i.e.*, the cultivator, the *samanta* and the king. Our main difficulty in arriving at a correct picture of the position of the cultivator as the owner of the soil in Mewar arises out of the absence of records for the sixteenth century. The word *Bhumia* no doubt is there, but it was used both for chiefs or holders of large tracts having with them a large number of tillers of the soil and for smaller peasants enjoying proprietary rights over their field from generation to generation in hereditary succession. The term *bapota* used to express the right of the *Bhumia* over the land which could not be taken away by the Maharana leaves out the position of the actual tillers of the soil who cultivated the land belonging to the *Bhumia Samantas*. The land which was with small *Bhumias* could be granted in *jagir* to the *samanta*. Thus in Rajput feudal system a *samanta* could have two types of holding. One, his ancestral land inherited by him and the other which was granted to him by the king for his personal maintenance as well as his soldiers. In the second case he could only collect the revenue from the cultivators but he could not transfer this right to others. Transference of land was a right which was enjoyed by the *Bhumia* of the *bapota* alone. Even the Maharana had a portion of land in *Bhumia* which was distinct from his right over the entire land constituting his kingdom.

Another factor which cannot be ignored is the existence of the Bhils who constituted the majority of the population of Mewar. These Bhils had been in possession of lands from times more remote than the emergence of the Guhilputras. They had a position in the social structure of Mewar which was quite formidable and whatever was their holdings could not be taken away from them.

Thus for the total picture with the existence of property right; the existence of intermediaries; the various types of grants made in perpetuity which is complex and suggests a socio-economic structure which we can call a feudal society. Tod when he made a comparison of the European feudalism with the political structure of Rajputana he tried to prove the existence of political feudalism but missed the basic point of socio-economic structure. Alfred Lylle on the other hand overstressed the point of non-existence of feudalism by stating that the strength of the holding depended on the amount of closeness the holder's blood with that of the Maharana.

7

Mewar and the British

Udaipur State was one of the twenty-three Native States under the Rajputana Agency of the British Government, before India achieved its freedom in 1947. Since its very inception in 568 A.D.[1], this State had been popularly called 'MEWAR'. Starting as a very small principality in the Aravalli hills under its founder Guhil or Guhdatta.[2] Mewar gradually developed in strength and extended its limits during succeeding centuries. During the reign of its rulers like Rana Kumbha (1433-68 A.D.) and Rana Sanga (1509-1528 A.D.), it enjoyed hegemony over its vast territory, which covered almost the whole of Rajputana and a part of Central India. In the days of its glory and prosperity the actual limits of the State of Mewar reached Beyana in the north-east; Rewa Kanta and Mahi Kanta in the south; Palanpur in the west, and Malwa in the south-east. However, the repeated invasions of the Mughals and the raids of the Marathas reduced the territory of Mewar to a narrow space between 23°-49' and 25°-28' north latitude and 73°-1' and 75°-49' east longitude bringing down area to 12,691 sq. miles.[3] Since Mewar entered into treaty relations with the British Government, its political limits had been like this; it was bounded on the north by Ajmer-Merwara and Shahpura Chiefship; on the west by Jodhpur and Sirohi; on the south-west by Idar; on the south by Dungarpur, Banswara and Pratapgarh; on the east by Neemuch, Nimbahera, Bundi and Kota, and on the north-east by Jaipur. The Gwalior paragana of

Gangapur consisting of ten villages lay almost in the centre of the State.[4] The most significant fact about this State was that its history covered a long period of over thirteen centuries, during which the rule of the family, which had founded it, continued without much interruption. During this long period, India was constantly subjected to foreign invasions and domination. The rulers and the people of Mewar always offered stiff resistance to the invaders, and played a heroic role in maintaining their independence.

After the fall of Chittor in 1568 A.D.[5] at the hands of Akbar, the capital of the State was shifted to Udaipur, a new city founded by the ruler of Mewar, Rana Udai Singh, and the State of Mewar gradually came to be called as the State of Udaipur. After the Treaty Relations of Mewar with the East India Company the British Government created a political Agency known as the Mewar Agency with its headquarters at Neemuch and placed under its political supervision the territory consisting of the States of Udaipur, Dungarpur, Banswara and Pratapgarh.[6] In 1860-61 the headquarters were transferred to Udaipur. The designation of the political charge was changed from Agency to Residency in 1881-82.[7]

The peculiar physical features of the land played a very prominent part in shaping its history. The nature has splitted up the State into two well-marked divisions. The northern and eastern portions consists generally of an elevated plateau of fine indulating country, watered by Banas and its affluents. The southern and western portions for the most part covered with rocks, hills and fairly dense jungle. The widest ridges of the Aravallis extended along the entire western part and formed the western border of the State.[8] This part of the land always made a natural bulwark of defence for the State of Mewar, which time and again afforded shelter to, and was the recruiting ground for its princes, when the sword of the enemy fell heavily on them. The long lines of the mountains and the wide dense forests isolated the people of this country from the rapid changes and movements taking place in other parts of India. In the isolation, the mass of the people developed a spirit of spartan simplicity, disciplined life and love for traditional glory of their ancestors. Virtues like courage, perseverance, straightforwardness, sense of service, and devotion to their class became a second nature with them. The rocky environments generated among the people of Mewar a spirit of independence which left its mark on Indian History.

The great watershed of India, dividing the drainage of the Bay of Bengal from that of the Gulf of Cambay runs almost through the centre of Mewar.[9] It has made the plains of Mewar rich in productivity, affording great facility for irrigation and contributing largely to the prosperity of the State. The rulers of Mewar during the times of peace erected magnificent dams and constructed lakes in different parts of land, such as Jaisamand, Rajsamand, Udaisagar, Pichola, Fatehsagar, etc., which helped the growth, productivity and prosperity of the State and well-being of the people. The big number of forts, temples, pillars, palaces and monuments found at various places in the territory of Mewar represent the erstwhile glory and prosperity of the land.

The whole history of the land of the Mewar, since its foundation was laid, until the Mughals and the Marathas wrecked the whole political fabric of the country, had been the history of heroic deeds of the ruling class, and of the people continuously fighting for their existence, honour and liberty. They carried on struggle for more than a thousand years during which this land presented many an example of great heroism, tenacity and self-sacrifice. Several kingdoms and principalities of India were laid low and vanished for ever before the invasions of the Turks, Afghans and Mughals, while many others compelled by circumstances preferred abject submission or change of religion to heroic resistance. Several of the Rajput rulers gave their daughters in marriage to the Muslim rulers, which the Rajputs of those days regarded very derogatory. But the Ranas of Mewar throughout the ups and downs of their career not only maintained and protected their State, but never deviated an inch from their cherished ideals, even at the point of death and destruction. This sustained effort for keeping high the banner of liberty and religion produced a deep impression on the minds of the people in other parts of India, and gradually the kings of Sisodia dynasty like Kumbha, Sanga and Pratap came to be regarded as the symbols of the struggle for liberty, and were hailed widely as the Hindua Suraj (Sun of Hindus).[10] Even the Mughal rulers like Babar and Jahangir were very eloquent in their praise of Mewar and its ruling dynasty.[11] Even the later Maratha leaders who wrecked and ravaged the territory of Mewar, never had reservations in showing respect to the dynasty. The British rulers had special regard for the Maharana of Udaipur. Aitchison has written: "the Udaipur family is the highest in rank and dignity among the Rajput Chiefs of India".[12]

The victory of Mughal Emperor Babar and the defeat of Rana Sanga in the Battle of Khanwa (1527 A.D.) resulted into a great set back to the State of Mewar. Henceforth a new leaf was turned in its history and the period of its gradual decline set in. Rana Pratap (1572-1597 A.D.) earned a great fame by his courage, sacrifice and heroic resistance which he offered against the power of the great Mughal. Though he never yielded yet his territory was considerably reduced. Peace was obtained by his son Amar Singh in (1614 A.D.), by tendering his submission to Jahangir on condition that he should never have to present himself in person, but send his son in his place.[13] However during Aurangzeb's reign, Rana Raj Singh again crossed swords with the Mughals, resulting in further loss of its territory. The greatest blow to the State of Mewar was given by the power of Marathas, which it could not withstand.

When the State of Mewar entered into the treaty relations with the British Government in 1818, it was a very critical moment of its history. For more than half a century the hordes of Holkar, Sindhia and Amir Khan had trodden, devastated and ravaged the land of Mewar. Within this short period they had pauperised the ruler, nobility and people of Mewar by plunder and by imposing excessive demands of tribute. Their demands and needs had no bounds and their greed and avarice required no excuse. When the State treasury became empty, they laid their hands on the jewellery of the royal family and began dividing the territories of Mewar among themselves, so much so that the actual rule of Maharana shrank to the valley of Udaipur city.[14] The position of Maharana became so pitiable that he had at times to depend upon the bounty of foreigners like Zalim Singh, the Regent of Kota in meeting his personal expenses.[15] During this time of turmoil and anarchy the nobles of Mewar had turned disloyal and refractory to the House of Mewar and were not slow in usurping the lands.[16] Besides, the wild tribes like Bheels, Meeanas and Mers indulged in ravaging activities. In short, Mewar was in a state of chaos by the beginning of 9th century. Tod described the condition of Mewar, in 1818, in these words, "But so much had it been defaced through time and accident that with difference could the lineaments be traced with a view to their restoration, her institutions a dead letter, the prince's authority despised, the nobles demoralised and rebellious, internal commerce abandoned and the peasantry destroyed by the combined operations of war, pestilence and exile".[17]

Under these circumstances Maharana Bhim Singh of Udaipur saw in East India Company a powerful ally who could save this state from total extinction and restore his domains, his authority and tranquility to his country. There was neither time nor question of giving thought to liberty, race of religion. There was only the desperate search for protection. As early as 1805, the Maharana tried to seek assistance from the British, when he sent Bhairon Baksh to the Camp of Lord Lake at Tonk,[18] but the obligation of their Treaty of 1803 with Sindhia prevented the British from entertaining the Maharana's request.[19] But in 1817 when the British Government decided to crush the power of the Maharana to seek, again, the friendship of the British. Now the British were also anxious to have alliances with the Rajput rulers.

On 13th January, 1818, the Treaty of Friendship, Alliances and Unity was concluded between Mewar and East India Company by which the British Government engaged itself to protect the principality and territory of Mewar and to use its best exertions for the restitution of those territories which had been seized by others by improper means during the times of turmoil. The Maharana of Mewar on his part agreed to act always in subordinate cooperation with the British Government and acknowledge its supremacy, while maintaining his sovereignty in his own country, to abstain from political correspondence with other chiefs or States and to pay the yearly tribute to the British Government amounting to one-fourth of the revenues of the State for five years and after that term three-eighth in perpetuity.[20]

The treaty of 1818 at once brought peace to Mewar. The Maratha incursions in the land stopped, and the Pindaris were eliminated. Colonel Tod, the first Political Agent of the British

Government in the State took the task of restoring peace inside the State by suppressing the activities of the tribes like Bheels, Meenas and Mers, who inhabited the wild regions of the State, to curb the rebellious nobility by compelling them to submit to order and surrender the usurped State lands, to put the whole administration into working order and revive the peaceful avocations in the country by calling in back peasantry and the trading class, giving them the necessary guarantees of protection and security. Under the instructions of Lord Hastings he was "to use more active interference to accomplish the success of measures in view" for restoring the prosperity to the State.[21] Col. Tod used both force and persuasion to achieve the desired results.

In May 1818, Tod negotiated a settlement between the Rana and the Chiefs of Mewar. By this agreement the Chiefs bound themselves to restore all the lands they had usurped or otherwise acquired during the preceding 50 years of turmoil, to submit to the laws of the State and the sovereignty of their ruler and to perform service (*Chakari*) for three months each year by turn with two horsemen and four foot soldiers for every Rs. 1000 of their annual revenue and to pay fixed tribute (*Chhatooned*) regularly to the ruler. The Chief also promised to restore all customs and other duties seized from the state and not to harbour thieves and robbers. The Maharana on his part promised to respect their ancient rights and privileges.[22] The conclusion of above agreement was a great success in persuading the Chiefs to submit to law and order, and maintaining internal peace. But the dispute between the Maharana and his Chiefs regarding service to be performed and tribute to be paid by the Chiefs regarding service to be performed and tribute to be paid by the Chiefs to the Maharana remained unsolved for about a century. Several attempts were made to negotiate the settlement between the Rana and his nobles about their rights and privileges as in 1827, 1845 and 1854, but none of them bore fruitful results. Thus one of the chief problems in the Mewar State which agitated the minds of the rulers, nobility and even the people for next hundred years was the undecided nature of the Rana's authority and the rights and privileges of his nobility. Many a time the internal peace was disturbed necessitating the interference of the British political officers.

Col. Tod took the task of suppressing the wild and turbulent tribes of Bhils and Graasias inhabiting the hills in south and south-west part of Mewar.[23] During the time of anarchy these people had done away with the institution of the State and had established their own. They levied a blackmail *'Rakhwali'* on the neighbouring villages and a tax called *'Bolai'* on the passage of goods and travellers, for whose safety they were considered responsible.[24] These taxes the Bhils realised by prescriptive right rather than by legal authority conferred by the Rana and the Rajput Chiefs, who were called Bhumias and who were in possession of the Bhomat part of the hilly area, received a share of the *Bolai* tax. These Chiefs owed a nominal allegiance to the Maharana of Udaipur and held the right of property in the land over which the Maharana had no power. Col. Tod in order to re-establish the Rana's authority in the hilly district decided to resume the above taxes and compel the tribes to pursue peaceful avocation. The Bhils as well as the Bhumia Chiefs refused to yield. In 1823, the British troops were employed against them and compelled them to surrender[25] but permanent peace could not be established. The Bhils being deprived of their means of subsistence, which they had enjoyed for years in this wild part of the country, did not reconcile completely to the above arrangement. Several times they defied the authority of the Maharana and force had to be used against them time and again. Finding that permanent peace could not be established in the hilly district under the authority of the Maharana, the British Government took the whole Bhomat area under the direct political supervision of the Mewar political agency[26], by giving the charge of the area to the Assistant Political Agent in Mewar, whose headquarters were established at Kherwara, keeping the same, in view, in the year 1841, the Mewar Bhil Corps were raised at the cost of Rs. 1,20,000 per year of which the Rana paid Rs. 50,000. The civil control over the Bhomat area was left with the Maharana.[27] However, the above arrangement, also, did not proved satisfactory. New problems cropped up, thereafter, which had to be dealt with during the succeeding Maharana, *viz.*, the problems of maladministration and oppression of the Bhils by the state officials in the hilly district, the struggle between the Mewar Government and the British Agent at Kherwara, the pauperised conditions of the Bhils in want of sufficient means of subsistence and undecided relationship between the Bhomia chiefs and the Maharana. Bhil disturbances continued to take place in various parts of the State which necessitated the use of force by the Mewar State and the intervention of the British Government time and again.

In 1818 the British Government, joined by Mewar and Marwar Governments took recourse to use of force in suppressing the predatory tribe of Mers inhabiting the district called Merwara, which belonged partly to Udaipur and Jodhpur States and partly to the British Government. The Mers had been a source of trouble for long. The wild, warlike and freedom-loving Mers usually took to revolt whenever they found the power of the ruler weakening. Mers were entirely subdued in 1821. Considering that the control of the three administrations on this district would not work successfully, it was taken under the British administration alone, and a local corps, Merwara battalion was raised to which Udaipur and Jodhpur States were required to contribute annually Rs. 35,000 each, out of the revenues of their parts of the district.[28] At the outset, the Maharana did not like the idea but in the end he acquiesced. The arrangement was made for ten years.[29] It was extended in 1823 for eight years more. In 1841, the period of the engagement expired, but it was not renewed. In 1847, the Maharana proposed the permanent cession of his villages of the Merwara district to the British territory on the condition of his receiving the former Mewar villages in the district of Jawad, Jeeran and Neemuch, which were then under the control of British Government, having been assigned by Sindhia for the payment of Gwalior Contingent. But this condition was not accepted by the British Government and in that unsatisfactory state, the British occupation of the Merwara continued.[30]

The recalling of the population, who had migrated from Mewar during the days of anarchy was the measure Col. Tod took simultaneously with the task of bring peace and order in the State. He issued a proclamation calling all the traders and peasants of Mewar to return and resume their avocations, guaranteeing them the safety and peace on behalf of the British Government.[31] The proclamation had its most favourable effect. All the deserted land and villages were again occupied. Foreign merchants and bankers established connections in the chief towns of Mewar. All restrictions on external commerce were removed, abolishing the old chains of stations for the collections of transit duties, except on the frontier, and the scale of duties was revised. Seth Jorawarmal of Indore was given the charge of the finances of the State, who advanced loans of the State on interest.[32] The revenues of the *Khalsa* lands which had been reduced to half a lakh of rupees by 1818 rose to Rs. 4,51,281 in 1819 and Rs. 9,96,640 in 1822.[33] This improvement became possibly largely due to Tod's active superintendence and also owing to the recovery of the *Khalsa* lands which had been grabbed by nobles, Marathas and Zalim Singh of Kota. However, Tod's efforts to restore the prosperity of Mewar were of no avail. Largely, this work was frustrated by the opposition of those for whom he laboured. The Rana proved inefficient and averse to business. Vain shows, frivolous amusements and an irregulated liberty alone occupied him. He had little steadiness of purpose and was particularly a prey to female influence.[34]

In 1821 Tod, acting under the instructions of the Supreme Government, relaxed his control over the internal administration of Mewar. Next year, Tod left India. When the new Political Agent, Captain Cobbe joined his duties, he found confusion all round. The State was involved in debt, the arrears of the British tribute amounting to Rs. 7,90,747 remained unpaid and the Rana was pawning his jewels and silver stocks again.[35]

The Political Agent again resumed the complete control of the administration and revived Tod's system. For the regular payment of the tribute and for liquidation of the arrears, certain *parganas* of the State were reserved. In 1826 Sir Charles Metcalfe visited Udaipur. The Rana presented him a memorandum of 10 articles, in which he requested the Government to reduce the tribute to a fixed sum instead of one-fourth of the State revenue, to restore his administrative authority and to get the ancient territories of Mewar restored to him which had been occupied by others during the times of turmoil.

The Maharana's memorandum was considered favourably. The tribute was fixed at Rs. 3,00,000 (Udaipur Rupees) a year. The oppressive dual Government in the country, whereby the British political officer maintained his own administrative machinery separately along with native officials, was abolished and the British servants were recalled. The reserved *parganas* were also returned to the Maharanas. Thus by the end of 1826 the minute interference of the Political Agent in the internal administration of the State was withdrawn.[36] The immediate results of this change were not found satisfactory, as the rulers and his officials, learning nothing from experience and time, again indulged in extravagance and oppression,[37] and the people were subjected to the conditions of medieval order, which naturally blocked the further progress of the State. However, the British Government did not revive its active interference in the internal administration of the State.

In 1828, Maharana Bhim Singh was succeeded by his son Jawan Singh, who gave himself to extravagance, debauchery and vice. The State got overwhelmed in debt, the tribute fell heavily into arrears and there was an annual deficit of two lakhs of rupees. In 1839 the Court of Directors ordered that, if Maharana should fail in his engagements to liquidate the arrears, a territorial or other sufficient security should be required.[38] When in 1838 Jawan Singh was succeeded by Sardar Singh, the latter inherited a total debt of Rs. 19,67,500 of which nearly eight lakhs were on account of tribute to the British Government.[39]

Rana Swaroop Singh succeeded Rana Sardar Singh in 1842. This ruler showed some improvement over his predecessors. He decided to check personally the State accounts and regulate the income and expenditure of the State at his own will, which had been hitherto solely the business of his Chief Minister. The *'Pradhan'*, or the Chief Minister did not like the idea of the ruler. He tried to evade the suggestion by saying, "Why His Highness should take pains to look after such petty affairs? It is the duty of loyal servants to provide him with and maintain all his comforts and requirements."[40] But Swaroop Singh looked personally into the details of the accounts and made certain changes in the administration by entrusting the State treasury to Kothari Chhagan Lal and establishing a State shop (*Rawla Dukan*) to regulate the State accounts.[41] During this time repeated applications were made to the British Government to reduce the amount of tribute, considering the financial embarrassments in which the Udaipur State was involved.

In 1846 the tribute was reduced to two lakhs of Government rupees from three lakhs of Udaipur rupees.[42] In 1851 the Maharana toured the district of the State to come personally in touch with the conditions of the State. He wanted to see that revenue was not misappropriated by the officials. He also introduced a new 'Swaroop Shahi Rupee' during his reign,[43] when he found that the previous currency was being counterfeited and the people were facing great hardship. Thus Swaroop Singh was the first ruler after 1818, who gave serious attention to the State affairs. He reduced extravagance, paid off the State debts, created a State treasury and introduced a new coin.

However, Rana Swaroop Singh was a deeply conservative ruler, strongly attached to ancestral customs and superstitions. He was perhaps the only ruler who evaded for about sixteen years the persuasion of the British Government to abolish the inhuman customs of immolating *Sati* and torturing of the so-called 'witches'.[44] He tried to defend the custom of *Sati* as being a religious rite of the people pleading that the Queen's proclamation of 1858 had promised not to interfere with the ancient customs of the people. However the latter, rejecting his plea, observed that the custom of *Sati* was not a religious observance but an act of suicide.[45] Consequently, the Maharana was compelled to issue orders prohibiting these practices. Rana's relation with the chiefs took a worse turn in his time. Having strong faith in the autocratic power of the ruler, Swaroop Singh pursued a discriminatory and repressive policy towards the nobility[46] to compel them to come to an agreement of his own liking. This policy caused him incessant troubles throughout his reign and consequently made an adverse effect upon his effort for the introduction of reforms in his State.

He was not popular with the British Political Agents as well.[47] He resented the pressure and interference of the Political Agents in the internal affairs of the State. This also caused him no little trouble.

The State of Mewar found itself in such conditions with the ushering in of the historic year of 1857. General peace and order had been established in the State, peaceful avocation revived and the authority of Maharana firmly established. This all could be possible with the assistance of the British Government.

However Mewar was still living in medieval conditions. Rana had not learnt to rule by legislation. His will was regarded as the law of the State and the same was true of the nobles in their respective estates. They took no interest in matters of political, social and economic development of the people. The society was divided into two classes, the oppressive class of feudal aristocracy at the top, and the pauperised and ignorant masses at the bottom.

The advent of British influence in Mewar added another element of oppression and complication. Rana's subordinate alliance with the British Government robbed him of all his real power and authority. In the name of maintaining internal peace and bringing order to the State, the will and authority of the Agent of the British Government began to rule supreme in the State. Rana's authority became nominal and the freedom of internal sovereignty provided in the Treaty of 1818 was reduced to naught for all purposes. Before taking any administrative measure, he was compelled to take the approval of the British Government and on the other hand he was bound to obey and implement all orders of the British Government regarding the internal administration of the State, which were generally imposed in the interests of the Imperial Government. The Rana was protected against external invasions and internal rebellions, but he was not entirely free to choose his own ministers. Thus he lost even that measure of freedom which he enjoyed in the days of Mughal domination and Maratha supremacy. Such conditions went to weaken the character of the ruler. As the initiative had been snatched from him, he lost all his imagination and sense of responsibility. He sank in his own esteem and lost that stimulus to good Government, which is supplied by the fear of rebellion and deposition, and he became sensualist, careless and lax.[48] The nobles, coerced by external ascendancy, also lost their self-respect and got degenerated like their master. Under these conditions the oppression and suppression of the masses increased a great deal.

Karl Marx in 1853 described the conditions of the native States of India in these words, "They (native States) virtually ceased to exist from the moment they became subsidiary to or protected by the Company.... The conditions under which they are allowed to retain their apparent independence are at the same time the conditions of permanent decay and of an utter inability of improvement. Organic weakness is the Constitutional law of their existence".[49] This was a true description of the State of affairs in Mewar, after 1818.

However, as the conditions in the state began to get stabilised and improved, the ruler and the nobility were gradually awakened in regard to their rights and privileges. A re-study of the terms of the Treaty of 1818 was begun and the demand of implementing it in its true spirit was raised. Eventually a struggle started against the undue interference of the Political Agent in the internal affairs of the State. This struggle during its course got mixed with the struggle against the reforms initiated by the Political Agents and thus assumed a dual character. As we would see in the ensuing chapters the cause of internal sovereignty and the cause of conservation upholding the old beliefs and traditions got united against the interference of the Political Agents which they continuously made in the internal affairs of the State in the name of reforms.

NOTES AND REFERENCES

1. *Udaipur Rajya ka Itihas* by G.H. Ojha, Part I, p. 67.
2. *Ibid.*, p. 93.
3. *A Gazetteer of the Udaipur State* by Major K.D. Erskine, p. 5.
4. *Ibid.*
5. *Udaipur Rajya ka Itihas* by G.H. Ojha, Part II, p. 417.
6. *A Gazetteer of the Udaipur State* by K.D. Erskine, p. 1.
7. *Ibid.*
8. *Ibid.*, p. 5.
9. *A Gazetteer of the Udaipur State* by K.D. Erskine, p. 5.
10. *Udaipur Rajya ka Itihas* by G.H. Ojha, Part I, p. 68.
11. *Ibid.*
12. *Treaties, Engagements and Sanads* by Aitchison, Vol. III, p. 3.
13. *Udaipur Rajya ka Itihas* by G.H. Ojha, Part I, p. 506.
14. *Annals and Antiquities of Rajasthan* by James Tod, Vol. I, p. 378.
15. *A Gazetteer of the Udaipur State* by K.D. Erskine p. 25.
16. *Ibid.*
17. *Ibid.*, p. 378.
    During the last hundred years the successive Sisodia Rulers developed the worst vices of false pride, narrowmindedness, parochialism to the extent that all their actions ran counter to the larger interests of anti-Mughal and anti-Maratha struggle of the Rajputs.
18. *The Rajput and the East India Company* by A.C. Banerjee, p. 296.
19. *Ibid.*, p. 297.
20. *Treaties, Engagements and Sanads* by Aitchison, Vol. I, pp. 17-18.

21. *The Rajput and the East India Company* by A.C. Banerjee, p. 309.
22. *Treaties, Engagements and Sanads* by Aitchison, Vol. III, p. 9.
23. *Ibid.*, p. 6.
24. *Ibid.*
25. *Treaties, Engagements and Sanads* by Aitchison, Vol. II, p. 9.
26. *Ibid.*
27. *Ibid.*
28. *Udaipur Rajya ka Itihas* by G.H. Ojha, Vol. II, p. 712.
29. *Ibid.*, p. 713.
30. *Treaties, Engagements and Sanads* by Aitchison, Vol. III, p. 6.
31. *Udaipur Rajya ka Itihas* by G.H. Ojha, Vol. II, p. 6.
32. *Ibid.*, p. 709.
33. *Annals and Antiquities of Rajasthan* by James Tod, Vol. I, p. 399.
34. *Ibid.*
35. *The Rajput States and the East India Company* by A.C. Banerjee, p. 312.
36. *Treaties, Engagements and Sanads* by Aitchison, Vol. III, p. 7.
37. *Ibid.*
38. *A Gazetteer of the Udaipur State* by K.D. Erskine, pp. 26-27.
39. *Treaties, Engagements and Sanads* by Aitchison, Vol. III,
40. *Vir Vinod* by Shymal Das, p. 1923.
41. *Ibid.*, p. 1927.
42. *Treaties, Engagements and Sanads* by Aitchison, Vol. III, p. 8. Government rupees were called 'Caldar' rupees in Mewar. Two lakhs of British rupees were equivalent to about two and a half lakhs of Udaipur rupees in value—*Itihas Rajasthan* by Charan Ramnath Ratnu, p. 72.
43. *Udaipur Rajya ka Itihas* by G.H. Ojha, Vol. II, p. 740.
44. *Rajputana ka Itihas* by J.S. Gahlot, p. 280.
45. F.D. Pol., Jan. 27, 1860, No. 80-85.
46. *Udaipur Rajya ka Itihas* by G.H. Ojha, Vol. II, p. 786.
47. *Ibid.*, p. 776.
48. Brookes writes; "It is probable that the very state of dependence in which the Rana was placed, chafed his spirit, and induced many of those evils of which the Agent complained" (*History of Mewar*, p. 27).
49. *India Today* by R.P. Dutt, p. 407.

8

Rising of 1857 and Mewar

The rising of 1857 was an unprecedent upsurge of the Indian people against the foreign Government. The chief theatre of the struggle was the territory consisting of British provinces and the main causes lay in the policies persued by the British Government. The despotic and exploiting Government of the East India Company which was termed as "a universal landlord" by Sir J.R. Seelay,[1] resting mainly on military forces, the imperialist zeal of the British to bring the whole of India under direct subjection; and the arbitrary suppression of the ancient traditions and beliefs of the Indian people, and the proselytising fervour of the Englishmen; the social arrogance of the English, and maltreatment with the soldiery and many other factors combined to bring about the rebellion. According to historian, Mellason, it created a 'bad faith,' which roused on sentiments of the people. The revolt started in the native army, the cross-section of the Indian people and soon it took a wide character. The case greased cartridges and compounded chaptis was immediate cause and Manghal Pandey lighted the fire, when he shot a British officer. The general revolt broke out on 10th May at Meerut and at once spread to other cantonments, which was gradually joined by various sections of the people.

When the revolt broke out, the situation in Rajasthan was

not just the same as in the provinces directly ruled by the British. Here the British rulers lacked direct touch with masses and were only the overlords of the rulers of the eighteen native States of this region. The result was this that the people's disaffection in this region generally remained blunted and could not take the character, it took in the Northern India. Seventeen States were ruled by the Rajput princes and the eighteenth, *i.e.*, Tonk by Mohammedan descendant of the famous freebooter Amir Khan. To most of these States were assigned political officers, the chief of them being the Governor General's Agent for Rajputana, George Lawrence in May 1857.[2]

There was a small area, in this region, under the direct British administration, to hold the general political and military control over the whole region. The British area consisted of three important military stations, *e.g.*, Ajmer, Nasirabad and Neemuch. The importance of Ajmer could scarcely be overestimated for what Delhi was to North, Western India. Ajmer was to Rajputana.[3]

In the old and dilapidated fort of Ajmer was an arsenal capable of furnishing a siege train of great strength, guns and muskets and ammunition. The war material was abundant and fortunately for the British, it did not fall into the hands of the rebels. 'If the arsenal at Ajmer had fallen into the hands of the mutineers and within the city. Rajputana would have been lost for the time.[4] There were, within this area, about five thousand native troops of all arms, belonging to the British army, with some twenty English sergeants attached to them. The nearest station where the English troops were available was Deesa in the Presidency of Bombay, thirty miles from Abu and a hundred and twenty from Ajmer.[5] Arsenal at Ajmer was under the charge of two companies of the 15th Regiment of Native Infantry, which was stationed at Nasirabad, and which had lately come there from Meerut. The garrison of Nasirabad consisted of the 15th and 30th Regiments of the Native infantry, a battery of Native Artillery and the first Bombay Lancers, while the troops stationed at Neemuch consisted of 72nd Regiment N.I., the 7th Regiment of the Gwalior contingent and the wing of the First Bengal Cavalry.[6] In addition to these, the Cantonment of Deoli, about seventy-six miles from Ajmer was held by a regiment of native covalry and one of Infantry, known as the Kota

Contingent. A similar force of less strength composed of irregular troops maintained by Jodhpur State and known as the Jodhpur Region, held Erinpura, fifty miles from Abu. All of these were destined to revolt and spread the flames of rebellion within a short time of the outbreak of Meerut. Two local corps, Mewar Bhil Corps at Kherwara and Merwara Battalion at Beawar under British officers, composed of men of inferior caste, having no affinity with the Hindus and Muslims of northern India, also proved a reliable source of strength for the British in this grim hour of peril.

Thus when the rebellion broke out, the British position in Rajputana was very insecure and critical, not only in view of the disaffected native troops, but also due to the fact that they were situated in a remote corner of Rajputana surrounded by semi-independent States. Rajputs had always been regarded to be deeply attached to their religious sentiments and beliefs, and as great lovers of freedom. Had they responded to the call of religion and freedom. British authority would have vanished from the desert area stretching from Delhi to Gujarat,[7] which would have immensely affected the destiny of the British in India.

Several factors worked in favour of the British in this region. It was not long since these stations had been emancipated from the plunder and dissolution at the hands of Maratha and the Pindaris by the British, and they were now enjoying peace and order after passing through the trouble and turmoil of more than half a century. They feared that complete success in the field of military hordes would be a prelude to the revival of the condition of rule without law. Most of the rulers, bound by the subsidiary alliances, were no better than the puppets in the hands of British Government, having neither courage nor resources to stand against the British. Also the rulers of these States feared the revival of the Mughal power at Delhi, which had kept them enslaved for over three centuries, when the last scion of the Mughal dynasty, Bahadur Shah was declared the Emperor of India by the rebels, these fears were confirmed. Another factor which greatly moulded the decision of the rulers, was the refractory activities of their chiefs, who, in some of these States, specially Mewar and Marwar, planned to take advantage of this critical situation to get their grievances redressed and interests fulfilled. Despite their moral and martial degeneration, the Rajput Chiefs had still not lost entirely their traditional love for freedom and some of them, joined hands with the rebels and were responsible for many a setback, which the British authorities suffered in that region. Though many a ruler of Rajputana was chafing under the high handedness of the British political agents, yet the fate and time united the interest of those rulers and the British Government, and most of the people in these States either generally followed the directions of their sovereign or remained passive and neutral.

There was one more turbulent force in this area and that was the outside troops employed by the rulers in their respective States. These troops were quiet different from Rajputs, who could generally be believed to follow the orders of their sovereign. The soldiers of those troops were generally of the same stock as the soldiers of the British army,[8] and the former readily fraternised with the latter, whenever the opportunity presented itself.

Realising the imminent grave danger, George Lawrence, the agent to the Governor General for Rajputana called an official conference of the political officers in Rajputana States at Mt. Abu to discuss and decide the ways and means for the safety of the British authority in this area.

After the conference, on the 23rd May, Lawrence issued a proclamation to all the princes and nobles of the States of Rajputs as well as to all loyal Rajputs to show their fidelity to the paramount power by giving such assistance as might be immediately required by its officers. It called upon them to preserve peace within their respective States, for preventing the mutineers to enter their territories and capturing and destroying them.[9] George Lawrence made an urgent requisition on Deesa for a light field force to be sent to Nasirabad and urged the Government of Bombay to direct all the European troops proceeding to Agra to march *via* Gujarat and Rajputana.[10]

Maharana of Udaipur received a personal communication from the A.G.G. in which he was reminded that since the days of Peshwa, the princes of Rajputana had been much benefited and strengthened by their friendship with British Government. He promised that the integrity of all the States would endure for ever. He exhorted the Rana to assemble the troops and march them at once *via* Ajmer towards Delhi and cooperate with the

British troops.[11] Captain C.L. Showers, the Political Agent in Mewar arrived at Udaipur on 29th May in order to discuss the matter personally with Maharana.[12]

Situation in Mewar

The Political Agent was required to solve certain problems before he was able to receive the unstinted support of Maharana Swaroop Singh. Since Swaroop Singh came to power, his relations with the Political Agent had never been good on account of his opposition to and disdainment for the Political Agent's interference in the internal matters of the State. The relations grew bitter during 1850-57, when George Lawrence held the post of the Political Agent in Mewar. The latter had the audacity to express that the Maharana was in his 'black books'.[13] Now the same George Lawrence had been promoted as the A.G.G. in Rajputana by the British Government. Naturally the Maharana had his own fears and doubts. The British Government, however, was not disposed to keep such an influential and powerful ally as the Maharana of Udaipur in the State of suspicion and estrangement at such a critical hour and the Political Agent had to employ his best wits to convince the Maharana of security and integrity of his State.

There were other problems relating to the internal affairs of the State. Maharana Swaroop Singh, having faith in autocracy, adopted the policy curbing and minimising the powers of his nobility, which resulted into petty disturbances in the State between the servants of the rulers and those of several Chiefs. In 1855, when the Maharana exercised his prerogative by attaching some villages of the estates of Salumbar Deogarh, Bhindar and Gogunda in order to curb the defiance of their Chiefs, the latter forcibly drove out all their officials and troops sent to effect the orders of the *Durbar*. The British Political Officer, on this occasion, adopted the policy of neutrality, and the Maharana had to suffer the loss of his prestige.[14]

Another source of internal trouble was the succession disputes of the *Jagirs*, in which usually all the chiefs of the State got divided into two parties and they always took such an uncompromising attitude that minor warfare was generally the result. Maharana himself fell prey to these partisan conflicts and the confusion became worse confounded. Just on the eve of the rebellion, there arose the succession disputes in Amet and Bijollia,[15] threatening a warfare between the prominent Chiefs of Mewar.

Maharana's relations with Salumbar Chief presented another problem. Kesari Singh had a few months before, assumed the Chieftainship of Salumbar upon his father's death. Even prior to his installation as the Chief, Kesari Singh had associated with the party autognistic to the Maharana. The new Chief tried to use the occasion of his installation to reassert his traditional claims and privileges and demanded that the Maharana should personally visit his jagir to offer condolence for the death of his father, perform the ceremony of the binding of the sword and take him to Udaipur.[16] As Kesari Singh belonged to premier family among Choondawats, his demand carried weight and importance. But the Maharana declined and Kesari Singh nursed his defiance and disaffection which took menacing attitude during the period of 1857-58. In all such disputes, however, the nobility of Mewar always found itself equally divided and it generally so happened that the chiefs who supported the protection of a claimant in one case, found themselves ranged on opposite side in the other. Some of the most powerful chiefs in the State as of Salumbar. Deogarh, Bheendar, Begun, Gogunda found themselves thus situated.

Maharana Supports the Cause of the British

When Captain Showers arrived at Udaipur, he found the capital being filled with fanatic mercenary troops, Mohammedan and others, similar to those at the hands of whom his brother political agent Major Burton of Haroti and Captain Monck Mason in Marwar subsequently lost their lives.[17] Showers was hooted in the streets and the Maharana took great care for the safety of the British representatives at his court. The meeting between the Rana and Showers was arranged on the margin of the lake out of the gaze of the people, a spot to which he crossed in the boats.[18] Intelligence of the events at Meerut and Delhi had already reached Udaipur. Public excitement was great and was increased by the news, which reached the capital a day or two after his arrival, of the rising of the troops at Nasirabad on the 28th May, 1857. Then arose the rumours of the impending rising at Neemuch. These rumours served to intensify the excitement at

Udaipur, where quartered some of the *Durbar's* regiments of regulars, composed principally of the same classes of mixed Hindus and Mussalmans, as filled the British native army ranks.[19]

The Maharana was, naturally, interested first and foremost in his own society at such a critical time. He feared that the recusant nobles would take advantage of the situation in which the sovereign power was placed and could even attempt to dethrone him. The *Durbar* officers counselled him to concentrate his forces within the fortified gates of the Udaipur valley only.[20]

Showers discussed the situation with the Maharana and was able after much persuasion, to convince him about the final victory of the British and caused him to actively help the British cause. Showers' friendly and conciliatory attitude as a political officer of the British Government which was quiet different from his predecessors like George Lawrence, had also a favourable effect on the Maharana.[21]

Showers at once attended to the task of maintaining internal peace in the State. He issued a proclamation notifying to the disaffected Chiefs that on his early return to Udaipur, he would enquire personally into their grievances and that His Highness had promised to act on his counsel in each and every case. He advices them to rest upon his assurance and have patience. He further warned everybody that whoever ventured to disturb the peace, would be denounced as a rebel equally against the British Government as against his own sovereign.[22] The decision with regard to the succession disputes of Amet and Bijolia and the claims and privileges of Salumbar chief were thereby postponed. The Political Agent in order to dispel the fears of Maharana confided to him that the British Government held no prejudice against him and that nothing would be done in regard to his State without consulting him and against his wishes.

The Maharana issued a *ruqqa* in June 1857 to the chiefs of Deroo, Bangran, Bawal, Sevaloor, Benota, Surwanger and Athona of the Neemuch district to assist the British cause.[23] This area previously formed a part of Mewar, which was lost in the days of the Maratha turmoil. However, the traditional influence of the Rana of Udaipur over them was still there.

The Maharana placed his trustworthy troops at Showers' disposal, which was headed by one of his highest and trusted chiefs, Rao Bhakt Singh, the chief of Bedla.[24] Order under '*Khas Ruqqa*' (the royal sign manaal) were at the same time issued on the 27th May calling upon all his loyal chiefs and district officers to afford every aid in British operation and obey Showers' orders as his own.[25] A further precautionary measure was taken at Kherwara, the headquarters of the Mewar Bhil Corps. There was the danger of a rising of the troops of the 1st Bengal Cavalry on detachment duty at Kherwara, a wing of which had by then mutinied at Neemuch on the 3rd June. Captain Bookes, the Superintendent, Mewar Bhil Corps closed all the passes leading out of the hilly tract and the attempts of the Cavalry to rise were nipped in the bud with the assistance of the Mewar Bhil Corps.[26] They began by cutting-off the head of their Risaldar, as he refused to lead them, however, they were disarmed by the Bhil Corps. Bhil like Mers, having no sympathy with the Hindus or the Mussalmans, proved trustworthy for the British. Mers of the Merwara Battalion played the same part for the British in saving Ajmer, as noticed above. In October, the Maharana issued a *parwana* to Bhumia chiefs of Ogna, Panarwa, Jawas, Madree, Jarole and Ghanee in the hilly district of Mewar directing them to undertake effective measures for the native of the British party at Kherwara and Kotra and for the prevention of any disturbances in the hilly tracts.[27]

Mutinies at Nasirabad and Neemuch

The first outbreak took place in Rajasthan at Nasirabad on the 29th May. The removal of two companies of the 15th Regiment from Ajmer to Nasirabad became the cause of distrust. The elements of disaffection had already been working in the garrison there. Mysterious reports were circulated of bone-dust being mixed up with the *atta* sold in the market and of cartridges being composed of objectionable materials.[28] On the 27th May the troops heard of an European force coming to Nasirabad from Deesa. This rumour set the spark and next day the station was a mass of smoking ruins.[29] On the 28th May at 3 O' clock in the afternoon some men of the 15th N.I. suddenly rushed to the guns with loaded muskets. They were joined by the 30th Regiment at 4 O'clock.[30] The Light Company, the Granadier Company and the Flank Companies all refused to fire on the mutineers.[31] The 1st Bombay Cavalry, on being ordered to charge, failed to follow the lead of their officers, two of whom were killed and three were wounded, though they refrained from rebellion. The game was up the Europeans fled to the jungles, fugitives were escorted to Beawar by men of 1st Bombay Cavalry. Of the officers Newberry and Spottiswoode were killed and Captain Hardy and Lieutenant Lock were badly wounded. Thus Nasirabad went into the hands of rebels. The bungalows and Government buildings were plundered and burnt and thereafter the rebels with their women and children streamed off to Delhi. When on the 12th June a force consisting of 400 men of the H.M.'s 83rd, the 12th Bombay Infantry and a troop of European House Artillery arrived at Nasirabad, it was founded entirely deserted and was therefore reoccupied by them without fighting.[32]

The second outbreak took place at Neemuch on the 3rd June, which is about a hundred and forty miles south of Nasirabad. Rumour of Nasirabad revolt had reached the station. On the 2nd June Col. Abbot administered to the sepoys an oath of allegiance making them swear on the holy *Koran* and of the Ganges water and he himself swore on the Bible expressing his confidence in the faithful intentions of the sepoys.[33] But on the 3rd June when information regarding the events at Nasirabad and a rumour of the coming of European troops reached Neemuch the sepoys got exasperated. They rose in revolt at 10 O'clock in the night. The firing of gun-shots alarmed the British Officers. The British men and women flocked in the fortified square of the station, but that being in the charge of the 7th Regiment of the Gwalior contingent, which was in no case reliable, they fled from the station. A general uproar went up from all parts of the station and in an instance every house was in flames.[34] Some of the officers of the rebellion army approached the agents of Mewar *Durbar* present at Neemuch and proposed to establish the control of Mewar *Durbar* over Neemuch, which was, however, not accepted by the latter until they received the *Durbar* orders to that effect.[35] Among those who were killed were the wife of the Sergeant Sappal and his two children. The fugitives ran towards the villages of Dungia, Kesunda and Jamlavade on the Mewar border.[36] The insurgents of Neemuch also evacuated the station and made off for Delhi, halting in the way at Nimbahera, where they were entertained by the local authorities of the Tonk State. General George Lawrance caused that place to be occupied by the detachments from the contingents of Mewar, Kota and Bundi. But as he had no reliance on these troops as well he took an early opportunity of replacing them by a detachment of the troops which he had requisitioned from Deesa.[37]

Udaipur Troops Rescue British Refugees at Dungla

About forty Englishmen, women and children escaping from Neemuch reached Dungia being pursued by some of the rebels and were besieged there. Their fate was doomed, if the Udaipur troops had not reached there in time to rescue them. News of the Neemuch revolt had reached Udaipur and soon after on the 6th June, Showers received Captain Macdonald's letter containing the news of the Neemuch happening and asking him to proceed at once for the relief of Dungla. Shower's started from Udaipur on the 7th June accompanied by Rao Bakht Singh of Bedia at the head of Mewar troops. Mehta Sher Singh also joined them.[38] They reached Dungla the next day. The report of the Maharana's troops taking the field had preceded them and had warned the mutineers to beat a retreat before the country was roused against them. Consequently the Mewar troops faced no resistance.[39] Showers found the refugees in the last stage of destitution expecting no survival. Rao Bakht Singh and other Mewar officers made arrangements of palanquins, elephants, horses, carts and carriages and all Englishmen, women and children were sent to Udaipur the same night.

At Udaipur the Maharana received them with full care, kept them at Jagmandir Palace in Pichhola Lake and appointed Mehta Gokulchand to look after their requirements and safety.[40] "His Highness", the Maharana, paid us a very handsome compliment by coming here in person yesterday to ascertain that we were being provided with every comfort. He asked to see the children, and to each he gave, with his own hand, two gold *mohurs*. In the evening they were taken over to the Queen's, when the Rana again sent for each, two gold *mohurs* in his own name, and two in that of the Ranee's. In fact nothing could exceed his civility and kindness. Thus Captain Annesley one of the refugees reported to Showers.[41]

The protection extended to the British refugees by the

Maharana, was gratefully acknowledged at the time by the Governor General in a *Kharita* to the Maharana,[42] and afterwards draw from Her Majesty, the Queen, the expression of her "highest gratification in observing the support which he gave to her armies, the assistance which he rendered to her subjects and tranquility he maintained throughout his extensive dominions, and assuring His Highness that these proofs of his loyalty and devotion to the British crown would ever be held by Her Majesty in grateful remembrance".[43]

Rajput Chivalry Displayed at Kesunda

While Mewar officers were busy with rescue operations for the English refugees at Dungla a border village of Kesunda in Chhoti Sadri Tehsil of Mewar presented an example of Rajput Chivalry. Two of the English fugitives from Neemuch, Doctors Murray and Gane got separated from the main body and weary with their wanderings on foot and exhausted by anxiety they sought shelter and protection at the village of Kesunda. They asked the villagemen if they could take rest there for an hour or so. The latter readily complied with their wishes, treating them with great civility. They were boaded for their rest in a house which had a walled enclosure, and were given milk, *chapatis*, *dal*, rice and mangoes to eat.[44]

Meanwhile the pursuing mutineers arrived at the village and demanded fugitives, which the villagemen refused. They reassured the guests saying "You have eaten with us and are our guests and now if you were our greatest enemy, we would defend you".[45] And they manned the walls for their protection. The rebels threatened to bring guns, but nothing daunted, the villagers invoked the vengeance of their suzerain, the Maharana and maintained a bold attitude. Assistance came to the villagemen from the Rawat of Begam estate and the Hakim of Sadri and mutineers had to retreat without effecting their desired objects.[46] At nightfall the Englishmen were escorted to Chhoti Sadri, the nearest military post of the Mewar *Durbar*, whence they preceded and joined the other refugees at Dungla.

The persons mainly responsible for the protection of the Englishmen at Kesunda included Pandit Yadav Rao, Patel Ram Singh, Patel Kering and Onkar Singh, who received appreciation of the British Government for their conduct.[47] The Political

Agent invested them with robes of honour in a public *durbar* at Udaipur and the Maharana rewarded their services with the substantial grant of land. The British Government on its own part bestowed a money rewarded on these persons and at its own expense got constructed a well at Kesunda which was to be lasting monument to them.[48]

The treatment, these officers received at another village of Mewar, named Bhil ka Gaon, is given by Dr. Mutrray in his letter to the Political Agent in Mewar in the following words. "Here we were received with very great kindness. The Bhils seemed to vie with each other in their hospitality". Dr. Murray, in the end says. The conduct of Udaipur *Durbar* at this crisis, was beyond all praise. The Maharana entered heart and soul into our cause, and indeed, had it not been for his loyalty to the British Government and cooperation with the authorities, there is no saying what might have been the aspect of affairs in Rajputana at that moment".[49]

Pursuit of the Neemuch Mutineers

Having accomplished the relief of Dungla, Captain Showers directed the main body of the Udaipur troops, after beating up for quotas of horse at Bari Sadri and Chhoti Sadri, to proceed towards Chittor to pursue the Neemuch mutineers Captain Sir John Hill Burt and Ellice of the 1st Bengal Cavalry accompanied the troops, while he, accompanied by Lieutenant Barnes reached Neemuch.[50] There he heard that Mahedipur Cavalry, which was marching to reinforce Neemuch, had itself mutinied within a few miles of the station and murdered their officers, Lieutenant Bordie and Hunt.[51] Then they went back to Mahedipur, roused the remaining section of the contingent and returned to join the Neemuch insurgents Showers left at Neemuch, a confidential *Durbar* officer, the Mewar *Vakil*, Arjun Singh Sahiwala, having control over the Raj troops at the neighbouring Udaipur post, in attendance on Captain Lloyd, the Superintendent of Neemuch. Then Showers, accompanied by Lieutenant Stapleton and Mehta Sher Singh of Mewar rode on to join the advance party, pursuing the rebels in the direction of Chittor. They joined them there on the 12th June.[52] On their advance from Chittor a few miles beyond Gangrar, they learnt that a party of the rebelious cavalry had been there, only an hour or two hours their arrivals, hunting for their protection and for the security of the post in transit.[53]

On continuing the march without halt, stranglers began to fall into their hands. Among others were the two Mewar Agency *Chaprasis* who had been left in charge of General Lawrence's property and who joined the mutineers after plundering the same.[54] Property of every description strewed the road of retreating rebels. On their march, Mewar were reinforced at Sanganer by those of the Raos of Hamirgarh and Mahuwa, who joined them in person with their quatas of horse.[55] Showers could not intercept the insurgents. Learning the way of march of the mutineer to Delhi, he thought to occupy Kekree, where the rebels were expected to come and plunder it. In order to attain this object of obstructing the movement of rebels he requested General Lawrence and Brigadier Macan, the officer commanding at Nasirabad, to send the Brigade, recently arrived from Deesa, to Kekree, so that a combined attack could be made on the mutineers.[56] However, Lawrence disapproved of his plan, as in his view the preservation of Ajmer was of primary importance, and that depended mainly upon the brigade, requisitional by Showers.[57] When Showers arrived at Shahpura, a Chieftainship holding villages both from Mewar and Ajmer and owing a divided allegiance, therefore equally to the British Government and to the Maharana of Udaipur, he found the gates of fort closed against them. No, reception was given to them by the chief and no supplies were offered. Showers learnt that the rebels had halted there.[58] From Shahpura he proceeded to Jahajpur.

The Neemuch mutineers arrived at Deoli, plundering and burning in the way the Government bungalows at Chittor. Hamirgarh and Banera and halting at Shahpura for two days.[59] They burnt the cantonment of Deoli and after seizing two pieces of ordnance and the whole magazine in store, proceeded on their march to Agra, facing no resistance. One Staff Sergeant with ten women and children, in all eleven Europeans, who fled from Deoli, were rescued by the Udaipur authorities of Jahajpur. They were brought to the Political Agent's Camp there,[60] whence they were sent to Udaipur. The Maharana received them with all cordiality.[61]

Showers now retraced his march and returned to Neemuch. On the way Showers halted at Begun, where he was well received by the Rao of the place, Maha Singh. This chief guarded the frontier passes of Mewar preventing the mutineers to enter into the territory and offered shelter and security to the Englishmen, women and children, who came as refugees from the side of Mandsore after the outbreaks in Malwa.[62] In lieu of this service, he afterwards was awarded a Khillat of the value of Rs. 2000 by the British Government.[63]

Learning that the mutineers were still entering the territory of Mewar, Showers wrote to Maharana from Neemuch to take necessary measures to fortify all the strongholds of the State.[64]

Stir in Udaipur Troops at Neemuch

At Neemuch were stationed the troops of Mewar, Bundi and Kota along with one Company of H.M.'s 83rd Regiment and a detachment of the Bombay Native Regulars, Cavalry and Infantry.[65] The situation of the adjacent areas of Malwa had become critical due to the mutinies at Indore, Mhow and Augur, which once again threatened the peace at Neemuch. There were sporadic attempts of incendiarism and the atmosphere remained filled with rumours. At this time in July, there were nine English officers present at Neemuch. The only reliable force there was the Mewar troops which consisted of 450 horses and 1600 infantry.[66] A rumour was spread among the Mewar troops that the English were bent on destroying their caste and religion and had for this purpose mixed human bone-dust in the flour served to them. This news created uproar among them and they even thrashed the *baniyas* selling the flour. Captain Showers requested Arjune Singh Sahiwala, the Mewar *Vakil*, to pacify the Mewar troops. The *Vakil* arrived at the Bazar asked the suspected flour to be produced and having a handful of it, kneaded and made into bread, ate it himself before them. This act dispelled their doubts.[67]

Salumbar Chief Threat to the Maharana

Just after his arriving at Neemuch, Showers received a confidential message from the Rana. At such a critical time when the British Government and her officers were engaged in quelling the rebellion, and the most trustworthy troops and officers of the Maharana were at Neemuch helping the British cause, Rawat of Salumbar, Kesari Singh saw an opportune moment to reassert his demands. He went so far as to threaten the Rana to set up a rival on the throne of Mewar at the ancient capital of Chittor, if within the period of eight days his demands were not accepted.[68] Showers, also received a report from Captain Brookes, Superintendent of Mewar Bhil Corps at Kherwara that Salumbar was instigating an attack on his post of Kherwara and the State of affairs there was critical.[69] Thereupon Showers wrote a bold and threatening letter to Kesari Singh reminding about Sir Henery Lawrence's report of the 5th Feb., 1857, in which Sir Henery had suggested the expulsion of the chieftains of Salumbar and Bheendar from Rajputana and confiscation of their *jagirs*. He warned the chief that if he did not stop plotting against the Maharana, he might be punished accordingly.[70] The Salumbar chief in his reply, however denied the charges levelled against him and affirmed that he would do nothing against the Maharana.[71]

British Reverses at Auwa and Kota

In the month of August, the flames of rebellion spread far and wide in the province. The native troops of the princes of Rajasthan now took the field and the anti-British outbreak took place in the troops of Jodhpur and Kota. On the 21st August, the infantry portion of the Jodhpur Legion,—stationed at Abu, mutinied and joined the main force at Erinpura, imprisoning the Englishmen and their families, who were however set free unhurt. These rebels then entered into alliance with the disaffected chiefs of Marwar led by Khushhal Singh, chief of Auwa. They jointly defeated the troops sent by Jodhpur prince at Pali, and fell on Auwa fort, where the British suffered an inglorious defeat and loss of prestige, when General Lawrence, the highest Military authority of the British Government in Rajputana marched on Auwa on the 18th September and failed to storm it.[72] He was compelled to march back from Auwa at once.

The big casualty of this campaign was Monck Mason, the Political Agent at Jodhpur, who was scheduled to join Lawrence at Auwa. When he reached the place, Lawrence had already withdrawn and the Agent fall into the hands of the rebels and was killed. His head was cut-off and placed over the gateway of the fort of Auwa.[73]

On the 12th September, 1857 the rebels issued an appeal to

the people of Marwar and Mewar in the name of Risaldar Abdul Ali Khan, Sheikh Mohammad Bux and *Subedars, Jamadars* and Hindu and Mussalman sepoys who were 3,000 in all to give them aid and shelter.[74] The Appeal read, "The sardars in Mewar and Marwar are on our side. Those who will give us aid for the sake of religion will gain reward in the heaven and the king will consider them loyal and will honour."[75]

Next month on the 15th October the disaffected forces of Maharao of Kota rebelled, attacked the Residency and killed the Political Agent, Major Burton with his two sons,[76] along with all other Europeans present in the city. Maharao Ram Singh himself was imprisoned in his place by the troops sent by the Karoli ruler for his help.[77] The Maharana of Udaipur, on receiving a letter from Kota Maharao, offered to bring his family to Udaipur as the privacy of the Kota *zanana* was not secure. But considering that the royal ladies would need in their escort a large retinue from Kota, Showers suggested to the Rana not to mix himself up in the Kota affairs at such a time and the Rana gave up his offer.[78]

The rebels indulged indiscriminately in plunder and arson and even the local business class was not spared. The misfortune which befell the town assumed an unrestricted magnitude when the British troops entered the town after a few days and in order to avenge the violence of the rebels they resorted to misdeeds of limitless proportions by plundering, burning and razing the town and not even sparing the honour of the women. About 500 women jumped in the Chambal river in order to save their honour.[79]

The disaster which the British suffered at Auwa was a great blow to its prestige in Rajputana, which was aggravated by the successful revolts of Kota troops and the murder of the Political officers. A reverse so aggravated was obviously calculated, in the inflammable State of country arising from the general rebellion, to excite a combination of all the disaffected elements in Rajputana spreading a general conflagration.[80] The success gained by Auwa chief and his allies might have emboldened of the rebellious chiefs of Mewar to take advantage and make common cause with the rebels. That they were urgently invited to do so with the assurance that the aid of the king of Delhi had been solicited is proved by the intercepted letters from the Auwa chief to the chief of Salumbar of Mewar, despatched immediately after his repulsing of General Lawrence's attack. Had Mewar Chiefs of Salumbar, Bheendar, Kotharia and other estates joined with the Marwar chiefs of the province in their train, the consequences of such a combination in the situation would have been disastrous for the British. But that was not to came-off.

On the 16th October, General Gerrard defeated the Thakur of Auwa at Narnol, who had, by then, been deserted by the Mutineers of Jodhpur Region. The fort of Auwa was invested and stormed and its fortifications were blown up and destroyed.[81] Khushhal Singh and the Thakurs of Gular, Asop and of other estates repaired towards hills on the Mewar-Marwar boundary near Roopnagar. Thence they passed unobstructed through the *jagirs* of Mewar State and took refuge there.[82] Khushhal Singh, the Auwa Chief took shelter with the Rawat of Kotharia. Having come to learn that Auwa Chief was hiding at Kotharia, the troops of the Jodhpur ruler along with the British Cavalry came to Kotharia in Mewar on the 8th June, 1858 to aprehend him.[83] At this the relatives and adherents of Rawat Jodh Singh of Kotharia assembled in the fort. The English officer was allowed to see the Kotharia fort but Khushhal Singh could not be detected there, and the troops were quietly withdrawn. The sentiments of the Rajputs were excited by the movement of the foreign troops in their territory in order to apprehend a shelterer, thereby violating their century old custom.[84] Khushhal Singh surrendered in 1860 and, after being tried by a court martial held at Nasirabad was acquitted of his offences against the British Government but he was expelled from Auwa, which was restored to him after several years.[85]

In Kota the authority of Maharao of Kota was reestablished, when on the 27th March, 1858, General Roberts gave a crushing defeat to the rebels.[86] The Maharao, in the beginning, was suspected of having espoused the cause of the rebels, but after investigation, he was declared to be free of having any complicity with the rebels. However, his salute was reduced from 17 to 13 guns, as he was found not to have performed his duty perfectly.[87]

Maharana's Counsel to other Rajput Rulers

Maharana Swaroop Singh, in the crisis of 1857-58 not only

extended his own moral and material help to the British but exhorted other Rajput rulers as well to follow him. When in the month of June, 1857, he received a communication from Maharaja Raghuraj Singh of the Rewa State seeking his advice in the crisis, the Maharana in his reply, stated "through the good fortune of the Sirkar (Paramount power) it is hoped that everything will speedily be settled. The advent of the British power has proved beneficial to all Rajwara and has been the means of restoring tranquility to the chiefs in the country. On this account we earnestly wish and pray to Sreejee (the deity) for the stability of the British power. I hope you will bear in mind what I have written".[88] Maharana's reply being late, the Rewa Maharaja sent another communication on the 20th August, stating, "I look upto no one else for advice but yourself in the present crisis. Myself and my troops are at your disposal". The Maharana in his reply reaffirmed his support to the British Government and advised the Maharaja to follow his example".[89]

Similar communications were received by the Maharana from the rulers of Jodhpur and Kota States. Just after the defeat of the British troops at Pali and Auwa and the murder of the Political Officer Monck Mason, the mission of an accredited minister Pancholee Kuber Mal, from the Jodhpur Maharaja Takhat Singh reached Udaipur on the 6th October, to have consultation with the Maharana Swaroop Singh conveyed the same view to the Jodhpur Maharaja as to the Rewa ruler.[90] A communication was received by the Maharana from the Kota ruler just after the October events. The Kota Maharana stated, "You are the head of the native chiefs...favour me with the good advice on this occasion". The Maharana in his reply regretted the events at Kota and observed that Rajasthan had gained by the friendship of the British Government and in that only lay their welfare and prosperity. Mehta Murlidhar was sent to Kota by the Maharana as his personal representative to hand over his reply and convey his views, orally, in detail.[91]

Occupation of Nimbahera by Mewar Troops

The situation at Neemuch continued to be disturbing. In the month of September it again became menacing, when it was threatened from the side of Mandsore.[92] At that place one Firuz Shah having announced himself as the king, invited all the neighbouring rulers and chiefs of Pratapgarh, Jawra, Sitamau, Ratlam and Salumbar to acknowledge his authority and attack the British positions.[93] The chief of Salumbar of Mewar was particularly called to attack the station of Kherwars, an important strategic military station in the area, and was threatened if he failed to comply with.[94]

The number of Firuz's followers gradually rose to about 18,000, and an attack on Neemuch was imminent.[95] At this time the Neemuch Authorities came to learn that there was a hostile intrigue at work at Nimbahera, a town and district of Tonk State, about 16 miles north of Neemuch, in communication with the rebels at Mandsore in the south.[96]

As Nimbahera lay on the road between Neemuch and Nasirabad, Neemuch was in danger of being attacked from two sides.[97]

To avert the two-fold danger Captain Showers, the Political Agent in Mewar and Colonol Jackson, the Commandant at Neemuch in consultation with the Mewar *Vakil* Arjun Singh. The Mewar *Durbar* was requested to despatch additional troops from Udaipur. The *Durbar* hesitated on account of unceasing internal trouble being caused by the chiefs. However, he was prevailed upon and two guns, a company of infantry and 50 horsemen were despatched with the instructions to halt at Sadri and keep alert to assist, when called upon. The Chiefs of Sadri, Kanor, Bansi, Begam, Bhadesar, Athana, Sarvanya, Daroo, Banota and other estates of Neemuch district and lying on Mewar border were invited to join the expedition against Nimbahera with the assurance that sufficient reward in form of land, etc. would be granted to those who joined it.[98] Neemuch was placed under the charge of a trustworthy force with a body of Mewar troops and British officers marched on Nimbahera on the 18th September, 1857 with about 60 horsemen, two guns, some Englishmen and Mewar officers. Next day they were joined by the contingent of Mewar troops and the levies of various Chiefs as of Athana, Daroo and Chhoti Sadri. Later Sawai Singh from Chittor also joined them with a number of troops. Their number reached 3000 before the siege operations started.[99]

The suspicion of the British Officers came to be true. The garrison of Nimbahera took to defiance, assaulted the messengers sent by the British Officers inside the fort and closed the gates. The guns of the invading force commenced their operations.[100] The garrison fired gunshots from the fort and killed the Englishmen of 83rd Regiment and a peon of Mewar troops. The invaders failed to capture the fort. However, realising further resistance fruitless the garrison evacuated the fort at night to join the Mandsor rebels. The assailants occupied the fort next morning. The fort was ordered to be plundered. The old *patel* of the fort was accused of having assisted in the escape of garrison and in spite of pleading of the Mewar officers on his behalf the *patel* was shot dead at the public parade of the troops.[101]

In view of the geographical position of the place, Maharana's influence over the subjects, and unreliability of the Mohammedan officers of the Tonk State, the possession of Nimbahera was made over temporarily to the Mewar officer Mehta Sher Singh, subject to the approval of the British Government. Various chiefs and Mewar officers, participating in the expedition were given cash rewards from ten to two hundred rupees. The promise of award in form of land was not fulfilled. The decision in that regard was put-off until the future position of Nimbahera was settled by the British Government.[102]

Attack of Neemuch

The rebels of Mandsor attacked Jiran, near Neemuch, on the 22nd October and defeated a British force, killing British Officers Tucker and Reade. They hung Tucker's head over the gate of Mandsor.[103] Encouraged by the victory the rebels, 2,000 in number,[104] marched against Neemuch under Firuz Shah. On hearing of their approach, the regular Cavalry, 250 sabres under Captain Bannister and 300 Mewar horse under Captain Showers, moved out and met the rebels about a mile or two from cantonments.[105] But finding the number of the rebels overwhelming the British troops shut themselves into the fort. Showers, Jackson, Mewar *Vakil* Arjun Singh and other Mewar officers escaped to Daroo in the night and other officers and servants fled pell-mell towards Athana, Piplia, Jawad and Chittor.[106]

The rebels advanced unresisted and unobstructed, burnt the station and laid siege to the fort but failed to capture it. The seige of the fort continued for about a fortnight, until Colonel Durand leading the Mhow Column arrived on the scene and inflicted a crushing defeat on the rebels at Mandsore.[107] The rebels withdrew and the fort of Neemuch was saved. In the meanwhile Showers and other British Officers left Daroo, finding it unsafe and proceeded to Kesunda and thence to Lasarvan. Soon after they received the news of the withdrawal of the rebels, from Neemuch and they return.[108] In April, 1858 the first detachment of the reinforcements from England, detailed for Rajputana, arrived and a wing of the 72nd (seaforth) Highlanders marched into Udaipur in progress to Neemuch under Captain Crombie. They were received very hospitably by the Maharana and were taken in boats and State barges to have a view of the Island palace, where previously the Neemuch refugees had been sheltered.[109]

Tantia Tope in Mewar

After the battle of Jawra Alipur on the 22nd June, 1858, Tantia Tope, accompanied by Rao Saheb, at the head of the rebels directed his activities towards Rajputana. They expected active cooperation and backing of the Chiefs and the people of this region. They were aware of the British reverses at several places in Rajputana, the rebellious activities of Marwar and Mewar Chiefs, and the revival of the plunder by some of the wild tribes of hilly tracts in Rajputana. Kherwara in Mewar had ever been a source of trouble for Mewar and the British authorities.[110] Just after the rebellion at Kota, the Meenas in the adjoining area revived their plundering activity and began coming murders and obstructing trade in and through that area.[111] By this time, however, the position of the British had amply improved by the reinforcements of the European troops and the pursuing British army was sufficiently strong in number and equipment. They, however, had still to depend upon the native rulers for supplies and information about movements of the rebels in the hilly country, cavared with ravines, defiles and forests and the Maharana afforded every facility to the British in that connection.

Being pursued by Colonal Holmes and General Roberts, Tantia Tope and Rao Saheb entered Mewar at the head of a force about 8,000 men,[112] passed through Jalindnari Pass and reached Mandalgarh, where they stayed for two or three days on account of heavy floods in Banas. They did not disturb the local authorities, fearing that such an action might alienate the Rajputs. Mehta Swaroop Chand and Gopal Chand collected about 2-3 thousand Rajputs and strengthen the defences of the fort.[113] As Udaipur was threatened by the rebels Captain Annesley, the Asstt. Political Agent in Mewar requested the officer commanding the Mahikanta Field Force at Tintori to despatch troops to Udaipur at once.[114]

Tantia and his party had the object of marching on Neemuch by way of Ratangarh-Singoli Passes, but Brigadier Parke and Major Taylor closed the way and Showers strengthened the defences of Neemuch with the help of Mewar troops.[115] The rebels, changing their route crossed Banas River near Baraundani and reached Bhilwara on the 8th August, 1858. They were about 8000 to 9000 in number and had ample cash and ornaments with them. But they were experiencing great scarcity of food and clothing. The men wore female *sarees* for turbans on their heads and were prepared to pay for the *chapatis* at the rate of one rupee each.[116]

General Roberts, pursuing the rebels reached Bhilwara on the 9th August and defeated and routed the rebels on the bank of Kotashwari near Sanganer.[117] The rebels fled towards Nathdwara, where they paid on homage in Vaishnawa Temple of Goverdhan Nath on the 13th August, and turning back arrived at the village of Kotharia on the Banas river[118] about 4 miles north from Nathdwara. The Chief of this place, Rawat Jodh Singh was already known for supporting the cause of all anti-British elements. It is believed that the Chief of Kotharia gave necessary provision to Tantia Tope before the latter encountered General Roberts.

On the 13th August, the battle took place, near Kotharia resulting in the victory of the British troops. The rebels were killed in great number and they lost four guns to the enemy.[119] The cavalry led by Colonel Nayler pursued them for 15 miles, killing a number of stragglers and capturing three elephants and a quantity of baggage. Thereafter they had to abandon the pursuit on account the steep hilly tract, which impeded the swift movement of cavalry. The place, where this battle took place lies on the northern side of Khari River, a tributary of Banas. This place is called "Rukamgarh-ka-Chhapar" and also Kala-gora-ka-Chhapar (the place where the white and the black fought).

Thence the rebels moved towards Akola, in the south of Chittor. In the village of Pur, Dulichand and Badriji Kamdar opened the State stores for the rebels out of fear that they might plunder the village. The rebels along with the above Kamdars left the place before the British troops arrived there. The rebels, however, left a gun behind them.[120]

After crossing the Chambal River and plundering Singoli the rebels appeared at Jhalawar, being pursued by the flying columns of Brigadier Parke. The Raja's troops readily fraternised with the rebels[121] and the great grandson of the famous Zalim Singh, Rajrana Prithi Singh was made captive. The Raja was compelled to surrender five lakh rupees, ample war material, a number of elephants, horses and twenty seven guns and the rebels left the place, before Parks arrived on the spot. They proceeded towards Indore, but General Mitchel intercepted their movement and defeated them at Beawar on the 15th Sept., 1858, whence they retreated towards Bundelkhand, and thence further south.[122]

After the reverses at Chhota Udaipur on the Narmada River, on the 3rd December, Tantia Tope re-entered Mewar territory from the south near Kushalgarh.[123] A bold attempt was made by the Rao of that place, to check his advance, for which the Rao received afterwards an honorary reward from the Government.[124] The rebel force was too strong for the native troops and Tantia Tope occupied the town on the 11th December.[125] However, the arrival of a British detachment under Major Learmouth saved the town and the Palace of Maharawal from being sacked. The rebels plundered 17 camel loads of cloth coming from Ahmedabad, before they left the place.

Tantia Tope, thence, proceeded towards Salumbar, Gingla and Bheender.[126] At Salumbar the rebels were furnished freely with supplies, collected from far and near. An advance party of rebels, disguised as *fakers*, had come to Korawar in November, in concert with the chief of Bheender took opportunity to reassert his demands and assume a threatening attitude. Political Officer Showers received letters from Salumbar and Bheender Chiefs by the hand of one and the same messenger at Udaipur. Showers summarily dismissed the messenger with a verbal admonition and pregnant warning.[127]

Tantia, collecting sufficient supplies from the Mewar Chiefs marched towards Udaipur. On the 29th December Captain Muter, at the head of a field force arrived at Salumbar in pursuit of the rebels. Having learnt that the Chief had assisted the rebels and that some wounded men and women were being sheltered in his fort the Captain decided to ascertain the truth. He found the fort closed and was allowed to enter it with 15 guards only to meet the Chief. The Chief admitted to have rendered supplies to the rebels, under threat, Muter on his part could not obtain supplies from the Chief easily until he threatened the Chief by sending guns on high ground to fire.[128]

Tantia Tope could not fulfil his desire to surprise Udaipur. The Maharana, in the meanwhile, had made requisition for British troops for his personal protection from the intrigues of his hostile Chiefs and foreign troops and thereupon the Neemuch Field Forces had covered the Capital.[129] The arrangement frustraced the plan of Tantia, who turned his way at Gingla, moving towards Bheender whence he reached Pratapgarh. Here the rebels were joined by some 4000 Bhils, who gave them refuge in the jungle and accompanied them to share the plunder of Pratapgarh, showing them the pass to reach there.[130] But Major Rocke's detachment overtook them at Pratapgarh on the 23rd December, 1858 and saved the rich Capital from being sacked. He inflicted a crushing defeat on the rebels. In this battle Tantia lost most of his men and material. Thence Tantia fled to Zirapur passing by Mandsor. On the 13th January, 1859 at Indergarh, he was joined by Firuz Shah with his 2,000 followers and they began to sweep round through upper and western Rajputana.

Tantia Tope and his party entered Mewar for the third time from the west in February, 1859. They reached Kankroli, forty miles north of Udaipur on 17th February.[131] Brigadier Somerset's coloumn was at the time in the field in Mewar in observation of the ghats, Showers proceed to help him. Learning that the rebels were advancing from the west, Lieutenant Collin reached Amet with some troops to guard the passes while the main force remained at Kosithal, [132] 20 miles from Kankroli. Here the British guards and officers experienced hostile treatment from the local people. Some of the advance guards were shut up in the fort, when they entered it to get supplies.[133] The guards were allowed to go out after about three and a half hours with nothing. Collin soon after found armed people challenging him and he had to call the force from Kosithal to Amet, in the meantime the rebels safely reached Kankroli, where they were well fed by the local people[134] and got enough time to flee from there before the British troops reached there from Amet. The rebels fled toward south-east, but their retreat towards Banswara jungles was cut-off by the British troops.[135]

Eventually rebel force got disorganised and disheartened on account of the unflagging and unrelenting pursuit of the British troops. After the second day of pursuit by the flying column of General Michel the stragglers began to fell into the hands of the British troops at every mile. One leader Nawab Abdul Sattar Khan broke off with his followers from the main body, while in mid-flight, and surrendered.[136] Rao Saheb and Firuz Shah had separated from Tantia Tope after the severe defeat at Sikar in January, 1959.[137] Tantia found himself now exhausted, weak and frustrated. The British had already quelled the rebellion all over India. On the first November a great change occurred in the Political set-up of India by Queen's proclamation, and many a rebel leader surrendered under the terms of the amnesty of the above declaration. Tantia Tope now saw that the game was over. When he was in Paron Jungle with Man Singh, the Chief of Marwar he was betrayed by the latter and Tantia was arrested on the 7th April, 1859, while he was asleep. He was tried before a court martial at Sipri and was hanged.[138]

Queen's Proclamation

On November 1, 1858 was issued the Queen's Proclamation which transferred the power from the hands of the East India Company to the British Crown. The passages of the Proclamation relating to the Native States read:

"... We hereby announce to the native princes of India that all Treaties and Engagements made with them by or under the authority of the Honourable East India Company are accepted by us and will be scrupulously maintained and we look for the like observance on their part.

"We desire no extension on our present territorial possessions, and while we will permit no aggressions upon our dominions or our rights to be attempted with impunity, we shall sanction no encroachment on those of others. We shall respect the rights, dignity and honour of the native princes as our own, and we desire that they, as well as our own subjects should enjoy that prosperity and that social advancement, which can only be secured by internal peace and good Government.

"We hold ourselves bound to the natives of our Indian territories by the same obligations of duty which bind us to all our other subjects, and those obligations by the blessings of Almighty God, we shall faithfully and conscientiously fulfil.

"Firmly relying ourselves on the truth of Christianity and acknowledging with gratitudes the solace of religion, we disclaim alike the right and desire to impose our convinctions on any of our subjects ... that all small alike enjoy the equal and impartial protection of the law ...

"And it is our further will that, so far as may be, our subjects, of whatever race or creed, be freely and impartially admitted to offices in our services, the duties of which they may be qualified by their education, ability and integrity, duly to discharge.

"We know and respect the feelings of attachment with which the natives of India regard the lands inherited by them from their ancestors, and we desire to protect them in all rights connected therewith, subject to the equitable demands of the State, and we will that, generally in framing and administering the law, due regard be paid to the ancient rights, usages and customs of India."[139]

Maharana's Congratulations

The proclamation was received with a great sense of pleasure and enthusiasm by the Maharana, like other rulers of Rajputana. The princes and landowners regarded it as a charter of their rights and possessions.[140] The Maharana publicised the royal proclamation along with the statement of the Viceroy, Lord Canning in his State with all fanfare. Then he expressed his sentiments of trust, pleasure and satisfaction in the '*Khareeta*' of congratulations, sent by him addressed to the Queen Empress, on the occasion of her assuming the direct Government of India. The '*Khareeta*' read:

"(After dutiful respects and compliments.) The announcement made in the Royal word, that the Queen of England is coming to rule over us, has shed light and joy over this darkened land like the moon rising upon the night. Impelled by the emotions which fill my breast I hasten to offer my humble tribute to loyalty to Your Majesty, and with the spontaneous outpouring of my day, I desire to give expression to my grateful feelings for your sense of solicitude for your Indian subjects, evinced by the act which your Majesty has taken us all under your immediate protection, and has thus removed the intermediate link and has riveted the chain of affection by which my humble throne is brought nearer, and bound inseparably to your high throne.

"The gratification at this proof of your regard for our welfare, which all the princes of India will, I believe share equally with myself, is enhanced by the assurance so graciously given by your royal word that Your Majesty will respect the rights, dignity, honour and religion of Indian princes as your own. Not that the assurance was needed for my own satisfaction for I had ever confidence in the magnanimity of England's Queen who, as the ruler of almighty a nation, had feelings of generosity towards her protected princes.

"I desire to offer my congratulations on the crushing of the head of the great rebellion, which has swept like a vengeful *avatar* over this land. I had no doubt myself of the end that has been accomplished no entirely is accordance with my hopes and prayers. It was equally a gratification to me, as it seemed also a duty, to reassure in that dark hour of danger, many of my brother sovereign who, when cut-off from the accustomed support of British troops, applied me for counsel, and I reminded of the benefits we had all experienced under British protection. I advised all to stand firm with me in our loyalty to Your Majesty's throne and royal person. All of these have shown their fidelity accordingly standing steadfast through all difficulties. But to a few only it was given what fell my good fortune, to be able to show by unalterable attachment to the British *Raj* by extending my humble aid and protection to the British refuges when they were betrayed by the rebellious soldiery stationed within my territories.

"That the auspicious change in the Government now inaugurated may prove to India, still smouldering from the recent configuration, like rain from heaven at once quenching the fire and renovating the soil, that the consciousness of the benefits Your Majesty will have extended to millions by that act, may increase the happiness of your own heart, and reflected, create an additional source of gladness and guardian interest throughout your Royal Family, in the earnest hope and prayer of Your Majesty's faithful and most devoted servant."[141]

Khillat to Maharana

Upon the inauguration of the new Government in India, the British Government made grants of lands, money and titles to various princes in appreciation of their services to her in the period of rebellion. The Maharana of Udaipur received a "*Khillat*" of the value of Rs. 20,000 from the British Government.[142] This reward by the British Government to the Maharana was regarded by the latter as inadequates compared to those received by other rulers, in view of the services he had rendered, for the British cause.[143] The hostile attitude of George Lawrence, the A.G.G., towards the Maharana and constant controversy between him and Captain Showers the Political Agent in Mewar over Udaipur affairs during that eventful period were largely responsible for it.

The Governor General acknowledged the services of Mehta Sher Singh, Gopaldas and Arjun Singh Sahiwala and left to the Maharana "the pleasing duty of rewarding these mortorious officers." Begun Chief Maha Singh got a reward of Rs. 2,000 for his services. A sword of honour was presented to him in the full *durbar* of the Maharana. A further reward of dress of honour of the value of Rs. 300 was given to Rangoo Rao of Dungla.[144]

Nimbahera taken back from the Maharana

As Nimbahera was one of the Mewar territories lost during the Maratha turmoil, the Maharana taking opportunity of his temporary possession of this place during the rebellion requested the British Government for its permanent restoration, pleading that the British Government had assumed under article 7 of the Treaty of 1818 to us its best exertions for the restoration of Udaipur places which had failed into other hands by improper means. The Maharana also pleaded that he might receive it in reward for the services, he rendered to the British. Captain Showers, the Political Agent had been given charge of Nimbahera to Mewar troops on 21st September, 1857, which continued for about two and a half years. Handing over of the entire possession of Nimbahera to Mewar authorities became a point of controversy among the British officers and the British Government disapproved of her Agent's action.[145] In one of his communications to the British Government the Maharana emphasised that Nimbahera was contiguous to Mewar territory of Chittor and the administration of two years by Mewar authorities had produced such peace and order in the area which was wanting under the Tonk administration.[146] The Maharana's request was not acceded to and he was informed that the possession of Nimbahera was given to Mewar only temporarily and the action did not mean the handing over of the district to the Maharana by dispossessing the Nawab of Tonk.[147]

The Maharana adopted an attitude of lingering and procrastinating the matter and the Mewar authorities at Nimbahera behaved as if they had acquired complete and permanent restoration of the place. Several times did the Political officers write to the Maharana to send accounts of income and expenditure of the district to the Government but nothing was done by the officers of the Maharana.[148] The Political Agent also complained that the arrangements at Nimbahera was quite inefficient and unsatisfactory, that the soldiers had not been paid for some time and the quantity of the ammunition was found insufficient.[149] Nawab of Tonk on the other hand was incessantly appealing to the British Government for the restoration of the district along with Rs. 5,50,000 on account of its revenue for the last two and a half years. The British Government finally ordered the Maharana to return Nimbahera to Tonk at once and withdraw his officers and soldiers, which was eventually done.[150]

Though the Maharana evacuated Nimbahera, the reluctance on his part to pay the money on account of revenue continued for some time. When Maharana Swaroop Singh adopted Shambhu Singh as his heir, Major Taylor, the Political Agent, advised the British Government to refuse to recognise the adoption until the dues on account of Nimbahera revenue had been paid, which was, however, not approved of by the Governor General.[151] The amount was, at last, paid by the Maharana after much procrastination and evasion.

Recalcitrant Chiefs of Mewar

It is clear from the foregoing pages that some of the prominent Chiefs of Mewar actively defied the orders of, and acted against the interests and safety of the British Government. One thing is undoubtedly clear that for long some of the Chiefs of Mewar as of Salumbar, Bheender, Kotharia etc., had been at daggers drawn with their ruler, Maharana Swaroop Singh. As the Maharana actively took side of the British Government, these Chiefs in their zeal to bend him, found their position in the opposite camp, which was no doubt utilised by the rebels. They likewise had happened in the Jodhpur State too.

The hopes were roused by the rebels in these Chiefs that the rule of the British would be overthrown, and the Mughal Emperor Bahadur Shah would again come to power, following which all the grievances of the Chiefs would be favourably looked into and settled. Consequently, though many other Chiefs of Mewar actively obeyed the orders of their sovereign to help the British cause, these Chiefs helped the rebels whenever they passed through their estates. It is said that on the occasion of the General Lawrence's attack on Auwa, the troops of Mewar Chiefs as Salumbar, Roopnagar, Lasani, etc. were fighting on the side of Auwa Chief and the rebels.[152] Tantia Tope and his troops had stayed at Salumbar in December, 1858, and took supplies. That occasion was tried to be exploited by the Chief in extorting from the Maharana the fulfilment of his demands.

An intercepted correspondence is found in the records between the Chief of Auwa and Salumbar as well as between their officers, which shows that they were planning in October, 1857 in alliance with the rebels of Jodhpur Legion to instigate all the Chiefs to rebellion and bring about 25,000 troops from Delhi for their help, and that Khushal Singh, Chief of Auwa was moving with his troops to Salumbar to make junction with the troops of Salumbar and other defiant Chiefs.[153] In the same way a letter from Nawab Rahmat Ali Khan to Salumbar Chief was intercepted, in which he asked the Chief to join him promising that "in concert with you, measures may be adopted for the settlement of affairs in Mewar. Join us, Khushal Singh has already joined us."[154]

However, the Political Agent, remarking on the above letter, opined that it should not be taken at once as genuine, because the rebels were tactfully acting to incite the Government to act against the anti-Maharana nobles so that they might be forced to rise in rebellion.[155] Not only that the Political Officers of the British Government were of opinion that Maharana Swaroop Singh had his hand in spreading many of the false rumours and getting forged letters written concerning the activities of the Chiefs of Salumbar and Kotharia, so as to tempt the British Government to crush the defiant Chiefs. For long the rumours were in the air that Rao Saheb had taken refuge at Salumbar and the Maharana requested the British Government to help to drive the rebels out from the estate. In July 1859 the Political Agent Showers recommended that a brigade should march to punish the Chief for his indirect hostility. But Major Taylor after enquiring into the charges concluded that he could find no proof of Rao Saheb having entered the fort of Salumbar.[156] The British Government regarded as fabrication on the part of the Maharana, a letter assumed to have been written by Rao Saheb from Salumbar calling upon Holkar to attack Mhow, assuming him that they would reach Ujjain to join him with 50-60 thousand men.[157]

The other Chief of Mewar who actively helped the rebels was Jodh Singh of Kotharia. He is said to have given supplies to Tantia Tope before the battle at "Kala Gora ka Maidan". Rao Saheb and other rebel leaders were always seeking assistance from him. The rumours were generally taken as genuine that Rao Saheb had, for long, remained in hiding in the hills of Kotharia *Patta*.[158] Hearing the news that the Auwa Chief was at Kotharia, troops of the Jodhpur prince along with a British Cavalry reached Kotharia on the 8th June, 1858 to seize him, though they could not find him.[159] On the 21st April, 1859, Maharana's *Vakil* again wrote to the Political Agent that the family of Auwa chief was residing at Hamirgarh, and that the Chief himself was moving around the Kotharia *Patta* (estate). The Maharana also complained that Bhemji Charan, who participated in the plunder of the property of the British Officers at Gangapur, fled to Kotharia and despite the request of the British Officers he had not arrested him and the culprit was hiding there.[160]

The Political agent in his despatch to the A.G.G., however, expressed that the Maharana in asking for British troops to help to capture the Auwa Thakur had intention of punishing Kotharia Rao. "If we do hastily, the nature of the action will be such that all anti-Maharana disaffected nobles might join Kotharia Rao and a general rebellion might break out against the Government at such a critical time."[161]

Towards a New Awakening

The bold anti-British attitude, which Rawat Kesari Singh, the Chief of Salumbar, Rawat Jodh Singh, the Chief of Kotharia and others adopted during the period of rebellion created a deep impression on the freedom-loving people of Mewar specially on the martial races. We have seen that the pro-British attitude of the Maharana kept the National feeling of the people generally subdued during the revolt. There are instances of active sympathy of the local people for the cause of the rebels but they are very few. The people in general either remained passive or assisted the British cause on the orders of the Maharana. However, the events in Mewar during the time of the rebellion and the anti-British attitude of some of its nobles had far-reaching effects on the minds of the people. We see onwards a new resurgence, though slow, of the nationalistic feelings of the people in Mewar as in the other parts of Rajputana. Contemporary Rajasthani poets like Surajmal, Bankidas, Raghodas and others wrote highly of the activities of the nobles like Khushal Singh, Kesari Singh and Jodh Singh and depicted them as the national leaders fighting against the foreign Government.

It is true that the new anti-British nationalism, which surged in the mind of the people still based itself on the narrow medieval outlook, if we see it in the light of the nationalism, which was then developing in Europe and which had begun taking its shape in India as well. The poets and the people talked of the glorious and heroic traditions of the Rajput race and compared the degraded conditions of the contemporary Rajput rulers and the nobles with their heroic ancestors, thus rousing their feelings to unite and fight for freedom.

NOTES AND REFERENCES

1. *Expansion of England* by Sir J.R. Seeley, p. 221.
2. *Reminiscences of Forty Three Years in India* by George Lawrence, p. 278.
3. *Ibid.*, p. 279.
4. *Mutiny in Rajputana* by Prichard, pp. 39-40. Ajmer was, in fact,

saved by the sagacity of Col. Dixon, the Commissioner of the British district of Ajmer-Merwara, who, rightly fearing the fall of Ajmer at the hands of disaffected elements of the 15th Regiment, at once replaced its two Companies by Merwara battalion—an act destined to be of the highest consequence.

5. A chapter of the *Indian Mutiny* by Col. G.H. Trevor, p. 2.
6. *Ibid*, p. 168.
7. *Eighteen Fifty Seven* by S.N. Sen, p. 308.
8. A missing chapter of the *Indian Mutiny* by C.L. Showers, p. 11.
9. F.D., See, June, 26, 1857, No. 113-116. *Reminiscences of Forty Three Years in India* by George Lawrence, p. 279.
10. A chapter of the *Indian Mutiny* by Col. G.H. Trevor, p. 3.
11. F.D., See, June 26, 1857, No. 113-116. The Maharana of Mewar maintained a force of 263 guns, 1338 artillery men, 6240 Cavalry and 13900 infantry (Kaye and Malleson's *History of Indian Mutiny* Vol. VI, p. 155).
12. A missing chapter of the *Indian Mutiny* by C.L. Showers, p. 9.
13. A missing chapter of the *Indian Mutiny* by C.L. Showers, p. 184, about, for two years 1854-56, the Maharana was not allowed to dismiss Mehta Sher Singh from the post of Prime Minister of the State. In 1855 the Political Agent threatened the Maharana that he would get the orders of the British Government to take the Jahajpur paragana of Udaipur under its management on the pretext of 'Meena troubles' there (Sahiwala, *Arjune ka Jiwan Charitra*, pp. 50-52.)
14. Sahiwala, *Arjune ka Jiwan Charitra*, pp. 52-53.
15. *Udaipur Rajya ka Itihas* G.H. Ojha, Part II, pp. 765-766.
16. *Ibid.*, p. 752
17. *Ibid.*, pp. 9, 10.
18. *Ibid.*, pp. 10, 11.
19. *Ibid.*
20. *Ibid.*, p. 13.
21. *Ibid.*
22. *Ibid.*, p. 15.
23. *Rajputana Agency Records*, April 1860, No. 556-60.
24. A missing chapter of the *Indian Mutiny* by C.L. Showers, p. 13.
25. *Ibid.*, p. 13.
26. *Ibid.*, p. 17.
27. *Rajputana Agency Records*, April 1860, No. 556-60.
28. *Mutiny in Rajputana* by Prichard, p. 21.
29. *Ibid.*, p. 42.
30. *History of Indian Mutiny* by Malleson, Vol. III, p. 168.
31. *Mutiny in Rajputana* by Prichard, p. 42.
32. A Chapter of the *Indian Mutiny* by Col. G.H. Trevor, p. 5.

33. *Eighteen Fifty Seven* by S.N. Sen p. 312.
34. A missing chapter of the *Indian Mutiny* by C.L. Showers, p. 21.
35. Sahiwala, *Arjune Singh ka Jiwan Charitra*, p. 56.
36. *History of the Indian Mutiny* by Malleson, Vol. III, p. 171.
37. *Udaipur Rajya ka Itihas* by G.H. Ojha, p. 769.
38. Ibid.
39. A missing chapter of the *Indian Mutiny* by C.L. Showers, p. 20.
40. *Vir Vinod* by Shymaldas, p. 1956.
41. A missing chapter of the *Indian Mutiny* by C.L. Showers, pp. 23-24.
42. Ibid., p. 23.
43. Ibid., p. 189.
44. A missing chapter of the *Indian Mutiny* by C.L. Showers, p. 29.
45. Ibid., p. 30. Dr. Murray's letter to C.L. Showers.
46. Ibid., Sahiwala, *Arjune ka Jiwan Charitra*, p. 57.
47. C.L. Showers: Letter to the Maharana, Aug. 18, 1857 (Bhakshi Khana Udaipur), Sahiwala, *Arjune ka Jiwan Charitra*, p. 57.
48. A missing chapter of the *Indian Mutiny* by C.L. Showers, pp. 30-31.
49. Ibid.
50. A missing chapter of the *Indian Mutiny* by C.L. Showers, pp. 26-27.
51. Ibid.
52. *Udaipur Rajya ka Itihas*, G.H. Ojha, Part II, p. 769.
53. A missing chapter of the *Indian Mutiny* by C.L. Showers, p. 33.
54. Ibid.
55. Ibid., p. 39.
56. Ibid., p. 38.
57. Ibid., p. 42.
58. Notes of Muni Dhanraj, *Shodh Patrika*, Vol. XIV issue, pp. 157-58.
59. Ibid.
60. A missing chapter of the *Indian Mutiny* by C.L. Showers, p. 41.
61. C.L. Showers to Maharana, June 30, 1857 (Bakshi Khan Udaipur).
62. *Vir Vinod* by Shymal Das, p. 1967.
63. F.D., *Pol*, April 1860, No. 607-652.
64. C.L. Showers to Maharana, July 13, 1857 (Bakshi Khan Udaipur).
65. A missing chapter of the *Indian Mutiny* by C.L. Showers, p. 85. *Reminiscences of Forty Three Years in India* by George Lawrence, p. 286.
66. C.L. Showers to Maharana, July 5, 1857 (Bakshi Khan Udaipur).
67. *Udaipur Rajya ka Itihas* by G.H. Ojha, Part II, p. 770, Sahiwala, *Arjune Singh ka Jiwan Charitra*, p. 59. Showers is wrong in telling Arjun Singh Sahiwala a Brahmin. He was a Kayasth.
68. A missing chapter of the *Indian Mutiny* by C.L. Showers, p. 67.
69. Ibid.
70. C.L. Showers to Kesari Singh, July 12, 1957. (Bakshi Khan Udaipur).

71. A missing chapter of the *Indian Mutiny* by C.L. Showers, p. 67; *History of Indian Mutiny* by Malleson, Vol. IV, p. 388.
72. *Ibid.*
73. A missing chapter of the *Indian Mutiny* by C.L. Showers, p. 108.
74. *Ibid.*, See., Nov. 27, 1857, No. 249-51.
75. *Ibid.*
76. *History of Indian Mutiny* by Malleson, Vol. IV, pp. 398-399.
77. *Ibid.*
78. A missing chapter of the *Indian Mutiny* by C.L. Showers, p. 216.
79. Notes of Muni Dhanraj, *Shodh Patrika*, Vol. XIV, p. 158.
80. A missing chapter of the *Indian Mutiny* by C.L. Showers, p. 216.
81. *History of Indian Mutiny* by Malleson, Vol. IV, p. 397.
82. *Marwar ka Itihas* by Bisheshwar Nath Reu, Part II, p. 452.
83. *Vir Vinod* by Shymal Das, pp. 1991-2.
84. *Ibid.*
85. *Rajasthan's Role in the Struggle of 1857* by H.K. Khadgawat, pp. 46-48.
86. *History of Indian Mutiny* by Malleson, Vol. IV, p. 399.
87. *Ibid.*
88. *Rajputana Agency Records*, April, 1860, No. 556-60.
89. *Ibid.*
90. *Ibid.*
91. *Ibid.*
92. *History of Indian Mutiny* by Malleson, Vol. IV, p. 403.
93. *Eighteen Fifty Seven* by S.N. Sen, p. 311.
94. A missing chapter of the *Indian Mutiny* by C.L. Showers, p. 93.
95. *Eighteen Fifty Seven* by S.N. Sen, p. 311.
96. A missing chapter of the *Indian Mutiny* by C.L. Showers, p. 97.
97. *Ibid.*
98. *Ibid.*, Sahiwala, *Arjune Singh ka Jiwan Charitra*, p. 59.
99. C.L. Showers to Maharana, Sept. 17, 1857 (Bakshi Khana Udaipur), Sahiwala, *Arjune Singh ka Jiwan Charitra*, pp. 59-61.
100. A missing chapter of the *Indian Mutiny* by C.L. Showers, p. 102.
101. *Ibid.*, p. 62. It appears that Rajput Chiefs were offered allurement of getting villages in *jagir* in the district of Nimbahera for their military assistance with the belief that Nimbahera would be returned to Mewar at this juncture, which the Mewar Durbar had been demanding since 1818.
102. Sahiwala, *Arjune Singh ka Jiwan Chritra*, p. 63.
103. A missing chapter of the *Indian Mutiny* by C.L. Showers, p. 63.
104. *Ibid.*, p. 119. Ten thousand according to Sahiwala, *Arjune Singh ka Jiwan Charitra*, p. 64.
105. *Ibid.*
106. Sahiwala, *Arjune Singh ka Jiwan Charitra*, p. 65.

107. A missing chapter of the *Indian Mutiny* by C.L. Showers, p. 128.
108. Sahiwala, *Arjune Singh ka Jiwan Charitra*, p. 65.
109. A missing chapter of the *Indian Mutiny* by C.L. Showers, p. 133.
110. Captain Annesley to Maharana Swaroop Singh, Jan. 8, 1859 (Bakshi Khana Udaipur).
111. Report of the Political Agent in Haroti, March 15, 1860. (Bakshi Khana Udaipur).
112. *Vir Vinod* by Shymal Das, p. 1977.
113. *Ibid.*, pp. 1976, 1977.
114. *Rajputana Agency Records* (*Mutiny*) 1859, No. 32.
115. *Vir Vinod* by Shymal Das, p. 1977.
116. *Ibid.*
117. *Ibid.*
118. *Ibid.*
119. *Reminiscences of Forty Three Years in India* by George Lawrence, p. 30.
120. *Rajputana Agency Records* (*Mutiny*) 1859, No. 32.
121. *A Chapter of Indian Mutinty* by G.H. Trevor, p. 15.
122. *Eighteen Fifty Seven*, S.N. Sen, p. 372.
123. *Vir Vinod* by Shymal Das, p. 1978.
124. *Ibid.*
125. A missing chapter of the *Indian Mutiny* by C.L. Showers, p. 138.
126. *Ibid.*, p. 138.
127. *Ibid.*
128. *Ibid.*
129. *Vir Vinod* by Shymal Das, p. 1978.
    A missing chapter of the *Indian Mutiny* by C.L. Showers, p. 199.
130. A missing chapter of the *Indian Mutiny* by C.L. Showers, pp. 140-41. Malleson gives different version "Bhils far from binding Tantia followed his tract as the vulture follows the wounded hare (*History of Indian Mutiny*, V.)
131. A missing chapter of the *Indian Mutiny* by C.L. Showers, p. 1978.
132. C.L. Showers to Maharana Swaroop Singh, March 29, 1859, (Bakshi Khana Udaipur).
133. *Ibid.*
134. Entries in the Daily Accounts Register of Kankroli Thikana of Mewar show that the rebels offered presents in money to the Vaishnawa deity of Dwarkanath at Kankroli and that the Thikana had to provide supplies of grass, wood, etc. for the British troops (*Kankroli ka Itihas* by Kanthamani Shastri, Part II, p. 13).
135. A missing chapter of the *Indian Mutiny* by C.L. Showers, p. 144.
136. *Ibid.*
137. *Eighteen Fifty Seven* by S.N. Sen, pp. 374-375.
138. A missing chapter of the *Indian Mutiny* by C.L. Showers, p. 147.

139. *History of Indian Mutiny* by Malleson, Vol. V, pp. 275-276.
140. *Ibid.,* p. 277.
141. A missing chapter of the *Indian Mutiny* by C.L. Showers, pp. 158-160.
142. F.D., *Pol.,* April, 1860, No. 607-52.
143. *Udaipur Rajya ka Itihas* by G.H. Ojha, Part II, p. 776.
144. F.D., *Pol.,* April, 1860, No. 607-52.
145. W.F. Eden to Maharana Swaroop Singh, March 27, 1860 (Bakshi Khana Udaipur.)
146. Swaroop Singh to C.L. Showers, Nov. 6, 1859 (Bakshi Khana Udaipur.)
147. W.F. Eden to Maharana Swaroop Singh, March 27, 1850 (Bakshi Khana Udaipur).
148. C.L. Showers to Maharana Swaroop Singh, July 25, Oct. 1858 and Nov. 6, 1859.
149. C.L. Showers to Maharana Swaroop Singh, July 25, 1858 and Nov. 6,1859.
150. *Rajputana Agency Records,* Nov. 20, 1861, No. 85.
151. *Ibid.*
152. *Rajasthan's Role in the Struggle of 1857* by R.R. Khadgawat, p. 50.
153. *Rajputana Agency Record* (Mewar) 1837, No. 81; *Rajasthan's Role in the struggle of 1857-97* by N.X. Khadgawat, pp. 15-92-160.
154. *Ibid.*
155. *Ibid.*
156. *Ibid.*
157. *Ibid.*
158. *Ibid.,* Rao Saheb's letter to Jodh Singh, dt. V.S. 1916 (A.D. 1859) Pos. Vid. 9.
159. *Ibid.*
160. *Ibid.,* Several contemporary couplets in Dingal language describing Jodh Singh's bestowal of shelter to Khushal Singh are still memorised by Charans and others.
161. *Ibid.*

9

Resistance to the British

The transfer of power from the East India to the British Crown in 1858 commenced a new Chapter in the Indian History, especially with regard to the British relations with the Native States of India. The policy of "expanding absorption of the decaying Native State into British territory under any pretext" was abandoned and the Queen's Proclamation guaranteed the rulers of the Native State their rights, dignity and honour. To remove further the cause of distrust, the British Government granted 'Adoption Sanads' to the rulers, by which a solemn assurance was given to them by the Queen that they would continue to enjoy heredity rights perpetually ever their ancient possessions, and that, on failure of natural heirs, they would have the right to adopt successors according to the Hindu Law and the customs of their races.[1]

The above change of policy was largely the result of the Indian Rebellion of 1857. Already in the years just before the revolt Sir Willion Sleeman had put forward the view that the Indian State should be regarded as "break-waters," since "when they are all swept away, we shall be left to the mercy of the native army, which may not always be sufficiently under our control."[2] The warning had come out true. Another lesson was learnt by the British Government that the feudal forces in India no longer presented the main potential threat to the British rule. They foresaw a new potential danger in the awakening of the

Indian masses, which was rapidly taking place under the leadership of the educated classes in India. Hence the policy was consciously adopted of building more and more decisively on the feudal elements, on the preservation of the Princes, as the bulwark of the British rule.[3]

The object of the new policy was rightly described by Lord Canning, the Governor General of India in these words: "It was long ago said by Sir John Malcolm that if we made all India into Zillas (or British Districts) it was not in the nature of things that our Empire should last fifty years; but if we could keep a number of Native States without political power, but as royal instruments, we should exist in India as long as our naval supremacy was maintained.[4]

The new policy had its inevitable consequences. We see that the Native States were preserved, but they were internally so weakened and emasculated that no semblance of real power was left with the rulers. The interference of the Agents of the paramount power in the internal administration of the States became obdurate and instead of acting in the character of ambassadors, they assumed the functions of the Dictators, interfering in all their concerns, private or public.

However the British authorities acted, as before, very shrewdly in every State to attain their purpose. As we have stated above, the State of Udaipur was still living in medieval conditions and several in human practices and customs were in vogue. They declared that it was highly necessary on the part of the State Government to improve the conditions of the people and introduce reforms in the State. They interfered with the right of the royal family to select its successors, favoured the "minority" Governments and appointed Regency Councils of their own choice. They, in the name of internal reforms, imposed their orders on the State Government or refused to approve of any decision or measure of the latter which they disliked. The Political Agent, as we would see in the ensuing pages, became so powerful and audacious that he began listening to the complaints of the people against their ruler or the Chiefs. Several times he interfered with the private life of the ruler, dismissed or expelled his counsellors and favourites and directed him to act on his instructions and advice. No doubt this State of affairs proved much helpful to the British Government, whenever any question of Imperial interest relating to the State of Udaipur arose. When the proposals in connection with the salt manufacture, opium trade, opening of the railway line, extradition treaty, etc. were put forth by the British Government for the acceptance of the ruler, the latter could never dare to refuse, though he found them largely against the interests of his State and the people.

The credit of introducing the reforms in the State goes to the efforts made by the British Agents from time to time. However, in the fairness of the things, it must be said that once the initiative of the ruler of State was crushed, it could hardly be expected from him that he would show his zeal and inclination towards the progress of the State. On the other hand, chafing under the dictatorship of the Agent, be generally fell prey to the forces of reaction and conservation. Hence it was inevitable that the resistance came forth from the ruler, nobility and people of the State to the introduction of the direct Government in the State by the British and violation of the internal sovereignty of the Maharana.

Accession of Rana Shambhu Singh

On the 16th November, 1861, Maharana Swaroop Singh breathed his last. He was succeeded by his adopted son Sambhu Singh at the age of 14 years. Just a month before his death the last ruler had adopted Shambhu Singh, who was the grand-son of Swaroop Singh's elder brother Maharaj Sher Singh and son of Maharaj Shardul Singh of Bagore. Some Chiefs belonging to the Salumbar party; *e.g.*, the Chief of Kurawar, Amet, Bijollia, Basee, etc. raised objection to the Maharana's choice and demanded postponement of the decision until Rawat Kesari Singh, the premier Choondavat Chief of Salumbar agreed to it. However, the Maharana rejected their pleas and announced his decision. Consequently most of the Chiefs paid homage to the Crown Prince.[5] The Maharana's decision was approved of by the British Government.[6]

It had been customary in Udaipur that as soon as a ruler died, his successor should accede to the throne instantly as the throne was never kept vacant. In Mewar there was no interregnum. "The king is dead, long live the king" was the usual tradition. The would-be ruler did not follow the funeral procession, but ascended the throne while the funeral ceremony was still in process. All mourning was to be performed at the house of *Purohit*. At this moment the party of nobles, opposed to the succession of Shambhu Singh, tried to delay his installation. But Rao Bakhta Singh of Bedla along with some other nobles backed by the Political Agent acted with firmness and promptitude, and seated Shambhu Singh on the throne and paid him homage, which led other Chiefs to follow suit.[7] George Lawrence, the A.G.G. in Rajputana and Major Taylor, the Political Agent in Mewar reached Udaipur on the 21st December, 1861. Neemuch movable column was also despatched to Udaipur to give eclat to the installation ceremony.[8] On the 26th December, a grand assemblage was held which was attended by the majority of the Chiefs of Mewar. The Chiefs of Salumbar, Bijollia, Kurawar, Asind and Amet did not attend it.[9] In the *durbar* the A.G.G. presented *khillat* to the Maharana on behalf of the British Govt. Speaking on the occasion, George Lawrence said: "This is a most auspicious day for your country. For many years Mewar has never seen so many Chiefs assembled to meet their king." He asked them to forget the past, as there had been errors on both sides, pay their tribute regularly and render becoming services to their sovereign. Lawrence further stated that it had not been the policy of the British Government to interfere between *Rajas* and their subjects, except to ensure the safety of those enjoying guarantee, which would be held. At the end he expressed his hope that the differences between the Maharana and his Chiefs would be resolved soon.[10]

On the 27th December the Governor-General of India sent a message to the new ruler expressing condolence at the death of the late ruler. He further stated in his letter, "You have succeeded to the '*gadee*' at a very early age, when you perhaps cannot fully realise the responsibility of power. I enjoin you to rule justly in the sight of God and be guided by the friendly counsel of the Political Agent."[11]

Sati Affair on the Death of Maharana Swaroop Singh

For long there had been the tradition of *Sati* in the Sisodia House of Mewar. When a Maharana died, his wives and even concubines immolated themselves as *Satis* by burning themselves along with the dead body in the funeral pyre. It is recorded that as many as four wives and four concubines committed *Sati*, when Maharana Bhim Singh II died, three wives and six concubines immolated on the death of Jawan Singh, and one concubine immolated on the death of Sardar Singh.[12] It was considered dishonourable, if the dead Chief was burnt alone.

When Maharana Swaroop Singh breathed his last, Khuman Singh, the Chief of Asind estate personally intimated the inmates of *'Rawla'* (Royal palace) about the death and requested their intention.[13] No response seems to have come from the *Maharanis*. Thereupon Gopaldas, a favourite courtier of the late ruler encouraged a slave girl to commit herself *Sati*.[14] Gopaldas happened to be her close relative. Gopaldas himself walked by the side of her palanquin in the funeral procession. *Pradhan* Kesari Singh, was also present when this act of immolation took place.[15] British Government took a grave view of this happening. The late ruler had been persuaded by the British Government to proclaim the rite of *Sati* as inhuman and illegal and to make efforts to stop its performance in the State. Now the act of immolation had taken place in the royal house itself. Gopaldas was at once put under surveillance by the order of the British Government, and, expelled from Udaipur.[16] The council of Regency afterwards ordered confiscation of his two villages, and further, he was forbidden to return to Udaipur during the minority period of the Maharana. The Thakur of Asind was also forbidden from entering Udaipur for the same period and was excluded from the council of Regency. *Pradhan* Kothari Kesari Singh was ordered to be dismissed and exiled for the same period. He was, however, reappointed in April, 1862, as no other capable man was available in the State to carry on the administration of the State.[17]

Appointment of the Council of Regency

As the new Maharana was a minor of 14 years at the time of his accession, the British Government decided to appoint a council of Regency to govern the State during the minority of Maharana Shambhu Singh. The Governor General of India issued orders to this effect.[18] Col. George Lawrence in consultation with prominent Chiefs and officers of the State appointed a council of Regency under the presidentship of the Political Agent, Major Taylor.[19] The council included Rao Bakhta Singh of

Bedla. Rawat Ranjeet Singh of Deogarh, Maharaja Hameer Singh of Bheender, Rawat Amar Singh of Bhensrorgarh and Rao Lal Singh of Gogunda. Mehta Sher Singh, Kothari Kesari Singh and *Purohit* Shyamnath were appointed as the executive officers in the council.[20]

Much interest was taken by the Salumbar Party of Chiefs for the appointment of the Asind Thakur, but as the chief failed to attend the installation ceremony and as he took part in the *sati* affair on the death of the late Maharana, he was excluded from the council. Two of the councillors, the Maharaj of Bheender and the Rao of Gogunda also had been previously refractory, but since the death of the late Maharana, these nobles had assumed a conciliatory attitude. George Lawrence, the A.G.G. thought it just and wise to encourage this feeling by giving them share in the temporary Government.[21]

The council of Regency began working under the presidentship of the Political Agent, Major Taylor. At the outset the councillors submitted a memorandum to the British Government by which they requested the latter to furnish them with a document protecting them against oppression thereafter of the Maharana, when he became Major, for acts which they performed in their official capacity. The British Government granted the same, however, with the condition that it would be limited to the acts done with the cognisance and approval of the Political Agent and the council of Regency.[22]

Regarding the remuneration to the members of the council, it was first proposed to exempt them from their personal services to the Maharana and remit half their tribute during their tenure of office. But as the tribute of individual members differed in amount and the members preferred to be paid all alike in money, the Government sanctioned the sum of Rs. 45,000 per year to be paid collectively to the members while in office, *i.e.* Rs. 25 daily to each member.[23]

The council fixed a daily allowance of Rs. 1000 for the Maharana. Pandit Ratneshwar was appointed as his preceptor.[24] The first measure of reform in the State was taken with the council sanctioning for building of a Varnacular School in the city at an outlay of Rs. 12,000.[24]

The Government of Regency council worked for about one and a half year. From the very outset the members tried to make it an instrument to gain their selfish ends. They began using their authority to crush their antagonists in the State. Rawat of Deogarh got the amount of *chhatound* payable by him for his estate, reduced from Rs. 99,661 to Rs. 38,366. He took back from the State treasury the amount of Rs. 25,000 which the late Maharana had charged from him for *Talwar Bandai* (Sword binding ceremony) and got this levy exempted for ever. He got back all the villages, which the late ruler had confiscated on account of his failure to pay the tribute and render his services to him.[25] In the same way the other Chiefs also reopened the cases of lands previously confiscated for their grave offences.[26]

Commenting on the above affair, the Governor-General expressed his view that no good would come from reopening the cases of the Chiefs of Deogarh, Bhensrorgarh, Kannore, etc.[27] However, he approved of the above settlement regarding Deogarh, keeping in view the recommendation of the Political Agent[28] that the example of loyalty and respect to his Government by this principal Chief of the State would have a salutary effect on others.[29] The executive officers of the Council also did not lag behind the Chiefs in misusing their authority and misappropriating the State money. Mehta Sher Singh's son Sawai Singh withdraw Rs. 3 lakh from the State treasury, which had been exacted by the preceding Maharana as a fine from his father.[30] The young Maharana himself was working under vicious influences. *Purohit* Surendranath became his chief favourite and began issuing orders in his name. At times orders were issued from the *zanana* also. Thus the work of the State Government soon found itself in the State of chaos and confusion.[31]

On the 20th April, 1862 Lieut. Col. Eden took charge of the office of the Political Agent in Mewar, replacing Major Taylor.[32] A definite change set in with Eden's taking charge of the presidentship of the Regency council. From the very beginning Lieut. Col. Eden decided to pursue a policy of vigorous interference in the internal affairs of the State in order to improve the work of the council, check the corrupt practices of its members and officials and to bring the young Maharana out of the influence of the vicious characters. Eden's active interference, consequently, resulted in a struggle between the members of the Regency Council and others opposed to foreign interference in the State on the one hand and the Political Agent and his supporters on the other.

Measures to Suppress the *Sati* Custom

In the year 1862, several cases of *Sati* were detected by the British Government, which took place at various places in the territory of Udaipur State *e.g.* at Bhadesar in March, at Bhensrorgarh and Bheender in April and at Khairalia in September. In the first case the Rani of the deceased Chief of Bhadesar was immolated. To apprehend the offenders, troops were sent from Udaipur, withholding temporarily the sword-binding ceremony on the succession of the young Chief. Two persons, Feiza and Kripashankar *Purohit* were arrested for the complicity in the happening and were sentenced to one year's simple imprisonment by the Regency Council, which punishment was regarded, by the British Government as inadequate.[33]

The second event took place at Bhensrorgarh on the 5th April, 1862 where the wife of a *Kamdar* committed *Sati* on her husband's death, Rawat Amar Singh, the member of the Council of Regency was present in the village at the time of the occurrence. The Political Agent took a serious view of this happening. Rawat Amar Singh was forthwith removed from the membership of the Council and was forbidden to enter into the capital until further orders. The Chief culprit Ram Gopal was sentenced to one year's imprisonment and a fine of Rs. 1,000 was imposed on him. At Bheender, a woman of low caste committed *sati* on the 17th April, 1862, two months after the death of her husband. Maharaj Hameer Singh, the Chief of the estate and the member of the Regency Council was not present in the village at the time of its occurrence. However, the Governor-General conveyed his resentment to Maharaja Hameer Singh for the happening and his inability to prevent it. The abettors were sentenced to imprisonment.

In case of a *Sati* at Kharalia under Banera *Jagir*, which occurred on the 24th September, 1862 on the death of a Bhumia, Regency Council had to send a '*Dhonsa*' or a threatening party of 5 horsemen and 17 soldiers on the expense of the Banera Chief to apprehend the culprits, and a fine of Rs. 500 was imposed on the whole village.[34]

On the 26th April, 1862 the Council of Regency issued a proclamation regarding the prohibition of *Sati*. It said: "Be it known to all Chiefs, *Sardars, Jagirdars,* the ministers of the Crown, Bhumias, *Patels, Patwaries* and whole population that a proclamation for prohibition of *Sati* was twice issued by the late Rana Swaroop Singh, but as yet the practice has not been arrested. Now for the third time orders are issued to the effect that whenever any person is found ready or desirous to sacrifice herself, the Chief of the village or his agent will be responsible to prevent the consumation of the crime, exercising his proper authority. He who neglects his responsibility will be fined and imprisoned."

Maharana's Attendants and Relations Expelled from Udaipur

Some complaints were made to the British Government regarding the private life of the young Maharana, some parasitical persons surrounded young Shambhu Singh during his minority and certain events of very disgraceful nature occurred at the Udaipur place. These individuals and personal attendants encouraged the Rana to lead a licentious course of life. As soon as Lieut. Col. Eden reached Udaipur, he called on the young Maharana and pointed out to him the "folly of his Act" and "great impropriety of his behaviour." The Rana at once submitted and promised to follow the advice of the Political Agent. The objectionable individuals were dismissed and expelled from the city, who included the mother and the uncle of the Rana himself, and *Purohit* Surendernath, Saroopnath and Ratan Lal. The Council of Regency was asked by the British Government to take care that the young Maharana was kept aloof from the undesirable persons.[35]

Direct Interference in the Internal Affairs

The above action of the Political Agent was resented by the people in the State as such interference was a great derogation of the Rana's authority. Some other events of the high handedness on the part of the Political Agent occurred, which enhanced the resentment in the people. Before his death, the late Maharana was said to have been given some lakhs of rupees for religious and charity purposes to the concubine who afterwards committed *Sati*. That money went into the hands of her mother. When the Political Agent came to learn about it, he, despite opposition from some sections, forced out the money from her, and spent it on the maintenance of dispensary and school at Udaipur.[36]

In July, 1862, Lieut. Col. Eden got the resignation of the *Raj* of Gogunda from the membership of the Regency Council. The Political Agent represented to the British Government that he, besides being old, nearly blind and feeble, was obstinate enough to obstruct the transaction of the public business and belonged to the Salumbar party. His resignation was approved of by the British Government.[37]

On the 28th April, 1863 Eden informed the British Government that he had been compelled to suspend the Maharaja of Bheender from the membership of the Regency Council on account of his persistent disregard of the interests of the State and his devotion to those of his family and friends and recommended that Raj Behari Lal of Delwara might be appointed in his place. The G.O.I. approved of the recommendation of the Political Agent. Maharaj Hameer Singh of Bheender was the leader of the party in the Council who opposed the assumption of direct control of Mewar Government by the Political Agent.

Thakur of Badnore Sentenced

At the end of 1862, the Deputy Commissioner of Ajmer called the attention of the Political Agent in Mewar to the inhuman act of the Thakur of Badnore in having cut-off the arm and leg of a Bhil of Ajmer for cattle-stealing. The Political Agent sent the paper to the Regency Council calling their attention to the case. The Council, on its part, replied that it had always been the practice in Mewar to mutilate the robbers. As the hills were full of Bhils, Meenas, Mers and other wild tribes who were used to indulging in robbery, the mere punishment of fine was not a sufficient check on them. The Political Agent rejected the Council's observation and remarked that it should not take into consideration the old usage, as the crime of mutilating of a human being was a very grave one and it was highly desirable and absolutely necessary that the offending persons in the case in question were severely punished by the Council to prevent similar occurrences in future. He further suggested that a proclamation be issued by the Council forbidding such cruel and inhuman practices.[38]

Thereupon the Regency Council revised its view. It fined the Rao of Badnore by Rs. 1,000 and he was bound to pay Rs. 5 per month to the incapacitated Bhil for his subsistence for his life time.[39] This punishment meted out to a noble of the State for his action in his own estate had no precedent and was against the traditional law of the State and was greatly resented in Mewar as derogatory for the dignity and status of a noble.

Dismissal of Kothari Kesari Singh

As we have mentioned earlier, Kothari Kesari Singh was re-employed in April, 1862.[40] However, the designation of the *Pradhan* (Prime Minister) was not restored to him. The following year grave charges of peculation of State money were made against him. He was placed under surveillance and investigations were started into the charges made against him. A case of embezzlement was made out against him as a difference of about Rs. 200,000 was found in the State accounts.[41] Kesari Singh, on his part, tried to defend himself on the plea that it was an ancient custom in the State to allow the minister to reap profit.[42] However, there was lack of unanimity in the Regency Council in making the various acts of embezzlement, the subject of formal and specific charges against him. The British Government chided members who evinced sympathy with the delinquent minister and commended the efforts of the Political Agent, Rao of Deogarh, Mehta Sher Singh, Ramnath *Vakil* and Lachhman Rao Sharistadar for exposing the gross misconduct of Kothari Kesari Singh. The latter was immediately dismissed and expelled from Udaipur with the order that he should never be re-employed by the State.[43] It was, however, argued by the rival party that Kothari Kesari Singh was mainly the target of ultra zeal of the Political Agent Lieut Col. Eden in his efforts to break the official party which surrounded the young Maharana.[44]

British Government Approved Eden's Policy

At this stage there developed a disagreement on various issues between the Political Agent in Mewar and the Agent to the Governor-General in Rajputana.

The harsh attitude adopted by the Political Agent Lieut. Col. Eden in the administrative affairs of the State antagonised a large number of the nobles, the officials of the State, and the members of the Regency Council who began complaining to George Lawrence, the A.G.G. against the high handedness and ultra zeal of the Political Agent.[45] Their main complaint was that Eden was interfering with their precious hereditary rights and usages and undermining the prestige of the ruler and the nobility of the State. The A.G.G. took notice of the direct petitions being submitted to him against the Political Agent. Consequently, various rumours gained currency and confusion and commotion spread in Udaipur. In the beginning of 1863 the A.G.G. reported to the Government of India that Dr. Ogilvy, the Agency Surgeon was giving advice to the Rao of Bedla and other persons on political matters with the sanction of the Political Agent, which was not desirable. The British Government, thereupon, asked the Political Agent not to act in a way which helped to develop the anti-British sentiments in the State.[46]

Various other complaints were made against Lieut. Col. Eden on behalf of the Maharana. Eden had refused to receive the Maharana unless the latter took off his shoes on entering his room, which was regarded as a disgrace to the ruler.[47] Eden arrived upto the royal stables mounted on the elephant which was considered as an usual precedent.[48] The Political Agent had got employed in the State service several foreign officials such as Pundit Lachhman Rao, Govind Rao, Maulvi Nizammuddin Khan and others, against the wishes of the Rana and the council. And lastly that the Political Agent had got Rana's favourites expelled from Udaipur unjustly.[49]

In the course of June, 1863 George Lawrence sent a series of letters to the British Government representing that the affairs in Udaipur had come to a deadlock. He attributed this to the failure to the Political Agent Lieut. Col. Eden to work well with the Regency Council and recommended the transfer of that officer and the dismissal of the Maharana's tutor, of Sharishtadar Lachhman Rao and of all other foreign officials who were employed by Lieut. Col. Eden in the State administration. Lieut. Col. Eden, however, on his part attributed the deadlock in the administration of the State and the contumacy of the Regency Council to the A.G.G.'s practice of listening to and taking action on the reports carried to him directly by the intriguers at Udaipur.[50]

The Government of India on receiving these papers decided

on the 28th July, 1863 that the charges made against Lieut. Col. Eden were frivolous and vexatious.[51] It expressed its surprise and disapproved of the A.G.G.'s practice of receiving direct communications from the people at Udaipur. The Government approved Lieut. Col. Eden's proceeding and remarked that, in expressing an opinion in favour of managing a native State through the people of the country, it had not, of course, intended to cramp the improvement of native administration. It also expressed regret on the fact that the selection of the members of the Regency Council by George Lawrence and Major Taylor had been very unfortunate at the contumacious Chief like those of Gogunda and Bheender had been included in it. In the end, Government of India instructed the Political Agent to submit his proposals regarding the re-organisation of the administration of the State.[52]

Mehta Ajeet Singh's Case

Hardly had the Government of India issued the above orders when it received a despatch dated the 20th July, 1863 from the A.G.G. in Rajputana reporting that one official Mehta Ajeet Singh, the adopted son of Mehta Sher Singh, the member of Regency Council in Mewar, had committed barbarous atrocities over the people in the Pur district of Mewar. Ajeet Singh was working as the Hakim of that district, having been charged with the duty of taking measures for the suppression of dacoity and highway robbery.[53]

The Pur district had always been a source of trouble for the people and the State, being inhabited by the tribes who indulged in highway robberies and other lawless activities. Mehta Ajeet Singh apprehended some persons who were charged with murder, robbery mutilation and cow-killing.[54] The *Hakim* ordered one of the offenders, Gomla Naik, to be tied to the leg of an elephant and dragged through the streets of the village. He then ordered him to be buried alive with his head above the ground in which state the man survived for two days. Another man, Kripa Naik's teeth were extracted by his order, who also died four days after the tortures, to which he was subjected.[55]

When this news reached the Political Agent at Udaipur, he at once asked the Regency Council to enquire into the matter and take necessary measures. The latter did nothing except delaying the enquiry. The Political Agent Lieut. Col. Eden sent a full report of the happening and the obstructive attitude of the Regency Council in the matter to the British Government. The Political Agent clearly told the Council that capital sentences could not be carried out without the report to and the sanction from the Supreme Government.[56] He ordered the head of the Criminal Court to go with some other persons to Pur to enquire into the affair and summoned Ajeet Singh to Udaipur. Ajeet Singh was ordered to be kept at Udaipur under heavy security pending enquiry. But on the 26th July, 1863 he escaped towards the hills from the house of Mehta Sher Singh, where he had been detained by the Council with the complicity of the young Maharana and some of his favourites. Mehta Sher Singh was forthwith dismissed from the Council and ordered to leave Udaipur. On the 27th July some members of the Regency Council who included Chiefs of Bedla and Deogarh, coming to know that the British Government was contemplating to take action against the members of the Regency Council, pleaded non-guilty in regard to Ajeet Singh's escape.[57]

Dismissal of Regency Council

The Political Agent's reports regarding Ajeet Singh's case set the British Government thinking seriously over the Udaipur affairs. The Governor-General issued a proclamation on the 14th August, 1863 declaring that instance in which the Council of Regency at Udaipur had failed to administer justice, criminal and civil, had been brought to the notice of the Supreme Government.[58] The Governor-General, therefore, deemed it necessary to confer on the Political Agent the full powers of a Sessions Judge in criminal cases, of a Superintendent of Police and the Commissioner and of Civil Judge in revenue and civil suits and such other powers to be exercised by him until the Maharana came of age and be capable of undertaking the responsibility of the administration of the State. The local courts at Udaipur were to be continued but the appeals against the decision of these courts could be made before the court of the Political Agent. All the cases of heinous offences and the civil suits exceeding in value of Rs. 1,000 were to be tried by the Political Agent. The Judgment of the Political Agent were to be considered final except in cases of capital punishment which were to be submitted for the sanction of the supreme Government through the A.G.G.[59]

In the same proclamation the Governor-General expressed his abhorence at the atrocities committed by Mehta Ajeet Singh in the name of Justice. He called upon all the Chiefs and people of Mewar and those of the neighbouring States to deny shelter to the outlaw Ajeet Singh and help the Government in effecting his capture. The Governor-General also made it known to all that the 'Kine-killing' should not be regarded as a capital offence. The A.G.G. was instructed to come to cordial understanding with the Political Agent in Mewar so that in future no advantage be deliberately taken by "the designing and unscrupulous persons" in the State.[60]

The Secretary of State, H.M.'s Government, London, receiving report from the G.O.I. about the Udaipur affairs, sent the following instructions to the Governor-General of India on the 16th March, 1864 "Your excellency is aware that the principles in accordance which H.M.'s Government desire to regulate your dealings with Native States are those of non-interference. No measures which only tend to degrade a Chief in the eyes of his subjects and retainers and impair his feelings of self-respect have to be adopted. But when occasions arise to correct the flagrant instances of misrule and friendly advice and solemn warning fail to have the effect, it is incumbent on the British Government to adopt more active measures." Approving the proceedings of the G.O.I., the Secretary of State further remarked to the effect that though Lieut. Col. Eden's proceedings were generally satisfactory, but indications of the harshness and want of due consideration for the rank and position of those with whom he was brought into collision, were visible in his dealing which were calculated to alienate the Chief from the Political Agent and add to his difficulties.[61]

Political Agent's Government (August 1863 to Nov. 1865)

On 19th August Lieut. Col Eden issued a public notification which read "Upto now the Government of Mewar has been carried on by a Council of Regency. An order of the Government has now arrived for a new arrangement, either of a new Council of several Chiefs or one as a Regent as may appear to us most desirable. Until the new arrangements shall be completed, the whole administration devolves on me."[62]

Lieut. Col. Eden proposed to appoint Rao of Deogarh as the Regent and Mehta Gokulchand as the executive, but the Governor-General did not approve of the idea, as the Rao had been one of the unreliable members of the late Council. However, he preferred a three men council under the presidentship of the Rao of Deogarh.[63] Failing to bring about any such arrangement, by which Mewar Chiefs could be associated with the administrative work of the State, the Political Agent created an executive body named *"Ahilyan Shri Durbar Rajya Mewar"* to work the administration of the State. Mehta Gokul Chand and Pandit Lachhman Rao were appointed as the officials to work for the executive.

Unrest in Udaipur

The assumption of direct control of entire administration of the State created a great unrest in the nobles as well as the people of the State. As the Dussehra festival was approaching the Political Agent feared that some disturbances might occur on that occasion, when the whole nobility of the State assembled in the capital. He at once procured a considerable temporary increase in his escort from Neemuch.[64]

There was a great uproar in Udaipur on the occasion of the Dussehra colebrations.[65] The whole atmosphere was filled with the feelings of resentment. Some posters were put on the walls of the city upbraiding the Maharana and the Chiefs for sitting silent, while the English Raj was being introduced in Mewar. However no disturbances took place and the assembled Chiefs dispersed peacefully.[66]

Lieut. Col. Eden seems to have attempted to utilize this occasion to review the long-standing questions of the *chhatooned* and personal service to be rendered by the Chiefs to their ruler. The Chief presented a memorandum of grievances to the British Government stating that, lately, the terms of the Treaty of Alliance and Friendship of 1818 were not being fully observed and that several such steps had been taken by the Political Agent which went contrary to the terms of the Treaty. They demanded that the State affairs should be conducted with the advice of five Chiefs, as had been the custom of the Mewar State that excessive fines in cases of *sati* should be stopped and that no change be made in the system of customs duties being levied in Mewar.[67]

Reforms by the Political Agent

Lieut. Col. Eden had initiated certain administrative reforms during the Government of Regency Council. He called some foreign officials and entusted them with responsible post in the Government, as no able and educated persons were available in the State. Eden gave special attention to the improvement of the administration of justice in the State. The justice was being administered in the old way, basing itself on ancient usages and customs without any definite law. Several barbarous and uncivilized practices had come into usage, in meeting out of the punishment to the guilty. He stopped such practices, put the courts into the hands of foreign officials employed by him and introduced certain rules of the Indian Penal Code in administering justice to the people.[68]

During this period the first Government School called "*Shambhu Ratna Pathshalla*" was started and a dispensary was opened. Improvements in the Jail and police arrangements were made. Mounted Police guards were posted into the city so as to provide greater safety of life and property to the people.[69] Attempts were made to improve the sanitation of the city. A department of *Deosthan* was established to manage the income and expenditure of the religious temples in the State and it was decided that the savings of this department would be spent in charity at the time of natural calamities as famine, flood, etc.[70]

Public works also received attention. The construction work of the road from Udaipur to Neemuch and from Udaipur to Kherwara was commenced. It was decided that a portion of the Mewar land be given free of cost to the British Government required to complete the project Rajputana-Malwa Railway line.[71] Efforts were made to curb the practices of bribery and embezzlement in the Government and steps were taken to manage and supervise the collection of revenue efficiently. The leases of the defaulting "*moostagirs*" (farmers of revenue) were annulled. In five *parganas* a summary settlement of land revenue was concluded with the heads of the villages, which was however opposed by the *Durbar* officials.[72] The State income rose to Rs. 24,75,000 with a saving of Rs. 3,00,000 per year. When in 1865 the reins of Government were handed over to the young

Maharana, there was a cash balance of about Rs. 30 lakhs in the State treasury.

The Political Agent continued his vigorous policy towards eliminating the inhuman practices of *Sati*, witch-swinging and slavery in the State by sternly bringing the offenders to justice. A proclamation regarding the prohibition of the sale of children was made in the month of Sept. 1863.[73]

Strike and Disturbance in Udaipur City

The administrative and judicial reforms introduced in the city of Udaipur (districts were still being administered in the old way) by the Political Agent worked to enhance the dissatisfaction particularly of the privileged classes, specially the chiefs, officials and businessmen. The will of the privileged could no longer be the rule. The chiefs had lost their hereditary right to give counsel and assist in governance of the State. Foreign officials had replaced the more or less hereditary official or favourite courtiers of the Maharana. On 23rd December, 1863 Nizamuddin Khan, the Superintendent of Police, Udaipur issued a notification, by which the system of the imposition of *"An"* was abolished.[74] The *"An"* was imposed in the name of the Maharana for stopping a man or men from doing certain act. Whenever a dispute arose between persons, any one so wishing could impose *"An"* on the other. The latter was then powerless to act. Traders and other wealthy classes misused this system to exploit and harass the poorer classes. According to the notification, it became compulsory for all to refer all the complaints in the proper and legal manner to the concerned courts. *"An"* was declared contrary to law and subversive of good Government and any one practising it was liable to punishment. This announcement was made in the city by beating of the drums.[75]

The order to abolish the *"An"* stirred the mercantile class of the city. A unity of interests was brought about between various interested classes who involved the young prince also in their plan. On the 30th March, 1864 instigated by officials, Chiefs and traders and with the moral support of the Maharana himself a general strike was observed in the city. All shops remained closed. About 2000 to 3000 people marched under the leadership of Seth Champalal, the *'Nagar Seth'* to the Residency outside the city. Leaders of the movement put the following demands before

him:
1. The ancient custom of "*An*" should be resorted.
2. The harassment of the traders by the policemen should be stopped.
3. Mortgages and names of the parties concerned in the transaction should not be recorded in the *Kotwali* office.
4. The order prohibiting slavery and buying and selling of children should be rescinded.
5. Settlement of the cases connected with caste and mercantile transactions should be conducted according to the old custom of Rajwara as before.
6. Complaints that can be settled, assembling at the "*Sethaji's* shop" according to the practice of Panchayat should be so settled, so also cases concerning quarrel between a husband and a wife.
7. In regard to *Fiuzdari*, *Diwani* and *Kotwali* courts, the old custom of employing some man of position and inhabitant of the city as judge to preside over them should be restored.[76]

Lieut. Col. Eden tried to explain them the Government's policy but the people were not satisfied. Gradually, the mob became menacing and boisterous. It is stated that abuses were hurled at him and even shoes and stones were thrown.[77] Eden used his guards to remove the strikers out of his residence. People then moved towards the garden of "*Sahiliyon-ki-Bari*" whence they intended to proceed to the A.G.G. in Rajputana to submit their complaints.[78]

The strike continued, though two or three days after the above incident the Bohra and Gujarati traders opened their shops.[79] But they were few in number. The situation continued to be tense and negotiations continued. On the 6th April, the Political Agent accompanied by the young Maharana went to the leaders of the movement camping at the gardens to conciliate them. Some promises were made and the leaders came back to the city and the strike was withdrawn.[80]

The event of general strike at Udaipur compelled the British Government to review the Udaipur affairs. The officiating A.G.G. wrote to the Political Agent on the 24th May, 1864, "You have been attempting too much, more than contemplated by the Government order of August, 1863." The Governor-General in his despatch of the 23rd June, 1864 made his observations in these words: "On the whole, there is no real ground for the complaint against Eden ... (but) Eden's conduct has not been judicious with the Chiefs, the leading courtiers and so many of the influential classes against him." The Governor-General further opined that Eden should endeavour to associate the Maharana with him in all he does, gain his assent in all such changes which were likely to prove unpopular and orders should be carried out with the name of Maharana himself.[81]

Col. Elliot, the A.G.G. proceeded to Udaipur to make on the spot study of the State of affairs at Udaipur and to soothe the feelings of the people.[82] No major changes were however made except that some nominal changes were made in the rules and Maulvi Nizammuddin Khan was relieved of his services.[83]

Punishment of Begun Chief

On the 18th April, 1864, a woman at Begun committed *Sati*. The Rao of that place afterwards sent the offenders to Udaipur, having received the orders of the Political Agent. After enquiring into the matter, the Political Agent held, along with the others, the Chief himself responsible for the crime and sentenced him to 9 months imprisonment and levied a fine of Rs. 5,000 on him. This action spread consternation among the nobles of the State finding a Chief so severely sentenced for a crime which took place in his own estate. Similar heavy punishments were meted out to other offenders. All of them were sent to Ajmer to be kept in jail there.[84]

The Chiefs of the State addressed a joint communication to Col. Eden on 7th March, 1865, protesting against the unusual punishments being inflicted on the chiefs in whose estates the cases of *Sati* took place. They wrote, "On no former occasions did we or any of our ancestors ever experience such a disrespect as has been shown to us by you in the present instance. Besides you have sent the criminals of this State to Ajmer. Such a thing had never before occurred in any of the Native States." The Governor-General upheld the proceedings of the Political Agent.[85]

Resistance Calms Down

The vigorous measures adopted by the Political Agent, Lieut. Col. Eden in the minority of Shambhu Singh with the sanction and approval of the British Government brought home the point to the mind of the young Maharana, the Chiefs and others that it was now no longer possible to carry on the administration perfectly in the old way. They also came to realise that it was the keen desire and the point of interest of the British Government to bring the Indian States out of the medieval order and re-organize their administration in such a way as to suit the Imperial needs and the set up of the British India. A definite change of outlook came in the mind of Shambhu Singh, and he began working solely on the advice of the Political Agent.

The changed attitude had its effect on the British Government. John Lawrence, the Governor-General of India wrote a *Kharita* in April 1865 to Shambhu Singh expressing the feelings of gratification for his good attitude and cooperation with the Political Agent and promised to entrust him with the management of the State administration at an early date.[86]

By the middle of the year 1865, the resistance to the changes and reforms initiated by the British Government had calmed down. The ruler, nobility and other privileged sections of the people had bowed before the inevitable. Lieut. Col. Eden by his bold and energetic measures prepared within three years, the ground for the modernisation of the State administration and the introduction of the reforms. The British influence in the internal affairs of the State reached its climax during the minority of Maharana Shambhu Singh. When the latter came of age and some questions of Imperial interests were taken up with him, the Maharana could not but yield to every demand that the British Government made.

NOTES AND REFERENCES

1. *Treaties, Engagements and Sanads by Aitchison,* Vol. III, pp. 19-20.
2. *India Today* by H.P. Dutt, p. 408.
3. *Ibid.*
4. *Ibid.,* p. 409.
5. *Ibid.,* p. 2043.

6. *Rajputana Agency Records (Mewar)* 1860, Vol. II, No. 85 (Swaroop Singh in a letter to the A.G.G. sought his advice whether it was necessary for him to address the Governor-General on the subject.)
7. *Vir Vinod*, p. 2058.
8. F.D., *Pol.*, Dec., 1861, No. 1,2.
9. *Ibid.*
10. *Rajputana Agency Records (Mewar)* 1860, Vol. II, No. 85.
11. F.D., *Pol.*, Dec. 1861, No. 135-138.
12. *A Gazetteer of the Udaipur state* by Major K.D. Frankine, p. 27.
13. F.D., *Pol.*, May 8, 1862, No. 59.
14. *Rajputana Agency Records (Mewar)* 1861-62, Vol. III, No. 85.
15. *Ibid.*
16. F.D., *Pol.*, Dec. 8, 1862, No. 130.
17. *Rajputana Agency Records, (Mewar)* 1861-62, Vol. III, No. 85.
18. *P.L.*, April 1862, *Her.* 93-95.
19. *Ibid.* On the occasion, the office of the Political Agent in Mewar was shifted from Neemuch to Udaipur: (*Itihas Rajasthan* by Charan Ramnath Ratna, p. 73; *The Residing Udaipur*, p. 1.)
20. *Ibid.* French Traveller Louis Rousselet says of Rao of Bedla; "Being both clever and polite, he managed to gain the entire confidence of the young prince and at the same time to keep on the most friendly terms with the British Government. In fact he represents two parties, "A Liberal conservative," he would like to see European Commerce and Industry introduced into his country on the condition that his privileges were respected" (*India and Its Native Princes*, pp. 160-161).
21. *Ibid.*
22. *Ibid.*
23. F.D. *Pol.*, April 1862, No. 93-95.
24. F.D. *Pol.*, Oct. 1862, No. 81-83.
25. *Ibid.*
26. *Vir Vinod* by Shyamal Das, p. 2063.
27. *Udaipur Rajya ka Itihas* by G.H. Ojha, Part II, p. 787.
28. F.D., *Pol.*, April 1862, No. 67-69.
29. *Ibid.*
30. *Vir Vinod* by Shyamal Das, p. 2063. There had been a practice in Mewar to impose fines on the high officials like the Pradhan by the ruler. It was believed that the officials made personal profits out of their employment in the State service. This practice resulted in greater corruption, as the officials took for granted that they would be fined by the Maharana one day or other. Thus even the honest learnt to became the dishonest.
31. *Udaipur Rajya ka Itihas* by G.H. Ojha, Part II, p. 788.

32. *Rajputana Agency Records* (General), Vol. III, No. 43.
33. *Ibid.*
34. F.D. *Pol.,* May 1862, No. 181-184.
35. F.D., *Pol.,* August 21, 1865, No. 206-96.
36. F.D., *Pol.,* August 1862, No. 73-75.
37. F.D. *Gen.,* March 1863, No. 108-110.
38. F.D. *Gen.,* Dec. 1863, No. 62-63.
39. *Rajputana Agency Records (Mewar)* 1861-62, Vol. III, No. 85.
40. *Vir Vinod* by Shyamal Das, p. 2065.
41. F.D., *Pol.,* July 1863, No. 100.
42. F.D., *Pol.,* May 30, 1886, No. 106.
43. *Vir Vinod* by Shyamal Das, p. 2066.
44. F.D., *Gen.,* Sept., 1863, No. 53-55.
45. *Ibid.*
46. *Ibid.*
47. *Vir Vinod* by Shyamal Das, p. 2066.
48. *Ibid.*
49. F.D., *Gen.,* Sept. 1863, No. 53-55.
50. F.D., *Pol.,* Sept. 1863, No. 1-42.
51. *Ibid.*
52. *Rajputana Agency Record (Mewar)* No. 132.
53. *Ibid.*
54. F.D., *Pol.,* July 25, 1863, No. 184.
55. *Rajputana Agency Records (Mewar),* No. 132.
56. *Ibid.*
57. *Ibid.*
58. *Ibid.*
59. *Ibid.*
60. F.D., *Pol.,* Sept. 1183, No. 1-42.
61. F.D., *Pol.,* Aug. 21, 1863, No. 206-96.
62. F.D. *Pol.,* Aug. 31, 1863, No. 214.
63. F.D., *Pol.,* Dec. 1863, No. 43-47.
64. *Vir Vinod* by Shymal Das, p. 2068.
65. F.D., *Pol.,* Dec. 1863, No. 43-47.
66. *Ibid.*
67. *Ibid.*
68. *Vir Vinod* by Shyamal Das, p. 2074.
69. F.D., *Pol.,* March 1862, No. 39-42.
70. *Udaipur Rajya ka Itihas* by G.H. Ojha, Part II, p. 792.
71. *Ibid.*
72. *Mewar Agency Report* (1864-65) by Major J.P. Sixon.
73. *Rajputana Agency Records (Confidential),* 1846, Slewazy, No. 2.
74. F.D., *Pol.,* July 1864, No. 30-42.

75. *Ibid.*
76. *Ibid.*
77. *Ibid.*
78. *Vir Vinod* by Shyamal Das, p. 2069.
79. F.D., *Pol.*, July 1864, No. 30-42.
80. *Vir Vinod* by Shyamal Das, p. 2070.
81. F.D., *Pol.*, July 1864, No. 30-42.
82. *Ibid.*
83. *Vir Vinod* by Shyamal Das, p. 2070.
84. *Rajputana Agency Record*, 1868 (*Sati*), No. 74.
85. F.D., *Pol.*, April 1865, No. 71-73.
86. Governor-General's letter to the Maharana, April 4, 1865 (*Bakshi Khana Udaipur*).

10

Beginning of Reforms

On the 26th November, 1865, Maharana Shambu Singh was invested with full powers of his State by the British Government.[1] On that day an assemblage was held, in which Lieut. Col. Eden read the *Kharita* of the Governor-General conferring on the Maharana the right to govern his State independently. To give eclat to the occasion two field guns, a troops of Native Cavalry, a company of British Infantry and two companies of Native Infantry were called to Udaipur.[2]

Re-appointment of Kothari Singh

Having been invested full powers, Maharana Shambhu Singh reconstituted the executive council of the State as "*Khas Kachahari*" (chief executive) and appointed Zalim Singh, the Chief of Bemali, as his chief advisor. A concession was made to the feelings of the local people soon after by removing Mehta Gokul Chand and Pandit Lachhman Rao from their posts, who had been appointed to the executive council by Lieut. Col. Eden, the Political Agent in Mewar. He re-appointed Kothari Kesari Singh on the 21st December, 1867 as the *pradhan* and entrusted him with the work of the Council.[3]

As the appointment of Kothari Kesari Singh would have been in contravention of the orders of the British Government passed during the minority of the Maharana, by which his re-employment in the State had been interdicted, the Maharana sought permission from the British Government to re-investigate his case, as it was believed that the Political Agent in his decision against Kothari Kesari Singh had been misled by some of the members of the Regency Council.[4] The new enquiry found him guiltless, which cleared the way for his re-appointment by the Maharana.[5]

Lieut. Col. Keatings, the A.G.G. reported the above matter to the British Government. The latter took a lenient view of the case and asked the A.G.G. to allow the Maharana to obtain the services of Kothari Kesari Singh. The A.G.G. approving of Kesari Singh's appointment wrote to the Maharana, "In so doing, I have been mainly guided by the expediency of having in Mewar a minister of sufficient influence with the Chiefs and the people to secure a moderately strong Government."[6]

Maharana and the Chiefs

The reign of Shambhu Singh marks an improvement in regard to the relations of the ruler with his Chiefs. In his minority he had been able to cultivate good relations with various sections of his nobility. He adopted generally a policy of compromise and canciliation, though in several cases he also succumbed to the partisan spirit. The Chiefs still maintained their attitude of defiance and independence, which had no parallel in any other State of Rajputana.[7] The British Government pursued generally the policy of neutrality and non-interference in the matter of Maharana-Chiefs relations in so far as the general peace in the State was not disturbed. However, the policy was largely influenced by Imperial interested, *i.e.*, to help and induce the Maharana in curbing the Chiefs having anti-British sentiments and promoting those who were pro-British. As the Maharana was the chief source of strength in the State, the British Government played its game in such a way that the weak and emasculated Maharana had to seek assistance from the British authorities in order to maintain his sovereignty over his chiefs. The situation of factionalism and civil strife among the chiefs and between them and the ruler was in the interests of the foreign power, which utilized it to promote its own interests in the State. The British Government neither helped fully the Maharana in subduing totally the refractory chiefs in order to strengthen the authority of the centre, which was the crying need of the time, nor encouraged the chiefs in their defiance to the extent that the authority of the Maharana collapsed. Consequently the militarily and politically weak Maharana remained entirely dependent on the support of the British Government and the latter in that condition came to the former's assistance, whenever the situation required it, in order to maintain his apparent sovereignty over his subjects.

Reconciliation with the Salumbar Chief

The reconciliation of the Maharana with the Salumbar Chief was an important event during his reign. During the Government of the Regency Council there arose a succession dispute in Salumbar State. Rawat Kesari Singh, the defiant chief of estate died issueless on the 20th July, 1862.[8] Rawat Jodh Singh of Bambora was chosen as his successor by the members of the late Chief's family. Zalim Singh, the Chief of Bamboli and a favourite of young Shambhu Singh supported Jodh Singh's succession. However, the Regency Council decided in favour of Bhopal Singh, the Chief of Bhadesar. Jodh Singh and his followers defied the orders of the Regency Council. The British Government was requested to provide British troops to suppress his defiance and maintain the authority of the *Durbar* council. Thereupon the Political Agent and the A.G.G. in Rajputana both put themselves in communication with commanding officers of the Bombay army asking them to hold themselves in readiness.[9]

The British Government, however, disapproved of the above measure of its Agents, without first obtaining the sanction of the Government with regard to the armed intervention in the affairs of Udaipur. The Governor-General observed that it was not the duty of the British Government to interfere in the internal disputes between the Maharana and his refractory chiefs, "except when the peace of neighbouring country is endangered by their strife."[10] Thus the Regency Council was left to itself to take action against Jodh Singh's defiance. Nothing could be done against him as the Council had not the sufficient strength and unity to suppress Jodh Singh as the prominent chiefs of the State were divided on the issue.[11] Subsequently, the Regency Council had to revise the earlier decision. Jodh Singh was accepted as the chief of Salumbar, with the condition that if he died issuesless, Bhopal Singh and his descendants only would have the right of succession to the Salumbar chiefship.[12]

Maharana Shambhu Singh, decided to close the old feud with the chief of Salumbar which had been cause of incessant trouble. The premier Chundawat family of Salumbar had always claimed and enjoyed some special privileges. Whenever a chief of the estate died and a new one succeeded, the Maharana was required to visit Salumbar personally to express condolence on the death of the late chief, fetch the new chief to Udaipur and perform the ceremony of *'Talwar Bandai'* etc.[13] This had been the main cause of strife between Maharana Swaroop Singh and Rawat Kesari Singh, which did not subside throughout the former's reign. Maharana Shambhu Singh visited Salumbar on 27th October, 1866 in person, thus giving recognition to the special privilege of the Salumbar family and brought Jodh Singh to Udaipur, where the ceremony of 'Sword binding' was duly performed.[14]

The Succession Case of Amet Reopened

In 1865, the succession dispute of the estate of Amet was reopened. When Rawat Prithvi Singh of Amet died in 1856,[15] there were two claimants for the *Jagir*, Rawat Zalim Singh of Bemali, who was distantly connected with the Amet family, had placed his son Amar Singh in possession of Amet with the concurrence of the members of the late chief's family. But Chatra Singh of Jilola, a near relative of the deceased Rao also presented his claim to the succession. A court intrigue at Udaipur procured decision in favour of Chatra Singh who armed with an order of Maharana Swaroop Singh proceeded to Amet, attacked the place and forcibly ejected Amar Singh and his family, killing his brother Padam Singh and two other men. Amar Singh afterwards several times fruitlessly attempted to regain the possession of the *Jagir*.[16]

In 1865, Amar Singh was able to find favour with the new ruler, Shambhu Singh, as his father was his chief advisor. Maharana Shambhu Singh declared Amar Singh to be the rightful heir of Amet and ordered Chatra Singh to leave Amet. Chatra Singh, however, refused to obey and the atmosphere in the State became tense. All the Chiefs of the State, as usual got divided into two parties and the clash became imminent. However, the Maharana revised his decision in order to avert much an occurrence. He conferred the *Jagir* of Meja, Sindha etc. on Amar Singh from Khalsa lands, having the income of Rs. 20,000 per annum and created him the chief of first rank. He however, ordered Chatra Singh to part with a portion of *Jagir* worth Rs. 8,000 and give it to Amar Singh in consideration of the latter's renunciation of his claim on Amet. Chatra Singh, though, agreed to give Rs. 8,000 cash annually to Amar Singh but refused to part with any portion of his estate. No compromise could be brought about and the strife continued.[17]

In 1871, Rawat Chatra Singh complained that both Zalim Singh and his son Amar Singh had entered the estate with their followers and plundered the territory. The Maharana finding himself unable to stop the disturbance requested the Political Agent, Major Nixon to bring about a settlement of the dispute. Major Nixon, having intervened in the affair, induced Chatra Singh to agree on the condition that Amar Singh would not make any claim to Amet thereafter, to grant two villages of Toongarh and Shodas for his life time yielding an income of Rs. 8,000 per annum approximately. However, if the income of the above villages fell short of the above amount, Chatra Singh was bound to make good the deficit. It was also provided in the proposed agreement that Amar Singh would pay Rs. 3 lakhs to Chatra Singh on account of the damages caused by him to the latter. Amar Singh, however, refused to agree to Chatra Singh's claim of the compensation and to the condition relating to the life tenure. On the contrary he laid claim for blood-money on account of his brother and two men killed by Chatra Singh in 1856. Thus the dispute still remained unsettled.[18]

In 1873, Chatra Singh died and was succeeded by a five years old boy, Sheonath Singh. The management of the estate was put under the *Durbar* administration during the minority. Amar Singh thought it an opportune moment to seize possession of Amet by force. The A.G.G. in Rajputana, having come to know of his intention, warned Amar Singh against taking such a measure.[19] Lieut. Col. Rutchinson, the officiating Political Agent in Mewar, was induced again to intervene in the affair. According to his advice the two important stipulations of the proposed agreement of 1872 were placed before a council of ten nobles, consisting of representatives of both the parties. The council, having met in Udaipur on Dussehra festival decided that the grant of the villages to Amar Singh should be made for perpetuity and that the claim for compensation by Chatra Singh amounting to 3 lakhs must be set off against the claim preferred by Amar Singh on account of the blood money. This decision was approved of as a final settlement of the case by Maharana Shambhu Singh and orders were passed accordingly. On the 16th February, 1874 the proceedings were sent to the A.G.G. by the Political Agent and were confirmed by the former.[20]

Reopaheli-Lamba Case

Another case of a border dispute which had occurred during the reign of Maharana Swaroop Singh was reopened in Shambhu Singh's time. In 1856, there occurred a factional clash between the families of the chiefs of Lamba and Reopaheli over the dispute of some border land, in which a son of the chief of Lamba and three men of his party and three men of Reopaheli party were killed.[21] An enquiry was instituted into the affair by Maharana Swaroop Singh which resulted in awarding the village of Taswaria, belonging to Reopaheli to the chief of Lamba as compensation for blood-money. But the orders of the Maharana could not be enforced at that time.[22] However, in Maharana Shambhu Singh's time Bagh Singh, chief of Lamba, represented his claims and demanded *"Moond Catti"* (Blood-money) for the murder of his son and brothers by Reopaheli men.[23]

Maharana Shambhu Singh appointed a *panchayat* consisting of Rao Bakhat Singh of Bedla, Maharaj Madan Singh of Bheender, Mehta Zalim Singh, Kothari Chhaganlal, Bakshi Mathurdas and Dhinkaria Udairam to enquire into the case. The committee endorsed the previous decision of Maharana Swaroop Singh by which the village of Taswaria belonging to Reopaheli was given in compensation to the chief of Lamba.[24] However, the chief of Reopaheli refused to comply with. Thereupon the State troops with 4 guns, 148 cavalry and 568 infantry proceeded to the *Jagir* under the command of Mehta Gokulchand to subdue the defiant chief. Levies of the Chiefs of Deogarh, Badnor, Banera, Asind, Bhensrorgarh, Bhagwanpura, Daulatgarh and Sangramgarh also joined the State troops. They collectively invested the village of Reopaheli on the 15th May, 1872 and the chief submitted.[25]

The Chief appealed to the Political Agent against the decision of the Maharana, which was, however, rejected by the British Government.[26] The A.G.G. on the other hand found it to be a case in which the Maharana should receive support of the Government, and asked the Political Agent to issue a proclamation to the *Kamdars* and *Fauzdars* of the Reopaheli *Jagir* ordering them to abide by the judgment of the Maharana. The Political Agent issued orders to the same effect.[27] The village of Taswaria was taken away from Reopaheli. As the chief of Lamba, the claimant was a minor, the village was kept under State administration for the time being.[28]

Deogarh Chief's Succession Fee Case

During Maharana Shambhu Singh's minority the Regency Council of which Rawat Ranjeet Singh of Deogarh was a member, decided to exempt the Deogarh Chief from paying succession fee to the Maharana. The Rawat also withdraw the sum of Rs. 25,000 from the State treasury which the proceeding Maharana had exacted from the Chief of Deogarh on account of the succession fee. Thus the orders of a former ruler were reversed during the Regency Council administration headed by the British Agent.

Rawat Ranjeet Singh died in the month of September, 1867, and was succeeded by his son, Kishan Singh.[29] Maharana sent as usual the sequestration party to the *jagir* and demanded the succession fee from the new Rawat, which the latter declined to give on the plea that his family had been exempted from this levy during the Regency Council administration. Consequently, neither the chief came to Udaipur for the purpose of tendering allegiance and performing the usual ceremony of 'Talwar Bandai' not the Maharana raised the 'Dhons' party from the *Jagir*, which he had sent.[30] Regarding the Regency Council's decision in favour of Deogarh chief the Maharana ordered that it was taken during his minority. The Rawat sought the Political Agent's intervention to remove the sequestration party from his *jagir*. The Political Agent reported the matter to A.G.G. in the beginning of 1869. The latter observed that it would not be advisable for the Maharana to reopen the question as the above decision of Regency Council had been approved of by the British Government. Commenting on the *Durbar's* reasoning that the

1862 decision was illegal because it was taken during his minority, the A.G.G observed that such an idea was most subversive of all good order. If such a reasoning was allowed them all decision taken during minority administration would be illegal and liable to be reversed.[31]

The above observations of the A.G.G. were conveyed to the Maharana. The latter, however, pleaded that such a decision would lower his prestige and would have a bad effect on his prerogative as the sovereign and credit of his administration. Rejecting the Maharana's plea, the A.G.G., Mr. Kestinge replied that the Maharana's dignity was, in fact, simply what the British Government had made it. He quoted in this connection, the remarks of Lieut. Col. Lawrence which he made about the Udaipur State in 1853, that the State had been reconstructed by the British Government and existed only by the pressure from without. Had the Political Agents not exerted their efforts and the British Government not assisted in preserving the State, it would not have survived. The A.G.G. therefore, asked the *Durbar* to remove the '*Dhons*' party from the *jagir* at once. The Maharana complied with the wishes of the British Government.[32]

The Maharana Asserts his Suzerain Rights over Shahpura

In 1869 there arose some differences between the British Government and the Maharana of Udaipur with regard to the latter's claim of suzerain rights over Shahpura.[33] In that year Rajadhiraj Lachhman Singh of Shahpura died, and his adopted son Kehar Singh, a minor succeeded. The Maharana of Udaipur raised certain objections with regard to the succession proceedings at Shahpura and advanced his own prerogatives in that respect.[34]

Originally the ruler of Shahpura was a grantee of the Mughal Emperor. During Maharana Ari Singh II's (1761-73) reign the ruler of Shahpura was granted the *Jagir* of 'Kachhola' from Udaipur State lands by the Maharana. Afterwards Maharana Bhim Singh conferred the title of '*Rajadhiraj*' on the ruler.[35] Thus the '*Rajadhiraj*' of Shahpura on the one hand enjoyed the status of a native feudatory having direct relations with the British Government and on the other hand he held the position of a *jagirdar* of the Udaipur *Durbar* by virtue of holding the estate grant of Kachhola from the Mewar State. The *Rajadhiraj* paid tribute and performed useful services to the Maharana like other Chiefs of the first rank in the State.

When in 1869, the British Government confirmed Nahar Singh's succession to the *gadee* of Shahpura State, the Maharana also asserted his own suzerain rights, which he enjoyed over Shahpura. He advanced claim for his rights of giving consent to the adoptions and successions in the Shahpura family, of levying 'Nazarana' on the chief at the time of his accession and of performing the '*Talwar Bandai*' (Sword-binding) ceremony. The Maharana as well demanded that a Mewar official should be included in the Government of the Shahpura State to look after Mewar interests until the minor chief attained his majority.[36]

The Government of India decided the case on the 14th May, 1870, observing that the plea advanced by the Maharana in the matter of succession of *Rajadhiraj* of Shahpura was entirely destitute of foundation. The Paragana of Phulla, previously a grant of the Mughal Emperor, was now held directly by a Sanad of grant from the British Government. The fact that the chief also held a estate in Mewar, gave the Mewar *Durbar* no more voice in the succession to Shahpura than the fact that Holkar held a village in Barwani gave the chief of that petty State a voice in the succession of Holkar's territories.[37] However, after subsequent correspondence between the British Government and the Maharana of Udaipur the former agreed that their relations refer only to the part of the estate held by the *Rajadhiraj* from Mewar, the payments demanded by the Maharana from the *Rajadhiraj* of Shahpura must be made, which however should be usual, customary and fair. Consequently, the *Rajadhiraj* of Shahpura paid amount Rs. 18,000 for succession fee and fine imposed on him for his act of disobedience.

In 1874, there occurred another dispute between Mewar and Shahpura over a village named Ubla, situated in the Kachhola paragana of Shahpura. In 1831 the then *Rajadhiraj* of Shahpura Madho Singh made a grant of the village of Ubla on Mehta Sher Singh of Mewar for the services performed by him to the former in getting the paragana of Phulia restored to Shahpura from the British Government.[38] When in 1856, Mehta Sher Singh incurred displeasure of Maharana Shambhu Singh the *Rajadhiraj* took opportunity to reoccupy the village of Ubla.

Mehta Sher Singh complained that this action was unjust and requested the *Rajadhiraj* to restore the village. The latter, however, rejected his request, replying that he had forfeited his right to hold the villages by displeasing the Maharana.[39]

The dispute of the village of Ubla took a different turn in 1871, when it was attached by the Maharana of Udaipur as a security for the defrayal of expenses, incurred in connection with some border disputes. In 1874, when the village was still lying attached to the Mewar State lands, the claim for the restoration of the village was again advanced by Zalim Singh on behalf of Mehta Sher Singh. When Maharana sought a reply from the *Rajadhiraj* in this connection the Shahpura authorities pleaded that it was merely a grant and therefore was liable to be resumed at the pleasure of the donor. However, the Maharana decided in favour of Mehta Sher Singh observing that he had been deprived of his village without any cause and as he had possessed it for a long time, cultivated and improved it, it must be restored to him.[40]

The relations between Mewar and Shahpura got thereby strained. Shahpura authorities were not willing to accept the Maharana's decision. In July 1874, about 30 armed men of Shahpura State assembled near the village of Ubla to cultivate the land in dispute.[41] The Maharana reported the event to the British Government. The Political Agent in Haroti intervened and persuaded the Shahpura authorities to withdraw their armed men from the village. However, the situation remained tense. On the 22nd September, 1874, the A.G.G. directed the Political Agent in Mewar to take whatever steps necessary for the preservation of peace on Mewar-Shahpura border. The British Government, after full consideration of the matter, declined to intervene in the matter, and observed that it was the duty of Shahpura authorities to pay tribute regularly and perform other customary services to the Maharana of Udaipur.[42]

Trial of Mehta Ajeet Singh

Mehta Ajeet Singh, as we have stated earlier, had escaped from Udaipur in 1863 during the Regency Council's administration. He had been accused of murder and inhuman atrocities over certain people. The British Government after his flight from Udaipur, declared him an outlaw and ordered all the Chiefs of

Mewar and of other neighbouring States not to give shelter to him. Ajeet Singh wandered about the wilds of Mewar till about 1865, when he found an asylum with the Rao of Kotharia.[43] The right of giving sanctuary to criminals was still an acknowledged institution in Mewar.[44] Rao Jodh Singh, the Chauhan chief of Kotharia was already known for giving shelter to several anti-British elements, specially during the time of the revolt. In the reign of Maharana Shambhu Singh also, Kotharia Rao gave shelter to Mehta Sher Singh who was said to have committed embezzlement of about Rs. 1,50,000 out of the revenue collections of the State, as a '*Hakim*' at Chittorgarh. In 1865, when State servants went to set up Lieut. Col. Eden's camp on the lands of Kotharia, the Rao threatened to kill them, and the Political Agent had to report the case to the A.G.G. about Kotharia Rao's defiance and disobediance.[44]

When the Political Agent came to know that Ajeet Singh was residing at Kotharia, he asked the Maharana to take measures to apprehend him. The Maharana showed reluctance on the plea that the case had occurred during his minority and therefore it belonged to the Agency. This argument was not accepted by the British Government.[46] In October, 1868, the A.G.G. suggested occupation of the Rawat's estate by a military force, but his proposal was not executed because such an action might provoke the national feeling of the Mewar chiefs.[47] The Maharana was compelled to send an ultimatum to the Rao. He simultaneously issued orders for the confiscation of two villages of his *jagir* and despatched a '*Dhons*' or imposing party to his estate. At last, after six years of defiance Ajeet Singh surrendered himself on the 1st November, 1869 to the Maharana of Udaipur. Having received reports of Ajeet Singh's surrender, the Governor-General wrote to the A.G.G. to find out and report whether the *Durbar* had held out any inducement to Ajeet Singh to surrender. He also instructed the A.G.G. to make the Maharana understand that the British Government would hold him responsible for the safe keeping of the accused.

Ajeet Singh was tried by the court of the Political Agent, Lieut. Col. J.P. Nixon on the 2nd May, 1870. Ajeet Singh tried to challenge the authority of the Political Agent to try him, as it was contrary to the terms of the Treaty of 1818, which recognized the sovereign authority of the Maharana in all the internal affairs of the State. He also argued that according to the Extradition Treaty of 1868 concluded between the British Government and Mewar Government it was required that the subject of Mewar territory should be made over for trial to the Maharana. The Maharana on his part expressed reluctance to deal with the case, implicitly consenting to his trial by the court of the Political Agent. The latter interpreted Maharana's reluctance as the delegation of the authority by the Maharana to himself in the case of trial of Ajeet Singh. Lieut. Col. Nixon acquitted Ajeet Singh on the charge that he cruelly executed Gomla, finding that he had acted under the due written authority from the Regency Council in this connection. He was, however, sentenced to three years imprisonment for the cruel treatment meted out by him to Kirpa.

The Governor-General was not satisfied with the judgment of Lieut. Col. Nixon in the case of Ajeet Singh. He observed that Nixon had placed undue credence in the statement of the accused that with regard to the first charge, he had got written orders from the Regency Council. However, the proceedings were approved and the Governor-General directed the Political Agent that Ajeet Singh be kept in detention at Udaipur and *Durbar* should be distinctly informed that he would be held responsible for properly carrying out the sentence and not allowing the criminal to escape again. A general order was issued disqualifying Ajeet Singh for any further public employment.[48]

Ajeet Singh, in December, 1871, appealed to the G.O.I. against the judgment of the Political Agent and afterwards to the Secretary of State, London, but his petitions were rejected.[49]

Extradition Treaty, 1868

There had been no definite system of extradition of offenders between the Native States and the British Government, which always caused several complications with regard to tracing the culprits and producing them before the courts for trial. The offenders, after committing murder, dacoity or theft in one territory fled to another for shelter. In order to curb the crime effectively, the British Government entered into negotiations with the native States of Rajputana.[50] On the 30th October, 1866 the Political Agent in Mewar was directed by the A.G.G. to enter into negotiations with the *Durbar* and settle an extraditions agreement. As the Maharana had certain misgivings with regard to the proposals, he showed little interest in the matter. Thereupon the A.G.G. asked the Political Agent to meet personally the Maharana and if he had apprehension that such an agreement might in future operate in a manner prejudicial to his interests, the Political Agent might call attention to 7th article of the proposed treaty which left it in the power of either contracting party to bring the engagement to a close at any time. Maharana Shambhu Singh on his part again put forward his objections and the Political Agent complained to the A.G.G. that no response was forthcoming from the *Durbar*.[51] Thereupon the British Government took the matter seriously with the Maharana. An English draft of the agreement was presented to the Maharana. The Maharana then insisted on having the draft of the Treaty in the vernacular language. In this connection the A.G.G. wrote on the 26th June, 1868, "Chiefs who hold positions which make it possible for them to be called upon to enter into treaty engagement with the British Government may certainly be expected to have in their service persons capable of accurately explaining to them the meaning of English documents. In a treaty with the British Government the English version would be binding on both parties. A translation of the draft would, therefore, be of no practical use for the native Government."[52]

The Extradition Treaty was concluded on the 16th December, 1868, between Mewar Government and the British Government which was forwarded to the A.G.G.[53] However, the Treaty contained no seal and signature of the Maharana. Returning the draft Keatinge, the A.G.G. wrote to Hutchinson, the Political Agent, "If the H.H. should have refused to sign it on account of any prejudice the treaty can be made out again as concluded between you and the minister whose signature would then suffice." Eventually the Maharana signed the Treaty which was ratified by the Governor-General on 22nd Jan., 1869.[54]

The Treaty provided for the arrangement of tracing the offenders, who passed from one territory to another after committing offences, transferring them to the Government, in whose territory the offence was committed and the mode of their requisition and trial. In Article 5 of the Treaty the description of the offences which were deemed to be heinous, was made. In Article 7 of the Treaty it was provided that "the Treaty shall continue in force until either of the high contracting parties would give notice to the other of its wish to terminate it." The Maharana, it seems, had objections to and misgivings about provisions in Article 3 of the Treaty by which any person other than a Mewar subject committing heinous offence within the limits of Mewar State was required to be tried by such court, as the British Government might direct.

As the procedure prescribed by the Treaty for the extradition of the offenders from British India to the Udaipur State was found subsequently "by experience to be less simple and effective than the procedure prescribed by the law as to the extradition of offenders in force in British India." an Agreement supplementary to the Treaty of 1869 was concluded in 1887 between both the Governments. By this agreement the original provisions of the Treaty regarding the procedure for the extradition of offenders from British India to the Udaipur State were made ineffective and in its place the procedure followed in British India was provided.[55]

Bhil Disturbances in the Hilly Tract

A stated earlier Bhils living in the Hilly tract of Mewar remained a continual source of trouble for the State administration. As the State officials were generally inefficient, cruel and corrupt, the tribesmen were provoked to rise against the State administration.[56] In 1868, Bhils of Karwar Pal in the Hilly district of Mewar indulged into lawless activities, and began defying the State authorities. Major Mackenzie, the Superintendent, Mewar Bhil Corps wrote to the Maharana that the administrative arrangement in the district was loose and ineffective. State officials like Mehta Raghunath Singh and Moti Singh were acting cruelly and unjustly with the tribesmen. The officials were charging double taxes and imposing heavy fines on the people by employing force. The Maharana at once sent 200 infantry and 150 cavalry to suppress the Bhils. For some time the disturbance of the Bhils continued. The State troops resorted to brutal measures against them and suppressed their resistance entirely.[57]

Lieut. Col. Mackeson, the Offg. Pol. Supdt. of Hilly Tract, Mewar, reported in May 1871, that the punishment meted out to the Bhil Pal had resulted in general specification. However, the attitude of the Mewar officials had not changed. Mirza Rahim Beg, the Police official was indolent and was becoming the source of unrest while Pandit Anand Rao, the Civil official was nowhere seen fulfilling his duties.[58]

Illegal Detention of the British Prisoners

In the year 1869, a case of illegal detention of three Agency prisoners in the Udaipur jail was detected. In 1865 three Moghia tribesmen were arrested in connection with a mail robbery and detained in Udaipur jail as Agency prisoners. They were acquitted on the 2nd June, 1866 by the court of *Vakils* at Abu (a type of interestated court of Rajputana States presided over by the A.G.G.). Lalchand, Mewar *Vakil* at Abu sent the copy of the decision to the *Durbar* executive. But the prisoners were released. When in half yearly statement dated the 30th June, 1869 of the Udaipur jail *Daroga*, having Agency prisoners under his charge the names of the above prisoners appeared, the British Government felt annoyed.[59]

The A.G.G. explained to the British Government that the prisoners were not released on account of the neglect of Lieut. Col. Nixon, the Political Agent (who was at this time on leave and was being officiated by Hutchinson). However, Nixon made himself clear of the charge, as soon as he resumed his duties and put the blame on the State authorities, on account of whose careless attitude the prisoners were not released. The British Government entered into communication with the Mewar *Durbar* in this connection. The Maharana in the end admitted that the whole thing happened due to the carelessness of the *Durbar* executive. The prisoners were forthwith released.[60]

After the above event the British Government adopted a specific procedure in regard to the keeping of the Agency prisoners in the jails of the native States. The A.G.G. directed all the Political officers under Rajputana Agency to follow a system of issuing warrants to be addressed to the *Vakils* of the States concerned in regard to the decisions of the court of Abu and in regard to the release of the prisoners. They should get monthly statements about Agency prisoners from the State Governments concerned and make on official of the Agency staff responsible with the Political Agent to check such statements.[61]

Maharana's Severe Measures against *Sati*

In August 1868 there occurred a case of *Sati* at Salloda in the paragana of Kumbhalgarh where a Brahmin woman immolated herself. At about the same time some more cases of *Sati* took place in different parts of the State, Maharana Shambhu Singh paid active attention to the occurrences and took strong measures against the offenders and inflicted heavy punishments on them. In the case of Salloda itself as many as 68 persons were apprehended including *Patel, Patwari* and other Government servants who were sentenced to from 3 to 7 years rigorous imprisonment.[62]

The prompt and strong actions taken by the Maharana earned gratification from the British Government, though in her opinion unusually large number of criminals had been tried and sentenced to severe sentences.[63] The British Government opined that the sentences should be reduced. However, the Secretary of State, London, while concurring with the appreciation of the ruler made by the G.O.I., observed that the sentences passed on the persons found guilty did not appear to him to be more severe. He further remarked, "although the Political Agents may advantageously use their influences in securing the infliction of suitable punishment on offenders of the character, I think it open to question whether it is altogether expedient, as a general rule, to interfere with sentences once promulgated and to lower the authority of the *Durbar* by so interfering with the sentences passed." He again wrote on the 6th May that "the desire of H.M.'s. Government is that any such reduction (in the sentences already passed by the Maharana) should proceed from the Maharana rather than from our side."[64]

Lieut. Col. Hutchinson, the Political Agent met the Maharana to convey views and wishes of H.M.'s. Government regarding the cases of *Sati* and remarked that the sentences were heavier and it was advisable to reduce them for which the Maharana agreed.[65] He was requested to State his wishes in writing to the British Government. Thereupon the minister of the State sent a letter to the Political Agent stating that the object of heavy punishment was to deter others and it had its desired results. But the punishment had driven the families of the prisoners to great distress, besides the sentences were severe. It was, therefore, the *Durbar's* wish to extend leniency towards those who were in custody. The Political Agent expressed his concurrence with the *Durbar's* wish and the suggested reductions in the punishments were carried out.[66]

Cases of Witch-hunting

The barbarous system of witch-hunting was greatly prevalent in the territory of Mewar as in other parts of Rajputana. Whenever a woman fell seriously ill in a village, she was thought to have been bewitched by some other woman. The suspect was then caught by the villagers and put to several types of ordeals. There used to be a '*Bhopa*' or witchfinder priest who practised the savage ordeals by brutally beating her. Generally she was hung by feet in tree or compelled to dip her hands in the boiling oil etc. Usually the so-called witch was, in this cruel way, put to death.[67]

In November 1862 two women of the village of Beechiwara in the Jharole estate were accused of being witches. Their hands were immersed in boiling oil. As their hands were burnt, they were considered to be guilty and were swung by the servants of the Chief of Jharole. One of the two died and the other managed to escape. When the news reached Udaipur, the Regency Council issued orders for the arrest of the witch-finder and others involved in the case.[68] The Governor-General receiving the news of the happening asked the Council to take measures to bring to account the culprits and to eliminate the practice in the State.

In August, 1868, a case of witch-swinging took place in the village of Roheenala, in the Panarwa estate of Mewar where a woman was brutally murdered on the suspicion that she had bewitched the wife of a soldier of the Bhil Corps.[69] The Chief of Panarwa did nothing to prevent the ordeal and to apprehend the culprits. When the news of the happening reached Udaipur, the Political Agent suggested the temporary attachment of the whole or a portion of the Panarwa estate as a warning and lesson to the Chief. Two sepoys and four other *grassias* were arrested for the crime and brought to Udaipur, however, the *durbar* was not able to secure the attendance of Chief of Panarwa or those of his subjects who had witnessed the outrage. Capt. Bettye, the officiating 2nd Assistant Political Agent, Mewar, reported from Kherwara that "He has been unable to produce further evidence in the case. In the wild tract of country known as the Panarwa estate, law and order are unknown and the Bhils disregard both the authority of the Kurabar and that of the Rana of Panarwa and it is impossible to secure the attendance of any Bhil and any attempt to seize the culprits scares the whole community who betake themselves to the fastness and defy pursuit.[70]

Having received the report about the happening the Governor-General expressed his serious displeasure at the conduct of chief of Panarwa for his non-cooperation with the Mewar *Durbar* in tracing out the culprits. However, he deemed it inadvisable to use coercion to bring the Chief to Udaipur lest the peace of wild tract might be disturbed and the Chief of Panarwa might be driven to outlawry. He spined that imposition of a small fine on the Chief, as a sort of punishment would do.[71]

Thereafter the Chief of Panarwa was fined Rs. 250. Two sepoys of the Mewar Bhil Corps were arrested and tried by the court of the Political Agent. They were sanctioned to 10 years rigorous imprisonment; four *grassias* were tried and punished by the Udaipur *Durbar*.[72]

Despite severe measures adopted by the Political Agent the Udaipur Government, the ordeal of witch-hunting continued in the Bhil tribes of Hilly Tracts. On the 28th Jan. 1874 the officiating Political Superintendent, Hilly Tracts, Mewar, Major Gunning, received information that a case of witch-swinging took place at a Pal in Jawas about 14 miles from Kherwara.[73] This Pal had always been regarded as the most defying and turbulent one. Mewar *Vakil* along with the sepoys of Mewar Bhil Corps and armed men of Jawas Chief reached the place. It was found absolutely deserted. Hundreds of Bhils were shouting ('Kilkeeing') in the surrounding hills. Major Gunning himself arrived at the place and called the Bhils to come down but with no response. He was treated with an insulting behaviour by the Bhils and one Bhil even shot an arrow at him. Eventually they had to return without accomplishing anything.[74]

On the 10th March, 1874, the Governor-General wrote to the A.G.G. to call upon the Mewar *Durbar* to force the refractory Bhils in order to stop the evil practice of witch-hunting and to punish them for the insults hurled at the English officer. He directed that the *Durbar* troops assisted by the levy of Jawas Chief should take prominent part in such an operation and Mewar Bhil Corps should act as a support.[75]

Ajmer *Durbar* of 1870

On the 22nd October, 1870 Lord Mayo, the Governor-General and Viceroy of India held a viceregal *Durbar* of Rajputana Chiefs at Ajmer. The Maharana of Udaipur was invited by the G.O.I. to attend the *Durbar*. The invitation created of great ideal of excitement at Udaipur.[76] Several of the old and freedom-loving Chiefs of the State opposed their ruler attending a Public *Durbar*, which they argued, was against the tradition and dignity of Sisodia House of Mewar. They held that the former meeting of the Maharana Jawan Singh with Lord William Bentinck in 1832 was private one and the latter had promised that the Maharana would not, in future, be called to meet the Viceroy outside his State.[77] After a great deal of pressure and persuasion by the Political Agent, the Maharana consented to attend the assemblage. He wrote to the A.G.G., Col. Breokes that it would give him great pleasure to meet the Governor-General at Ajmer, however, the same dignity and honour should be accorded to him at Ajmer, as was done in 1832 and the same ceremonies should be adhered to. He further requested him that he should not be required to present *Nazarana* personally to the Viceroy and the interview should not take place in the open *durbar*.[78]

The A.G.G. in his reply to the Maharana observed that the Maharana should recognise the fact that the position of the British power in 1870 was very offerent from what it was in 1832. Now the ruler of India was not the servant of the company, but the Viceroy of the Queen and as such entitled to the same honours as Her Majesty would receive. However, the A.G.G. assured the Maharana that due consideration of his rank and dignity would be taken and the ceremonial which would be accorded would be such as to enhance the Maharana's rank and dignity in the eyes of the beholders. Having received the suggestions from the A.G.G., the Governor-General decided that the Maharana of Udaipur would take precedence over all the other Chiefs of Rajputana at the assemblage, that he would present no 'Nazar' and that he would generally be received with all the distinction and honour due to his exalted rank. However, the request of the Maharana to be exempted from appearing in the general *durbar* could not be acceded to.[79]

The *durbar* was attended by the ruler of Udaipur, Jodhpur,

Bundi, Kota, Kishangarh, Jhalrapatan, Tonk and Shahpura.[80]

At the assemblage the Maharana was treated as the first ruler in Rajputana.[81] He was given the first seat on the left side of Lord Mayo in the *durbar* and foreign secretary sat next to him. In the ceremonials observed at the time of exchange of visits and making presents, the same consideration was made. A salute of 19 guns was fired at the time of Maharana's arrival at and the departure from Viceroy's camp and the Viceroy received him at the door of the tank, while the next highest Chief of Rajputana, the ruler of Jodhpur was saluted with 17 guns and the Viceroy received him at the edge of carpet.[82]

In his address at *durbar*, Lord Mayo, the G.G. laid particular emphasis over the duties and responsibilities of the rulers of Rajputana. He said, "If we support you in your rights and privileges, you shall also respect the rights and the privileges of those who are placed beneath your care. We demand that everywhere throughout the length and breadth of Rajputana, justice and order should prevail that you should make roads and undertake the construction of works of irrigation and encourage education and provide for the relief of the sick."[83]

The lower States accorded to Maharaja Takhat Singh of Jodhpur in the assemblage at Ajmer displeased the latter. He abstained from attending the public *durbar*, as his seat had been arranged below that of the ruler of Udaipur. Kaviraja Shyamaldas, in his history '*Vir Vinod*' States that at 10-30 P.M. the same day, the Maharana of Jodhpur came to see the Maharana at his camp to dispel his misunderstanding. He told the Maharana that the cause of his absence in the *durbar* was not that he did not wish to sit next to him but that he thought it objectionable that a Political officer should occupy a seat between the Maharana and himself.[84]

The Governor-General expressed his displeasure at Jodhpur Maharaja's conduct and sought explanation from him.[85] In his reply, the Maharaja disclosed that he felt it derogatory to set below the Maharana of Udaipur, as he was in every respect equal to him. The Governor-General, however, observed that the ruler of Udaipur had always been regarded as the '*Patwee*' and the most respectable ruler in Rajputana. Therefore, he would be considered above all other Chiefs and would take precedence over the Maharaja of Jodhpur.[86]

In the assemblage at Ajmer the Viceroy announced the establishment of a college for the education of the children of princes, Chiefs and leading sardars of Rajputana befitting their rank and position. The Maharana on his part declared to contribute a sum of Rs. 1,00,000 towards the fulfilment of the project of the proposed Mayo-College.[87]

An event of some significance took place at Ajmer, which displayed the respectable position which the Maharana enjoyed among the Rajputs and their rulers. The ruler of Jhalrapatan attending the *durbar* was Rajrana Prithvi Singh, the successor of Madan Singh on whom the British Government had conferred the rulership of Jhalrapatan State. Madan Singh was the descendant of Zalim Singh, the famous minister of Kotah during the period of Maratha hegemony. But no Rajput ruler had accepted Raj Rana's position as a sovereign of his State, equal in rank to them in their class. Hence the ruler of Jhalrapatan found himself like an outcast in the Rajput Society.[88] On the occassion of Ajmer assembly the Rajrana requested the Political Agent of Mewar, Lieut. Col. Nixon to use his influence with the Maharana of Udaipur to receive him.[89] The Maharana agreed to it. Several Chiefs of the Maharana opposed this move, the Maharana, however, received the Rajrana at Nasirabad on equal footing of a ruler. Rajrana was given a seat on Maharana's left side permitted to use *Chamar, Morchal*, etc., and was presented an elephant, horses and *Khillats*, all the honours due to a Raja. This honour accorded to the Rajrana by the Maharana Shambhu Singh at once brought the change in the former's position and he was now regarded as having entered the Rajput society as a full-fledged ruler.[90]

Establishment of Opium Scales at Udaipur

In several parts of the State of Udaipur, opium was grown by local people, most of which was exported to Bombay, Previously it was grown for local consumption only. However, after the establishment of the British Government encouraged the cultivation of poppy.[91] In Mewar gradually it came to be the most important and valuable of the cold weather crops and in some parts of the State almost as common as wheat or barley. The Mewar opium passed by a long and circuitous way through Central India, as there was no British depot at Udaipur to weigh the opium and issue permits for the passage through the British territory after levying transit duties on the articles.[92] The opium trade in India was gradually turned into a source of huge profit by the British Government. It exported Indian opium largely to China. Opium which was grown in British territory at Banaras and Patna, was the direct monopoly of the Government while the opium which was grown in the Native States of Central India and south-east Rajputana was taxed heavily when it passed through British territory.[93]

In 1868 negotiations took place between the British Government and the Udaipur *Durbar* regarding the establishment of an opium depot at Udaipur.[94] As the Mewar opium passed through a longway in Central India and thereby suffered intermediate petty taxes on the way, it was thought advisable to export the Mewar opium through the direct route of Udaipur-Ahmedabad road passing though the hilly tracts of Mewar.[95]

Next year, however, the British Government began reconsidering the advisability of retaining the depot at Udaipur, as some of the Rajput chiefs in the hilly tract of Mewar levied transit duties on the opium passing through the route, despite the orders of the Maharana to the contrary.[96] The Udaipur-Ahmedabad route had no proper roads in Mewar and there was no guarantee of security of the goods passing through the Bhil territory. Smuggling was also resorted to by the people. In view of these conditions it was considered that there was no use of maintaining the depot at Udaipur. However, there was a proposal under consideration of the Government of India at that time regarding the Ahmedabad-Udaipur-Ajmer railway project, so the depot was not immediately removed from Udaipur.[97] The British Government, however, asked the Maharana to provide proper security on the roads and take proper measures for manufacturing and despatching the opium and preventing its smuggling in the State territory.[98] The depot was shifted in 1883 to Chittor a railway station as the proposed railway project from Ahmedabad to Ajmer had not been carried out and the conditions on the Mewar route had not improved.[99]

The State derived yearly revenue of about 3 lakhs from the export duty and transit levied on the opium during 1881 and 1890. Subsequently owing to general depression in the opium trade the opium revenue came down to about 2 lakhs. The

Mewar Government levied Rs. 48 and Rs. 20 per cent as export duty and transit duty respectively. The British Government charged export duty of Rs. 600 per chest on opium going out of India and Rs. 700 per chest on opium for consumption in British India.[100]

The growth of opium trade had harmful effects on the economy of the State. Some of the big chiefs and landlords and the native brokers earned profits from the trade, however, the production of the grains fell down on account of the cultivation of the poppy. Consequently, the famines stalked the land repeatedly and with more ferocity and the poor people died in great number.[101]

Administrative Reforms

Maharana Shambhu Singh acting on the advice of the Political Agent at Udaipur, began to show zeal and active interest in further renovating and improving the State administration. The resistance to reforms had calmed down, but the covert opposition still continued, so much so that after Shambhu Singh's assumption of full powers several Chiefs began to clamour for the removal of British Agency from Udaipur, as its existence there was the main source of interference.[102] Lieut. Col. Nixon, the Political Agent reported to the British Government on the 16th May, 1870 that there had been much opposition to the new laws which had been promulgated shortly. The main opposition to the new changes came from the Chiefs, who feared that the changes would have adverse effects on the privileges enjoyed by them and on their autocracy in the estates. The Agent suggested that administrative changes should be effected simultaneously in the *jagirs* and a State official should be posted at every estate to supervise the administrative work there.[103]

Administration of Justices

The year 1869 marks a turning point in the administrative history of Mewar. Maharana Shambhu Singh under the guidance of Lieut. Col. Nixon, the Political Agent prepared an outline of the administrative changes for the State and began implementing them step by step, thus laying the foundation for the modernisation of the State. On the 23rd December, 1869, the Maharana announced for the establishment of a new executive council called *'Mahakma Khas'* and appointed Mehta Pannalal as its *Munshi*.[104] In July 1870 Kesari Singh resigned from his post of *Pradhan* as he was opposed to the new changes in the administration of Justice. The post of *Pradhan* was not immediately filled up and the *Munshi* acted as the medium of communication between the ruler and the various branches of the administration.[105]

In 1870 measures were taken for the proper functioning of Civil and Criminal Courts headed by Arjun Singh and Samin Ali Khan respectively.[106] The former was empowered to settle cases amounting to Rs. 2000 and to fine to the extent of Rs. 1000 while the latter was empowered to fine upto Rs. 500 and to give the punishment upto one year's imprisonment. A new code of law for the State of Mewar compiled by Lieut. Col. Keatinge, the A.G.G. was introduced. A draft of the new rules was sent by the A.G.G., which was translated into Hindi. The Maharana issued orders for the promulgation of the new rules and regulations. All the punishments of physical tortures were abolished and those of fine and imprisonment were introduced instead. Thus onwards the administration of justice came to be regulated collectively by the codes of British India, Hindu Law and local customs.[107]

In August, 1873 the stamp regulations were introduced. Previously a cash fee amounting to ten per cent of the value of suit was charged from the plaintiff and five per cent of the same value was charged from the defendant. According to the new rules only the plaintiff was required to pay the Court fee. It was ordered that the plaintiff should affix stamps to his petition of the value of five per cent of the total amount claimed by him in his suit.[108] The services of an experienced man from Benaras, Mohammad Kudra Tulla were acquired to carry out the work of the stamps department.[109]

Revenue Settlement

The advantages of a regular settlement of revenue in *Khalsa* (State) lands was continually discussed between the British Officers and the *Durbar* authorities which was considered gainful both for the State and the farmers. In 1871-72 the Udaipur *Durbar* took measures to carry it through.[110]

It would not be out of place to mention here, briefly about

the then prevalent system of the land revenue in the State. The principal tenures in the State were *Jagir, bhom, sasan* and *Khalsa*. The *Jagir* land was held chiefly by the Rajput nobles of the State, who paid to the ruler a fixed annual tribute called '*Chhatoond*' (one-sixth of the annual income of an estate) and offered personal services to the ruler with their fixed contingent for a certain period in the year. They also paid certain other taxes to the ruler such as '*Nazarana*' on the occasion of a new Maharana and '*Kaid*' on the succession of a new Chief to the estate. The holders of the '*bhom*' tenure were of two kinds, namely, the petty Chieftains of Kherwara and Kotra, the hilly district of the State, who also paid a small tribute to the *Durbar* and were liable to be called on for local service, and the *bhumias* in other parts of Mewar who paid a nominal quit-rent and perform certain service for the State such as guarding the villages and roads etc. *Sasan* or '*muafi*' land was held by the Brahmins, Gosains and other religious classes and by the Charanas, Bhats, etc. The *Muafidars*' paid no tribute to the ruler and were generally free from all taxes. Lastly, the '*Khalsa*' was the land directly administered by the ruler and revenue collections were made by the *Durbar* officers appointed in the districts.[111]

The tenure in the '*Khalsa*' was *ryotwari* which was of two kinds, '*Pukka*' and '*Kachcha*.' The former gave the occupier rights of mortgage and sale and permanent title to the land, while under the '*Kachcha*' tenure the occupier was little better than tenant at will. In former days the land revenue was usually realised in kind and the share of the State varied in every district and nearly every village for almost every crop and for particular castes. The agriculturist by profession always surrendered the largest share, while Brahmins, Rajputs, Mahajans, etc. were required to pay less. The State demand ordinarily ranged from one-fourth to one-half of the produce. The latter was most common and it was realised in one of the two following ways, namely, by an actual division of produce called '*batai*' and by the division based on a conjectural estimates of the crop on the ground known as '*Kunt*.' Several other cesses were levied on the farmers by the State varying from place to place. Cash rates were applied to valuable crops such as sugarcane, cotton, hemp, vegetables, poppy and tobacco; etc.[112]

In a system of revenue collection like the above, a regular

settlement could hardly have a place. The State revenue was entirely dependent on the crops grown, the amount of land under cultivation and the chances of seasons. A remedy was from time to time attempted by resorting to the system of farming entire districts for fixed annual sums. However, under this system the *ryots* had to suffer greater oppression and exaction, at the leases were mostly *Durbar* officials, rarely men of wealth and responsibility. These conditions resulted in the decline of produce, poverty of the people and the accrual of the arrears of the State demand.[113]

There were about fourteen '*moostagirs*' or farmers of revenue during the Government of Regency Council, who held the leases. They owed to the State about Rs. 592,030 as the balance payment of the State demand. Consequently the losses of some of the defaultory '*moostagirs*' were annulled. An attempt was made to conduct a summary settlement in some of the districts of the State, but could not be carried out owing to the opposition of the State officials and other vested interests.[114]

In 1871, the Maharana decided to take measure to make a regular settlement of the land revenue in the *Khalsa* land. The cultivated area of the villages was roughly measured and the soils classified in accordance with the current usage of the people. An average of the actual collections in each village for the previous ten years was in most cases adopted as the revenue demand and summary rates were fixed for each class of soil in accordance with its estimated value. The arrangement was introduced in various districts for time ranging from 3 to 10 years.[115]

The scheme was once again opposed and attempts were made to sabotage it by the State officials and other exploiting classes in the land. When Mehta Pannalal, the Secretary to Maharana Khas left Udaipur in 1874, the plan almost collapsed and the following year the scheme was abandoned. The lands were now farmed to the *ryots* direct at easy rates for a money payment instead of in kind as had hitherto been the practice.[116] However, the system of farming the lands at cash rates also failed and in the year 1875-76 the matters reverted to the old system of levying the dues in kind.[117]

Changes in District Administration

Administrative conditions in the district of the State were more deplorable. There was no proper division of the districts. The *Hakims* appointed by the *Durbar* generally enjoyed enormous powers over the life of the people in the absence of any definite law to regulate their functions and on account of the weak and inefficient Central Government. These district officials were generally found to be corrupt, inefficient and oppressive. Hence it was found necessary to effect improvement in the district administration. The services of two English officials Captain Charles G. Strahan and Lieut. Holdich were sought to prepare a topographical survey of the State in order to redivide the districts on a proper basis.[118] In accordance with the survey report prepared by the English officers, the *Khalsa* part of the State was divided into 7 divisions, five of them were put under the charge of Police Magistrates, who were made wholly responsible for the administration of their respective areas. However, no changes were made in the administration of two hilly districts of Jahajpur and Kherwara. In order to generate the sense of responsibility and integrity, definite pay scales of the district officials were fixed. The Police Magistrate got Rs. 150 per month while a *Jamadar* got Rs. 30 per month.[119]

As we have said earlier, the first Government school in the State '*Shambhu Ratna Pathshala*, was opened in 1863 at the Capital. Prior to the opening of the Government school, there used to be some private Hindu '*Pathshalas*' and Muslim '*Maktabs*' in which reading, writing and a little simple arithmetic was taught, generally in the open air. In the Government school instruction was given in Hindi, Urdu, Persian, and Sanskrit. In 1865 English was also introduced. Another school was opened for the girls in 1866 at the capital. In 1873-74 two more schools were opened at Bhilwara and Chittor.[120]

The first dispensary was opened at the capital in 1862, in which accommodation for in-patients was provided in 1864. The same year another branch dispensary was opened at the capital. A small hospital was started at Kherwara in 1869-70 for the civil population, which was maintained partly by a monthly grant of Rs. 4 from the *Durbar* and partly from the private subscriptions. At Kherwara and Kotra in the hilly tracts, regiments hospitals were being maintained, which had been opened since Mewar

Bhil Corps were raised. Introduction of vaccination was opposed vehemently by the people in the beginning.[121]

A department of '*Kamthana*' or Public works was established at Udaipur to undertake the construction works of the roads, buildings, etc. Construction of the Mewar portion of Udaipur-Ahmedabad Road was started and similarly the projects of the construction of some other roads as Udaipur to Desuri and Udaipur to Chittor were undertaken.[122]

Attention was given to the sanitation of the city. Arrangements were made for the establishment of a suitable conservancy in the city. An officer was appointed under the supervision of the city magistrate, to superintendent the conservancy. A large staff of sweepers and *chaprasis* was employed and a small duty was levied on some articles being imported into the city to meet the expenses. This measure was also opposed by the conservative opinion of the people in the beginning.[123]

The State troops were reorganised during Shambhu Singh's reign. Regularly trained troops had virtually ceased to exist after the Treaty relations with the British. Consequently, it was always found difficult to curb effectively the refractory activities of the chiefs and the wild tribes of the State. Hence an infantry "*Shambhu Paltan*" was established consisting of 299 sepoys.[124]

The mining work at Jawar had always been a good source of the revenue for the State, yielding revenue of about 2 lakhs in former times which stopped working during the times of turmoil.[125] The Maharana was advised to restart the work of Jawar mines. The services of an Englishman, Mr. Bushell was acquired, under whose supervision the work was started on 31st January, 1873 and about Rs. 15,000 were spent for it. However, the experiment proved a failure. Difficulty arose in removing the water from the mines by manual labour and the Maharana was not disposed to incur the cost of providing machinery, finding that the venture would not be much profitable as the quantity of silver in the galena was found to be in a very small proportion.[126]

In 1873-74, the revenue of the State rose to Rs. 26,51,382 of which Rs. 24,23,829 were spent in the current years.[127]

Maharana Awarded with the Title of G.C.S.I.

The British Government, in appreciation of Maharana's

loyal attitude and behaviour and his policies of internal reforms, honoured the Maharana by conferring on him the title of Grand Commander of the Star of India (G.C.S.I.) in 1871. Col. Brookes, the A.G.G. came to Udaipur to present the title to the Maharana. The Maharana and several of his chiefs objected to such a title being conferred on him, as the title of his race had traditionally been *"Hindua Suraj"* (Sun of Hindus), hence it was felt derogatory for him to accept the title of 'Star.'[128] However, the Maharana was prevailed upon by the A.G.G. to accept the title, who impressed upon him the such titles were given only to the equals. In order to celebrate to occasion and to perform the title giving ceremony, a *durbar* was held on the 6th December, 1871 in which Col. Brookes decorated the Maharana with the badge of the title and presented a flag having the Mewar State emblem.[129]

Maharana's Serious Illness an Arrest of Mehta Pannalal and others

During 1873-74, Maharana Shambhu Singh fell seriously ill. Maharana was being incessantly made to believe by some of his counsellors that some mischievous persons were attempting to make use of witch craft and poison to do away with his life. He was told that several of his relatives including his uncles Sohan Singh and Sakat Singh were involved in the affair. Mehta Pannalal, Secretary of *Mahakma Khas* was also suspected to be one of the conspirators.[130] Pannalal was at once arrested and imprisoned on the 9th September, 1874 in the Karanvilas palace.[131] However, Maharaj Sohan Singh found time to flee from his house and got shelter in the garden next to the Residence and begged for the Political Agent's protection.[132] Lieut. Col. Wright, the Political Agent counselled the Maharana not to punish Pannalal and others until an open and fair trial had been held. Afterwards a rumour was spread by some people that Sakat Singh, Rana's another uncle, was administering poison to the Maharana. The Political Agent got the Maharana's system fully examined by the doctors and found that no symptom of poison was traceable. The Political Agent came to the conclusion that the rivalry between two uncle of the Maharana and their parties had led to the above confusion and intriguing situation. The situation by then became very tense and the parties would have come to blows resulting in bloodshed but for the intervention of the British Agent.[133]

Maharana Shambhu Singh could not recover from his illness and breathed his last on the 7th October, 1874.[134] He was only 27 years old when he died.

Personalty of Shambhu Singh

Maharana Shambhu Singh was a minor, when he was installed. He was surrounded in his minority by mischievous people under whose influence he began indulging into a licentious type of life which ultimately ruined his health. In the beginning of his reign Shambhu Singh found himself allied with the anti-reforms party in the State which vigorously opposed the reforms. However, the anti-reforms party in the State was curbed and the Maharana was brought round in favour of reforms. Since he was given full powers, he generally worked under the guidance of the Political Agent. Thus he was the first ruler of Mewar during whose reign the initial effective measures were taken towards the modernisation of State administration. Though himself illiterate, he opened schools to impart primary education in Sanskrit, English and Hindi. By his association with the Political Agents and other English officers he became adept in talking in English language.[135] The offg. Political Agent Major Bradford reported in 1874 that Maharana Shambhu Singh was in favour of innovation and improvement. Only the want of knowledge acted as a check upon their introduction.[136]

Like his predecessors he was a deeply religious and superstitious ruler.[137] The atmosphere of his court always remained filled with various types of rumours and intrigues, which also had adverse effects on his thinking and activities.

NOTES AND REFERENCES

1. F.D., *Pol.*, Nov. 1865, No. 48. *Vir Vinod* by Shyamaldas, p. 2072.
2. *Ibid*.
3. *Vir Vinod* by Shymaldas, p. 2077. Lachhaman Rao is referred to as Dewan by Louis Rousselet, the French traveller in his memoirs, "*India and its Native Princes*" (p. 153). He visited Udaipur in the beginning of Jan. 1866.
4. *Rajputana Agency Report* (1867-68) by Lieut. Col. Keatings.
5. *Vir Vinod* by Shymaldas, p. 2080

6. F.D., *Pol.*, November 17, 1868, No. 212.
7. *Vir Vinod* by Shymaldas, p. 2075.
8. *Udaipur Rajya ka Itihas* by G.H. Ojha, Part II, p. 789.
9. *Ibid.*
10. *Ibid.*
11. *Udaipur Rajya ka Itihas* by G.H. Ojha, Part II, p. 79.
12. *Ibid.*, p. 790.
13. *Ibid.*, p. 793.
14. *Vir Vinod* by Shymaldas, p. 207.
15. *Rajputana Agency Records*, 171-0, No. 79.
16. *Ibid.*
17. *Ibid.*
18. *Ibid.*
19. *Ibid.*
20. *Ibid.*
21. F.D., *Pol.*, June 1873, No. 47.
22. *Ibid.*
23. *Udaipur Rajya ka Itihas* by G.H. Ojha, Part II, p. 2.
24. *Ibid.*
25. F.D., *Pol.*, June 1873, No. 47.
26. *Ibid.*
27. *Ibid.*
28. F.D., Pol., June 1873, No. 1-4.
29. *Ibid.*
30. *Ibid.*
31. *Ibid.*
32. *Ibid.*
33. F.D., Pol., July 1872, No. 120-122.
34. *Ibid.*
35. *Udaipur Rajya ka Itihas* by G.H. Ojha, Part II.
36. *Ibid.*
37. *Ibid.*
38. *Rajputana Agency Records*, year 1874, No. 190.
39. *Ibid.*
40. *Ibid.*
41. *Ibid.*
42. *Ibid.*
43. F.D., *Pol.*, Aug. 13, 1868, No. 133.
44. F.D., *Pol.*, Oct. 23, 1868, No. 132.
45. F.D., *Pol.*, Aug. 13, 1868, No. 133.
46. *Ibid.*
47. F.D., *Pol.*, Oct. 23, 1868, No. 132.
48. *Ibid.*

49. F.D., *Pol.*, Dec. 1872, No. 384-385.
50. *Rajputana Agency Records* (General), 1869-1873, No. 623.
51. *Ibid.*
52. *Ibid.*
53. F.D., *Pol.*, Jan. 13, 1869, No. 45.
54. *Rajputana Agency Records* (General), 1869-73, No. 623.
55. *Treatise, Engagements and Sanads* by Aitchison, pp. 32-33 & 38-39.
56. Major Mackeson's letter to Maharana Shambhu Singh, April 20, 1868 (Bakshi Khanna Udaipur).
57. *Ibid.*
58. *Mewar Agency Reports*, 1870-71 by Major J.P. Nixon.
59. *Ibid.*
60. *Ibid.*
61. *Ibid.*
62. *Ibid.*
63. *Ibid.*
64. F.D., *Pol.*, March 11, 1869, No. 47.
65. F.D., *Pol.*, July 6, 1869, No. 89.
66. *Ibid.*
67. *Vir Vinod* by Shyamaldas, p. 2039.
68. F.D., *Pol.*, Jan. 1863, No. 116-118.
69. F.D., *Pol.*, Sept. 1869, No. 72-79.
70. *Ibid.*
71. *Ibid.*
72. *Ibid.*
73. F.D., *Gen.*, March 1874, No. 1-3.
74. *Ibid.*
75. *Ibid.*
76. *Mewar Agency Report*, 1870-71 by J.P. Nixon.
77. *Ibid.*
78. *Rajputana Agency Record*, 1870, No. 12, List 2.
79. *Ibid.*
80. *Rajputana Agency Records*, 1879-71 by J.C. Brookes.
81. *Rajputana Agency Records*, 1870, No. 12, List 2.
82. *Ibid.*
83. *Ibid.*
84. *Rajputana Agency Report*, 1870-71 by J.C. Brookes.
85. *Rajputana Agency Records*, 1870-73, No. 10.
86. *Ibid.*
87. *Rajputana Agency Report*, 1870-71, by J.C. Brookes.
88. *Vir Vinod* by Shymaldas, p. 2104.
89. *Mewar Agency Report*, 1870-71, by J.P. Nixon.
90. *Ibid.* In the assembly of princes the Rana always occupies the seat

of honour and has the right of speaking and in the discussions on the points of caste or religion, he is the sole arbitrator (Louis Russelet's *India and its Native Princes*, p. 155).

91. *Hamara Rajasthan* by Prithvi Singh Mehta, p. 227.
92. *A Gazetteer of the Udaipur State* by Major K.D. Erskine, p. 44.
93. *The Economic History of India* by Ramesh Dutt, p. 73.
94. F.D., *Pol.*, Jan. 1869, No. 380-382.
95. *Rajputana Agency Report*, 1870-71 by J.C. Brookes.
96. *Ibid.*
97. F.D., *Pol.*, June 1870, No. 82.
98. *Ibid.*
99. F.D., *Pol.*, Dec. 1883, No. 12-14.
100. *A Gazetteer of the Udaipur State* by Major K.D. Erskine, p. 75.
101. *Home Rajasthan* by Prithvi Singh Mehta, p. 227.
102. *Mewar Agency Report*, 1870-71, by J.P. Nixon.
103. *Mewar Agency Report*, 1870-71, by J.P. Nixon.
104. *Vir Vinod* by Shymaldas, p. 2097.
105. *Mewar Agency Report*, 1870-71, by J.P. Nixon.
106. F.D., *Pol.*, May 1870, No. 119-122.
107. *Ibid.*
108. *Mewar Agency Report*, 1873-74 by Major Bradford.
109. *A Gazetteer of the Udaipur State* by Major K.D. Erskine, p. 73.
110. *Ibid.*, p. 73.
111. *Ibid.*, p. 72.
112. *Ibid.*
113. *Ibid.*, p. 73.
114. *Ibid.*
115. *Ibid.*
116. *Mewar Agency Report*, 1873-74, by Major Bradford.
117. *Mewar Agency Report*, 1875-76 by Major C.G. Gunnings.
118. *Mewar Agency Report*, 1873-47, by Major Bradford.
119. *Vir Vinod* by Shymaldas, p. 2119.
120. *A Gazetteer of the Udaipur State* by K.D. Erskine, p. 82.
121. *Ibid.*, p. 85.
122. *Ibid.*
123. *Mewar Agency Report*, 1873-74 by Major Bradford.
124. *Udaipur Rajya ka Itihas* by G.H. Ojha, Part II, p. 805. In order be sure of keeping the sepoys of "Shambhu Paltan" in a State of efficiency the Maharana employed them to surround the forests and drive the beasts during his hunting expeditions. (*India and its Native Princes* by Louis Rousselet, p. 186).
125. *A Gazetteer of the Udaipur State* by Major K.D. Erskine, p. 53.
126. *Mewar Agency Report*, 1873-74 by Major Bradford.

127. *Ibid.*
128. *Vir Vinod* by Shymaldas, p. 2192.
129. *Ibid.* Before the assemblage was held, the A.G.G. asked the Maharana to make some changes in the usual arrangements of the *durbar*, suggesting that the Maharana should not sit on the silver throne and no canopy should be raised over his seat etc. The A.G.G. previously sat on a gilded chair in the *Durbar* placed next to but lower than the Maharana's seat. As changes suggested by the A.G.G. were unusual contrary to the tradition and derogatory for the Maharana's dignity, consultations were held with the A.G.G. who agreed to the changes proposed by the Maharana by which his chair was to be of silver and raised high on the level of the Maharana's throne. This new arrangement was introduced which continued thereafter (*Sahiwala Arjun Singh ka Jiwan Charitra*, Part II, p. 18).
130. *Rajputana Agency Records,* (Mewar), 1874-84, No. 1.
131. *Vir Vinod* by Shyamaldas, p. 2122.
132. *Rajputana Agency Records,* (Mewar), 1874-84, No. 1.
133. *Ibid.*
134. *Mewar Agency Report,* 1874-75, by Col. G. Herbert.
135. *Itihas Rajasthan* by Ramnath Ratnu.
136. *Mewar Agency Report,* 1873-74, by Major Bradford.
137. *Vir Vinod* by Shymaldas, pp. 2123-4.

11

Maharana Sajjan Singh: Interference and Reforms

Shambhu Singh was succeeded by Sajjan Singh, a minor boy of 16 years.[1] Shambhu Singh had no son and adopted none. Once again the problem of adopting the successor arose in the royal house. There were rival claimants and there was a possibility of a clash between them.[2] The old and influential chief of the State, Rao Bakht Singh of Bedla again took initiative and brought about a settlement. He did not join the funeral procession and had consultations with Lieut. Col. Wright, the Political Agent, several prominent Chiefs then present in Udaipur and the royal ladies.[3] By their choice Sajjan Singh, the son of Maharaja Sakat Singh of Bagore was adopted as the successor to the late Maharana.[4] After all necessary and traditional ceremonies, Sajjan Singh was installed on the throne on the 8th October, 1874.

Attempt to Commit *Sati* by the Palace Ladies

On the death of Maharana Sambhu Singh, there arose, once again, the problem of immolation of royal ladies as *Sati*, as it had been a custom in the House. It is stated that as many as four palace ladies sought to burn themselves with the deceased ruler.[5] They attempted to escape from the palace, but were prevented from doing so by the vigilance of the Political Agent, Lieut. Col. Wright and some of the chiefs. Even then Bhoori Bai, one of the Maharana's concubines persisted in her attempts to come out to commit herself *Sati*. Thereupon the Political Agent threatened to imprison her. However, the tradition of *Sati* had come down from generation to generation and the members of the family, specially the palace ladies were deeply attached to the custom. The mother of the late Maharana felt much exasperated when she learnt that the "performance of the sacred rite" was being prevented by the English. She demanded that she should herself be allowed to commit *Sati* with her son, as no Maharana of Udaipur upto that time had died alone, and his memory, country and people would be disgraced for ever by this interference. Her Plea was of no avail and no lady was allowed to immolate herself.[6]

Succession Dispute

Sajjan Singh's installation was not acceptable, as was the situation in Mewar, to each and every noble of Mewar and a rival claimant was produced.[7] He was Sohan Singh, the Chief of Bagore, who had made off from Udaipur in 1874, when he was charged with being involved in the conspiracy of attempting to poison the late Maharana. To press his claim Sohan Singh threatened to use valance with the backing of several Chiefs. The Political Agent requested the British Government to grant an early recognition so as to avoid any disturbance.[8] The Governor-General asked the A.G.G. to furnish him with full information stating whether the late Maharana had expressed any wish about the adoption and whether Sajjan Singh's claim to the *gadee* was fully justified. He further directed him that Political Agent in Mewar, in the mean-while, should in conjunction with the minister take necessary steps for preserving peace and carrying on the administration of the State. The Political Agent was further authorised to call, if required, two companies of Bhil corps from Kherwara for that purpose. On the 18th October, the A.G.G. sent a telegram to the Governor-General stating that the late Maharana had expressed no wish regarding the adoption of Sajjan Singh, the latter was qualified and had the strongest claim to succession.[9]

On the 16th October, 1874, Maharaj Sohan Singh of Begore

sent a telegram to the Governor-General pressing his claim to the *gadee* of Mewar. He said that he had a paper in his possession to support his claim for the succession, in which the late Maharana had acknowledged his right. However, he further said, by means of false accusations his enemies were trying to impress the Political Agent in Mewar to confirm the nomination of Sajjan Singh and set his claims aside.[10]

Strongly recommending Sajjan Singh's claim, the A.G.G. in his letter dated the 15th October, 1874 wrote to the Governor-General, "Among the advantages incidental to the succession of Sajjan Singh would be that we should have a minority in Udaipur State and I would recommend that in event of His Excellency being pleased to recognise Sajjan Singh, a firm and experienced Political Agent should hold at Udaipur a sort of guardianship of the minor and ample powers under the general supervision of the A.G.G. in the administration of the Mewar State." He further stated the Supreme Government might thereby hope to see the Mewar borders really sat in order, the refractory and powerful feudal barons brought into real and proper subordination to the central power, and the material improvement of the country practically attended to.[11]

On the 24th October came the telegram of Viceroy's confirmation of Sajjan Singh as the successor to the late Maharana. In his letter following the telegram, the Governor-General observed that as Sajjan Singh was not full of Age and educated, he should not be at once entrusted with full powers of administration. He, therefore, asked the A.G.G. to make, in conjunction with Council, such arrangements as the circumstances might require.[12] On the 30th October, the accession *durbar* was held in the palace, which was attended by almost all the Chiefs and the officials of the State.[13] Lieut. Col. Wright along with Lieut. Yate, Commander of Mewar Bhil Corps attended the *durbar*. In the *durbar* an uproar took place on account of a dispute which arose between some Chiefs about the arrangements of seats in the assembly. The situation became so tense that a clash appeared imminent, which was averted by the intervention of the Political Agent, Lieut. Col. Wright, who led Megh Singh, the Rao of Begun and Kunwar Madan Singh of Bheender, the main disputants, out of the *durbar*. Two more *durbars* celebrating the installation were held afterwards, first on the 29th November, and the second on the 28th December.[14] In the first *durbar* the Khillat of accession sent by Queen Victoria was presented to the Maharana and in the second the Kharita of the Governor-General, Lord Northbrooke addressed to the young prince was read.[15] The Governor-General, conveying his congratulations, advised the Maharana to work under the direction of the Political Agent until he came of age and be capable of discharging the duties of the Government which would thereafter would develop on him. Notwithstanding the above proceedings the disturbances on the part of Sohan Singh did not cease and the Political Agent called two companies of the Mewar Bhil Corps under the command of Major Gunning from Kherwara to compel him to submit.[16]

Upon the installation of Maharana Sajjan Singh the British Government decided to levy 'Nazarana' fee on the State. The Maharana and the council of Mewar Chiefs, however, raised objections to the decision on traditional grounds and the Governor-General conceding to their plea exempted Mewar successions observing that Mewar was the oldest State in India and its ruler was the head of all the Rajputs.[17]

Action against Sohan Singh

In order to curb the refractory activities of Sohan Singh the Mewar Government at the outset ordered confiscation of the Bagore house at the Capital, which was placed in the possession of Sakat Singh, father of Maharana Sajjan Singh.[18] Sakat Singh was also granted the Jagir of Sonyana and an allowance of Rs. 65,000 per year was fixed to be paid from the State treasury. Sohan Singh was ordered to retire to Bagore his Jagir, and stop his disloyal activities.[19] But no change came in his attitude. In the meanwhile companies of Mewar Bhil Corps requisitioned by the Political Agent arrived at Udaipur. On the 18th September a force consisting of 975 infantry, 437 cavalary and six guns of the State along with the contingents of 106 feet and 109 horsemen supplied by the nobles and 275 men of the Mewar Bhil Corps was despatched under the command of Major Gunning the commanding officer of the Mewar Bhil Corps to reduce him to submission. He was arrested at his *Jagir* without a shot being fired and was brought to Udaipur on the 8th October. He was exiled to Banaras and the *jagir* of Bagore was attached and placed under the charge of an agent of the *durbar*.[20]

In 1880, Sohan Singh was allowed to return to Mewar by the British Government after getting from him a written undertaking to the effect that he would not take to lawlessness in future and that he would renounce his claim to the *gadee* of Mewar as well as to the Chiefship of Bagore. An annual allowance of Rs. 10,000 was fixed for his maintenance of which a village yielding not less than Rs. 2000 would form part. Sajjan Singh confirmed the Chiefship of Bagore on his own father, Sakat Singh in 1881 obtaining from him an undertaking to the effect that only his descendants would hold the estate.[21]

Regency Council's Government (Oct. 1874–Oct. 1876)

The British Government appointed a Council of Regency consisting of four *sardars* and two officials under the presidentship of the Political Agent to carry on the Government of the State until Sajjan Singh came of age.[22] The members appointed to the council were Rao Bakhta Singh, of Bedla, Ranawat Udai Singh of Kakarwa, Maharaj Gaj Singh of Shivarati and Moti Singh 'Bhanej'; Mehta Gokul Chand and Saheewala Arjun Singh. The last two had been appointed secretaries to the Mahakma Khas after the dismissal of Mehta Panna Lal shortly before the demise of the late ruler. They were confirmed on their posts to carry on the work of general administration under the Council.[23]

The Council, usually, met once a week. The Political Agent laid before the Council all cases of importance, of unusual expenditure, of disagreements between chiefs and others of position, of disputes connected with caste, religion and customs of the country, etc. However, the council was not empowered to pass an official opinion upon any subject nor to entertain any case except which was laid before it by the Political Agent for its consideration.

Thus during the minority of Maharana Sajjan Singh the British Government acted with caution. Though it appointed a State council, the powers of the Government were practically wielded by the Political Agent "so as not to allow the disturbing conditions to recur which marked the beginning of the late ruler's reign. The councillors were expected only to advise. Another caution was also taken. The Maharana was generally present in the meeting of the Council to associate himself with the work of the Council and the Government. Sometimes, various files of the Government work were sent to him at his palace for his study and perusal. By this procedure the young Maharana came into touch with the work of the State and got a gradual training in administration.[24]

The civil and criminal courts functioned separately as they did in the previous reign. The former was headed by Mathuradas and the latter by Maulvi Abdul Rehman.[25] *Mahakma Khas* worked as the Appellate Court.[26] As Sahiwala Arjun Singh could not fit himself in the new system of work and atmosphere dominated by the Political Agent, he resigned from Mahakma Khas in the month of July, 1875. Kothari Chhagan Lal who was working as the head of the Finance department was appointed as the Secretary in his place.[27] However, neither he nor Mehta Gokal Chand could work satisfactorily. Col. Herbert, the Political Agent, therefore, called Mehta Panna Lal back from Ajmer, obtaining the consent of the young Rana and re-appointed him on the 8th September, 1857 as the Secretary to *Mahakma Khas*.[28] Mehta Panna Lal had been released from imprisonment after the death of Maharana Shambhu Singh. An attempt on his life was made by some person at the instigation of *Zanana*. However, he escaped and had thereafter left Udaipur for Ajmer on the advice of the Political Agent.[29]

Some changes were made in the State Council in the year 1875. As Maharaj Gaj Singh expressed his desire to go to Banaras on pilgrimage, he was replaced by Manohar Singh of Lawa as the Councillor. Parsoli Rao who went to Abu owing to ill-health was replaced by the Delwara Chief.[30]

The functioning of the Council did not prove successful, as the councillors generally remained silent on the matters placed before them. To bring this situation to an end, the Political Agent began sending the cases to the Maharana prior to placing them before the Council, to allow him to form an independent opinion and to encourage the councillors to participate actively. However, it did not produce the desired results.[31] Col. Herbert, the Political Agent found himself thus isolated and unsupported in the whole work. In his despatched of the 4th August, 1875, he complained, "The people of all grades insist upon looking to the Political Agent for Justice and redress of their grievances. I find that all power in the State is thrust into my hands and that I necessarily occupy in the administration the position of the *durbar* or ruling power.[32]

Arrangements for Maharana's Education

The Secretary of State, London in his despatch of the 23rd December, 1874 wrote to the Governor-General that it was regrettable to learn that the new Maharana was 'uneducated' and possessed no 'particular ability'. It was, therefore, necessary to take such steps during the period of his minority as were possible to qualify him for the discharge of his important duties as a ruler.[33] Dewan Jani Behari Lal, a Nagar Brahman and Vakil of Bharatpur State at Abu, was appointed in February, 1875 as tutor of the young Maharana.[34] His monthly salary was fixed at Rs. 500 which was afterwards raised to Rs. 700. The Political Agent instructed him to do his duty by endeavouring to obtain influence over the mind of the young Chief, to keep him away from the palace ladies as much as possible, to advice him to avoid excesses of every kind and to induce him to take interest in the Government of his country.[35]

Beharilal was well versed in Sanskrit, Hindi, Persian and English languages and had sufficient administrative experience. His appointment as the tutor of the Maharana produced 'restraining influence' over the palace ladies and the courtiers. He stayed at Udaipur for about one year. During this short period he gave sufficient training to the Maharana in dealing with the administrative work. He assisted Sajjan Singh in understanding and forming opinion about the State matters which were sent to him by the Political Agent for his study. Beharilal's services were cut short in October, 1875 as the ruler of Bharatpur called him back on duty. He was replaced by Framji Bhikaji, the second class Assistant Political Agent in Mewar.[36]

Maharana attends Prince of Wales' Reception at Bombay

On the 8th November, 1875 H.R.H. Prince of Wales Edward Albert arrived at Bombay to pay a royal visit to India. All the princes of India were invited to assemble at Bombay to give him a royal reception. Maharana Sajjan Singh was also requested by the British Government to attend the Bombay reception.[37] The Maharana and his prominent Chiefs raised the question of the dignity and status of the Mewar ruler which he claimed to enjoy among all the rulers of Indian States and begged assurance to the effect that he would be treated as the first ruler in India as had been done at Ajmer in 1870.[38] The request was not conceded to. However, he was assured that he would be given equal honours with the rulers of Hyderabad, Baroda and Mysore.[39]

The Maharana arrived at Bombay on the 30th October. There he exchanged visits with the Governor-General Lord Northbrooke and the Governor of Bombay Sir Philip Woodhouse. On the above occasions customary practices of reception and offering of presents were duly observed.[40] On the 8th November, Prince Albert landed at the port. The Maharana, however, came to know that at the place of reception, arrangement of seats had been made contrary to the assurance given to him by the British Government. Therefore, he did not take his seat and kept on strolling. When the Prince landed, the Maharana "got into a great scrape for refusing to walk after the Gaikwar of Baroda" to receive the Prince.[41] On the November, the Maharana paid his personal visit to the Prince of Wales, which the latter returned on the 10th, customary practices of reception being duly observed.

Viceroy's Visit to Udaipur

Lord Northbrooke, the Viceroy and Governor-General of India paid a State visit to Udaipur on the 23rd November, 1875 on his way from Bombay to Udaipur. He was received with all fanfare and rejoicing. Preparations for the reception of the Governor-General caused considerable labour and anxiety to the *Durbar* Government specially in putting in order the roads which had been greatly damaged by the recent disastrous flood.[42] The Governor-General stayed for three days at Udaipur. Whole of the city was illuminated with lights to celebrate his visit. Visits were exchanged between the Maharana and the Viceroy. On every occasion a salute of 21 guns was fired for the Viceroy and of 19 guns for the Maharana. After seeing various places in the city, the Viceroy left Udaipur on the 26th November.[43]

Gosain of Nathdwara

For several years the Gosain (head of a Vaishnav religious seat) Girdharilal of Nathdwara had been adopting attitude of disloyalty and insubordination towards his sovereign, the Maharana of Udaipur.[44] In 1671 Goswami Damodar of Vaishnav sect fled from Giriraj, with the idol of his deity, Goverdhannath (Shrinathji) and came to Udaipur, being threatened by the iconoclastic frenzy of the Mughals.[45] Rana Raj Singh of Mewar gave him shelter at a place about 30 miles north of Udaipur which later came to be known as Nathdwara. Sufficient *jagir* was conferred on him to meet the expenses of the shrine.[46] Thus the Goswami was also created *thikanedar* (Chief of an estate) any by virtue of his later position he enjoyed powers almost equal to any other Chieftain in the State. In one respect he enjoyed an exceptional privilege. As he was a religious priest, he was not required to render personal services or pay tribute to the Maharana like other Chiefs.[47]

By the end of the year 1874 it was brought to the notice of the British Government that Gosain Girdharilal had assumed the attitude of independence from the authority of the Udaipur *Durbar*,[48] that he was indulging in licentious sort of life and that he had thrown away the spirit and devotion of his fore-fathers in the service of Nathdwara temple. He had arbitrarily reduced the quantity of the daily offerings to the deity, was oppressing the people of the land attached to the shrine and was acting in a tyrannical manner to extract money from the pilgrims. He assumed supremacy in civil and criminal affairs of the *Thikana*. He unjustly imprisoned some persons at Nathdwara and when complaints were lodged with the *Durbar* and the latter asked him to explain the reasons of their detention, he refused to comply. Lastly, he employed many Pathan sepoys in his service against the orders of the *Durbar*.[49] His disobedience and insubordination went to the extent that he thought of seeking himself fully independent of the Mewar State and for that he requested the British Government to take his estate directly under the British sovereignty. His request was rejected by the British Government.[50]

In the year 1871 the *Durbar* attached some villages of the priest and withdraw from him the privilege of having a representative (*Vakil*) with the Political Agent.[51] But these measures did not produce the desired results. In the year 1874 the priest arrested a discharged servant named Parshuram, in defiance of Maharana's orders and cruelly treated him. He was released only on the orders of the Political Agent.[52] In the month of December preparations were made to despatch a force to the place to compel him to submit. However, to avert this action the Political Agent induced the Goswami to write a letter to him acknowledging his subordination to the Maharana in all temporal matters and agreeing to obey his orders, to release all the prisoners, to cease oppressing his people, to submit the files of civil and criminal cases to the *Durbar* and to dismiss all foreign soldiers from his service.[53]

In the beginning of 1876, the Political Agent received petitions from various places of India on behalf of the people of Vaishnav sect protesting against the action of Mewar Government in taking away the temporal supremacy of Nathdwara Gosain and the attachment of his villages in Mewar. After receiving relevant reports pertaining to the matter from the Political Agent in Mewar, the British Government observed that the matter was one in which the British Government was interested in so far as good Government of the State under his Political Agent's superintendence and preservation of peace and order generally was concerned.[54] The Gosdain on his part continued his attitude of insubordination going back on the promises he had made to the Political Agent. The British Government thereupon decided to use force to bring him to submission.[55]

On the 8th April, 1876, the officiating Political Agent, Major Gunning, the members of the Regency Council including Rao Bakhat Singh of Bedla, Mehta Pannalal and Mehta Gokul Chand proceeded to Nathdwara with State troops, guns and a detachment of the Mewar Bhil Corps.[56] The priest was besieged along with his 200 men outside the town in the Lalbag garden half of the troops and guns were sent under the command of Lonergan to take possession of the temple, where the Pathan soldiers closed the gates from within and refused to submit.[57]

The Goswami was arrested and sent to Udaipur. His guards either surrendered or were disarmed. His minor son Goverdhanlal was installed in his place who was induced to accept the following conditions offered by the Council.

1. He (Gosain) would act in accordance with the orders of the *Durbar*.
2. There would be no reduction in the services and offerings to the deity and the previous status would be restored.

3. Foreign soldiers would not be employed by him. The *Durbar* would appoint the officials and guards, who would be paid by him.
4. The Maharana would appoint an officer to manage the work of civil and criminal justice, who would act in consultation with him.

The Council decided that the power of civil and criminal justice would be vested in him as soon as he came of age, but the appeals in all cases would be heard by the *Durbar* Government. A *Durbar* force was left for the protection of the shrine. The *Durbar* control over Nathdwara remained for about five years, after which Goverdhanlal was given the powers of internal administration. Girdharilal, the deposed priest, being exiled from Mewar, was allowed to proceed to Mathura. An allowance of Rs. 1000 p.m. was fixed for him.[58] As he did not desist form his objectionable activities and began intriguing against the arrangements made by the *Durbar*, this allowance was also stopped later on. Mehta Gopaldas was appointed as the *Durbar* official in the Thikana at the outest, who was later on replaced by Mohan Lal Pandya. Arrangements were made for the education of the young Goswami by an intelligent tutor and for his protection from being influenced by vicious persons.[59]

Expulsion of Maharana's Favourites from Udaipur

In 1875 Maharana attained the age of Majority to be invested with ruling powers. The Political Agent, however, found that the Maharana was surrounded by elements and the persons in whom he reposed confidence were of objectional character.[60] One of them was the Maharana's father, Sakat Singh himself, who was considered to be a man of loose character and it was feared that he misguide his son and play intrigue in the Council.[61] Among others were Dhabai Badanmal (a mali or gardener by caste) and his son Rooglal. Badanmal had been in charge of the royal Kitchen in Shambhu Singh's time. Since then he gained gradual ascendancy in the royal House so much so that he became a favourite of the young Maharana. In May, 1876, Major Gunning, the officiating Political Agent suggested Badan Mal's expulsion from the city. In August, Col. Herbert, the Political Agent reported that Badanmal was not so offensive, as was his son Rooglal, who was very much insolent and oppressive and held pernicious influence over the Maharana. Col. Herbert called Rooglal to the palace in the presence of the Maharana and reproved him for his insolent and oppressive dealings and his interference in the matters with which he had no concern. He was warned by the Political Agent that unless he followed suit, he would be banished from the country and serious consequences would follow for his family.[62]

The Governor-General Disapprove's Col. Herberts Dealings

When the reports of the above treatment meted out to Rooglal reached the British Government, the Governor-General disapproved of the action. In his despatch of the 16th September 1876 he observed, "Nothing short of grave political exigency would justify the adoption of threatening attitude towards a chief in the personal matter, such as the choice of his friends and associates. And the circumstances must be indeed serious which would demand the interposition of the paramount power for the purpose of expelling a favourite of the Maharana from Udaipur. "He further directed that" the Political Agent should exert in a kind and friendly way whatever influence he may have with the Maharana for the purpose of removing reasonable and well grounded causes of discontent, avoiding vexatious interference in the personal concern of the chief.[63]

In October, 1876, Maharaja Sakat Singh was compelled to leave Udaipur for Sonyana but was afterwards permitted by the orders of the Governor-General to return to Udaipur in July, 1877.[64] The Governor-General; Lord Lytton, in November, again resented Col. Herbert's attitude. He strongly objected to the adoption by the Political officers of a threatening tone towards native chiefs, unless such proceedings were expressly sanctioned by the Government of India.

Maharana Invested with Ruling Powers

On the 30th October, 1876, Maharana Sajjan Singh was entrusted with direct control of the administration of the State by Col. Herbert, the Political Agent, without any formality being observed in that connection. Some restrictions were, however, placed on him which were regarded as an unwarranted and derogatory precedent. The restrictions placed on the Maharana included his taking advice of the Political Agent in all important matters of the administration and seeking prior concurrence of the Political Agent before reversing any decision of the Regency Council taken during his minority or replacing the secretaries of *Mahakma Khas*, who had been working for last few years. In his communication of the 30th October, 1876, addressed to the Maharana Col. Herbert explained that these conditions had been temporarily imposed in accordance with the order of the Supreme Government. Whether the duration of these conditions should be short or long would depend upon the degree with which the Maharana gained the Political Agent's confidence by proper discharge of his duties as a ruler and thereby satisfied the British Government. Then only the arrangements would be made to bestow full control of the Government of the State on him.[65]

Thus the formal installation of Sajjan Singh with full powers was put off, though Sajjan Singh was, in practice, allowed, hereafter, to enjoy the powers of a ruler to the extent the British Government was allowing the rulers of other Native States to enjoy. The confusion in this matter continued to prevail for some years and nothing was done by the British Government to remove restrictions despite repeated appeals of the Maharana in this respect. As late as May, 1884, the Maharana again requested the Political Agent to get the restrictions formally removed. The Political Agent Lieut. Col. Walter wrote to the G.O.I on the 1st May, 1884 "For many years past these conditions have been, of course, a dead letter, yet they still remain on record and Maharana on several occasions asked that he might receive a formal *Kharite* from the British Government withdrawing or cancelling those conditions. The British Government consented and the restrictions were formally withdrawn by a communication addressed to the Maharana by the Political Agent on the 26th July, 1884.[66]

Maharana attends Delhi *Durbar* of 1877

The British Government held an Imperial *Durbar* at Delhi on January 1, 1877 to proclaim the assumption of the title of 'Empress of India' or 'Kesari Hind' by Queen Victoria. All the princes, Chiefs and distinguished persons of India were invited to attend the *durbar*. Maharana Sajjan Singh received a communication from Lord Lytton, the Governor-General of India, requesting his presence at the assemblage.[67] At first the Maharana expressed his reluctance to go to Delhi almost on the same grounds, which his predecessor Shambhu Singh had raised before going to Ajmer.[68] However, the G.O.I. pointed out to Maharana that there could be no demur in accepting the invitation and it was obligatory for him to attend the assemblage. At this juncture the British Government found some of its Political officers in the Native States behaving as "the partisans and advocates" of their Rulers and encouraging and supporting the Ruler's grievances regarding their status and dignity. Lord Lytton directed all the political officers to stop such activities.[69] The Maharana arrived at Delhi on the 18th December by a special train. Here he exchanged visits with the princes of Jodhpur, Rewa, Jaipur, Jhalawar, Kishangarh and Indore and also with Lord Lytton, the Governor-General.[70]

On the 1st January, 1877, sixty-three princes of Native States attended the *Durbar*. The Governor-General distributed badges, flags and presents to all the princes in accordance with their status and services to the British Government. The Maharana took his seat in the *durbar* with nine of his Chiefs while eight of his attendants stood beside him with traditional royal paraphernalia. Maharana Sajjan Singh's salute was raised from 19 to 21 guns. Rao Bakht Singh of Bedla was awarded the title of 'Rao Bahadur' and Mehta Pannalal and Kothari Chhaganlal received the titles of 'Rai'. On his way back the Maharana paid a visit to Jaipur on the 8th January on the invitation of Maharaja Ram Singh where Jodhpur prince Jaswant Singh was already staying as a guest. The Maharana stayed there for one day and reached Udaipur on the 20th January.[71]

Re-organisation to the State Council

Soon after his return from the Delhi *Durbar*, the Maharana began to take keener interest in the work of the State Government. He appointed Kaviraj Shymaldas, a charan by caste, who afterwards, wrote *'Vir Vinod'*, the official history of Mewar, as his Chief counsellor.[72] The Political Agent Lieut. Col. Impay became his main guide, friend and Philosopher.[73] The Maharana announced the constitution of a new State council, namely, *'Ijlas Khas'* (Privy Council) on the 10th March, 1877. It consisted of 14 members both Chiefs as well as officials, who included:

1. Rao Bakhta Singh of Bedla.
2. Rao Laxman Singh of Parsoli.
3. Rawat Arjun Singh of Asind.
4. Maharaj Gaj Singh of Shivarati.
5. Thakur Manohar Singh of Sardargarh.
6. Raj Devi Singh of Tana.
7. Ranawat Udai Singh of Kakarwa.
8. Raj Fateh Singh of Delwara.
9. Kaviraj Shymaldas.
10. Bhanej Moti Singh.
11. Arjun Singh Sahiwala.
12. Dhabai Rao Badanmal.
13. Mehta Padam Singh.
14. Purohit Padmanath.[74]

All the above members were nominated as honorary members. Munshi Ali Husain was appointed as the *'Shrishtadar'* of the council. Mehta Rai Pannalal who was hitherto working as the secretary of *Mahakma Khas* was confirmed on his post. The Maharana issued *'Khas ruqquas'* (Special orders signed by the Maharana himself) the newly appointed members of the Privy Council by which they were directed to give him such good counsel as would help his subjects in getting full justice, and peace and prosperity might prevail in the country. Measures were taken for the improvement of various departments of the Government as Civil and criminal courts, *Mahakma Khas* departments of Public Works, Revenue, Accounts, Police, Army and *Deosthan*, etc., of which was placed under the charge of one or two responsible officials.[75]

Efforts made by the Maharana for improvement of the administration marked slow progress. In his report for the year 1877-78, Major Cadell, the Political Agent, stated, "The Privy Council has proved rather a difficult institution to deal with. Class interests have, at times, interfered and decisions on matters, where its support was most needed, have with difficulty been elicited. Still it has been of considerable assistance to the administration and has decided under the Maharana's presidence many important cases." The Political Agent further remarked that the most active element in the administration had been the Maharana who had displayed imagination and perseverance. He had been seeking the aid and advice of the Political Agent unreservedly.[76]

Oppression of the Bhils in the Hilly Tract

In the beginning of 1876, the *Durbar* forces were despatched to suppress the refractory Bhils of the Pals of Mandawa and Bakol in the hilly tract where, it was reported to the Political Agent, some cases of witch-hunting had occurred and Bhils were least disposed to submit to law and order.[77]

The Bhils on hearing the arrival of State troops prepared themselves to face the attack by dividing their bulk of cattle and goods among their friends and relations in the neighbouring Pals and by storing grains for their own consumption, in anticipation of their being compelled to take to the hills. The expedition was successful in crushing the defiance of the Bhils. The ring leaders were caught and several hundred heads of the cattle and most of the unharvested grain were seized. This was the first time when guns were used against bows and arrows of the Bhils in the hilly tract.[78]

Looking at the recurrence of Bhil uprisings, the Political Agent advised the Mewar *durbar* to find out the causes of Bhil unrest and redress their just grievances. The findings of the enquiry revealed that the administration in the hilly tract was too much corrupt and oppressive.[79] Several complaints were received during enquiry against Pandit Raghunath Rao, the *Hakim* of the district. It was found that he was using cruel and inhuman methods in dealing with the people and was extorting money illegally and forcibly from them. The oppression of the Bhils was reported to have reached to such an extent that these people had to sell their children to fill the pockets of the State officials. Raghunath Rao was found guilty of embezzlement of State money amounting to 3 lakhs. He was forthwith dismissed from the service and, along with his guilty subordinates, he was punished with imprisonment.[80]

During the proceedings of the above enquiry a case of misappropriation by several persons of the money of *'Rikhabdeo'* temple, lying in the hilly district amounting to about Rupees one lakh came to notice. The Mewar *Durbar* appointed prominent businessmen and officials of Udaipur to go into the affairs of the temple and the management of the temple was placed under the supervision of the *'Deosthan'*, department of the State.[81]

Akshya Singh was appointed as the new *Hakim* of the District. A new department namely, *'Shail Kantar Sambhandhini Sabha'* or 'council concerning hilly area' was constituted to give proper attention to the affairs of the district. Jani Mukund Lal was appointed as the head of this department, under the direct supervision of the Maharana himself.[82]

Another source of trouble in this district was the exploitation and oppression of the Bhil subjects by *Vilayatis* (Pathans) who were employed as soldiers by the Mewar Government. These Pathans, along with their Government duties, also carried on money-lending business with the local people on very high rates of interest. They committed every type of fraud in the accounts and claimed payment as high as five times of the principal. They used force to extort every pie of their fabricated accounts and turned them into slaves. Such a brutal treatment provoked the Bhils to retaliate who killed some of these Pathans at different places. The State official's thereupon used force to destroy Pals of the Bhils. This action caused a great stir in the entire area and the situation threatened to turn into a wide Bhil uprising.[83] The Mewar Government, however, acted cautiously and warily. The Maharana ordered all the Pathans to be called to Udaipur and instituted an enquiry into their dealings. Most of them were found guilty. At this juncture about 200 Pathans tried to creat disorder in Udaipur, whereupon guns and troops had to be employed against them. These found guilty were either sentenced to imprisonment or expelled from the country and those found non-guilty were re-employed.[84] These eneasures had the effect of temporary pacification among the people in the area.

Settlement Operations and Stir in the Peasants

We have seen the efforts to settle the land revenue in the *Khalsa* area of Mewar had failed during Maharana Sambhu Singh's reign. In the year 1877 Maharana Sajjan Singh was advised to take up the work in order to enhance the revenue of the State and improve the conditions of the subjects and the country. Col. Impey, the Political Agent drew a scheme. The A.G.G. Mr. Lyall advised him to act slowly and cautiously and asked the Mewar *Durbar* to obtain a comprehensive survey report on land and revenue questions in Mewar.[85] With this subject in view Mr. W.H. Saith, first grade settlement officer in N.W. Province who had just completed settlement operations in Dholpur State was called to Udaipur and employed in *Durbar* services in February, 1878. He toured the country for about a month and submitted a preliminary report to the Mewar Government.[86] Maharana himself toured his country between November, 1878 and January, 1879. The keen interest and zeal displayed by the ruler in the matter received appreciation of Lieut. Col. Walter, the Political Agent who reported to the British Government on the 1st May, 1880. "It is so rare that a Chief will leave his capital except for sporting or other purposes of amusement, that few of them have a really practical knowledge either of the requirement or want of the country over which they are called upon to rule."[87]

In August, 1879, Mr. A. Wingate, C.I.E. of the Bombay Civil Service joined the Mewar services as the Superintendent. Settlement Operations in Mewar receiving Rs. 1250 as his monthly pay.[88] An unprecedented service condition was, in regard to his employment thrust upon the *Durbar*, which ran counter to the established rules and the spirit of Treaty relations. Though Wingate was in the State employment, he was required to work under the political supervision of the A.G.G. This practice eventually led to great bitterness and apprehensions afterwards. Wingate commenced his work on the 24th September in *Chhoti Sadri* area. He had to face stiff opposition from the local people. Villagers displayed a spirit of non-cooperation in the measurement work. Amins and labourers were not made available. However, the *Durbar* authorities stuck to their position firmly. In April 1880 the work was stated in Chittor district also.[89]

The resistance to the settlement operations continued and the peasants threatened to suspend the cultivation. In the same year a forest officer was appointed by the Mewar Government who started his work zealously by taking out land in every village for grass and forest conservancy and punishing those who disobeyed the orders.[90] This added fuel to the fire. People were accustomed to the old order for hundreds of years and got alarmed at the new changes. *Baniya, Hakims*, officials and Rajput chiefs, *e.g.* of Salumbar, Bheendar, etc. were instigating the peasants to oppose the land settlement work by spreading various types of rumours. Great discontent amounting almost to rebellion among certain classes prevailed in July, 1880. All the Jats of Mewar united in refusing to cultivate until the 'obnoxious' orders were withdrawn. On the 22nd June, 1880 at the holy place called *'Matri Kundia'* in Rashmi Paragana, hundreds of Jat peasants swore in the light of full Moon and the lunar Eclipse that they would not plough or furnish any assistance to the *amins* until they had gone to Udaipur and got their grievances redressed by the *Durbar*.[91] A deputation of about 250 cultivators including a number of *Baniyas* came to Udaipur on or about the 1st July, 1880 and presented their demands before the Maharana. The Maharana along with Shymaldas, Mehta Pannalal and Wingate patiently heard and discussed their grievances with the deputationists. He tried to convince the peasants that the measures for the settlement of revenue would result to their advantage. He assured them that no harm would be done, in any way, to their ancestral rights in the land, as they had been led to believe. He also promised to make such changes in the work of the Forest Department which would go to redress their grievances. But, the Maharana refused to accept their demand to suspend the land settlement operations.[92]

The *Durbar* authorities announced that they would not hesitate to use force wherever people tried to obstruct the operations. However, promises and threats produced little effect. Various other causes worked to enhance the dissatisfaction of the people. The Political Agent in his report of the 3rd July, 1880, drew the attention of the British Government to the serious situation prevailing in Mewar. He stated that it would have been more advisable if survey operations had not been started in a region which was more backward and deeply bound to old traditions. The *Hakims* were mainly of *Baniya* class, who were all against the settlement because it went against their own self-interest. The Political Agent further observed in his report that it was very unfortunate that so many new things should have been introduced simultaneously. The Salt-agreement with the Mewar Government had resulted in many complaints by the people. Sardars and peasants had disliked the project of railway, having little hope of compensation for their land from the *Durbar*. The forest rules and the settlement operations had produced further dissatisfaction and excitement in the people.[93] By this time the Political Agent had received orders from the British Government to commence the census operations in Mewar. He requested the Government to allow him to keep the census work in abeyance for some time, keeping in view the unrest prevailing in Mewar lest it might aggravate the crisis.[94]

However, after some time the resistance of the people began claiming down. Mr. Wingate and Rai Pannalal went from village to village explaining the policy of the Government, which had its effect. *Patels* began quarrelling among themselves. Consequently the settlement work progressed rapidly.[95]

The Maharana made necessary changes in the work of Forest Department by which he limited the duties of the ranger to conserving the larger forests and looking after the grass lands belonging to the *Durbar* only. Preliminary operations of the settlement were completed in 1884.[96]

Agreement Regarding Railway Line

In 1864, the extension of the B.B. & C.I. Railway line passing through Rajputana States was contemplated by the British Government and the correspondence was started with the States concerned regarding the lease of land and other relevant matters.[97] The then *Durbar* Government under Regency Council headed by the Political Agent agreed to bestow land for the proposed railway line passing through Mewar territory, free of cost and settle the matters in the manner as would be done by other States in Rajputana. However, the British Government was then requested to give an assurance that the line would not disturb or harm temples and other religious buildings and needles destruction of the property would be avoided, which was agreed to by the British Government.[98]

The British Government proposed the following three conditions for the acceptance of the *Durbar* to arrive at an agreement:

1. That the necessary extent of land averaging 200 feet in breadth for the construction of railway line would be given up by the *Durbar* Government free of all costs. All necessary compensation for occurring loss thereby to the owners of lands, homes, gardens, etc. in the State

territory would be defrayed and borne by the ruler.
2. That full jurisdiction in such leased lands, short of sovereignty right, would be made over absolutely to the British Government.
3. That all transit and other duties on goods passing through would be surrendered to the British Government. However, duties on good breaking bulk and being conveyed to and from the railway might be charged by the State at the usual rates and according to a fixed tariff, to be settled thereafter.[99]

The above conditions were accepted by the *Durbar* Government during the minority of Shambhu Singh, in July, 1865, when the Political Agent held the entire control of administration in his own hands. From the very beginning, various chiefs and people of the State raised objections to imposition of such arbitrary conditions which were considered not only harmful and derogatory for the State, but were regarded as distinct violation of the spirit and conditions of the Treaty of 1818. The introduction of British jurisdiction in the State and other rights and privileges to be obtained by the British Government inside the State were the points which were vehemently opposed. It appears that the opposition had its effect and the matter was put-off for some years.

In 1879 the negotiations regarding the construction of railway line passing through Mewar State were resumed.[100] Maharana Sajjan Singh requested the British Government to reconsider the three conditions proposed by the latter in 1865. The Maharana, on his part suggested the following changes in the conditions:

1. That no stipulation should be made enforcing payment by the *Durbar* for losses to its subjects in land, houses, etc. and that 200 ft. of land seemed to be more than was required and requested that such land only as was actually needed should be taken up. The *Durbar* also hoped that, by the liberality of the British Government, he might receive compensation for the land so taken up and for the losses of the transit duty.
2. That no detail was given of the authority which the Government would wield in the land so taken up, the

Durbar requested full explanation on this point.

3. That *Durbar* would not levy transit duty on goods passing through Mewar, however, it should be allowed to levy duty on goods exported from and imported into Mewar at the usual rate or at such rates as might be thereafter decided upon.[101]

The Political Agent Lieut. Col. Walter had an interview with the Maharana on the 17th November, 1879 in this connection. He sent a communication to the Maharana on the next day in which he said, "I have examined the papers relating to the case and found an original *Kharita*, dated the 15th July, 1865 in which all the three points to which objections are now made, were cordially agreed to by the late Maharana. Objections raised by the *Durbar* are, therefore, uncalled for. As regards compensation to his subjects, it is the matter of the decision by the Maharana himself. As regards quantity of land, presently 50 ft. land to the each side of the line would suffice. Regarding the transit duties the late Maharana had agreed to the condition that no compensation would be demanded. It, therefore, behoves the present chief to carry out the agreements so made by his predecessor. "He further informed the Maharana that the British Government would exercise full powers in the land thus made over, in the same way as it did in the territory actually belonging to itself."[102]

On receipt of this letter, the Maharana found himself helpless to maintain his position with regard to the objections he had raised and he gave in. The line was opened in 1881 which crossed the eastern half of the State from north to south having the length of 82 miles in Mewar territory.[103]

The introduction of the railway line in the backward and feudal economic conditions of Rajasthan created a great havoc in this part of the country. Several classes who dealt in the export and import trade in the area got ruined economically, specially the numerous 'Banjara' and 'Gadolia' people who used to carry goods from place to place and supplied all the articles of necessity to the people. Several of the erstwhile business centres became deserted.[104] In the absence of investment opportunity in other spheres, the moneyed classes began leaving Rajasthan to explore opportunities elsewhere. The industry and manufacture in Rajasthan also suffered badly, as the foreign manufactured goods were dumped in the market. The export of food grain and other agricultural products increased greatly in exchange of the imported foreign goods resulting in the scarcity of food grains in Rajasthan. Thus the poverty and destitution of the peasantry increased and whenever there was the deficiency of the rains, famines stalked the land and thousands died of hunger. No doubt the introduction of railway lines had its own advantages for people, particularly in the famine days, when they proved very useful in swift movement of grains from one place to another. Basically introduction of railway lines in India and the Native States was to fulfil the imperial interests of the British Government and naturally its imposition on the Native States had adverse effects on the latter in all respects, legal, political, economic and social.

Slavery, Traffic in Women and Cases of Infanticide

In 1863, the Udaipur Government had issued a notification by which the practice of selling children was prohibited by law.[105] In the year 1876 a case of the sale of two girls belonging to Mewar territory but sold in Cutch in the Bombay province was reported to the Supreme Government. This case raised a problem as to what attitude should be taken by the British Government regarding the system of slavery of women prevalent among Rajputs of Cutch and Rajputana. It was a custom among Rajputs to give girls in dowry of their daughter's marriages as '*golis*' or slaves. The Political Agent in Kathiawar commenting on the custom suggested that whatever their (Rajput) tradition and custom might be, the delivery of human beings into slavery should not be tolerated by the British Government. However, the Bombay Governor in Council observed in reply that the Government did not consider it necessary or expedient that notice should be taken of the '*golis*' then in the houses of the Rajputs in Cutch in Bombay province, but decided measures should be taken to secure the punishment of persons who were found guilty of kidnapping or abduction for traffic in girls.[106]

As early as the year 1847 the British Government had urged the Native States to take vigorous steps to stop the cases or infanticide and foeticide. There were not definite rules in the

States of Rajputana regarding the prohibition of those practices.[107]

In 1882, the Political Agent informed the British Government that during 1876 to 1881, 42 cases of abortion and four cases of infanticide after birth took place in Mewar. He disclosed that the punishment being given for these orgies was 3 years maximum imprisonment and maximum fine of Rs. 500. The cases were tried by the criminal court and appeals lay with the State Council.[108]

The practice of infanticide was specially prevalent among the Rajputs. The victims were generally the female children. The birth of a daughter was regarded a calamity in the house, because the father of the daughter had to pay a heavy dowry in the marriage and no Hindu could keep his daughter unmarried as it amounted to committing a sin. Another cause of foeticide and infanticide was illegal pregnancy. The British Government urged the *Durbar* to take vigorous measures to check the above inhuman and barbarous practice.[109]

Salt Agreement

Among the sources of British Government's revenue in India, their monopoly in salt had been very important.[110] Salt was manufactured at several places in the British India and the Native States. The British Government levied heavy duties on the article at the time of its passage from the Native States into the British territory. Salt was being imported from England also along with other manufactured goods to India.[111] The monopoly of the Government in salt with its policy of heavy duties as high as three times its cost price fetched high profits, but the poor people in India suffered badly. The duties were so levied on the article that the salt which was sold 30£ per ton in England was sold in India as high as 21£ per ton.[112]

The British Government maintained an Inland custom line to raise the duty on salt imported into British India from the Native States. This inland custom line, about 2500 miles long, extended across the whole of British India from Punjab to Madras, consisting of thorny trees and bushes, stone walls and ditches and it was guarded by an army of about 12,000 officers.[113] In the seventies the British Government decided to abolish this system firstly by fixing the duties equal in the different parts of India and secondly by agreements with Native States in Rajputana and Central India under which the British Government obtained leases and control of all the important sources of salt manufactured.[114]

In Rajputana almost every State had its own salt works, which apart from supplying salt for the consumption of the people of the States also exported it, specially to Oudh and Central India. Every State used to draw sufficient revenue out of the salt trade by levying duties on the article before its export. The British Government, in order to gain monopoly over the salt manufacture in Rajputana also, started negotiations with the rulers of Native States. The famous Salt Lake of Sambhar was thus taken under the management of the British Government from Jaipur and Jodhpur States.[115]

In Mewar, there was numerous petty works owned by about forty-three Chiefs and other manufacturers. The salt works were scattered over Mewar territory specially between the Khari river and the Udaipur city.[116] On the 14th February, 1878, when Maharana Sajjan Singh was camping at Rajnagar, Mr. A.C. Hume, member of the Viceroy's Council and Lieut. Col. Impey, the Political Agent in Mewar arrived at the place to negotiate the salt agreement.[117] Kaviraj Shymaldas and Mehta Rai Pannalal discussed the question on behalf of the Maharana. Naturally, the State officers expressed anxiety over the huge loss of revenue to the State and ruinous effects over the people owing to the closure of the salt works. Discussions continued for some time. However the larger interests of the Imperial Government were made to prevail over the interests of the *Durbar* Government and the salt Agreement was signed between the British Government and the Mewar Government on the 12th Feb., 1879.[118]

The Salt Agreement closed all the salt works in Mewar. It was stipulated in the Agreement that no salt other than the salt, on which duty had been levied by the British Government would be exported from or imported into Mewar territory and that the Mewar Government would not levy and transit duty on the British Salt. In order to compensate the losses of the *Durbar* and other manufacturers of the salt, the British Government agreed to pay Rs. 2900 per year. In the same way the British Government agreed to pay Rs. 35,000 per year to the Mewar Government to compensate the loss of revenue to the State which it got from the transit duties.[119] It was also stipulated that the Maharana would get one thousand maunds of salt free of cost for his personal use and the salt purchased for the consumption of people of the State of Mewar at Panchbhadra would be taxed at half the rate of the duty.[120]

The Agreement was ratified on the 8th May, 1879. However, some difficulties were found in regard to the purchase of salt for consumption in Mewar and charging of half the tax on it. Therefore, the Agreement had to be amended. It was decided that the British Government would charge full duties on the salt of Mewar and Maharana would get, in compensation, a sum of Rs. 2,04,150 per year in all, which included Rs. 2,700 to be paid to the Chiefs and others as compensation for closing their salt works. The Maharana on his behalf agreed to abolish transit duties on various articles in Mewar to make good the losses suffered by the people owing to the price rise of the salt.[121]

The closing of salt works in Mewar had its adverse effects on the country. The salt trade mainly run by 'Banjara' community, came to a standstill and the old distributary organisation existing in Mewar was shattered. Consequently, the salt became scarce and the price of the salt rose high as much as three times.[122] The labourers became unemployed, the traders lost their trade and several places were totally deserted. A general unrest spread throughout the country. In order to alleviate the suffering of the people, the Mewar *Durbar* exempted duties on essential articles in March 1880, except on opium, cotton cloth, tobacco, timber, iron, mahuwa ganna, milk cloth, etc.[123]

However, continues complaints poured in from the districts about the scarcity of the salt and rise of prices. The Maharana sent Mehta Rai Pannalal in the July 1880 to the districts to make a careful enquiry on the subject of salt trade. A month later he submitted a report in which he suggested the proper distribution of salt in the country.[124] Thereupon the Mewar Government took measures to achieve the object. Each paragana of the State was divided into circles, each circle having a depot of salt to supply the surrounding villages. The Government expressed its desire to give credit on easy interest, to the merchants who volunteered to import salt in the State. The *Hakims* of the districts were ordered to keep sufficient stock of salt at the depots, to take steps to encourage salt trade and to report periodically to the

Government about the prices of the salt. The immediate result of these measures was the reduction in the price of the salt upto almost the prevailing rate.[125]

Bhil Disturbances in Hilly Districts

For the first time in 1881 a census was attempted in Mewar. In the prevailing backward and conservative atmosphere of the State, it also became the cause of dissatisfaction in the people.[126] It was found difficult to make the people understand its objects and advantages various types of doubts were created and rumours were spread, as soon as the operations were started by the State officials. Some of the leading nobles of the State considered it as the British Government's desire to levy a 'Barar' (tax) for contribution towards the cost of Afghan war, while among the Bhils a general apprehension arose that numbering was being attempted to see how many able bodied men could be recruited to fight for the British Government at Kabul. Not only this, some strange rumours prevailed among the Bhil population. Some thought that fat women would be assigned to the stout man and the lanky to the lean, etc. There was a general apprehension that new taxations would follow the Census. Though other classes of people were, somehow, specified but the work among the Bhil population was found difficult and some of the enumerators really brought a crisis by their over-zealous and atrocious dealings.[127]

The Government soon realised the impending danger. In the hilly district the house to house census and actual counting of individuals was abandoned and the Government directed the officials to ascertain through the principal gametis or the headmen the number of Pals and huts in each 'Pal', by which a rough idea could be made of their number. Thus, Census operations, which caused many alarms in the Bhils, passed-off quietly but they left in its train elements of distrust and resentment which, in an accidental collision occurring afterwards led to a wide-spread out-break.[128]

By 1881 several factors combined to bring about a critical situation in the hilly district. The barbarous social practices prevailing in the Bhils were being ruthlessly suppressed by the *Durbar* Government under the supervision of the Political Agent. The Mewar *Durbar* had issued orders prohibiting manufacture of liquor, which the Bhils regarded as their age old freedom and right. The rise in prices of salt taking away of the freedom of salt manufacture and mismanagement in its distribution enhanced their dissatisfaction. Lastly, the census operations caused great uproar among them and only a spark was needed to light the fire of a general uprising.[129]

The *thanadar* of Barapal, 14 miles south of Udaipur, in the month of March 1881, sent a mounted policeman to summon a gameti of another 'Pal', Paduna, 9 miles away to appear as a witness in a land dispute.[130] The Gameti concerned refused to comply. When the Policeman tried to use force, it resulted in his murder by the Bhils standing by. This event alarmed the whole Bhil population of this area who feared reprisals from the State. Several thousand Bhils assembled at the temple of Mother Goddess and took oaths to fight as one man the armed attack by the State troops. The emissaries of the Bhils of Barapal and Paduna scattered in all the parts of the area and instigated the whole population to join their defiance.[131] The *thanadar* of Barapal was killed along with the *kalal* (liquor contractor) and several other persons and the post was burnt down. Bhils of Asirgarh, Kotra, Payee and other places also joined them. At Asirgarh a *Kamdar* and some police constables were done to death. Bhils burnt the police posts of Kewra Pas. Akshya Singh, the *Hakim* of the hilly district was besieged in the village of Parsad. The chief leaders of the upsurge were Neema Gameti of Beelak Pal, Khema of Peepli and Joyata of Sagatari. The Road between Udaipur and Kherwara was closed by them.[132]

The news of their widespread disturbances reached Udaipur on the 26th March 1881. Next day a force of *Durbar* troops consisting of two guns, 150 cavalry and 500 infantry, left Udaipur with orders to open the roads and suppress disorder at the insurgent pals avoiding clash with the peaceful Bhils.[133] Troops were placed under the command of Lonargan and Raja Aman Singh. When they reached Barapal and Paduna, they found the pals deserted. The troops burnt a few road-side huts of those pals to terrify the Bhils. As the troops proceeded further the Bhils cried 'faire, faire', shot arrows and disappeared in the hills. News was then received that the Bhils intended sacking the villages of Parsad and Rikhabdeo, and were threatening to attack the post of Kherwara itself.[134] Consequently the troops were divided. Rawat Pratap Singh of Bhensrorgarh, Maharaj Rai Singh of Shivpura and Maulvi Abdurrahaman Khan were sent with a party of troops towards Kotra, while Rawat Ratan Singh of Kurabar, Mehta Takhat Singh and Madan Singh of Bathera proceeded towards Kewara Pass.[135]

In the meanwhile, Shymaldas, the Maharana's personal secretary accompanying the troops received a letter from the Maharana on the 29th March, in which the Maharana expressed his dissatisfaction at the slow movement of Mewar troops and directed them to save Hakim Akshaya Singh at Parsad. The remaining troops, thereupon advanced towards the valley of Gadhera on the 30th March, fighting their way out and killing several Bhils, whose dead bodies the Bhils carried away.[136] However, the troops were insufficient in number and the Bhils continued to block their advance and interrupt the communications.[137] There were no reinforcements coming from Udaipur. On their arrival at Rikhabdeo, the Mewar troops found about 6 to 7 thousand Bhils assembled there. The later attacked the State troops, but were repulsed. For three days the 'Bhils' were chased and fired at by guns and muskets but to no consequences. Following their usual practice the Bhils disappeared in the fastness while being attacked and then reappeared suddenly and attacked the unwary enemy.[138]

Having realised that the Bhils would not be suppressed in that way, Shyamaldas entered into negotiations with the Bhil leaders through Khemraj Bhandari, the priest of the Rikhabdeo temple. The Bhils put forth some 24 demands. They asked the Government to cease interference with their practices and usages as witch-hunting. Census work should be stopped, barar tax (war-tax) should be withdrawn and the State troops should be pulled back.[139] As the negotiations commenced the Bhils agreed to open the roads on the condition that the movement of the State troops would be withheld, so as to enable the State officers to send their demands to the Maharana for 'consideration'. Both parties agreed to suspend their hostilities until the 17th April, during which period negotiations would continue in order to arrive at an amicable settlement.[140] On receiving the reports of the disturbances in the hilly area of Mewar the Governor-General expressed resentment at the conduct of the British officers in Mewar Agency who were not looking carefully after their business. He observed that it was perfectly well known in Rajputana that if Darbar officials were not guided and controlled by our Political officers in their dealings with the Bhils, they would mis-manage and bring in trouble. The A.G.G. arrived at Udaipur under the G.O.I. instruction and took the affairs in his own hands.[141]

Negotiations at Rikhabdeo continued. On the 19th April Lieut. Col. Blair, the First Assistant Political Agent in Mewar and the commandant of the Mewar Bhil Corps, arrived on the scene from Udaipur accompanied by Mewar Settlement Officer. Mr. Wingate[142] Blair tried to contact the Bhil leaders directly through his trustworthy Bhil officers. Apprehension arose in the minds of the *Durbar* officers lest the British Government might make direct settlement with the Bhils and the hilly district of Mewar might be taken away from Mewar, as was done with the Mewar part of Merwar during the time of Maharana Bhim Singh.[143] Regardless of the objections of Mewar officials, Blair entered into talks with the Bhil leaders and asked the Mewar officials to remit the taxes and stop census work for the time being. On the same day some disorder took place in the conference between State officials and the Bhil representatives. Blair feared that disturbances might again break out. He telegraphically summoned British troops from Erinpura with the intimation that a serious rising was imminent on account of the deceitful tactics of the Mewar officials in dealing with the Bhils. At Udaipur, Col. Walter, receiving the news of the failure of talks of Udaipur officials with the Bhils, persuaded the Maharana to permit Blair to supercede Shyamaldas, if necessary in bringing about a settlement with the Bhils.[144] It instantly broke down the morale of the State officials, who immediately come to an agreement with the Bhils.[145]

Mewar Government agreed to remit half the Barar, and to stop census work while the Bhils agreed to pay fine to compensate the killing of the State persons and promised to refrain from the lawlessness in future to abide by the State law and not to help the offenders. An inscription was raised at Rikhabdeo announcing the settlement. The settlement was a cheering news for the Governor-General who observed that Col. Walter had done well in keeping the *Durbar* in front and himself acting as mediator, thereby the British Government had been prevented from coming into direct collision and exacerbation with the Bhils.[146]

The above settlement did not atonce bring total peace in the hilly district. Disturbances here and there continued for some time. In the beginning of 1882 Bhils of Bhorai and Kathra Pals took to lawlessness. They besieged the house of Dayalal Chobisa, the '*girdawar*' of the district. Troops were again sent from Udaipur which suppressed the insurgence and punished their leaders.[147] The Maharana got a fort constructed at Bhorai and put a garrison of 300 troops in the fort in order to keep a constant restraint on the nearly pals.[148] Lord Ripon was gratified to learn the way the Maharana had punished the outrageous Bhil subjects and observed that he had "acted in those difficulties with energy, judgement and mercey ably supported and advised by Dr. Stratton, the officiating Political Agent.[149]

Col. Walter toured the hilly district in the winter of 1882-83, in order to bring about a permanent pacification in the district. He made necessary consultations with the Maharana before proceeding on tour. The latter, desirous of permanent peace in the area, agreed to allow him to act and decide on his behalf as he thought useful on the spot.[150]

At Rikhabdeo Col. Walter had a successful meeting with several of the gametis and a large number of Bhils. An agreement was arrived at the A.G.G. subsequently reported that "the Bhils put their turban on my feet begging pardon. My main object in assembling the Bhils was to tell them that the crime of witch-swinging must be put down. After several hours of discussion an agreement was arrived at, which was engraved on stone, put on the right hand side of the entrance of the temple with much ceremony." The agreement provided that the gametics (headmen of the Pals) and the Banjgaris (headmen of the hamlets) would never allow a woman being killed on the suspicion of her being a witch. If they had a suspicion on any woman, they would report it to the Government. They took the oath of 'Kalaji (their deity at Rikhabdeo)' that they would follow the agreement.[151]

The Case of Mewar Portion of Merwara

After the subjugation of the Mers by the combined armies of British, Mewar and Jodhpur Governments in 1819-21, the two

Native Governments agreed on 1823 to cede their portions in Merwara to the British Government for ten years in view of the maintenance of peace and order in the area.[152] The Maharana of Udaipur agreed to pay the sum of Rs. 15,000 (Mewar coins) or Rs. 12,000 (British coins) per year towards the maintenance of the Merwara Battalion and its share of the expenses for the civil administration of its area from the income of Mewar portion.[153] In the year 1833, again a formal engagement was entered into by which British management was extended for a further period of 8 years. The contributory payment towards the maintenance of the local corps and the cost of civil administration was raised to Rs. 16,000 (British coin) per year.[154]

In the year, 1841, while the 1833 engagement was still in force, both the Governments agreed to raise Mewar Bhil Corps at Kherwara under the management of the British Officers. It was expressly stipulated, at the time, that the surplus revenue of Mewar-Merwara should be placed at the disposal of the British Government to meet its share of the cost of the Bhil Corps, which was fixed at Rs. 50,000 per annum. The agreement of 1833 expired in 1841, but no talks were held for its further extension or otherwise. In the year 1845, when the question of the expediency of bringing the judicial and revenue administration of the whole Merwara on the same pattern as that of the Ajmer district under the British Government, was raised, the Udaipur *durbar* suggested the renewal of the engagement of 1833, with new conditions which the British Government did not accept finding them disadvantageous to itself. The British Government on her part proposed the permanent cession of the Mewar portion to the British territory. As no satisfactory arrangement could be arrived at, negotiations were suspended in 1848.[155]

The Mewar Government, thereafter sent several communications from time to time the British Government to return the Mewar-Merwara to the Mewar State. But nothing came of them and the question remained on an unsatisfactory footing. However, Maharana Shambhu Singh submitted a fresh appeal on the 7th January, 1872 to the British Government to restore the territory, when he came to learn that the British Government was making arrangements for a 30 year revenue settlement of the whole Merwara, which meant that the British Government wanted to keep the territory under its possession indefinitely.

However, the A.G.G. assured the Maharana that the settlement which might be made regarding the Government of the country.

In February, 1874, the Political Agent in Mewar informed the British Government that since 1868-69 there had been a great deficit in the revenue of the Mewar area of Merwara and, therefore, the surplus income of the area could not fulfil the share of the expenses of Mewar Bhil Corps which was Rs. 50,000 per year. He further stated that the Mewar Government was indebted to the British Government to the extent of Rs. 1,32,928 on that account upto the end of the year 1872-73. The Maharana was, therefore, asked to pay the above amount as per the agreement of 1841, pertaining to the Mewar Bhil Corps which provided that if the revenue of Mewar-Merwara exceeded after meeting the share of the expenses of Merwara Battalion, Merwara Civil Administration and Mewar Bhil Corps Government, the excess would be given to Mewar Government and if the revenue fell short, that would be made good by the Mewar Government. Maharana Shambhu Singh on his part proposed that as it would bring an extra drain on the State's resources, it was desirable that the area should be restored to the State.[156]

While the talks were continuing, Maharana Shambhu Singh died and the Regency Council took over the administration of the State during the minority of Sajjan Singh. The British Government tried to utilize the situation of the ruler's minority to their own advantage. On the 2nd March, 1875, the Political Agent called an urgent meeting of the Regency Council to make arrangements to meet the demand of the British Government to pay the amount of Rs. 1,32,928. Orders to that effect were issued and the amount was paid.[157]

In the year 1883, the British Government again made the demand of Rs. 76,000 on the Mewar Government to make good the balance on the same account as was done in 1875.[158] Thereupon Maharana Sajjan Singh again raised the question of restoration of the Mewar-Merwara. The Governor-General in reply of the Maharana's letter observed that the tenure on which the British Government administered the district of Mewar-Merwara was an intricate question and any discussion about it did not appear to be expedient.[159] Regarding the difficulties connected with the adjustment of the account of the district, however, he informed the Maharana that the British Government was ready to agree to the condition that the revenues of Mewar-Merwara should in future be accepted in full discharge of the contribution of the Mewar State towards Mewar Bhil Corps, Mewar Batallian and the cost of the administration of the district itself. The British Government would, in that case, forego the claim of arrears of Rs. 76,000 from the Mewar Government. He also proposed that, in future, the system of rendering accounts to the Maharana should be discontinued to avoid unprofitable discussions.[160]

The Maharana, on his part did not agree and expressed his apprehension of loss of his sovereignty over the said territory. He further observed that the proposals of the British Government regarding the adjustment of revenue of the district was not profitable to the Mewar Government. The Maharana, however, took opportunity to propose that the villages previously owned by Mewar, which were under the possession of Gwalior State, might be transferred to Mewar in exchange of Mewar portion of Merwara. On that condition he agreed to give away permanently the area of Mewar-Merwara.[161] In June, 1882, Lord Ripon, the Governor-General while disapproving of the Maharana's proposals, assured the later that his sovereignty would continue over the district. He also promised that if the receipt from the district exceeded, any time, Rs. 66,000 per year, which sum represented the amount of the contribution payable by the Maharana for all the expenses referred to the surplus proceeds would be made over to Mewar. He assured that the Maharana would be informed every year about the amount of revenue collections by the Political Agent.[162] This arrangement was, at last, accepted by the Maharana.

Kalambandi with the Chiefs

During Maharaja Sajjan Singh's reign, the Maharanas' relations with his Chiefs further improved. Shambhu Singh and Sajjan Singh both developed amity and good-will with them giving due regard to their traditional dignity and privileges. Most of the Chiefs also, on their part, began rendering personal services to him and paid their tribute regularly to the ruler. However, the problem regarding the extent of Maharana's Civil and Criminal jurisdiction in the estates of the nobles remained unsolved. This problem became more acute, owing to the progress of reforms in the State area, as the administration was being placed on a footing of definite rules and regulations and it was not possible to leave more than half the portion of the State in complete by medieval and lawless conditions. It was, therefore, considered necessary to introduce similar administrative rules and regulations in the *jagir* areas as well and Mewar *Durbar* to act as an appellate authority over them.

In 1878, Maharana Sajjan was able to persuade a large number of first class Chiefs to come to an agreement with him regarding their respective powers of civil and criminal jurisdiction. The Agreement (*Kalambandi*) was individually signed by 14 estates namely, Banera, Sadri, Bedla, Bijjellia, Begun, Badnor, Delwara, Amet, Kanore, Parsoli, Kurawar, Asind, Lava, and Shahpura.[163] The Chiefs of Salumbar, Kotharia, Deogarh, Gogunda, Bheendar, Bansi, Bhensrorgarh and Meja did not sign it. Several of the whom had been for long working as the anti-Maharana party. On May 1880, Lieut. Col. Walter reported that eight nobles of the first rank, the non-conformists, still held aloof because they objected to the new procedure as invasion on what they considered their rights.[164]

The agreement provided that the authority of the Maharana, Ijlas Khas and Mewar Government, would be supreme in the State and the orders of the Government would be obeyed by the Chiefs. The Maharana would not interfere with the civil and criminal cases of the *Jagir*, although he would hear appeals in such cases. But the cases of murder, *sati*, decoity, highway robbery, traffic in children and counterfeiting of the coins would have to be reported to the *Durbar* at once and proceedings in connection therewith would be submitted for the *Durbar's* approval. Laws which were framed for the whole of Mewar would be applicable to the *Jagir* area also. The rules also defined the procedure in cases in which one of the parties was a Khalsa subject or a resident of some other estate.[165]

The object of *Kalambandi* was to regulate the civil and criminal powers of the Chiefs and bringing the procedure in *Jagir* Courts on the lines of the State courts, which had been recently constituted. Through some of the nobles declined to sign it, however, the object was largely achieved and this agreement formed a good basis to determine the relations between the ruler and his Chiefs, in future.[166]

Title of C.I.E. Conferred on Bakhta Singh

Rao Bakhta Singh of Bedla the old and loyal chief of Mewar State was awarded the title of C.I.E. by the British Government on the 3rd September, 1878. A special *durbar* was held by the Maharana in which the Political Agent, Major Caddle performed the ceremony of the investiture. The Rao had received a sword as the prize from the British for his faithful services rendered by him during 1857-58 and in the imperial Assembly of 1877, at Delhi he was given the title of Rao Bahadur. Rao Bakhta Singh died on the 3rd February, 1880. Lieut. Col. Walter in his report of the 10th May 1880 wrote about him,'The gentleman had been a faithful servant to the Udaipur State under five of its rulers and proved the loyalty to the British Government in the stormy days of 1857-58. He took a prominent part in assisting the Political Agent in preventing 'Sati' on the occasion of Shambhu Singh's death."[167]

Banera Chief's Effort to be Independent of Mewar

Originally the estate of Banera was a Mughal grant to Bhim Singh, the fourth son of Maharana Raj Singh (1652-1650). During the reign of Rana Raj Singh II (1754-1761), the Raja of Banera accepted the sovereignty of the Maharana of Udaipur and thereafter he was treated as one of the first class nobles of the States. Raja of Banera paid the tribute, rendered personal services and observed all other duties and obligations as other first class chiefs in the State adid.[168] During Maharana Swaroop Singh's time, the Banera Chief, having fallen out with the ruler joined the anti-Maharana party and took to disobedience. In 1852, the Maharana ordered the Chieftain of Dabla, a vassal of the Raja of Banera to render his personal services to him directly and continue to pay as usual the yearly tribute of Rs. 300 to the Raja. This action further worsened the relations. In 1855, on the death of Raja Sangram Singh, Govind Singh was adopted and installed as the Raja without obtaining the prior approval of the Maharana. He did not go to Udaipur to pay homage to the Maharana and perform the 'Talwar Bandai' ceremony. It was a clear violation of the traditional practice and infringement of sovereign rights of the Maharana. Preparations were made by the Mewar *Durbar* to despatch troops to camel the Raja to submit. The Raja relented and came to Udaipur seeking his pardon and paid a fine of Rs. 21,000 for his disobedience. Regarding his rights on Dabla he continued to assert his claims.

About 1873, the Raja of Banera sent a 'dhons' party on Dabla with the intentions to restores his authority. The Mewar *Durbar*, however, again issued an order (*Parwana*) that Thakur of Dabla would render his personal services to the Maharana only and informed the Raja also about it. But the Raja did not raise his 'Dhons' party. In January, 1875, the Raja of Banera was again ordered to withdraw his men from Dabla but he did not comply with it and sent an additional number of Pathan soldiers to Dabla reinforcing the party. Clashes occurred at Dabla resulting into bloodshed. The Mewar *Durbar*, receiving complaints from the Dabla Thakur instituted an enquiry, which found Banera authorities guilty of bloodshed and disobedience of the *Durbar* orders. The *Durbars* Council, in punishment of Banera Chief's disobedience, passed orders freeing the Dabla Thakur from the vassalage of the Banera in all respects and requiring him accordingly to pay the tribute also to the Maharana.[169]

In 1876, Raja Govind Singh sent a petition to the British Government against the above decision of the Mewar *Durbar* along with the request to make him independent of Mewar *Durbar*[170] on the grounds that the Chiefship of Banera was a grant of the Mughal Emperor and as such he was entitled to pay his tribute and render services to the British Government directly. The Governor-General in his letter of the 3rd July, 1877, disapproved of the Raja's claim to be independent of Mewar State. However, he directed the Political Agent in Mewar to persuade the Maharana to restore his rights over the village of Dabla. In 1879, the Maharana agreed to issue orders to that effect, which were, however, not executed and the Raja continued complaining to the British Government.[171]

Succession Dispute of Bohera Jagir

In the year 1884 the attention of the British Government was drawn towards another trouble in Mewar which resulted in the disturbance of internal peace and bloodshed.

Upon the death of Udot Singh, the Chief of Bohera Jagir Kesari Singh of Sakatpura, his nephew assumed the Chiefship of the estate with the help of the late Chief's relations in defiance of Mewar *Durbar's* decision regarding Bohera sucession.[172] The

Maharana ordered Kesari Singh to retire from Bohera and come to Udaipur. Kesari Singh refused to obey his orders and continued his defiance. Thereupon the Maharana sent 'Khalsa' (troops and officials to attach the *jagir*) to the *Jagir* on the 19th March, 1884. The troops consisted of Shambhu Paltan, Sajjan Paltan, First Cavalary and two guns and were placed under the joint command of Lonorgan and Mehta Laxmi Lal. Levies of various Chiefs of the Chittor and Kherwara district also joined them. The village was attacked on the 6th April, which was boldly defended by about 400 men of Kesari Singh. However, Kesari Singh's men lost heart before the fire of the guns and the attack of Cavalry and fled leaving four persons dead and twelve wounded. The State troops pursued them and arrested several of them with their wives and children and brought them to Udaipur on the 12th April.[173] The Maharana sentenced Kesari Singh and his brother to imprisonment for indefinite period. Several of his men were expelled from Mewar while some of them sentenced to various terms of imprisonment.[174] The village of Mangalwar of Bohera estate was attached to Khalsa to compensate the expenses of the Bohera expedition. Rawat Ratan Singh of Bheender family was installed as the Chief of Bohera estate. Petitions were, thereafter, sent to the G.O.I. on behalf of Kesari Singh against the Maharana's action, but the G.O.I. declined to interfere "finding no sufficient cause to do that."[175]

Administrative Changes

In 1880 Maharana Sajjan Singh took further measures in order to improve the work of administration and to effect separation of the executive and judicial wings of the Government.[176]

On the 27th August, 1880, the Maharana announced the dissolution of 'Ijlas Khas' and establishment of '*Mahadraj Sabha*' in its place. On the same day the Maharana held a *durbar* which was attended in addition to the State Chiefs and officials by the Political Agent, Lieut. Col. Walter and some other Englishmen.[177] The Maharana declared the enactment of "Kwaid Intizam Mulk Mewar No. 1" (Rules for the Administration of Mewar State No. 1) Sambat 1937 (A.D. 1880) and its promulgation.[178]

According to the provisions of the new law, the administration under the *Durbar* was divided into two main departments, *Mahakma Khas* and *Mahadraj Sabha*. *Mahakma Khas* was to look after the executive branches of administration as Revenue, Foreign Relations, Military, Police, Treasury, Customs, Account, *Shail Sabha*, P.W.D., Forest, Mint, Press, Bakshi's office, etc. *Mahadraj Sabha* was entrusted with the work of judicial branches as *Sadar Faujdari*, *Sadar Diwani* and district courts along with the departments of Registration, Stamps and Jail.[179]

The head of the executive body, *Mahakma Khas*, was to be called the *Pradhan* (Prime Minster). The function of the *Mahadraj Sabha* were again divided into two branches:

1. *Ijlas Khas* (Special Council); and
2. *Ijlas Mamuli* (Ordinary Council).

The former was to be presided over by the Maharana himself with at least ten members present. It was empowered to dispose of all serious cases in which nobles, respectable officials, personal attendants of the Maharana were involved and also to deal with cases relating to other States. The *Ijlas Mamuli* did not essentially require the presence of the Maharana. It required the presence of at least 5 members and was empowered to give punishment of imprisonment upto 7 years, of fine upto Rs. 5,000 and of dozen stripes in criminal cases while in civil cases it could decide, finally suits upto the value of Rs. 15,000.[180]

The district *Hakims* could dispose of civil suits, not exceeding Rs. 5000 in value and pass sentences of imprisonment upto a term of one year and fine upto Rs. 500 in criminal cases. Appeals against the decisions of district *Hakims* were heard by either of the two courts at the Capital. The Civil Courts at the capital was empowered to decide civil suits not exceeding Rs. 10,000 in value and the criminal court could sentence upto 3 years imprisonment and 12 stripes and fine upto Rs. 1000. The appeals against the decision of these courts lay with the *Mahadraj Sabha*, the final court of Appeal. The functions of the members of the *Mahadraj Sabha* were also defined in the Rules.[181]

The following eighteen members were appointed to the council of *Mahadraj Sabha*:

(1) Rao Takhta Singh of Bedla;
(2) Rawat Arjun Singh of Asind;
(3) Maharaj Gaj Singh of Shivarati;

(4) Raja Devi Singh of Tana;
(5) Rajarana Fateh Singh of Delwara;
(6) Rao Ratan Singh of Parsoli;
(7) Thakur Manohar Singh of Sardargarh;
(8) Rawat Udai Singh of Kakarwa;
(9) Mama Bakhtawar Singh;
(10) Kaviraj Shyamaldas;
(11) Mehta Rai Pannalal;
(12) Sahiwala Arjun Singh;
(13) Mehta Takhta Singh;
(14) Purohit Padmnath;
(15) Pandit Brijnath;
(16) Mohanlal Pandya;
(17) Jani Mukundlal; and
(18) Maharaj Rai Singh of Shivpura.[182]

In order to improve the administration of districts the Maharana changed the previous set-up by dividing the *Khalsa* territory into eleven divisions and placed each under a *Hakim*. The monthly salary of the *Hakims* was fixed as Rs. 200 for the first class *Hakim* and Rs. 150 for the second class one.[183]

Various Measures of Reforms

The Census work, as has been stated earlier, was attempted in Mewar in 1880, according to which the population of the Mewar territory was counted to be 14,72,610. Despite stiff resistance on the part of the rural population the land settlement work was carried on, which was finally completed during Maharana Fateh Singh's reign. Revenue settlement operations greatly restricted the corrupt practices of the State officials and and the State revenue reached to about 30 lakhs in 1882-83. Annual State expenses in the year was about 25 lakh.[184]

During Maharana Sajjan Singh's time the Department of Public works was put on a systematic footing. The services of Mr. Williams an Englishman were obtained for this purpose, who worked as the head of the Public Works Department.[185] Several roads were constructed or completed such as from Nimbahera to Udaipur, from Udaipur to Kherwara and from Udaipur to Nathdwara.[186] Several irrigation works were started at various places. Old lakes were repaired and canals at

Udaisagar and Raj Samand Lakes were constructed. Irrigation Department was afterwards separately organised under the supervision of an engineer. An English engineer was also appointed to prepare a plan of a railway line between Chittor and Udaipur, however, the scheme got postponed owing to the untimely demise of the Maharana.[187]

Several buildings and fortresses were constructed during this period, Chief of which were Sajjan Niwas Palace at Jagniwas in Pichhola Lake, Sajjangarh at Udaipur, a fortress at Bhoraipal, etc. He spent about Rs. 2,00,000 in repairing the Jaisamand dam after the heavy rains of 1875 and Rs. 24,000 in repairing the old buildings at Chittorgarh.[188]

In the city of Udaipur, a vast garden called Sajjan Niwas garden was laid under the supervision of an European Engineer on the modern design. Cricket and football grounds were laid in the garden for the use of the students. A Zoo was built in the garden. Sanitary conditions of the city were further improved and attention was given to the planned development of the city.[189]

In order to expand the education, an Education Committee was appointed with the Maharana and the Political Agent as its Presidents. A compulsory course of education was introduced.[190] The school for males at Udaipur was raised to the status of High School and a separate "Sanskrit school" was opened in the city.[191]

In addition to the Hindi schools at Chittor and Bhilwara, schools were opened at Kotra, Jawar, Rikhabnath, Barapal and Paduna. A special class for the sons of Chiefs was started at Udaipur in 1877, which was however, abolished in 1882, owing to the poor attendance. The Maharana High School was afterwards affiliated to the Allahabad University.[192]

The Expansion of Medical facilities for the people received further attention. A larger "Sajjan Hospital" was opened replacing the previous small one. A hospital for ladies called Walter Ladies Hospital was opened. In 1877, the United Free Church of Scotland Mission established a dispensary at Udaipur. The Udaipur Government granted land free of cost to the Scottish Mission to open the hospital, a church and a School. Several medical institutions were opened in the districts, and by the end of 1891 there were about 18 hospitals and dispensaries in the

State in all.[193]

History Department

A History Department was established by the Maharana under the supervision of Kaviraj Shyamaldas to prepare the History of Mewar and sanctioned Rs. 1,00,000 to be expended over the work.[194] The scholars well-versed in Sanskrit, Hindi, Urdu, Persian, Arabic and English were employed to collect and edit the old and contemporary records and works. The prints of ancient inscriptions were made and various genealogists and Bhats of Rajput class were consulted. Shymaldas wrote the major part of the book during Sajjan Singh's time. The work was completed during his successor's reign.[195] The book was named *"Vir Vinod"* having two parts and 2259 pages. *Vir Vinod* was the first comprehensive history written in Mewar and was an improvement over the history of Mewar written by Col. James Tod. Shymaldas was a 'charan' by caste. He later on become a member of the Royal Asiatic Society and a fellow of the Royal Historical Society. He contributed several papers to the journal of the Asiatic Society of Bengal. He was given a title of "Maha Mahopadyaya" by the G.O.I. in 1887.

A library named "Sajjan Vilas" was established in Maharana palace under the supervision of Shymaldas, where standard book in various languages and by various authors were collected. He also started publication of an official weekly paper *"Sajjan Kirti Sudhakar."*

Among other things the Maharana established was *"Desh Hitkarini Sabha"* (Council for National Welfare) in 1877 with the aim of startling philanthropic and social welfare activities in the State. An orphanage and a lunatic asylum were also opened at Udaipur.[196]

Title of G.C.S.I Conferred on the Maharana

In 1881, the British Government conferred on Maharana the title of G.C.S.I. in appreciation of his policies and measures of reform in his State. The Maharana expressed his reluctance to accept it on the plea that it would be against his status and dignity. However, he agreed to accept it, on the condition that he would be formally invested with the Insignia by the Governor-General himself in a *Durbar* to be held at Chittor.[197] Accordingly an assemblage of the chiefs and officers of the Mewar was held at Chittor on the 23rd November, 1881. The Governor-General, Lord Ripon performed the ceremony of investiture in the *durbar*. The Political Agent, Col. Walter read the English version of the Maharana's speech in the *durbar* in which the Maharana said: "Today's meeting vindicates the friendship between Mewar and the British Government and awarding of the title of G.C.S.I. to me by the Queen Empress strengthens that bond of friendship."[198] Lord Ripon expressed his appreciation at the sentiments expressed by the Maharana and sense of gratification for the face that he was called upon by the command of the Empress to confer upon the Maharana with the full and complete ceremonial the distinction of such a high order, as he was the foremost representative of the ancient and noble race of Rajputs, one of the most famous races in the history of Hindustan. Lord Ripon in his speech spoke highly of the Chivalrous deeds of the Sisodia race of Mewar. Dealing with the doubts and objections raised regarding the propriety of the 'Order' he said,"It might perhaps have been thought by some that the scion of a race so ancient would have regarded the order of the Star of India as a recent creation, but His Highness has interpreted the true meaning of the decoration of the Star of India the very same insignia which are worn from time to time by our gracious Sovereign herself and members of the royal family of England as a proud distinction.[199]

Lord Ripon, returned on the 24th November, after seeing the historical places of Chittor. The Maharana stayed a few days more at the fort arranging for the repairing of the dilapidated mansions and monuments. He ordered Rs. 24,000 to be spent for that purpose.[200]

Personality of Sajjan Singh

Sajjan Singh's excessive indulgence and irregular habits affected badly his health and cut short his life. He died at the age of 26 on the 23rd December, 1884. Though his education was limited, yet he developed his taste in literature, philosophy and politics.[201] He himself grew into a good poet and literary critic. he always looked forward for the association with the scholars of the day and to gain knowledge from them. He duly honoured the celebrated scholars like Bhartendu Babu Harishchandra and

Dayanand Saraswati who visited Udaipur on his invitation. He patronised several scholars of Sanskrit, Hindi and Rajasthani at his court.

Sajjan Singh always cared to consult the Political Agents in the important matters of the State. The latter, during this period, found little difficulty in getting their schemes carried out. Col. Walter, the Political Agent, wrote in 1883, "My relations with the Maharana continue of a most cordial nature. He is a constant visitor at the Residency and in my interviews with him in officials matters, I always find him well acquainted with the subjects under discussion and his judgements are as a rule just and fair.[202] As we have seen it was during this period that the agreements pertaining to closure of salt work, and opening of railway lines were concluded in the Imperial Interests.

The reformatory attitude of Sajjan Singh was responsible for adopting such important measures as the enactment of the Rules for the Administration of Mewar State No. 1, the *Kalambandi* with the chiefs and the Revenue Settlement Operations. Sajjan Singh himself faced the resistance offered by the conservation opinion in the State.

As Sajjan Singh grew of age, he revived the pride and glory of his race. It is stated that on learning that the Rajput ruler of Jamnagar had appointed a son born of a Muslim concubine as his successor to the *gadee* of the State and the British Government had confirmed his decision, he raised his objection to it. When the A.G.G. Col. Bradford asked him as to why he should raise objection about a State lying outside Rajputana, he replied that as it was a Rajput State, it was his duty to see that it should not be blamed in any way.[203]

Notes and References

1. *Vir Vinod* by Shymaldas, p. 2255.
2. *Udaipur Rajya ka Itihas* by G.H. Ojha, Part II, p. 808.
3. *Vir Vinod* by Shymaldas, p. 2139.
4. *Rajputana Agency Records* (Mewar), 1874-84, No. 1.
5. *Mewar Agency Report*, 1874-75, by Col. C. Herbert.
6. Ibid.
7. Ibid., Princes (who visited in Udaipur in 1876) in his journal "Imperial India" (p. 159) writes, "His father (Sakat Singh) who was

a man of turbulent disposition and had been in disgrace was passed over (in the matter of succession). He lives away from Udaipur and is forbidden to see or in any way influence his son.

8. Ibid.
9. Ibid.
10. Ibid.
11. Ibid.
12. *Rajputana Agency Records* (Mewar), 1874-84, No. 1.
13. *Vir Vinod* by Shymaldas, p. 2141.
14. Ibid.
15. Ibid.
16. *Rajputana Agency Records*, (Mewar), 1874-84, No. 1.
17. F.D., *Pol.*, Feb. 1875, No. 197-198.
18. Sohan Singh, the uncle of Sajjan Singh was then the chief of Bagore estate, Sajjan Singh's father Sakat Singh was Sohan Singh's elder brother. The latter obtained Chiefship of Bagore, as he was adopted by Samarth Singh, the late chief of the estate.
19. *Udaipur Rajya ka Itihas* by G.H. Ojha, Part II, p. 808.
20. *Rajputana Agency Report*, 1875-76, Major C.G. Gunning.
21. F.D., *Pol.*, July, 1880, No. 48-51.
22. *Rajputana Agency Records*, (Mewar), 1874-84, No. 1.
23. *Udaipur Rajya ka Itihas* by G.H. Ojha, Part II, p. 807.
24. Ibid.
25. *Mewar Agency Report*, 1874-75 by Col. C. Herbert.
26. *Rajputana Agency Records*, (Mewar), pp. 874-84, No. 1.
27. *Mewar Agency Report*, 1875-76 by Major C.G. Gunning.
28. *Vir Vinod* by Shymaldas, p. 2146.
29. *Rajputana Agency Records*, (Mewar), 1874-84, No. 1.
30. *Mewar Agency Report*, 1875-76 by Major C.G. Gunning.
31. *Rajputana Agency Records*, (Mewar) 1874-84, No. 1.
32. Ibid. In practice total confusion prevailed in the administration. During these days orders were issued simultaneously from four quarters, *i.e.*, from the office of the Political Agent, the Maharana, Maharana's father Sakat Singh and Rajmata (late ruler's Maharani) *Sahiwala Arjun Singh ka Jiwan Charitra*, Part II, p. 28.
33. F.D., *Pol.*, Feb, 1875, No. 11-12.
34. *Mewar Agency Records*, 1874-75 by Col. C. Herbert.
35. *Rajputana Agency Records* (Mewar) 1874-84, No. 1.
36. *Mewar Agency Report*, 1875-76, by Major C.G. Gunning.
37. *Vir Vinod* by Shymaldas, p. 2141.
38. *Rajputana Agency Records*, 1875, No. 39.
39. Ibid.
40. *Vir Vinod* by Shymaldas, pp. 2149-2151.

41. *Imperial India* by Prince, p. 160.
42. *Mewar Agency Report*, 1875-76 by Major C.G. Gunning.
43. *Vir Vinod* by Shymaldas, p. 2153.
44. F.D., *Pol.*, Aug. 1876, No. 103-107.
45. *Vir Vinod* by Shymaldas, p. 2153.
46. F.D., *Pol.*, Aug. 1876, No. 103-107.
47. *Udaipur Rajya ka Itihas* by G.H. Ojha, Part I, p. 22.
48. F.D., *Pol.*, Aug. 1876, No. 103-107.
49. *Udaipur Rajya ka Itihas* by G.H. Ojha, Part II, p. 311.
50. F.D., *Pol.*, Aug. 1876, No. 103-107.
51. *Mewar Agency Report*, 1873-74, by Major Bradford.
52. *Mewar Agency Report*, 1874-75, by Col. Herbert.
53. *Ibid.*
54. F.D., *Pol.*, March 1876.
55. F.D., *Pol.*, 1876 No. 103-107.
56. *Ibid.*
57. *Vir Vinod* by Shymaldas, p. 2154. Lonergan, an Irish man was employed by *Durbar* in 1875 to drill Mewar troops: F.D., *Pol.*, Sept. 1875, No. 44-48.
58. *Vir Vinod* by Shymaldas, pp. 2155-2156.
59. *Ibid.*
60. *Rajputana Agency Records*, (Mewar) 1874-84, No. 1.
61. F.D., *Pol.*, July 1877, No. 91-93.
62. *Ibid.*
63. *Ibid.*
64. *Ibid.*
65. *Ibid.*
66. *Ibid.*
67. Governor-General's letter to Maharana Sajjan Singh, Sept. 18, 1876 (Bakshi Khana Udaipur).
68. *Udaipur Rajya ka Itihas* by G.H. Ojha, Part II, p. 813.
69. *Rajputana Agency Records*, 1876-77, No. 70.
70. *Vir Vinod* by Shymaldas, p. 2161.
71. *Ibid.*, 2162-2189.
72. *Ibid.*, p. 2190. In practice he acted as the Chief Minister *Itihas Rajasthan* by Ramnath Ratnu, p. 74.
73. *Mewar Agency Report*, 1877-78 by Major T. Cadell.
74. *Vir Vinod* by Shymaldas, pp. 2190-2191.
75. *Ibid.*
76. *Mewar Agency Report*, 1877-78 by Major T. Cadell.
77. *Mewar Agency Report* (1875-76) by Major C.G. Gunning.
78. *Ibid.*
79. *Vir Vinod* by Shymaldas, p. 2191.

80. *Ibid.*
81. *Ibid.*, p. 2192.
82. *Ibid.*
83. *Ibid.*
84. *Ibid.*
85. *Mewar Agency Report*, 1877-78 by Major T. Cadell.
86. F.D., *Rev.*, Oct. 1879, No. 1-17.
87. *Mewar Agency Report*, 1879-1889 by Lieut. Col. Walter.
88. F.D., *Rev.*, Oct. 1879, No. 1-17.
89. *Mewar Agency Report*, 1879-89 by Lieut. Col. Walter.
90. *Mewar Agency Report*, 1880-81 by J.P. Starrock.
91. F.D., *Rev.*, May 1881, No. 5-10.
92. *Ibid.*
93. *Ibid.*
94. *Ibid.*
95. *Ibid.*
96. *Ibid.*
97. *Rajputana Agency Records*, 1864, No. 4.
98. *Ibid.*
99. *Ibid.*
100. *Ibid.*
101. *Ibid.*
102. *Ibid.*
103. *A Gazetteer of the Udaipur State* by Major H.D. Erskine, p. 57.
104. *Hamara Rajasthan* by Prithvi Singh Mehta, p. 258.
105. *Rajputana Agency Records* (Confidential), 1846, Slavery, No. 2.
106. *Ibid.*
107. *Rajputana Agency Records* (Confidential), 1847, No. 1.
108. *Ibid.*
109. *Ibid.*
110. *The Economic History of India* by Ramesh Dutt, Vol. II, p. 107.
111. *Ibid.*, p. 108.
112. *Hamara Rajasthan* by Prithvi Singh Mehta, p. 226.
113. *The Economic History of India* by Ramesh Dutt, Vol. II, p. 393.
114. *Ibid.*, pp. 393-394.
115. *Ibid.*
116. F.D., *Pol.*, April 1880, No. 60-87.
117. *Vir Vinod* by Shyamaldas, p. 2194.
118. F.D., *Pol.*, April 1880, No. 60-87.
119. *Udaipur Rajya ka Itihas* by G.H. Ojha, Part II, p. 816.
120. F.D., *Pol.*, April 1880, No. 60-87.
121. *A Gazetteer of the Udaipur State* by Major K.D. Erskine, pp. 29, 76.
122. F.D., *Pol.*, July 1880, No. 186-188.

123. *A Gazetteer of the Udaipur State* by Major K.D. Erskine, p. 29.
124. *Mewar Agency Reports*, 1880-81 by Dr. J.P. Stratton.
125. *Ibid.*
126. *Ibid.*
127. *Ibid.*
128. *Ibid.*
129. F.D., *Pol.*, April 1881, No. 25-39.
130. *Mewar Agency Reports*, 1880-81 by Dr. J.P. Stratton.
131. *Ibid.*
132. *Vir Vinod* by Shymaldas, pp. 2220-2222.
133. F.D., *Pol.*, April 1881, 25-39.
134. *Mewar Agency Report*, 1880-81 by J.P. Stratton.
135. *Vir Vinod* by Shymaldas, p. 2220.
136. *Ibid.*, p. 2221.
137. *Mewar Agency Report*, 1880-81, by J.P. Stratton.
138. *Vir Vinod* by Shymaldas, p. 2221-2222.
139. *Ibid.*, p. 2226.
140. *Mewar Agency Report*, 1880-81 by J.P. Stratton.
141. F.D., *Pol.*, April 1881, No. 25-39.
142. F.D., *Pol.*, April 1881, No. 137-139.
143. *Vir Vinod* by Shymaldas, p. 2226.
144. F.D., *Pol.*, April 1881, No. 137-139.
145. *Vir Vinod* by Shaymaldas, p. 2227.
146. F.D., *Pol.*, April 1881, No. 137-139.
147. F.D., *Pol.*, June 1882, No. 83-92.
148. *Mewar Agency Report*, 1882-83 by Col. Walter.
149. F.D., *Pol.*, June 1882 No. 82-83.
150. *Mewar Residency Report*, 1882-83 by Col. Walter.
151. *Ibid.*
152. *Rajputana Agency Records*, 1874, No. 73.
153. *Ibid.*
154. *Ibid.*
155. *Ibid.*
156. *Ibid.*
157. *Ibid.*
158. *A Gazetteer of the Udaipur State* by K.D. Erskine, p. 64.
159. The Governor-General's letter to Maharana Sajjan Singh, Oct. 16, 1883 (Bakshi Khana Udaipur).
160. *Ibid.*
161. *Udaipur Rajya ka Itihas* by G.H. Ojha, Part II, p. 826.
162. The Governor-General's letter to Maharana Sajjan Singh, Oct. 16, 1883, (Bakshi Khana Udaipur).
163. *A Gazetteer of the Udaipur State* by K.D. Erskine, p. 66.

164. *Mewar Agency Report*, (1879-80) by Lieut. Col. Walter. Prince writes, "The feudal system holds good here as in all Rajputana. Each 'Thakoor' is independent and rules his State, administering the laws as though he were king." (*Imperial India*, p. 162).
165. *A Gazetteer of Udaipur State* by K.D. Erskine, p. 66.
166. *Ibid.*
167. *Mewar Agency Report*, 1879-80 by Lieut. Col. Walter.
168. *Rajputana Agency Records* (Mewar), No. 68.
169. *Ibid.*
170. *Mewar Agency Report*, 1876.
171. *Rajputana Agency Records*, (Mewar) No. 68.
172. F.D., Pol., June 1884, No. 23-28. In 1862 the Mewar Regency Council had decided that Udot Singh would be succeeded by Sakat Singh, the second son of Hamir Singh, the Chief of Bheender. However, as luck would have it, Sakat Singh passed away in young age leaving no issue behind. Udot Singh, upon his own, adopted his nephew, Kesari Singh of Sakatpura. Maharana Sajjan Singh, however, disapproved his proceedings and upheld the claim of Ratan Singh, the third son of Hamir Singh of Bheender.
173. *Vir Vinod* by Shyamaldas, pp. 2247-2248.
174. F.D., Pol., July 1884, No. 96-105.
175. F.D., Pol., June 1884, No. 23-38.
176. *Vir Vinod* by Shyamaldas, p. 2212.
177. *Ibid.*
178. F.D., Pol., Int., May 1905, No. 66-67.
179. F.D., Int., May 1905, No. 66-67.
180. *Ibid.*
181. *Ibid.*
182. *Vir Vinod* by Shyamaldas, p. 2212.
183. *Ibid.*, p. 2198.
184. *Mewar Agency Report*, 1882-83, by Col. Walter.
185. *Mewar Agency Report*, 1879-80 by Lieut. Col. Walter.
186. *A Gazetteer of the Udaipur State* by K.D. Erskine, p. 58.
187. *Udaipur Rajya ka Itihas*, by G.H. Ojha, p. 828.
188. *Ibid.*, p. 833.
189. *Ibid.*
190. *Mewar Agency Report*, 1877-78 by Major Cadell.
191. *A Gazetteer of the Udaipur State* by K.D. Erskine, p. 82.
192. *Ibid.*
193. *Ibid.*, pp. 85-86.
194. *Udaipur Rajya ka Itihas* by G.H. Ojha, Part II, pp. 829-832.
195. *Ibid.* The Publication of the volumes of *Vir Vinod* was completed

by 1894, however the next ruler Maharana Fateh Singh was averse to its circulation for certain reasons and, therefore, got the entire publication locked in a room. *Vir Vinod* came to public eye only after his death in 1930.

196. *Udaipur Rajya ka Itihas* by G.H. Ojha, Part II, pp. 837-838.
197. *Vir Vinod* by Shyamaldas, p. 2229.
198. Speeches by H.E. the Marquis of Ripon, pp. 144-147.
199. *Ibid*.
200. *Vir Vinod* by Shyamaldas, p. 2238.
201. *Vir Vinod* by Shyamaldas, p. 2255.
202. *Mewar Agency Report*, 1879-80 by Lieut. Col. Walter.
203. *Vir Vinod* by Shyamaldas, p. 2253.

12

Maharana Fateh Singh: Struggle for Internal Independence

The year 1884, marks the beginning of a new era in the history of political relations of Udaipur State with British Government. For more than twenty years the Agents of the British Government ruled supreme in the state. During this period various reforms were introduced in the State, respecting prohibition of age-old in human practices, such as, *Sati*, witch-swinging, slavery, infanticide, etc., introduction of a legal Code improvement of the administration, settlement of revenue and extension of social services in education, public health, communications and irrigation, etc. During this period, the State of Udaipur entered into agreements with the British Government with regard to prohibition of salt manufacture in the State, establishment of a depot of opium seales at Udaipur, opening of railway line in the state. These agreements, as we have seen, were concluded to enhance the revenues of the British Government, which, however, proved harmful to the interests of the state and its people. In the backward conditions of the State, they resulted in the greater misery and oppression of the people. Whatever good intentions the British Agents might have had in introducing reforms in the State, they were disliked by the conservative people of the state. They felt that the prohibition of age old usages and practices was the violation of their traditional privileges. They did not comprehend new rules and regulations, enacted on the pattern of those of the British India and they were, therefore, owing to their ignorance, subjected to greater oppression of the officials. The hatred and prejudice against the British intervention induced the people to oppose such beneficial measures as the revenue settlement. People of the state came to think that the British Government was gradually doing away with their time honoured political, social and cultural institutions.

With the accession of the new ruler of the State in 1884, a period of reaction set in. Unlike his two predecessors Fateh Singh who succeeded Sajjan Singh was a major. He was of 35 years, when he sat on the throne. He was of conservative outlook and believed in the medieval theory of personal rule and was against any interference with the sovereign powers of the ruler. He was ardently attached to and proud of the heroic and glorious traditions of his forefathers. From the very beginning of his rule he initiated a struggle to regain the dignity of his status and internal sovereignty of the state, which had been lost during his predecessors' reigns. After about ten years' struggle, he finally achieved his aim and thereafter, for about 20 years he enjoyed a large measure of independence in the internal affairs of the State, and the Political Department found it difficult to compel him to do what it desired and had to allow him to take his own course until the beginning of the First World War when the accretion of several factors brought above change in the relationship. The change of relationship resulted in the development of the crisis leading to the events of 1920-21.

Accession of Fateh Singh

Maharana Sajjan Singh also died without leaving a son after him. Besides, he did not adopt any body as his successor in his life-time. Consequently the problem of selecting a successor to the throne of Mewar arose again. As Maharaja Sakat Singh of Bagore had no son, the second choice of the palace, most of the chiefs and the British Resident went in the favour of the Shivarati family. Fateh Singh, the adopted son of Maharaja Gaj Singh of Shivarati was unanimously placed on the throne.[1]

On the 23rd December, 1884, the British Government confirmed his succession and a *durbar* was held on the 4th March, 1885 to celebrate Fateh Singh's accession. The A.G.G., Col. Bradford, the Resident, Col. Walter and some other Englishmen attended the assemblage.[2] The A.G.G. addressed the *durbar*. He advised the Maharana to be careful in the selection of his counsellors and to carry forward the work of reforms, initiated by his predecessor, Maharana Sajjan Singh, by enlarging internal communications, improving education and sanitation, establishing efficient police force and introducing further reforms in the criminal and civil Justice in the State. In the end he counselled the Maharana to take regular advice and guidance in his work from Col. Walter, the Resident and Mr. Wingate, the Settlement Officer of the State. At the conclusion of his speech, the A.G.G. presented the Maharana with the Governor-General's Khareeta, which, the Maharana placed for a moment upon his head. The Khareeta was read to the assembled *durbar*. The whole *durbar* stood up to honour it and a salute of 19 guns was fired. The A.G.G. then presented the Maharana with a Khillat, consisting of robes and jewels.[3]

The Maharana in his reply to the Governor-General's letter expressed his gratitude to the British Government. He wrote, "it is well known to everyone that the prosperity and advancement of this State are due to the assistance of the British Government and I, your friend, have every hope that your Excellency will continue your favour and assistance to me".[4]

Temporary Restrictions Placed upon the Maharana's Powers

At the outset, the British Government placed some temporary restrictions upon the ruling powers of the Maharana, requiring him to consult the Resident in all important matters, to follow his advice and to obtain his consent before any important measures of the late Maharana could be reversed and before any change could be made in the prevalent system of the administration in the state. The restrictions were intended to remain in force until the Maharana had gained sufficient acquaintance with the business of the State in order to qualify him for the exercise of full powers of the Government.[5] These restrictions were removed and full powers were conferred on the Maharana on the 22nd August, 1885, after the Resident and the A.G.G.

made favourable reports of his conduct with their recommendations to the G.O.I. to invest him with full ruling powers.[6]

On the 8th November, 1885, Lord Dufferin, the Viceroy and Governor-General of India visited Udaipur. In order to fulfil the wishes of Lady Dufferin, Maharana Fateh Singh agreed to erect a separate hospital building for the females which was afterwards opened on the 24th May, 1888 by the Resident Col. Miles.[7]

Queen Victoria's Jubilee Celebrations

In 1887, the fifty year jubilee of the reign of Queen Victoria was celebrated throughout the British Empire. The Native rulers of India participated in these celebrations to express their feelings of joy and loyalty Maharana Fateh Singh held a *durbar* on the 16th February in the palace. That day the whole city was illuminated, prisoners were released and alms were distributed. Elephant fishli and other sports were arranged. Bhil dances were held at the Residency.[8]

On this occasion the Maharana donated Rs. 10,000 to the funds of Imperial Institute, London and Rs. 5,000 to the Lady Dufferin Fund. In order to give a losting character to the memory of Jubilee celebrations, the Maharana announced to construct a museum in the Queen's name. The foundation stone of the museum, which was named "Victoria Hall Museum" was laid on the 20th June, 1887, in the Sajjan Niwas gardens. In front of the Hall a beautiful marble statue of Queen Victoria was laid. On the 22nd February, 1887, the *Mahakama Khas* of Mewar issued a proclamation, stating, "With a view to permanently commemorate the fiftieth anniversary of Her Most Gracious Majesty, Queen Victoria, Empress of India's accession to the throne, H.H. the Maharana of Udaipur has decided, from this date, to abolish the levy of transit duties on all articles of merchandize, with the exception of opium in this territory.[9]

The feelings and expression of loyalty of the Maharana towards the crown were reciprocated by the British Government. In December 1887 the Maharana was awarded the title of G.C.S.I. and his minister, Mehta Pannalal the title of C.E.I.[10]

Visits of the Duke of Cannaught and Prince Albert

In 1889, the Duke of Cannaught, son of Queen Victoria visited Udaipur. He was the first English Prince to visit the State.

The Maharana spent several lakhs in his reception. In order to commemorate his visit the Maharana constructed a dam named "Cannaught Dam" on the Dewali lake outside Udaipur. The Lake thereby got expanded and was renamed as Fateh Sagar Lake.

On the 18th February, 1890, Prince Albert Victor, the Heir Apparent of the British Crown visited Udaipur. He was received by the Maharana with all ceremonies and formalities. The prince unveiled the statue of Queen Victoria laid in the Sajjan Niwas Garden.[11]

Completion of Revenue Settlement

Mr. Wingate, who had been conducting settlement operations in Mewar since 1879, completed his work in five Khalsa parganas by 1885 and laid before the *Durbar* his report and proposals for the settlement of land revenues for a term of twenty years in that part of the State. His report was accepted by the Maharana, who issued orders on the 5th May, 1885 to give effect to his proposals.[12]

Wingate, while conducting settlement operations, measured each village and classed it according to its capabilities without any reference at first to previous records of revenue being realised, so as to ascertain what it was capable of producing upon its own merits. Then he took the average of last 20 years of revenues and modified the rates upon individual holdings, so as not to exceed these averages. By this process he convinced the ryots that the object of the settlement was not to impose fresh burdens upon them. According to the settlement, the maximum rate for wet lands was fixed Rs. 8 per *bigha*, for irrigable dry lands, Rs. 3 per *bigha* and for dry lands, pure and simple Rs. 1/3 per *bigha*. Wingate recommended the payment of fixed remuneration by the State to the Patels and Patwaris for their services in collecting the land revenue from the peasants, so as to liberate the latter from excessive demands, which the Patels and Patwaris made for themselves from the cultivators on account of their work. The settlement was to remain in force for next 20 years. In his proposals Wingate also suggested to levy a cess of half an anna on every rupee of the land revenue, which account was suggested to be spent on such useful purposes as schools and dispensaries.[13]

The results of giving effect to the Wingate's settlement proposals were encouraging. For the first time even handed justice was done to the rich and the poor alike in making demands. The demand was generally moderate and did not go higher than the previous realisations. The cash payment sanctioned for Patels and Patwaris for the services gave great relief to the peasants. Above all a fixed settlement for next twenty years freed them from the uncertainty of the revenue demands and a feeling of general security spread among the cultivators of the settled districts. New wells were dug in a large number and cultivators began approaching the Government applying for grants of the waste lands to bring them under cultivation.

The gains for the state were the definite ascertainment of agricultural resources of the state and its revenue, the enhancement of revenue due to the enlargement of cultivation as well as due to the curbing of intermediary corruption and finally the exact and timely collections. These reforms, however, adversely affected the Baniya class, and as most of the district officials belonged to this community, they tried to sabotage its successful execution for some time. However, the affairs improved gradually to the benefit of both the State and the cultivators.[14]

In January, 1887, Wingate resigned his office and was replaced by Mr. Buddulph on the 5th January, 1887, to complete the work in the remaining parganas of the state. However, when the work was in progress, Buddulph went abroad on 8 months' furlough in April 1890. As Mr. Buddulph expressed his unwillingness to rejoin the services, Mr. Wingate was recalled to Udaipur in February 1891.[15] By 1893 he completed the work in the whole Khalsa area except the hilly district. The latter was left out of the settlement operations, as the Bhil resistance was apprehended. *Jagir* area of the State remained out of the purview of these operations as the chiefs were opposed to the settlement work realising that they would be put to a great loss by fixing definite revenue demands on the cultivators and that they would be prevented from making arbitrary exactions from them on and often.[16]

Case of the 'Spurious' son of Sakat Singh

When Fateh Singh was chosen as the successor of Maharana Sajjan Singh, the royal ladies placed a condition before Fateh

Singh, that in case he had no male issue, the descendant of Maharaj Sakat Singh of Bagore would have the right of succession to the *gadee* of Mewar. Fateh Singh on undertaking to this effect.[17] In 1887 the Maharana was informed by Sakat Singh that his second wife was in the family way and had been taken to Bagore from Udaipur. The Maharana did not believe the statement. He thought that Sakat Singh was trying to bring forward a spurious child, so as to produce a future claiment for the chiefship of Bagore as well as for the *gadee* of Mewar.[18]

The Maharana decided to verify the truth. He consulted Col. Miles, the Resident, in this matter and then sent Takhat Singh, the *Girwa Hakim* to consult Col. Walter, the A.G.G. The latter in his letter to the Resident observed that as the son born to Maharaja Sakat Singh would have a claim to succeed to the *gadee* of Mewar, in the event of the Maharana having no male issue, the latter was justified in taking steps to assure himself and the British Government regarding the truth of his wife being really pregnant. The Maharana decided to have medical examination of Sakat Singh's wife. Sakat Singh opposed to get his wife medically examined on the plea that such a procedure would damage the prestige of his family. His plea was considered as untenable and on the 14th November, 1887, Mrs. Lonorgan, a certified medical practitioner and physician in the Walter Female Hospital, Udaipur proceeded to Bagore. She examined the lady and declared that she was not pregnant. Sakat Singh refused to accept the judgement declaring that as the examiner was a *Durbar* employee she could not have a true judgement. He, on his part, called another lady doctor from Ajmer to examine his wife, who declared that she was pregnant. Thereupon the Maharana called another lady doctor from Bombay, whose judgement was the same as that of Mrs. Lonorgan.[19]

About three weeks after the last medical examination Sakat Singh announced that his wife had given birth to a son. Before this announcement the Maharana as well as the Resident, Col. Miles had asked Sakat Singh to bring his wife back to Udaipur. Miles conveyed it to Sakat Singh that unless he brought his wife to Udaipur, he would recommend to the Government not to recognise any child, put forth by him, as genuine. However, Sakat Singh did not comply with the above orders and announced the birth of a son from Bagore.[20]

On the 22nd January, 1888 the Maharana, receiving the news of the birth of a son to Sakat Singh's wife, declared that the announcement could not be credited and finally on the 10th February he gave his judgement that the boy produced by Sakat Singh, as his son, was spurious. Col. Miles supported Maharana's announcement and the British Government approved of the decision.[21]

Maharaj Sakat Singh died of apoplexy on the 16th August, 1889. Maharana Fateh Singh passed orders for the attachment of the Bagore estate, as he had left no successor behind. Sohan Singh, who had been, in Maharana Sajjan Singh's time, disqualified for the chiefship of Bagore estate for his contumacious conduct and had himself given an undertaking to that effect, appealed to the British Government against the Maharana's orders. Mother and two widows of the late chief also sent petitions in favour of Sohan Singh. Sohan Singh, in order to assert his right, claimed to have a *ruqqua*, issued by Maharana Sajjan Singh in 1881 in which he favoured his and his descendants' right to succeed to the chiefship of Bagore, in case Sakat Singh died issueless. As to the previous orders of 1880 disqualifying him for the chiefship, the Maharana had promised not to enforce them. Thereupon the British Government directed the Resident to have a full enquiry into the affair.[22]

The *Durbar* appointed a committee consisting of Rao Takhat Singh of Bedla, Thakur Manohar Singh, Rai Mehta Pannalal, C.I.E. and Sahiwala Arjun Singh to examine the genuineness of the document produced by Sohan Singh. The committee, after examining the document, concluded that it was a forged one. The Resident concurred with the decision of the committee. He forwarded the proceedings to the British Government which decided not to interfere in the case.[23]

Maharana's Efforts to Gain Control of the Administration

For some years, in the beginning of his reign, Maharana Fateh Singh remained on good terms with the Residents and continued to take their advice in regard to the internal administration of the state. His relations with other English officials employed in the State such as Mr. Wingate, the Revenue Settlement Officer and Mr. Thompson, the P.W.D. Engineer also went on well for some time. However, owing to various factors, chiefly, due to the Maharana's ambition to region as well as to rule, there developed gradually a situation in which the Maharana found himself at logger-heads with the Resident and other English officials in the state, which subsequently developed into an open conflict between the Maharana and his party on the one hand and the Resident and English officials on the other.

As we have said earlier, Fateh Singh had come to adopt a conservative outlook in his early life and had a firm faith in personal rule. Called to govern the State from his feudal village, where he had led the simplest life, largely devoted to mainly sport, he had entered upon his difficult task with few educational advantages.[24] Influence of family traditions and bardic recitations of the heroic deeds of his ancestors had moulded his character and outlook, cherishing racial glory, austerity and notions of independence.

As a natural consequence, he began to assert his authority in the internal affairs of the States, just after his assumption of power. On various issues there arose differences between the Maharana and the Resident. The Resident, in his attitude, had the support of all the English officials employed in the State and the Prime Minister, Rai Pannalal C.I.E. An anti-English party developed comprising mainly of Maharaj Gaj Singh, Kothari Balwant Singh, Brijnath and Joshi Narayan Das, the last three being in the state employment. The Maharana had full support of the second party in his policy and worked with their consultation.[25]

Mehta Rai Pannalal, C.I.E. had been working as the Minister since Maharana Shambhu Singh's time. He enjoyed British support throughout the period of his state service as a minister. Gradually he came to be looked upon as a British 'Agent' in the State enjoying the powers of the '*Pradhan*', that the young Maharana Sajjan Singh never had the courage to oppose him outright. From the very beginning Maharana Feteh Singh was not reconciled to Pannalal and was particularly displeased with his over-bearing attitude. It seems, the Maharana, at the very outest, drew a definite conclusion, learning from the past history, about the post of the Prime Ministership. He decided in his mind to do away with the services of Rai Pannalal and along with him the post of Prime Ministership as well. He decided to be the Prime Minister of his own. If Fateh Singh was slow in taking decision he was firm in their execution. Once he got rid of Pannalal, he never, throughout next thirty years of his reign, employed an official as the Prime Minister despite continuous and threatens of the British Political officers.

Postponement of the Railway Project

On several administrative issues the conflict of policies appeared. A scheme of a railway line in Mewar from Chittorgarh to Udaipur had been approved by the preceding Maharana. Sajjan Singh had agreed to start the work and therefore, he had sought the services of an Engineer. Mr. Thompson from the British Government. Correspondence was still continuing regarding the question of civil and criminal jurisdiction on the line, when the A.G.G. informed the G.O.I. that Maharana Fateh Singh had decided to give up the idea of constructing the line. He stated that the scheme had never been popular with the officials of the State, the leading Jagirdars and the trading class. The A.G.G. also observed that the Maharana himself was not keen about the scheme and was prejudiced by unfavourable counsels.[26] The Maharana put forward the reason of inadequate funds in the treasury to start the work. The Political Department continued pressing him for some time. In January 1893, Col. Miles, the Resident again advised the Maharana to start railway work as in his opinion the latter had about ten lakhs of rupees with him.[27] By that time, however, several other events took place leading to further estrangement of relations.

Question of maintaining Imperial Service Troops

In response to the G.O.I's call in 1888 to the Native States of India to assist in the defence of Empire, the Maharana expressed his willingness to contribute Rs. 6 lakhs towards the frontier defence of India and place his troops at the disposal of the G.O.I.[28] The latter, however, did not accept the cash offer and preferred that the Maharana of Udaipur should maintain a small military Corps fully equipped and trained for the use of Imperial defence. The Maharana in his reply of the 20th June, 1889 expressed his readiness to maintain a force of 200 cavalry and 800 infantry which could always be kept in readiness for Imperial services and be sent to the frontier, when required.[29]

The Udaipur Government at that time was maintaining

about 300 cavalry and 1200 infantry.[30] But the reports received about the condition of the Udaipur troops revealed that they were being maintained very poorly. As such the G.O.I. did not agree to accept the Maharana's proposal and put an alternate proposal that Mewar might maintain a transport corps of about 500 ponies, under the supervision of the English officials. The Maharana in his reply intimated the Government that ponies were found in a very small number in Mewar and there was the deficiency of grass as well. The G.O.I., however, did not think the argument plausible as in its opinion, sufficient grass was available in Mewar specially near Roopaheli.[31] The Maharana, on his part, again submitted that the country did not suit ponies and proposed either to maintain a corps of 200 camels or to pay Rs. 24,000 cash annually towards Imperial defence. Neither of these proposals was acceptable to the British Government.

On the 2nd March, 1892, Col. Trevor, the A.G.G. held personal talks with the Maharana in regard to the Imperial Defence Corps. The Maharana told him that his state was not rich and as he was already contributing towards the maintainance of the Mewar Bhil Corps, it would be better if his contribution towards the Mewar Bhil Corps was reduced to make up the expenses for the maintenance of the Imperial Defence Troops in Mewar. He also desired that the British Government should compel the feudatories of Mewar to share the expenses towards Imperial defence. Two days after the above meeting the A.G.G. again called on the Maharana and proposed to enlarge the number of the Mewar Bhil Corps, the enhanced expenditure of which should be met by the Mewar Government.[32] The Maharana expressed reluctance to agree to it. He again advanced the previous proposal of maintaining 200 cavalry and 800 infantry for the Imperial defence. He also put forward the demand to restore the Mewar Bhil Corps to him, which he proposed to maintain as a police force.[33]

On the 10th May, 1892, the Governor-General intimated to the A.G.G. that the question of taking a contribution from Udaipur might be dropped. He asked the A.G.G. to inform the Maharana, if necessary, that it was not the desire of G.O.I. to press any Native State to supply Imperial Service Troops. If the Chief could not afford to do it or disliked the idea of doing so, there was an end to the matter. He further directed the A.G.G.

that, in regard to opening a railway line in Mewar also, he should stop pressing the Maharana, as the G.O.I. did not attach much importance to that branch.[34]

Seth's Affairs

In 1892-93, an administrative action taken by the Maharana against a trading firm brought about great bitterness between him and the Political Agent. There was a trading-cum-banking firm of Seth Jawaharmal Chhogamal at Udaipur, whose branches were scattered over the prominent towns of Mewar as well as in Central India. Jawaharmal was the descendant of Seth Jawaharmal Bapna who had come to Mewar to aid Maharana Bhim Singh in 1819 on the invitation of Col. Tod. Seth Jawaharmal had also been the treasurer of Residency at Udaipur and the banker, since 1861 to the Mewar Bhil Corps, Kherwara. He had also financial dealings with the Maharana of Udaipur. Revenues collected from the districts of Mewar were transmitted to Udaipur through his agencies. He used to take loans from the Maharana from time to time. In 1887, the Maharana, being counselled by the Customs Officer of the State, Brijnath, undertook to run a mail cart from Udaipur to Chittorgarh for the benefit of the railway passengers, as Chittor Station was about 69 miles from Udaipur and entrusted the Seths (Jawaharmal Chhogamal) to manage the *dak*. It was later disclosed that Brijnath had partnership with the firm in the business. Brijnath induced the Maharana to advance Rs. 40,000 to the firm from his privy purse to manage the mail cart. The firm made large advances to the dak contractor and others out of the *Durbar* funds with them. By the end of 1890 the liabilities of the Seths to the *durbar* amounted to about Rupees 5 lakhs. The Maharana came to know that state demands were falling into arrears and payments were not forthcoming from the Seths. He was also led to believe that the firm had manipulated to misappropriate State money. He at once issued orders to attach his *jagir* village of Parsoli and shop and to release then only when the Seths paid the whole amount.[35]

The above action was opposed by the Resident, Col. Miles. The Maharana was led to believe that Rai Pannalal was secretary involved in the Seth's scandal and that he was encouraging them to defy the orders of the state officials.[36] Wingate was appointed the president of a Commission to enquire into proceedings of the *Durbar* officials in connection with the claims upon the Seths' firm.[37] Wingate, after preliminary investigations, recommended that the Seths should be allowed and assisted to carry on their business pending full enquiry. These recommendations were not acceptable to the Maharana. When Wingate tried to impress upon the Maharana not to take severe measures against the Seths, until the full enquiry into the affair and Seth's accounts had been made by a Sahukar and two officials, other than Kothari Balwant Singh and Joshi Naraindas of the accounts office, the Maharana got suspicious of him, believing that he was also working in alliance with the Seths and Rai Pannalal.

The Seths, on their part, argued that much of the less incurred by the firm was due to the mail cart management and Pandit Brijnath's deception. Wingate on his own submitted a memorandum on the affairs to the G.O.I., which further exasperated the Maharana. Col. Miles, the Resident tried to press the Maharana to release Seths' shops, which the latter did not do. The Resident thereupon forwarded the Wingate report and his own comments on the case to the A.G.G. He observed that it was a just case for the Government's interference. The A.G.G. disagreed with the Resident's views and declined to interferes.[38]

Col. Trever, the A.G.G., wrote about the matter to the Maharana, stating that there were some reasons to believe in the fact that the Seths' difficulty had arise no wing, to a great measure, to the expenditure in the 'Dak' and the deception played by Pandit Brijnath. He advised the Maharana to release the Seth's shop, books and village from attachment and settle the case with the Seths on reasonable terms. He further remarked that if he sold the Seths' property and continued to keep their business closed, the whole case would be sent to the G.O.I. along with Wingate's report and the Maharana would stand the risk of disagreeable comments from the Government. Upon the recommendations of Col. Miles, the A.G.G., also asked the Maharana to dissociate himself from persons like Gaj Singh, Brijnath, etc. Subsequently Col. Miles got Gaj Singh removed from Udaipur.[39]

In March, 1893 Col. Miles left Udaipur on leave and Lieut. Col. Martelli arrived as the Offg Resident Martelli in his report about the affairs at Udaipur stated that the critical situation which had developed there Resident and other English officials were also to be blamed for it, as they had zealously and unwisely suppested the Seth's cause. He further stated, "it will be very difficult to heal the present unpleasant feeling which appears to exist between the *Durbar* and the British officers concerned. I cannot help thinking myself that the Seths have been strongly supported and it is a question whether their transactions have not made them amenable to the Criminal Court."[40]

The Maharana, on his part, remained firm on his decision and regarded the affair as an internal one in which he did not think necessary to carry out the suggestions of the Resident and the A.G.G. In the month of May, the Maharana desired to go to Simla to apprise the Governor-General of the real state of affairs, when he came to learn that Col. Miles was intriguing against him there, but later on, dropped the idea. Lieut. Col. Martelli used his good offices to bring about the settlement in the case. Seth's were distinctly told by him, on behalf of the A.G.G., that he would not interfere in the case and they ought to come to terms with the Maharana. Consequently in the month of May, 1893, a settlement of the case was brought about agreeable to the Maharana, by which the latter released some part of the dues by selling some of the Seth's goods, such as opium, gram, etc., and for some part he kept the village under mortgage.[41]

On the 27th June, 1893, Trevor reported to the G.O.I. in regard to the settlement of the Seths' case stating that Col. Miles would have done well not to have interfered in the matter. By examination of the case he had come to differ from Col. Miles and believed that the Maharana had just cause to feel annoyed. Trevor, in the same report, recommended that Wingate should be transferred from Udaipur, at the earliest.[42]

Disagreement between the Resident and the A.G.G.

The differences over the Seths' case between Col. Miles, the Resident and Col. Trevor, the A.G.H. led to personal embitterment. When in July 1893, Col. Miles rejoined his duties at Udaipur he wrote to the G.O.I. suggesting to disapprove of the settlement arrived at according to the wishes of the Maharana. He spread various rumours at Udaipur. He entered into direct communication with the Foreign Department of the G.O.I., when the A.G.G. directed him not to indulge in any activity, which affected adversely the settlement in the Seths' affair. Col. Miles wrote to the G.O.I. complaining against the A.G.G. that they had supported, throughout the case, the actions of the Maharana against his views. He further stated in his letter that the treatment experienced by Wingate and himself from the *Durbar* was but a feeble indication of the disloyalty and anti-English feeling that prevailed at Udaipur and had long prevailed in the State and which if allowed to continue to develop would result in its becoming a hot bed of sedition. He wrote, "Two centuries ago Mewar was the only Rajput State that refused to give daughters to Delhi. Today, it is the only large State that refuses to give Imperial Troops. The motive is the same. If troubles should arise in the future, it will be found that the Hindu, and not the Mussalman, is the enemy and that the rallying point will not be Delhi but Udaipur. Col. Miles recommended that Mr. Wingate should be retained at Udaipur despite the fact that his term of two years employment had expired so that, the Maharana could be kept under restraint.[43] The Maharana, was however reluctant to retain him. He also wished to get rid of another English official Mr. Thompson, who was also found actively helping the trouble on behalf of the anti-Maharana party at Udaipur.

Wingate and Thompson Retire from Udaipur

The G.O.I. uphold the views of the A.G.G. with regard to the Seths' case and refused to intervene further. The Wingate's term of employment for two years at Udaipur having been expired in June 1893, was relieved from the State services on the 8th August, 1895. Regarding Thompson the Resident impressed upon the Maharana to retain his services for Railway work, however, the Maharana did not agree to it, stating that the State was not in a position to pay heavy salary of Rs. 1200 per month, which the engineer was drawing. Thompson was the man who planned and executed the scheme of such important constructions as Victoria Hall, Fateh Sagar Lake and other works in the State. But his activities in alliance with Mr. Wingate had alienated the Maharana and he was also relieved of his services at Udaipur.[44]

Dismissal of Mehta Pannalal

In the month of August, 1894, the A.G.G. found it necessary

to meet the Maharana personally for reconciliation.[45] The new Resident Lieut. Col. Wyllie got on good terms with the Maharana and was trying to make good terms with the latter. When the A.G.G. Trever met the Maharana the latter expressed his desire to dismiss Mehta Rai Pannalal from the Prime Ministership, as in his opinion Pannalal was the evil spirit conspiring in everything against him and was corrupt to the core. The Maharana further stated that he would have dismissed Pannalal long ago, but for fear of the interference by the G.O.I. Trevor did not like the Maharana's idea, however, he found him firm on his decision to remove Pannalal. Thereupon the A.G.G. advised the Maharana to appoint some other man as the Prime Minister in his place, but the Maharana had got so much suspicious of the men, that he did not agree to it. He also did not agree to the A.G.G.'s proposal to appoint a three-men council instead of a Prime Minister. At the end, the A.G.G. told the Maharana that the *Durbar* would personally be regarded responsible for the affairs in the state after Pannalal had gone and that he would not interfere until they had been proved inefficient.[46]

In the month of September, Rai Pannalal Mehta, C.I.E., was relieved of his services. He was allowed to take an honourable retirement by taking leave for one and a half years and then resign.

During the above meeting with the Maharana Col. Trevor, however, achieved an imperial object. Conceding to the Maharana's demand to dismiss Pannalal, he was able to persuade the Maharana to agree to construct the long pending railway line from Chittor to Udaipur.[47] Trevor reported to the G.O.I. after his meeting with the Maharana, stating, "He has consented to construct the railway from Chittor to Udaipur to please me". In the same report Trevor further stated that time would show whether the Maharana would go better. If situation further worsened. The British Government would be in a stronger position to press for the appointment of a competent Dewan or a Council. He further opined, "Experiences has shown that he resents coercion and is one of those whom it is easier to lead than drive. I already find him extremely pleasant but he is narrow-minded, very suspicious and sensitive, as regards his dignity and has been nothing of the world."[48]

Construction of Railway line from Chittor to Udaipur

During Maharana Sajjan Singh's time, the *Durbar* Government had agreed to open a branch railway line connecting Chittor station, on Rajputana-Malwa Railway line of P.B.C.I.R. with Udaipur. In October, 1884, the G.O.I. lent the services of Mr. Thompson to Mewar state to carry out the work of surveys and estimates connected with the above branch line. However, as we have seen earlier, the scheme was abandoned after Fateh Singh's accession.

In August, 1894, the Maharana agreed to construct the line and discussions started with regard to its working. The British Government desired that the rules and regulations of Indian Railway Act of 1890 should be applicable to the new line. The Maharana, on the other hand, desired to frame a Railway Act of the Mewar state, itself, like the State of Mysore, on the lines of Indian Railway Act of 1890. But the G.O.I. observed that no native state except Travencore could be allowed to go in for high class legislation like Mysore and the Government did not expect such a thing from a backward State like Udaipur. Any attempt to frame an act of the state itself would result into endless references to the local authorities and also to the G.O.I.[49]

On the 25th January, 1895, the *Mahakama Khas* of Udaipur informed the Resident that Maharana had sanctioned the extension of the Indian Railway Act and the Rules to the Udaipur-Chittorgarh Railway, as had been done by Jodhpur state on its railway line and that a notice to that effect would be put on all the railway stations for the information of the public. The Maharana agreed that both during the construction of the line and after its opening for traffic, the consulting Engineer of B.B.C.I.R. would have right to periodically inspect the line and investigate the incidents, occurring on it. However, the Civil and Criminal jurisdiction on the line was retained by the *Durbar* itself.

The branch meter guage railway line, about 67 miles long, was constructed at the expenses of the Mewar State and was opened on the 1st August, 1895. It was maintained and worked by B.B.C.I.R. Company on behalf of Mewar state, upto by 31st December, 1897, after which the management was taken over by the *Durbar* Government. Initially the line extended from Branch near Chittorgarh to Debari near Udaipur. The final completion of the line was done in 1899 when Debari and Udaipur were also linked. Total capital expenditure incurred on the line by the Mewar State came to over Rs. 20 lakhs. The railway line after some years gradually became a good source of revenue for the State. The net earnings from the line rose from some thousands in the beginning to Rs. 1,03,551 in the year 1905[50] and Rs. 2,05,984 in 1919.[51]

The opening of the Udaipur-Chittorgarh Railway line had the same effect on the life of the people of the State as had the Khandwa-Ajmer line of the B.B.C.I.R. However, the line proved much useful during the famine of 1899-1900, providing rapid movement of grain in the parts of the state through which it crossed.

Progress of Reforms

Maharana Fateh Singh had a conservative outlook, he was averse to all innovation in the state. In his opinion the reforms introduced on the pattern of western ideas were against the culture and traditions of the Hindus and were, therefore, to be renounced. As the proposals for reforms generally came from the British Government, his struggle for achieving internal sovereignty of the State was identified with his opposition to the reforms. His success in achieving the internal independence had, therefore, its adverse effects on the progress of reforms. However, the progress was not totally arrested at once. During the initial ten years of his reign the progress of reforms was more or less maintained. After 1894 and specially after 1901, the progress of reforms gradually came to standstill.

As we have seen, it was in the beginning of Maharana Fateh Singh's reign that the settlement operations were completed and a twenty year settlement of land revenue was enforced in the State. The Maharana afterwards took up the project of the Udaipur-Chittorgarh Railway line and completed it. Though no new projects of the construction of major roads were taken up, however, the length of metalled roads fell down from 270 miles to 257 miles.[52] He spent about five lakhs over the construction of the embankment called "Cannaught Bandh" and completed the work of Fateh Sagar lake. By 1908 there were about 100 small and big lakes in Khalsa area of the State, the majority of which were built during 1888-1908. He constructed the building of Victoria Hall Museum. Lans Downe Hospital and Walter Female

Hospital.[53]

On the death of Maharana Sajjan Singh a sum of two lakhs had been put aside with the object of establishing new schools and dispensaries in the state. A cess of one anna per rupee of the land revenue payable by the agriculturists was being collected from them under the settlement towards the expenses of the progress of education and public health. Consequently, the number of educational institutions in the State increased from 16 in 1886 to 34 in 1894 and 42 in 1901, after which further progress was more or less held up. There were a High School at Udaipur, a Middle School at Bhilwara, 10 Upper Primary Schools and 30 Lower Primary Schools. Besides these, there were 10 private schools run by the United Free Church Mission and Church Missionary Society and 2 Regimental Schools of Mewar Bhil Corps.

Between 1884 and 1894 schools were administered by a special Education Committee, which was created by Sajjan Singh. However, the above arrangement ceased in July when the management was taken over by the *Mahakma Khas*. A normal school for male teacher was started at the Capital in 1885, but was subsequently closed in 1891.

In 1894, the Sujjan Hospital was replaced by the Lans Downe Hospital. The new hospital building was constructed in the memory of the Governor-General's visit to Udaipur in 1891. The total number of the hospitals and dispensaries in the state reached to 20 by 1901 including the three run by the G.O.I. in Bhil areas and one each run by the Mission at Udaipur and the Gosain of Nathdwara at his place. A new lunaticasylum was opened at Udaipur in the year 1899-1900. In May 1889, a Central Jail was opened by the Maharana and was placed under the superintendence of the Residency Surgeon. Manufacture of carpets, rugs, blankets and coarse cloth, etc., was started in the Jail for the benefit of the prisoners.[54]

During this period the number of Imperial Post Offices in the State increased from 18 in 1888 to 36 in 1908. The State also maintained a local postal system called Bramani dak, which was started during Maharana Swaroop Singh's time. It was managed by a contractor to whom the *Durbar* paid Rs. 1920 a year. There were over 40 local post offices in different parts of the State. By 1918 there were 20 telegraph offices at 20 Railway stations and four telegraph offices at Udaipur, Bhilwara, Chittor and Nathdwara.[55] A cotton ginning factory had been established in 1880 at Bhilwara by Maharana Sajjan Singh. However, it was sold to the Mofussil Company of Bombay in 1887 as it was running at loss. A press was added to it shortly afterwards and the Maharana purchased back the entire property in 1898 in which about six hundred hands were employed in the working season.[56]

NOTES AND REFERENCES

1. *Udaipur Rajya ka Itihas* by G.H. Ojha, Part II, p. 839.
2. F.D. *Int.*, May 1883, No. 147-151.
3. Ibid.
4. Ibid.
5. Ibid.
6. F.D., *Int.*, Aug. 1885, No. 152-154.
7. *Udaipur Rajya ka Itihas* by G.H. Ojha, Part II, p. 840.
8. Ibid.
9. F.D., *Int.*, May 1887, No. 178-181.
10. *Udaipur Rajya ka Itihas* by G.H. Ojha, Part II, pp. 840-843.
11. Ibid.
12. *Rajputana Agency Records*, 1879, No. 107.
13. Ibid.
14. Ibid.
15. F.D., *Int.*, Oct. 1893, No. 60-80.
16. *Rajputana Agency Records*, 1879, File No. 107 List 1.
17. F.D., *Int.*, May 1888, No. 248-260.
18. Ibid.
19. Ibid.
20. Ibid.
21. Ibid.
22. Ibid.
23. Ibid.
24. India—Step mother by Sir Claude Hill.
25. F.D., *Int.*, Oct. 1893, No. 60-80.
    Owing to various factors for which the Political Agents were no less responsible, the political atmosphere at the States Capital always remained filled with intrigues and various kinds of rumours. The Political Agents usually assumed the role of dictators and in furtherance of the same they always pursued the policy of keeping the ruler weak and dependent on themselves and eliminating or corrupting the pro-Maharana elements. They even went to the extent of expelling people from Udaipur to attain that object. They did so as we have seen during the previous

reigns. In the beginning of Maharana Fateh Singh's region as well as Political Agent got Balwant Singh Kothari and other expelled from Udaipur for some time (Kothari Balwant Singh, p. 59).

26. F.D., *Int.*, Sept. 1883, No. 228-236.
27. *Rajputana Agency Records*, 1892-1894, (Udaipur Affairs).
28. F.D., *Int.*, May 1888, No. 110-111.
29. F.D., *Int.*, May 1889, No. 129-135.
30. F.D., *Military*, Dec. 1883, No. 3-13.
31. F.D., *Int.*, Oct. 1889, No. 129-135.
32. F.D., *Int.*, May 1892, No. 130-131.
33. *Ibid.*
34. *Ibid.*
35. F.D., *Int.*, Oct. 1893, No. 60-80. *Kothari Balwant Singh ka Jiwan Charitra*, pp. 63-64.
36. F.D., *Int.*, Oct. 1893, No. 60-80.
37. *Ibid.* The Commission consisted of three members, Kothari Balwant Singh, Joshi Naraindas and Mehta Pannalal. The first two were opposed to Wingate's views (*Kothari Balwant Singh ka Jiwan Charitra*, pp. 63-64).
38. *Ibid.*
39. *Ibid.*
40. *Rajputana Agency Records*, 1892-1894 (Udaipur Affairs).
41. *Ibid.*
42. *Ibid.*
43. *Ibid.*
44. *Ibid.*
45. F.D., *Int.*, Sept. 1894, No. 173-174.
46. *Ibid.*
47. F.D., *Int.*, Sept. 1894, No. 173-174.
48. *Ibid.* "His Highness abhors railways and the telegraph is a mighty muisance to him. Yet after considerable pressure he consented to allow both the one and the other to approach his rock-crowned capital. But only to approach. The Maharana would almost renounce his genealogical tree rather than the venerable quiet of his Kingdom (*Though India with the Prince* by Abbott G.F.A.).
49. F.D., *Int.*, March 1895, No. 192-202.
50. *A Gazetteer of the Udaipur State* by Major K.D. Erskine, p. 57.
51. F.D., *Int.*, Jan. 1920, No. 272.
52. *A Gazetteer of the Udaipur State* by Major K.D. Erskine, pp. 58, 46.
53. *Udaipur Rajya ka Itihas* by G.H. Ojha, Part II, p. 856.
54. *A Gazetteer of the Udaipur State* by Major K.D. Erskine, pp. 81-86.
55. *Ibid.*, p. 59.
56. *Ibid.*, p. 55.

13

Setback for the Interference

Maharana Refuses to have a Dewan

In September, 1894 Mehta Pannalal went on leave and after a few days he submitted his resignation. The Maharana was then counselled by the British Government to appoint someone as the Prime Minister which the former declined to do. He had attained his coveted objective and was now not prepared to part with his ruling powers. He was well aware that the officials like the *Pradhan* or Prime Minister usually played into the hands of the British Agents to the detriment of the interests of the State and derogated the dignity and authority of the ruler. In some cases this official with the support of the British Agent usurped the entire authority of the State Government by reducing the ruler to the position of a nominal sovereign.

The Maharana appointed Kothari Balwant Singh and Sahiwala Arjun Singh as the secretaries to the *Mahakma Khas*[1] and took up the reins of the Government in his own hands. The above officials enjoyed no powers except submitting the files to the Maharana for his decision and carrying out his orders. He had another object in view in appointing two officials simultaneously and dividing the executive work of the Government between them. Being a man of suspicious nature and having little experience and knowledge of administration, he tried to play one official against the other, as a result of which the officials could not pull together and the work of the administration suffered. Confusion prevailed in all the departments of the Government which further increased on account of the Maharana's averse attitude to the reforms. His autocracy also led to the growth of friction and ill-feelings between him and his nobility which taxed much of his energy and affected adversely the work of the Government.[2]

Complaints began pouring in the Political Department of the British Government regarding 'the deterioration' of the administration of the State of Udaipur. The assumption of all the powers, legislative, judicial and executive by the Maharana himself resulted in the centralisation of the authority and the responsibility. The *Mahadraj Sabha*, the highest judicial council in the state, ceased to function properly. The highest officials of the state having no powers, became inefficient and irresponsible. The cause of education and public health suffered and progress was gradually arrested. The State Education Committee, appointed by Maharana Sajjan Singh was abolished and the control of the department was placed directly under the *Durbar*. Since then the funds, collected from the cultivators along with revenue demands, were not spent properly and began accumulating in the state treasury. Similarly, the P.W.D. and Revenue Departments fell into gross mismanagement and inefficiency. The former was placed, after the departure of Thompson, under the charge of an old Anglo-Indian gentleman Mr. Williams, who was entirely unqualified and inexperienced. No new major projects were undertaken thereafter and whatever small projects were taken up, specially during the famine days of 1899-1901, were 'badly managed'. Almost all the roads in the State were very poorly maintained. Collection of the revenues fell in arrears and the agrarian conditions in the State began to deteriorate. The work of civil and criminal courts almost came to a stand still and a large number of under trial prisoners were detained in the prison, without bringing them to the court.[3]

The Maharana well realised his difficulties. However, he was not prepared to trust anybody. He employed to tide over the difficulties. Some Indian officials from outside the State but it was also discontinued after a few years.

Shyamji Krishna Verma and Harbhamji in Udaipur Service

Shyamji Krishna Verma, an Oxford Graduate, was appointed by the Maharana as a member of *Mahadraj Sabha* in 1892. Shyamji relinquished the Udaipur services in 1894 to become the Prime Minister of Junagarh state.[4] Shyamji was remployed in 1895 by the Maharana seeking his assistance in a dispute with the Shahpura Rajadhiraj in which British Government was also involved. His appointment at Udaipur was resented by the Resident, Lieut. Col. Wyllie. The British Government was suspicious of his connections with the revolutionary elements and Shyamji had to leave Udaipur the same year.

In 1898 the British Government offered to lend the services of Shyamji, the Prince of Morwi State, who was then working as the Dewan of the Bharatpur State. The Maharana refused to appoint Harbhamji as Dewan. He was assigned the work connected with missions to the A.G.G. and the Resident and was appointed as a member of the *Mahadraj Sabha* in October, 1898.[5] He stayed at Udaipur for about two years and thereafter he resigned and returned.

Victoria's Diamond Jubilee Celebration

In 1897 Queen Victoria's Diamond Jubilee was celebrated all over India. On this occasion at Udaipur Pichola lake was illuminated, prisoners were released and charity was distributed to the poor. The British Government raised the Maharana's salute from 19 to 21 guns. The Maharani of Udaipur was awarded the title of Order of the Crown of India. She was first lady among the royal families in Rajputana who got such a title.[6]

Famine Relief Measures

In 1899 there was severe draught in Mewar, the rainfall being less than ten inches at the Capital and only four inches in some parts of the State. The prices of the grain rose high and it vanished from the market due to the manipulation of the traders. The people in rural areas of Mewar particularly in Hilly and Kherad districts suffered most. As there were few roads in the interior of the State, the grains could not be made available easily to the distant parts in the country. No proper administrative measures were taken to check the profiteering and herding activities of the traders and hundreds of the people died of starvation in all parts of the State. People survived by eating roots and leaves of the trees and the flesh of the cattle. Instances of people eating the flesh of died bodies of their kins were witnessed at several places.[7] The hilly district was filled with dead bodies lying on the paths and the hills. By December the people who migrated towards Gujarat and Mahikantha began to return in a state of destitution finding no food and fodder there.[8] The *Durbar* Government proved too a low in extending relief to the famine striken people. At the end of September, 1899, A.H.T. Martindale, the A.G.G. visited Udaipur principally with the object of inducing the Maharana to make adequate arrangements for providing relief to the people in distress, specially in the hilly district. He adviced the *Durbar* to give loans to the Bhumia Chiefs of the hilly tract, who held that part of the country under him. For three months, the Maharana continued arguing about the guarantee of the repayment of the money from the Chiefs and, therefore, no relief work could be started in the districts at once.

Major Dunlop Smith of the Rajputana Famine Commission afterwards observed in his report to the G.O.I. that Udaipur was the real bolt in famine administration in Rajputana. Most of the Rajput feudatories of Mewar displayed indifference towards the miseries of the people and did nothing for their relief for some months in the beginning. The wild tribes of Bhils and Minas getting desperate to save their lives indulged everywhere in clot and plunder.[9]

Initial steps for relief were taken in Khalsa area of the State. Relief works, such as, constraining of tanks, wells, canals and buildings were started. The Maharana made large advances to the traders to import grains from outside. Charity Houses were opened at several places where food was distributed free of cost.[10]

In December, 1899, Major Dunlop Smith, the Famine Commissioner in Rajputana along with Mr. Holderness, Secretary, Department of Revenue and Agriculture, G.O.L., visited Udaipur and held a conference with the Maharana and his officials. It was decided that *Durbar* would spend Rs. 2 lakhs on P.W.D. works, Rs. 4 lakhs on relief works and would advance Rs. 1 lakh for taquavi loans and gratuitous relief.[11] Upon the advice of the G.O.I., the Maharana constituted a special famine office under Mr. Wakefield, the officer lent by the British Government and Mehta Bhopal Singh, who undertook the whole management of relief in their hands.[12] Prompt measures were taken which had their good effects. Yet the ill, inadequate and corrupt management of the affairs in the rural areas brought little relief to the people. The Resident, during his tour of the country, found *Durbar* officials giving the most inhuman treatment to the famine stricken people. The Resident after his tour of Mewar reported that the contribution of the Mewar for relief was inadequate in comparison to requirements and that also was being misappropriated by the dishonest people.[13]

The Maharana obtained a loan of Rs. 5 lakhs from the G.O.I. on the condition that the money would be spent on relief works, to bring down the prices of grain, to give loans to cultivators to purchase seeds and bullocks and to *jagirdars* to spend on famine relief.[14] The Chiefs of Mewar were advanced a loan of rupees sixty thousand directly by the British Government to undertake relief measures in their estates.[15]

To add to the misery of the people, Cholera broke out in the summer of 1900. People who were saved in the previous year owing to the relief works, began dying even at the places, where the relief works were going on. The disease played so great a havoc that about 5 per cent of the people died at Udaipur and its suburbs in a fortnight. Even the Maharana's palace was not immune and five of his six personal attendants succumbed to the disease. As a result of the raysges carried by famine and cholera the population of Mewar was reduced to 10,18,805 in 1901 from 18,45,008 in 1891. The percentage of mortality in the hilly area was as high as 25 to 30 per cent of the people.[16]

The *Durbar* spent in all about 25 lakhs on relief measures and gratuitous relief. Commenting upon the affairs in Mewar the official famine report of the G.O.I. remarked, "No administration was subjected to more severe and searching criticism, both official and public, than that of the Mewar *Durbar*. There was unquestionably a large amount of mortality and suffering which should have been avoided. The *Durbar* was unable to shape its relief policy on the lines which the political authorities considered the most suitable for the emergency. Its strained relations with the leading *jagirdars* and the inefficiency of the subordinate officials largely contributed to bring about the above result.[17]

Major and Mrs. Hutton Dowson, the Major was second in command of the Mewar Bhil Corps, rendered praiseworthy services at Kotra during the days of famine and cholera. From the very beginning they unostentiously engaged themselves in saving lives of men, women and children with the help of private funds which they raised from all parts of India and even from England. They started a charity house and maintained about 600 persons on their rolls.[18]

British Government Presses for Reforms

The reports of mismanagement of relief measure in the State and heavy mortality during 1899-1900 drew the attention of the British Government towards the state of affairs inside Mewar. Major Pinhey, the Resident in Mewar reported in March, 1901 that the administrative conditions in the State had further deteriorated. Reforms and improvements initiated by Sajjan Singh had been gradually allowed to fall into abeyance. People were not getting justice in time. As many as 252 references in *Mahakma Khas* were lying unattended and about 2000 police cases were lying undecided. District *Hakims* were complaining that despite their requests for several months, money was not being advanced to the distressed cultivators to purchase bullocks and seed. The officials of the State, Pinhey reported, were corrupt and inefficient and the crimes were increasing in the hilly area, which suffered most during the calamity.[19]

Lieut. Col. Wyllie, the A.G.G. observed that since his accession Fateh Singh's ambition had been restore his position and dignity which his predecessors enjoyed before the Maratha wars. Being distrustful of his own officials, he had concentrated the administration in his own hands and was finding himself overwhelmed by a mass of confusing details and the wheels of the administration had ceased to revolve.[20]

Major Pinhey had an interview with the Maharana and discussed the State of affairs with him. He plainly told the Maharana that in the opinion of the British Government it was highly desirable that he appointed a responsible '*Dewan*' (Prime Minister) in the state and place the department of Public Works under qualified engineer. Pinhey counselled him to appoint any experienced local man or a trained graduate from Mayo College,

Ajmer as the '*Dewan*' of the State, if he was unwilling to appoint an outsider. Pinhey's efforts bore no fruits.[21] In June, 1903 he reported that no substantial progress of reforms could be expected during Fateh Singh's life-time, as his character and disposition were totally opposed to any extensive alteration in the existing regime. Notwithstanding that, Pinhey observed Fateh Singh's administration did not appear generally unpopular and that petitions from his subjects were comparatively rare.[22]

In 1903 a systematic examination of irrigation projects and resources in Rajputana was undertaken by G.O.I. The work was started under supervision of Mr. Manners Smith, the Superintending Engineer Protective Irrigation Works Rajputana and Mr. Jacob, the consulting Engineer. The immediate object of the survey, as expressed by the G.O.I. was to take stock of local conditions and ascertain the most promising irrigation schemes in order to protect the local people from the calamity of famine in future.[23] The survey report stated that Mewar had immense possibilities of irrigation. It suggested to start the following projects immediately, a canal from Naogam on the Banas, two reservoirs on the Kothari at Thala and Meja and a big reservoir on the Banas at Amarpura. The last, in its opinion, if carried out was to be one of the grandest works of its kind in India.[24]

In January, 1904, the A.G.G. asked the Maharana to establish a separate department of Irrigation, placing it under a qualified official and start work on the lines suggested by the Jacob Smith report. The Counsel again fell on deaf ears and in November, 1904 the G.O.I. expressed great disappointment at the fact that the Maharana of Udaipur had not adopted any of the measures suggested to improve the administration of the State and directed the Resident to induce him to realize the obligations of a ruler in the present day.[25]

In the beginning of 1905 the A.G.G. himself paid a long visit to Udaipur. He met the Maharana at his Jai Samand Camp and requested him to give practical evidence of his desire to meet the reiterated wishes of the G.O.I. The Maharana, at the end of the meeting agreed to replace the previous ministers Kothari Balwant Singh and Sahiwala Arjun Singh by Mehta Bhopal Singh and Mahasani Heeralal, to create a separate Irrigation Department and put it under the control of Mr. G.W. Wakefield, who was then working as the Boundary Settlement Officer in the state, to get plans and estimates prepared for three large irrigation projects, recommended by the Jacob-Smith's report, to create a Department of Court of Wards to look after minority administrations in various *jagirs* and put it under the supervision of Mr. Wakefield, to make arrangements for his son, Bhopal Singh's education, to appoint a qualified revenue officer in place of Mehta Bhopal Singh, to restore the effective functioning of the Mahadraj Sabha, to establish a school for the education of the children of the Chiefs and to improve the conditions of his regular troops, a portion of which was to be maintained as Imperial Service Troops.

In may 1905, the G.O.I. congratulated the Maharana on his decision to introduce administrative reforms. But after two years in April 1907 the succeeding A.G.G., Sir Elliot Colvin complained that no sufficient improvement was visible from the actions taken by the Maharana in fulfilment of his pledges except in one important particular of the Irrigation Department which had been placed under a British Officer, Mr. Wakefield.[26] Colvin reported that the Maharana was opposed to the education of his son by an European teacher. The two new ministers Mehta Bhopal Singh and Mahasani Heeralal had no more powers than their predecessors had, and the general position of the administration remained as inefficient as it was before.[27] The G.O.I., it appears, could do more than pressing the Maharana time and again to fulfil its desires and the latter adopted evasine tactics and half-hearted measures.

Withdrawal of Prohibitory Orders on Export of Cotton from Mewar

During the famine years of 1899-1900, the Mewar *Durbar* had prohibited the export of cotton and wool from the State.[28] Usually cotton and wool were exported from Mewar into the British territory of Ajmer-Merwara and formed the major part of supplies to run six cotton presses, two ginning factories and one spinning and weaving Mills at Beawar. The prohibitory order of the Mewar Government was not withdrawn thereafter and its continuation had an adverse effect on the cotton manufacture of that town resulting in slowing down of production, closing of some factories, unemployment of labourers and depression in the trade. The Maharana, in the meanwhile, in order to increase the State revenues, established a state press at Bhilwara and directed all the cultivators of his State to move their cotton to Bhilwara.

In November, 1900, Citizen's Cotton merchants traders and bankers of Beawar sent a memorial to the Governor-General submitting their grievances against the Udaipur *Durbar's* order and requesting the G.O.I. to persuade it to lift the ban on the export of cotton. Receiving the above complaints through the Commissioner of Ajmer, Merwara, the Resident in Mewar counselled the Maharana to remove the prohibitory orders on the export of cotton and not to induce by "artificial means" the cultivators to sell cotton at Bhilwara. The Maharana agreed unwillingly to the request but ordered that the exporters should get licenses from the Mewar Government. This procedure was found objectionable by the G.O.I. Though the Maharana issued no notification to that effect, he however, verbally conveyed to the Government that the Beawar merchants could freely export the cotton without any restriction. The A.G.G., in his reply, stated that he had accepted the assurance of the Mewar *Durbar* that the prohibition of the export of cotton had been withdrawn.[29]

The Maharana asserts his Sovereignty over his Chiefs

With the assumption of power by Maharana Fateh Singh, there occurred a change in the relationship between the ruler and the Mewar chiefs. Fateh Singh reversed his predecessors policy of conciliation and compromise with the nobles and began asserting his sovereign rights in the internal matters of the estates, big or small alike.[30] He disregarded the claims of some of the big chieftains of the first rank, of enjoying several traditional rights and privileges inside their estates, in which the Maharana could not interfere. Fateh Singh's attitude was in consonance with his idea of personal rule and his sovereignty inside the state.

The chiefs opposed the attitude of the Maharana. Death had, by that time, carried off the old and influential chiefs of Salumbar, Deogarh, Delwara and Bedla and the Maharana's position had thereby greatly strengthened. However, the attachment for their ancestral and traditional rights had always been great in the Rajputs and the chiefs resisted all those measures which affected their rights and privileges. Conflict appeared on several matters like tribute, personal services, Nazarana fee Talwar Bandai, Court etiquette, minority administration and civil and criminal jurisdiction. Both the parties began acting in disregard of the "*Kalambandi*" of 1878. Several of the chiefs finding it futile to make complaints to the British Government against the Maharana's actions adopted the attitude of defiance and disobedience. They ceased coming to assemble at Udaipur on the Dussehra festival and stopped rendering personal services. The Maharana complained to the G.O.I. against the attitude of his chiefs and sought its assistance to coerce them to submit. The latter declined to interfere. The Maharana, on his part pursued to repressive and coercive policy towards them and took every opportunity to impose his personal authority and judgements over them.[31]

In 1898 the Chiefs, jointly, submitted a memorandum of about 53 grievances to the G.O.I. complaining that the Maharana was acting against the traditions and customs of Mewar and against the *Kalambandi* of 1878.[32] They stated:

(i) That the *Durbar* authorities were interfering with their criminal and civil jurisdiction inside their respective estates contrary to the Agreement of 1878 and the ancient customs;

(ii) that irregularities were being practised in the settlement of boundary disputes;

(iii) that their rights to use Lawazima and Muratib (insignia) on the state occasions were being denied;

(iv) that *Mahakma Khas* was displaying discourtesy towards the Chiefs and delaying the decisions;

(v) that the Maharana was acting arbitrarily in regard to the question of *Nazarana, Talwar Bandai*, fines and renewal of *pattas* (grants) and the same was being done regarding taxes, lagat, irrigation works, shooting preserves, salt compensation, grants, etc.

(vi) that undue interference was being practised during the minorities in the estates ;

(vii) that much injustice was being done in regard to the settlement of debts due to *Durbar* and in regard to the services; and

(viii) that the nobles were not being consulted in the State matters.

The Maharana, on his part, complained that the Chiefs were not rendering appropriate services due to him and not paying full tribute, that they were adopting such attitude as lower his prestige, that they were not paying anything towards development works as irrigation, roads, education, etc., carried on by the state and that they were not living to the standard befitting *sardars* and were indulging in luxury and illness.[33]

In 1901, the A.G.G. Lieut. Col. Wyllie urged Captain Pinhey, the Resident in Mewar to try to bring reconciliation between the parties. The A.G.G. also suggested to seek the services of Sir Pratap Singh, the ruler of Idar, if required to settle the dispute as the latter was held in high esteem by the Maharana of Udaipur. Pinhey did dry but his efforts failed to produce the desired result.[34]

In July, 1913, the Maharana paid a visit to the Governor-General Lord Hardinge at Simla to enquire after his health.[35] He explained his position to the Governor-General regarding his relations with his Chiefs. He agreed to the institution of an enquiry into the case to ascertain to what extent the *jagirdars* had from time to time, failed in discharging their duties and obligations and how the *Durbar* treated them. After some correspondence in that connection in August, 1914, Lord Hardinge appointed two ruling chiefs *viz*., the Maharaja of Indore and the Maharao of Kota and a British officer Lieut. Col. H.L. Showers to go into the facts. Col. Showers spent five months at Udaipur. The proceedings of the enquiry, however, got stuck on account of the sudden demise of Mr. Showers and thereafter no other official was appointed to the committee and the matter remained in the sad state as it was before.[36]

Maharana Fateh Singh's long reign of more than forty-five years witnessed several confrontations between him and his Chiefs on various questions which brought in frequent interventions by the British Government. The Maharana is found, in almost all cases, asserting successfully his supremacy in the internal affairs of the state.

1. Banera

As stated earlier the *Durbar*, had during Sajjan Singh's reign issued orders for the restoration of the village of Dabla to Banera Chief. The village was, however, not restored. On the other hand, the *Durbar* afterwards appointed a Musarim to collect the tribute to which the Banera Chief was entitled. Further complaints were, thereafter, made by the Banera authorities that other chieftains under Banera, such as of Baldrakha and Bamnya were also being instigated by the *Durbar* to show insubordination to the Banera Raja.[37]

The affairs were further complicated and relations got more strained during Maharana Fateh Singh's time. Two villages called Muhwa and Sidriyars had been mortgaged by one of the ancestors of Banera family to that of Baba Gyan Singh's Chief of Udaipur. Now the new Banera Chief, Raja Govind Singh desired to redeem the above villages by paying mortgage money. But his desire was not fulfilled due to the reluctance of the Durbar.[38]

A boundary dispute between the village of Muhwa and other villages belonging to Banera arose in 1886. In June, 1886 Mehta Laxmilal, the Magistrate of Jahajpur district was appointed by the Mewar Durbar to decide the boundary dispute in question and the concerned parties were asked to refrain from lawless action. Two years passed and no decision was given, however, in July, 1888, a clash occurred between the two parties on the disputed land resulting into several people dead and wounded on both sides. Dr. J.P. Straton, the boundary Settlement Officer in Mewar at that time, was appointed to enquire into the case. According to his findings the Banera authorities were found guilty of the bloodshed and of disregarding the notification of the *Durbar*. Banera was punished with a fine of Rs. 10,000. The heir-apparent of Banera was deprived of the privilege of visiting Udaipur for one and a half years. All the Afghans in the service of Banera were ordered to be dismissed. Two weeks were given to obey the decision, failing which an additional village was to be forfeited as the penalty.[39]

As the Banera authorities did not pay the fine after the expiry of the period of about 3 months, the *Durbar* confiscated the village of Reechra. Banera Raja Govind Singh submitted a memorial of grievances to the G.O.I. in August, 1890, stating that Dabla had not been restored to him by the *Durbar* despite the

British Government orders of 1879, and that the Maharana was acting unjustly and arbitrarily in his relations with the Chieftains, particularly in regard to the boundary disputes. He requested the G.O.I. to interfere, in order to compel the *Durbar* to restore Dabla to him, to revise his judgement on Muhwa boundary dispute and to restore the mortgage villages getting payment from the Banera estate. At the British Government was already displeased with the refractory activities of the Banera chief, it declined to intervene. It desired, however, that the Raja should submit his grievances to the *Durbar* in a becoming manner and the Maharana in that case would be pleased to accord to them a patient hearing and just consideration. It also desired that the Raja of Banera fully acknowledged his subordinate position to the *Durbar*. Until he did so, the G.O.I. observed, it would be difficult to settle, in detail, the several questions which the Raja had raised. If the Raja of Banera acted as directed it would be pleased to appoint any English Officer to remove the remaining causes of dispute.[40]

The Raja and his son both came to Udaipur and presented their grievances personality before the Maharana. It, however, brought no change in the decision of the Mewar *Durbar*. In 1895 the Raja sent another memorial to the G.O.I. The Governor-General, while declining to intervene, observed that it was to be regretted that the Maharana was adopting an uncompromising attitude towards one of his principal Chiefs. He directed the A.G.G. and the Resident to try to bring about an amicable settlement.[41]

Efforts were, thereafter, made by the successive Residents to settle the matter, but no amicable settlement could be effected. The Raja wanted to adjust the fine of Rs. 10,000 against the revenue of the village Reechra, which the *Durbar* had been collecting since confiscation and wanted the repayment of Rs. 8,000, being the remaining amount of the annual income of the village for the period. But the Maharana refused to agree to it and even put forward the demand of enhanced Chhatoond, claiming that the previous amount of Chhatoond was to small and had been decided long back. He also desired that the Chief should share the expenditure on roads, railways, hospitals, schools, irrigation works, etc. In 1901, the G.O.I. received another memorial from the Raja of Banera but it was field under clause

2. Shahpura

For several years the Rajadhiraj had not been rendering personal service to the Maharana, thought in compliance of the decision of the G.O.I. of 1874 he was paying the tribute regularly to him.[43]

Maharana Fateh Singh asked the Rajadhiraj of Shahpura to serve him personally as the other Chiefs did. As the Rajadhiraj did not comply with the Maharana's demand, the latter attached the village of Phulia of Shahpura. This action on the part of the Maharana against the Rajadhiraj of Shahpura, who was also a feudatory of the British Government produced a constitutional tangle in which the British Government found itself involved.[44]

The Resident, Lieut. Col. Wyllie conveyed to the Maharana that the G.O.I. highly objected to the Maharana's step of attaching the village belonging to Shahpura. On the 18th Nov., 1894 the Maharana wrote to the A.G.G. requesting him to compel the Shahpura Chief not to raise unjustifiable objection about personal service due to him being a *jagirdar* of Mewar state. The A.G.G., however, asked the Maharana to first retrace the stop, he had taken, stating that as soon as the attachment was withdrawn he would be ready to do what he could to settle the differences. In the month of June 1895 the Maharana sent Kothari Balwant Singh to the A.G.G. to submit the Maharana's case before him. In July the A.G.G. again informed the Maharana that the question of the moment was that the *Durbar* released from attachment the village of Shahpura Rajadhiraj and then only their grievances could be attended to. The Maharana stated that it was perfectly justified on his part to punish the Rajadhiraj for his disobedience, as the latter was a *jagirdar* of his state. If he withdrew the attachment it would create a harmful precedent which other Chiefs might try to follow.[45]

At the end of July, Lieut. Col. Wyllie had a personal interview with the Maharana and told him plainly that the G.O.I. would directly intervene in the matter if he did not withdraw his action. The Maharana agreed to withdraw the attachment from the village of Phulia, however, on the condition that the

Rajadhiraj would come to Udaipur to settle the matter, which he did.[46]

Shyamji Krishna Verma was called back from Junagarh by the Maharana for his assistance in this case. The negotiations were held in August 1895. The Maharana proposed that Shahpura Raja Dhiraj should come to Udaipur himself to serve for two months every alternate year or send a jamiyat to serve for 3 months in a year in case he did not personally attend, that he should pay succession fee to the Maharana and that he should promise to send his troops to Maharana's services whenever called upon to do so in emergency. The Raja Dhiraj declined to agree to the above conditions and the talks failed. Thereupon the Resident repeated the demand of the withdrawal of attachment. On the 6th August, the Resident expressed his resentment to Shyamji Krishna Verma and Kothari Balwant Singh stating that the Maharana had gone back upon his words.[47]

Shyamji left Udaipur on the 7th August. On 17th August, Lieut. Col. Wyllie reported to the A.G.G. that he was sorry to state that all his powers of diplomacy had failed and the Maharana had acted most obstinately. He further stated that he had sent a warning to the Maharana through Balwant Singh that it would be the beginning of the trouble, the extent of which he little foresaw. The Government of India's decision in favour of Rajadhiraj would lead to a host of other affairs and the rotten state of administration in Mewar would not remain out of the gaze of the Governor-General. The Resident stated that the Maharana required to be "pulled with a round turn." At last the Maharana succumbed to the pressure and on the 19th August the Resident informed the A.G.G. telegraphically that the Rajadhiraj had left for Shahpura and Balwant Singh had verbally informed him that the attached village had been released.[48]

The G.O.I. appointed Sir Robert Crosthwait and Mr. Martindale to effect an amicable settlement between the two parties in regard to the service question, who also failed in their efforts. In 1903, Major Pinhey, the Resident in Mewar proposed the transfer of Shahpura from Haroti Political Agency to Mewar Agency in order to facilitate the settlement of the problem. In 1904, the G.O.I., approved of the above suggestion and decided that the Rajadhiraj would in future attend on Maharana every alternate year and remain subject to other obligations applicable to other Udaipur *jagirdars* of similar position, failing which the Maharana could levy a fine of Rupees one lakh on the Rajadhiraj.[49] This decision settled the case. The idea of the transfer of Shahpura from Haroti-Agency to Mewar Agency was, however, dropped.

3. Amet

As stated earlier, a settlement was brought about by the Regency Council in Mewar in 1874 in regard to the succession case of Amet, thereby the villages of Toongarh and Shodas belonging to Amet were given away to Amar Singh in perpetuity. Later on during the minority of Sheonath Singh, the authorities found that the said villages yielded only Rs. 2,500 yearly, whereas Amar Singh claimed the payment of Rs. 8,000 per year according to Maharana Shambhu Singh's decision. Consequently further orders were issued to the Amet management to pay an additional amount of Rs. 5,500 annually to Amar Singh from the Amet treasury.[50]

In 1886 Sheonath Singh attained his majority and the management of the estate was handed over to him. He put forward the claim that the village given to Amar Singh from Amet *jagir*, were worth Rs. 8,000 and not Rs. 2,500 as assessed by the *Durbar* management during his minority. He stopped paying the additional amount of Rs. 5,500 annually to Amar Singh. He proposed that either Amar Singh should retain the village without getting any additional money or return them to Amet and get Rs. 8,000 annually instead.[51]

Sheonath Singh's plea was not accepted by the *Durbar* and he was ordered to obey *Durbar's* decision. When the chief did not follow suit orders were issued in 1889 by the Maharana for the attachment of three villages of Amet, namely, Nari, Amarkhera and Parloda in order to make payment of Rs. 5,500 annually to Amar Singh. The annual income of these villages was claimed by Sheonath Singh to be Rs. 10,000. The Chief requested the Maharana to reconsider the whole case. Maharana Fateh Singh refused to revise the decision as it was taken during his predecessor's reign in 1874, and had been approved by the G.O.I.[52]

The chief appealed to the Resident the A.G.G. against Maharana's action. In April, 1892, Col. Miles, the Resident wrote to the A.G.G. stating that Sheonath Singh had been treated with injustice by the Durbar and that Amar Singh had been favoured and allowed to aggrandise at his expense. The resident opined that the case deserved the Government's sympathetic consideration, the A.G.G. differed with Col. Miles' opinion. He observed that the G.O.I. had approved *Durbar's* decision of 1874 and the Maharana was justified in attaching Sheonath Singh's villages on his failing to pay Rs. 5,500 to Amar Singh. In May, 1895 the chief submitted a printed memorial to the G.O.I. about his claims, but the latter refused to interfere and withheld the memorial under clause 7(3) of the Memorial Rules of G.O.I.[53]

4. Delwara

In 1899, Man Singh, a minor boy of 8 years succeeded to the *Gadee* of Delwara estate.[54] During his minority the estate was placed under the management of the Court of Wards and a Munsarim was appointed by the *Mahakama Khas* for the same. Man Singh died of consumption in 1913, when the *jagir* was still under the *Durbar* management. The Delwara family was in favour to seat Chanda Sen, the son of Bijay Singh the chief of Kunadi in the Kota State on the *gadee* of Delwara. Chandra Sen was a young educated man. However, before Delwara people could send their memorandum to the Maharana, the latter decided in favour of a boy of 10 years, who was the son of Jawan Singh, the Jhala chief of Bari Sadri estate in Mewar and issued orders to the effect. The Delwara family had been closely connected with the estates of Bari Sadri also. Several times, when succession failed in Delwara, it had been customary to adopt from the collateral family of Bari Sadri. The Maharana also claimed that Man Singh's widow had sent a written request in favour of Jawan Singh's son.[55]

Bijay Singh objected to the procedure and the Delwara family appealed to the Maharana to reconsider the case. However, the Maharana held that Bijay Singh and his son could have no right to Delwara, as he had been adopted in a *jagir* belonging to another State. The Delwara family produced a "will" said to be left by the late Raja Fateh Singh which stated that Bijay Singh or his son would succeed to the *gadee* of Delwara if Zalim Singh died heirless. The Maharana refused to accept the "will" on the plea that as Zalim Singh was succeeded by his son Man Singh, the "will" became ineffective. He also claimed that the widow of the late Man Singh had favoured his decision. The widow, however, declared that the letter referred to, was a forged one and she wrote another letter in favour of Chandra Sen. Bijay Singh attributed the real cause in selecting a minor to the fact that his son was disliked by the Maharana on account of his being educated as the Maharana was conservative and averse to western education.[56]

When the A.G.G. visited Udaipur in August 1913, Bijay Singh submitted a petition to him. The A.G.G., while declining to intervene, observed that the succession in question, seemed to have been decided with some precipitancy. There seemed to be some doubt as to the real wishes of the widow. The "will" laid down by Raj Rana Fateh Singh for the order of the succession, to which the *Durbar* agreed to, also had some weight, as Man Singh died without getting himself powers of administration in Delwara *jagir*. The position seemed to the A.G.G. very much the same as though Zalim Singh had died childless. He informed the Maharana verbally about his views, but he did not press them as he thought the case was one in which he had very right to decide as he liked. The Maharana on his part adhered to his previous decision.[57]

When Bijay Singh sent him memorial to the G.O.I., the latter, declined to entertain it stating that the case was not one in which it could interfere.[58]

5. Asind

Rawat Ranjeet Singh of Asind, the first class noble of Mewar died of influenza in November, 1918 leaving no male issue to succeed him.[59] His only son Bijay Singh, aged 16, had also died a fortnight before the Rawat's death. The Maharana ordered to take the management of the *jagir* under the Court of Wards. The ladies of Asind family conveyed their wishes to the Maharana in favour of Thakur Sajjan Singh of Kotra to succeed the late Chief of Asind. For some time the Maharana sent no reply and then finally, in March, 1919, the *Maharana Khas* issued orders to resume the *jagir* in Khalsa, stating the reasons that the line of Ajeet Singh, the original grantee, had exhausted, that the grant of Asind was of recent date and origin and that the late Rawat Ranjeet Singh took to a refractory and disobedient attitude towards the *Durbar*. The *Mahakama Khas*, elucidating the last reason, stated that the Rawat took 'tika' money from Sitamau against the decision of 'Walter krit Rajput Hitkarini Sabha' whereupon the *Durbar* had to attach the village of Changeri to compel him to return the money, that Rawat did not send 'Assamis' (persons of his *jagir* connected with criminal cases) when he was asked to do so and that he did not pay tribute regularly. The Rawat was subsequently debarred from coming to Udaipur.[60]

The ladies of Asind family sent petitions to the A.G.G. against the decision of the Maharana. A petition was presented to the Maharana by the chiefs of Salumbar, Bhensrorgarh and other *jagirs* submitting that the Maharana's action was against usage, custom and Dharma Shastra. They pleased that "such an order causes great detriment to our rights. Where there is issuelessness, the adoption is customary and it has been usually practised in every case." They requested the ruler to confirm the adoption decided by the ladies of Asind family. The Maharana rejected their plea arguing that the Dharma Shastra did not apply in such cases. It was the duty of a subordinate to render services and be loyal to the ruler and if he committed defaults, he should be punished.[61]

On the 24th March, 1919, the A.G.G. intimated telegraphically to the ladies of Asind that after enquiring into the matter, he saw no reason to interfere on their behalf in the case as the Maharana has resumed the *jagir* on the failure of the direct line.[62]

Jawas Succession Case

Several succession questions of adoption arose from time to time in Bhomat area of Mewar which raised certain questions regarding the precise nature of relations between the Maharana and the Bhumia chiefs on the one hand the Maharana and the British Government on the other in the area. When Mewar entered into treaty relations with the British Government, the Bhumia Chiefs holding the estates of Ogna, Panarwa, Jura, Jawas, Para, Madri, Chani, Thana, Patia and Sarwan were enjoying full freedom. There was then left no trace of Maharana's sovereignty over that area. It was the power of the British army that subjugated this trouble some area and Maharana's sovereignty was restored. But it was recognised that these chiefs had prescriptive rights in land and not by Sanad from the Maharana and that they paid no Nazarana on succession. However, they were required to pay the tribute (Chhatoond) annually.

After the subjugation of Bhomat by the British army, it was realised that the Mewar *Durbar*, upon their own, were unable to control the area. An arrangement was brought about by which the area was put under the charge of a British Political Superintendent, who held also the offices of the Commandant of the Mewar Bhil Corps at Kherwara.[63]

When in December, 1874, Bheron Singh, the Rao of Jawas died issueless, he was succeeded by his uncle, Amar Singh, the chief of Babulwara. The latter had been the regent in the late chief's minority. The Political Superintendent, Hilly Tracts, Lieut. Col. Gordon, was informed by the late chief's family that the chief had adopted his uncle before his death and was requested to confirm Amar Singh's succession. On the 10th January, 1875, Gordon wrote to Col. Wright, the Political Agent in Mewar that it was very unusual for a nephew to adopt an uncle and that Jawas succession was attracting attention in the neighbourhood. He further stated that under ordinary circumstances the succession of a Bhumia chief was marked by the present of a 'pagree' from the Political Superintendent and much importance was attached to this custom implying British protection. In the meanwhile, *Durbar* Council coming to know of the case addressed a letter to Amjar Singh calling upon him to explain upon what authority he had installed himself as the chief of Jawas.[64]

By then another claimant to the *gadee* of Jawas came forth. Lachhaman Singh, the chief of Para, challenged Amar Singh's succession. He applied directly to Mewar *Durbar* to recognise his claim. Col. Wright, the Political Agent, wrote a letter to the A.G.G. stating: "It is a question, whether they (*Durbar*) have the right to do so. These Bhumia chiefs have always regarded themselves as semi-independent and have always been the 'protected states' under the British Government. Their dependence on Udaipur had been nominal and in the absence of our assistance they would have never been subjugated by the *Durbar*.[65]

The *Durbar* Council desired that their sovereignty over the area ought to be recognised. Whenever a succession took place in any estate, it must be confirmed in the customary way by the

Durbar. The British Government saw no objection to it. Lieut. Col. Gordon induced Amar Singh to send a request to the Mewar *Durbar* in writing to confirm his succession to the *gadee* of Jawas. The *Durbar* Council approved of his installation as the chief of Jawas.[66]

In 1894, Amar Singh was succeeded by Ratan Singh, who was adopted from the Thana family. The Maharana raised his objection to the proceedings of adoption and installation by asserting his prerogative of sanction in such matters. Ratan Singh claimed that *Durbar* had no right to interfere in the question of adoption or succession in the *Jagir*. The case was referred to the British Government. In the September, 1897, the A.G.G. conveyed the decision of the Government stating that though the Jawas chief was subordinate to the Maharana, he, however, did not hold estate by a grant and as such the heir, whether natural or adopted, did not pay a *Nazarana* or any fine on his succession. In view of this the consent of the *Durbar* in the succession was not necessary. The *Durbar*, however, might be allowed to express their opinion before such a succession was finally sanctioned by the British Government. The Government decided that the *Durbar* should receive a formal notice of an adoption or a succession by an adopted son, which should be communicated through the Superintendent Hilly Tracts and the Resident. The concurrence or sanction of the *Durbar* in such a case was not required. Accordingly, Ratan Singh sent such a notice to the *Durbar* in a formal way.[67]

In 1919, Ratan Singh died leaving an infant son of $2^1/_2$ years, called Nobat Singh. The Political Superintendent Col. Hutton recommended the name of Kunwar Raghunath Singh of Thana to look after the management of the *jagir* in the Rao's minority. The Mewar *Durbar* represented verbally to the Resident that the management of Jawas in the circumstances of the case should remain under the *Durbar* management, i.e. Court of Wards. There had been no precedence of the *Durbar's* management during the minority in the Bhomat estates, since the area was placed under the Political Superintendence of the British Government. There were instances of some Bhomat estates, where regents were appointed in the minorities under the supervision of the Political Superintendent. In some estates during minorities, the Pol. Supdt. had exercised direct supervision and looked after the management of the estate himself. Consequently, the Maharana's objections were ruled out by the British Government. Lieut. Col. Spence, the Resident in Mewar wrote to the Maharana in May, 1919, "No review is called for in the case. But I think the *Durbar* may be held responsible uptodate for their own failure to obtain that further measure of authority which it has long been the desire of the Government and the Political Officer to extend them." The A.G.G. sent instructions to the Resident in Mewar that in future the procedure of sending an appeal or petition to the Mewar *Durbar* regarding any succession to an estate in Bhomat through the Political Superintendent, Hilly Tract and the Resident in Mewar should be strictly adhered to.[68]

Delhi *Durbar* of 1903

On the first January, 1903 British Officials, Princes, prominent chiefs and other dignitaries of India assembled in a *Durbar* held at Delhi to celebrate the accession of Edward VII as the Emperor of the British Empire. The younger brother of the Emperor, Duke of Cunnaught, arrived in India to grace the occasion. Maharana Fateh Singh like other Princes received an invitation to attend the *durbar*. The invitation created a sort of uproar at Udaipur. The Maharana felt it was derogatory to his dignity and position to attend such a *durbar*. Such an act, he thought, was not envisaged in the terms of the Treaty and Alliance of 1818 and would impair the prestige, which he enjoyed among the Rajputs and the Hindus of India. The Maharana was in a fix, however, as he is said to have consented verbally to Lord Curzon, the Governor-General, to attend the *Durbar* during the latter's visit to Udaipur in 1902.[69]

Maharana Fateh Singh put certain conditions before the British Government on fulfilment of which he was ready to attend the *Durbar*, that he must be given first position among all the Native Rulers of India that he must be excused from join the procession and that arrangement of his seat in the *Durbar* ought to be in keeping with his dignity of being the highest among the Native Rulers. Some assurances were conveyed to the Maharana and he decided to go to Delhi.[70] When he started for Delhi the poet Kesari Singh Barahat presented some verses entitled "*Chetavani ra Chungatia*" (urges to wake) to the Maharana reminding him of the glorious and heroic traditions of his ancestors, who never submitted to any power nor paid 'Nazar' to any king, but carried constant struggle to uphold their glory and fame.[71] The poem created a marked impression on the Maharana's mind and revived the sense of his ancestral glory in him.

Two special trains brought the Maharana's one thousand retainers and servants to Delhi and three elephants reached there by road. He reached Delhi on the 31st December, 1902 there he came to know that in both the assemblage and the procession he had been assigned a place below the rulers of Hyderabad, Baroda, Mysore, and Kashmir, which was quite contrary to the words given to him before he left for Delhi. He did not leave his railway carriage and decided to abstain from participating in both the State Entry and the *Durbar* giving out that he had fallen ill on account of the exteration of the journey.[72]

The Maharana's words were not taken as genuine. However, he could not be persuaded to leave the carriage and to the extreme vexation of the G.O.I., the Maharana left Delhi even before the first ceremony of the State Entry was accomplished.

Visits of various Viceroys to Udaipur

Several Viceroys of India visited Udaipur during Maharana Fateh Singh's time. Lord Dufferin came in 1885, Lord Lansdowne in 1890, Lord Elgin in 1896, Lord Curzon in 1902, Lord Minto in 1909, Lord Hardinge in 1912 and Lord Chelmsford in 1916. Lord Curzon visited Udaipur on the 15th November, 1902, just before the Delhi *Durbar* of the 1st January, 1903. Lord Curzon was a source of great awe for the Princes of India. It was his usual practice to give sermons to the Native Rulers in regard to their obligations to the sovereign power and their people. Sir W.R. Lawrence described the meeting of Lord Curzon with the Maharana in these words. "Lord Curzon met the Maharana for the first time. I watched him closely and saw with pleasure that he, who was no respector of persons, fell, at once, under the charm. He did not press the Maharana with questions of administration nor pointed out weak points in the state nor suggested reforms. Curzon, at the state banquet given in his honour, praised the Maharana as a conscientious and hard working ruler who led a simple and exemplary life and devoted himself assiduously to the interest of his people. He further said that he was an embodiment of the pride, dignity and patriotism of his race.[73]

However, Lord Curzon's visit left Maharana aggrieved about some changes made by the former in points of ettiquete to the detriment of the Maharana's status. At the time of the *Durbar's* courtesy visit to the Viceroy at the Residency, the latter came forward only to the edge of a small carpet, whereas previously the viceroy used to receive the Maharana at the door of the room.[74] Again the Maharana used to bring "*Chanwar*" men and two or three attendants with him who used to stand behind him when he interviewed the Viceroy. This time the above practice was not allowed as the Viceroy's chobdar stopped all the attendants at the door. This treatment left a bad taste behind.

During Lord Minto's visit to Udaipur in October, 1909, the Viceroy laid the foundations stone of a *Durbar* Hall in the Kunwarpada Palace, which was afterwards named as Minto Hall. During his visit the Maharana raised the question of restoring the custom of the Maharana having '*chanwar men*' and attendants with him during his interview with the Viceroy. Minto agreed to it. However, the practice of receiving the Maharana by the Viceroy at the edge of the carpet was not changed. The Maharana received the viceroy where he alighted. As usual 31 guns were fired for viceroy and 21 for the Maharana.[75]

Lord Hardinge visited Udaipur in November, 1912. As Maharana was ill at that time, the Heir apparent Maharaj Kumar Bhopal Singh performed all the ceremonies on behalf of the Maharana. Some modifications in the ceremonial were made necessitated by the lower status of the Maharaj Kumar. On the 15th Viceroy visited the ailing Maharana and decorated him with the collar of the title G.C.I.E., which was awarded to him at the time of Imperial *Durbar* of 1911 at Delhi.[76] The Viceroy made a present of Rs. 500 to the Vaishnav Shrine of Nathdwara when 'Samadhan' and 'Mahaprasad' from the Goswami of Nathdwara were presented to him.[77]

Lord Chelmsford visited Udaipur on 13th November, 1916 and stayed there for 3 days as the state guest.

H.R.H. Prince of Wales Visit

On the 18th November, 1905, Prince of Wales (later King George V) and Princess of Wales (Later Queen Mary) arrived at Udaipur. The Maharana received the royal visitors with all customary ceremonies. At the Banquet given by the Maharana the latter said, "This state has always been loyal to the British Government and will always remain so."[78] In reply, the Prince of Wales said, "We have heard much of the Rajputs and have had the pleasure of meeting those of your class in England but to realise the splendid traditions of chivalry, freedom and courtesy which are proud possessions of the Rajput, one must see him in his own house and that all we have heard and read in the praise of Rajputana is dwarfed by what we have seen in one short day." The Prince further observed, "It would be superfluous to speak to those present this evening about the noble reputation what your Highness has won for yourself in Rajputana and in India." He stated that what they had seen in their host were the great traditions being greatly maintained. The Prince and his wife left Udaipur on the 20th November.

Imperial Assemblage of 1911

On the 12th December, 1911 an Imperial *Durbar* was held at Delhi, which was attended by His Majesty the King Emperor, George V, and the Empress Mary. All the ruling princes of India were invited to attend the *durbar*. When Maharana Fateh Singh received the invitation, he clearly expressed his reluctance to accept a position below any other prince in India. In the 1903 *Durbar*, Maharana Fateh Singh had returned from Delhi station without attending it, because in the arrangement of seats the Rajputana block was not the first block on the right side of the Viceroy and because he would not have been the first chief to be presented to the Governor-General of India. The Maharana informed the G.O.I. that such an arrangement would lower the dignity of his status and requested that he might be excused from attendance and be allowed to present himself before his Imperial Majesty elsewhere.[79]

The seating arrangements in the 1911 Assemblage also followed the pattern of 1903. The Rajputana block was arranged further away from Royal dais in which the Maharana was to occupy his place. The G.O.I. informed the Maharana that he could not be excused from attendance at Delhi and that no chief could be permitted to dictate the terms on which he was to attend the *Durbar*. It told the Maharana that no change in the grouping could be made. The dignity of the Ruling Family of Udaipur would be fully maintained before public as the Maharana would head the line of the Rajputana Chiefs at the State entry and the *Durbar*.

Maharana Fateh Singh declined to attend the *Durbar* in such conditions and is stated to have threatened to commit suicide rather than allow the dignity of the House to get impaired. The news that Maharana Fateh Singh was threatening to commit suicide moved the G.O.I. The matter attained greater significance when several of the ruling princes of India began finding out whether the Maharana of Udaipur was coming to Delhi. The extremists in Foreign Department of the G.O.I. talked of giving a suitable punishment to the Maharana. However, it was carefully observed by Mr. Colvin, the A.G.G. in Rajputana in his note of 22-11-1911 that "Whatever punishment may be meted out to Udaipur, we can never dethrone him from his position in the hearts of the Rajput people. If we attempt to do this, we should find ourselves in collision with the Rajputs, the most loyal of all Indian communities."[80]

The G.O.I. was then compelled to revise its previous decision. However, the rulers of Hyderabad, Mysore, Baroda and Kashmir would have disliked giving the Maharana of Udaipur preference over them. At last the G.O.I. evolved a solution of the problem of precedence to which the Maharana of Udaipur as well as the other four major ruling Chiefs of India could agree. It was decided to present the Maharana and above four Princes at the Salingarh railway station as Aides-de-camp to the Emperor. The Maharana was to be assigned a place in the state entry procession and given a place in *Durbar shamiana* along with other Aides-de-camp. They were excused from doing homage. The Maharana was appointed as the "Ruling Chief in waiting", an "unusual honour" done to him. He was amongst the Indian rulers who was given place on the platform at reception and was the first Indian Ruler to be presented and introduced to the King and the Queen.[81] He, however, refrained from joining the procession as he found that his elephant was being placed in the procession after that of the ruler of Baroda.

He atonce made it known that he had taken ill all of a sudden. The Maharana did not attend the *Durbar* as well. He stayed at Delhi until the *durbar* was over. During his stay he was received by the King Emperor and his visit was returned by the Governor-General.[82] On the 2nd January, 1912, he left Delhi for Udaipur. In the *Durbar* he was awarded the title of G.C.I.E.

NOTES AND REFERENCES

1. *Kothari Balwant Singh ka Jiwan Charitra*, pp. 65-66.
2. F.D., *Int.*, July 1901, No. 125-126.
3. *Ibid.*
4. *Kothari Balwant Singh ka Jiwan Charitra*, p. 65.
5. F.D., *Int.*, Jan. 1900, No. 211-212.
6. F.D., *Int.*, Aug. 1897, No. 342-343.
7. *Fifty Years in Service of India* by G.E.C. Wakefield, pp. 62-72.
8. F.D., *Int.*, Jan. 1900, No. 44-47.
9. *Ibid.*
10. *Ibid.*
11. F.D., *Int.*, Jan. 1900, No. 44-67.
12. F.D., *Int.*, May, 1900, 301-303.
13. F.D., *Int.*, May, 1900, No. 58-101.
14. F.D., *Int.*, March, 1900, No. 190-206.
15. F.D., *Int.*, June, 1901, No. 3-8.
16. *A Gazetteer of the Udaipur State* by Major K.D. Erskine, p. 62.
17. *Ibid.*
18. F.D., *Int.*, July 1900, No. 138.
19. F.D., *Int.*, July, 1901 No. 125-126.
20. *Ibid.*
21. *Ibid.*
22. F.D., *Int.*, Feb. 1904, No. 51-56.
23. F.D., *Int.*, Nov. 1904, No. 51-52.
24. *Ibid.*
25. F.D., *Int.*, May 1905, No. 66-67.
26. F.D., *Int.*, May 1907, No. 77-78. Wakefield says that he was appointed the tutor of Maharaj Kumar by the Maharana in addition to his responsibilities of the Boundary Settlement Officer, Superintending Engineer, Irrigation and Confidential Secretary of the H.H. on the principle of preferring the devil he knew" (*Fifty years in Service of India* by G.E.C. Wakefield, p. 114).
27. *Ibid.*
28. F.D., *Int.*, May 1901, No. 235.

29. F.D., *Int.*, May 1901, No. 235.
30. F.D., *Int.*, Feb. 1904, No. 51-56.
31. *Ibid.*
32. F.D., *Int.*, Feb. 1904, No. 51-56.
33. *Ibid.*
34. F.D., *Int.*, July 1901, No. 125-126.
35. F.D., *Int.*, April, 1916, No. 52.
36. *Ibid.*
37. *Rajputana Agency Records* (Mewar), 68.
38. *Ibid.*
39. *Ibid.*
40. *Ibid.*
41. F.D., *Int.*, June 1896, No. 272-282.
42. *Rajputana Agency Records* (Mewar), 1968.
43. *Rajputana Agency Records*, 1894, List No. 9 File 10.
44. *Ibid.*
45. *Ibid.*
46. *Ibid.*
47. *Ibid.*
48. *Ibid.*
49. *Ibid.*
50. *Rajputana Agency Records*, 1908, No. 79.
51. *Ibid.*
52. *Ibid.*
53. *Ibid.*
54. F.D., *Int.*, Jan. 1914, No. 4142.
55. *Ibid.* Bijay Singh was the younger son of Rao Bahadur Raj Raja Fateh Singh of Delwara and was adopted by Kunadi family in 1887.
56. *Ibid.*
57. *Ibid.*
58. *Ibid.*
59. F.D., *Int.*, Oct., 1920, No. 201-203.
60. *Ibid.*
61. *Ibid.*
62. *Ibid.*
63. *Rajputana Agency Records*, 1874, File, No. 29, List No. 2.
64. *Ibid.*
65. *Ibid.*
66. *Ibid.*
67. *Ibid.*
68. *Ibid.*
69. *Fifty Years in Service of India* by G.E.C. Wakefield, p. 116.

Setback for the Interference ✦ 347

70. F.D., *Sec.*, May 1912, No. 11-15.
71. *Kothari Balwant Singh ka Jiwan Charitra*, p. 71. See appendix.
72. I. At Delhi by Lovat Fraser, p. 139.
    II. *Fifty years in the service of India* by G.E.C. Wakefield, p. 116, "He got a bad attack of fever (certified by two doctors deputed by Lord Curzon)".
    III. F.D., *Sec.*, May 1912, No. 11-15.
    IV. *History of the Delhi Coronation Durbar* by Stephenwheeler, p. 67.
73. *The India We Served* by W.R. Lawrence, p. 216.
74. F.D., *Sec.*, April 1907, No. 7-18.
75. F.D., *Sec.*, April 1910, No. 5-27.
76. F.D., *Int.*, May 1913, No. 68-69.
77. F.D., *Sec.*, June, 1913. No. 40-66.
78. *Royal Tour in India*, 1905-06 by Stanley Reed, p. 87. It was customary in Mewar that the Maharana decorated each parting guest's neck with a garland of gold thread and tafts of silk, and presented to each a packet of betel wrant up in green-leaf.
79. F.D.S., *Sec.*, May, 1912, No. 11-15.
80. *Ibid*.
81. I. *Ibid*.
    II. *The King and the Queen in India* (1911-12) by Stanley Reed, p. 129.
    III. Historical Record of the Imperial Visit to India, 1911, p. 68.
82. F.D., *Int.*, May, 1913, No. 68-69.

14

Political Unrest: Fateh Singh's Abdication

The Delhi Darbar of 1911 took place in the atmosphere of a tremendous growth of national awakening in India. Ideas of national unity and freedom were sweeping all over the country and anti-British movements were breaking out every-where. Indian people resisted boldly Lord Curzon's measure of divided Bengal and launched a movement of boycotting foreign goods. The defeat of Russia by Japan, a small Asian country, produced the feeling of self-confidence and determination in Indian people to attain their national freedom. The British object to hold an Imperial assemblage at Delhi, in such circumstances, was to restore confidence in the ruling classes of India and hold back the rising wave of nationalism in the country.

Anti-British Stir in Rajputana

The object of the British Government was, however, not realised. On the 23rd December, 1912, Lord Hardinge, the Governor-General was attacked with a bomb by the revolutionaries belonging to the terrorist group of Rasbihari Bose while he was entering into Delhi. The Governor-General was saved, yet the event greatly impaired the prestige of the Government and thrilled the patriotic sentiments of the entire people of India. In the beginning of the second decade of this century the terrorist wing of the revolutionary movement of India was spreading its activities in Rajputana, especially among the martial races. They lay their hopes, in this part of the country, on the support of the Rajputs and their chiefs having the traditions of chivalry and freedom-struggle. The bold and independent attitude adopted by Maharana Fateh Singh of Mewar encouraged the patriotic feelings of the people and exposed the latent Rajput love for freedom. The revolutionaries established a secret military organisation called *"Vir Bharat Sabha"* in Rajputana. They planned to bring about an armed revolt against the British Government and the new organisation was entrusted with the task of collecting arms from and getting support of the rulers, Rajputs and other martial races in this area. It is generally believed that several Rajput rulers of Rajputana such as of Jodhpur, Idar and Bikaner actively sympathised with the activities of *Vir Bharat Sabha* in Rajputana.[1] The principal workers in Rajputana connected with the terrorist activities were Rao Gopal Singh of Kharwa, Kesari Singh Barhat, Arjun Lal Sethi, Bhup Singh, Jorawar Singh Barhat, Pratap Singh Barhat (son of Kesari Singh) and Swami Kumaranand. Several revolutionaries secretly got employment in the services of the Rajput rulers.[2] The efforts of Dayanand Saraswati and his Aryasamaji followers at the close of the 19th century and aroused national consciousness in Rajputana. The revolutionaries further heightened that consciousness.

In 1914, when preparations to attack the British posts in Rajputana and to bring about mutiny among the soldiers stationed at various cantonments were still under way, the British Government received information of the plan. Thakur Gopal Singh of Kharwa, Kesari Singh Barhat of Shahpura, Bhup Singh and others were atonce arrested. All precautionary measures were taken by the Government and the plan of the armed revolt was scotched. The activities of *Vir Bharat Sabha* eventually came to an end. Several revolutionaries were jailed and subjected to inhuman tortures while others were driven to underground life.[3] With the launching of the non-violent civil disobedience movement by Gandhiji against the British, most of the revolutionaries abandoned terrorist methods and began organising mass movements, particularly of the peasantry in the rural areas. The peasant movement had twin aims of freeing the rural masses from age-old bondage and exploitation of feudalism and compelling the British to quit India. The agitators saw Mewar as one of the best fields for their work and soon launched their activities in the Bhil and Jat masses of the State.

Mewar: A Source of Trouble for the British Government

Maharana Fateh Singh was proving a source of trouble in several ways for the British Government. While he had refused to appoint a *Dewan*, he had associated himself directly or indirectly with people of anti-British convictions as Shyamji Krishna Verma, Kesari Singh Barhat, etc. Fateh Singh had already become known through India for his independent attitude and defiance of the orders of the British Government relating to the internal affairs of the state. British Agents several times complained that Udaipur was the only state in Rajputana which had been adopting a disloyal attitude. Little was known to them with regard to the internal conditions of the State and they were being prevented from having a direct say in its affairs for several years. He had not fully carried out the measures of reforms suggested by the British Government as early as 1905. British Agents were desiring the change of the headship of the state. However, Fateh Singh, despite his advancing age, was perfectly healthy and energetic and the British Government was finding no way to do anything in that regard.

Several factors were responsible to prevent the British Government from laying its harsh hand on Fateh Singh. During closing years of the 19th century and the first decade of the 20th century, Fateh Singh came to enjoy a leading place among the rulers of India and specially in Rajputana. Owing to his bold and firm attitude in his resistance to the interference of the British Agents in the internal affairs of the State. Traditionally the Sisodia family enjoyed the highest place among the Rajputs, which position he maintained by his noble character, attachment to ancient traditions and regard for his ancestral glory. Any action taken against him by the British Government in such circumstances would have antagonised a large section of the people of India. People of his State, despite his opposition to change and reform and his antiquated methods of administration loved and respected him, as they saw in him an upholder of the traditions of Sisodia glory. His Chiefs also, despite being opposed to his repressive policies, supported him for several years.

In the second decade of the 20th century, however, the position changed. The massive upsurge of national movement in India had its political repercussions on the Native States of Rajputana. Gradually, a new leadership began to emerge in the masses, especially among the cultivators who were groaning under an inefficient and corrupt administration. Thereby the traditional leadership belonging to the Ruler began to lose that support of the people which he enjoyed in the beginning of his reign. Secondly, as a result of the new awakening in India, the demand of internal reforms and change in the Native States increased consequently the progressive rulers began to acquire greater importance in the comity of the Princes.

As Fateh Singh was always opposed to change and he remained indifferent to the new trends developing in the Princes of India, he gradually lost his previous status, which he enjoyed among them. Soon he lost the support of his Chiefs as well owing to his continued autocratic behaviour towards them. His gradual estrangement from his people, chiefs and Ruling Princes weakened his position and made it possible at the end of the second decade of this century for the British Government to realise its wishes to compel the Maharana to submit. He was eventually deprived of his ruling powers in 1921.

In depriving Fateh Singh of his ruling powers, the British Government was actuated by some other factors also. The First World War resulted in a great deal of economic hardship for Indian people. Unemployment, rising prices and other factors were giving impetus to the growth of anti-British feelings in India. The Bolshevik Revolution in Russia, in 1917, also had a great impact on Indian people and their movements. The British Government had the apprehension of the Bolsheviks in India turning the backward Native States, like Udaipur, into the field of their activities where opposition to the British hegemony on emotional grounds was already great. When the peasant movements began to grow in the State, apprehension of the British Government was all the more confirmed.

Imperial Interests and Mewar

1. Imperial Service Troops Raised in Mewar

As we have stated earlier, Maharana Fateh Singh continued to carefully evade the question of raising Imperial Service Troops at Udaipur. In 1905, the Maharana, being pressed too much, agreed to raise them on the lines of the other Native States. Consequently, the G.O.I. recommended that Mewar *Durbar* should maintain a detachment of cavalry of 150 strong at Udaipur.[4] The Maharana agreed to the proposal verbally but no written acceptance was sent to the British Government. In July, 1908, Brigadier General Drummond visited Udaipur in order to assist and advise the *Durbar* in implementing the scheme.[5] Lord Minto, the Governor-General during his visit to Udaipur in 1909, took opportunity to make a formal announcement of the G.O.I.'s appreciation for the Maharana's proposal of raising imperial Service Troops at Udaipur.

Preparations to raise the detachment at Udaipur continued but there was no formal correspondence on record in that connection. It was found necessary to get the offer in writing from the Maharana, which the latter did in August, 1911. In September, 1911, Captain Webber of 3rd Skinner's Horse was sent to Udaipur on deputation to train the squadron, initially for $3\frac{1}{2}$ months, which period was later on extended for 2 years more.[6]

The squadron of Siladar Cavalry raised at Udaipur (consisting solely of Rajputs) had the strength of 5 officers, 20 non-commissioned officers, 5 frarriers, 2 trumpeters and 122 sawars. The expenses of the state over the troops were estimated to be Rs. 88,340 (Imperial).[7]

2. Maharana's Cooperation in the Great War

Whenever the British Empire went to war with another power in any part of the world, it was obligatory for the Native Rulers of India to offer their military assistance for the defence of the Empire. As early as 1880 the G.O.I. appealed to all the Native Rulers of India to raise Imperial Service Troops in their States for the defence of the British Government. The Maharana then offered to contribute Rs. 6 lakhs in cash towards Imperial defence. The cash offer was not accepted by the G.O.I.[8]

During the Great War of Europe which broke out in 1914,

the Maharana assisted the British Empire militarily and financially. In August, 1914 at a banquet given to the A.G.G. at Udaipur, the Maharana said, "England may with confidence count on the hearty support and confidence of its friends and allies. I also desire to express that the State of Mewar is ready, on the present occasion, with all its heart to render every help and assistance in its power."[9]

A detachment of the Udaipur Imperial Service Lancers was despatched to accompany Government remounts to Europe. Mewar detachments were also employed on remount duty at Bellary.[10] "The *Durbar* undertook to exchange trained horses for untrained ones for war services. He supplied on requisition about 1300 maunds of 'babool bark' from his state.[11]

The Maharana subscribed Rs. 1,00,000 to the Rajputana Aircraft and Machinegun Fund and contributed Rs. 2,00,000 to the Imperial Indian Relief Fund.[12] About 8 lakhs were given by him and the Maharaj Kumar towards war loans, the interest of which was allowed to be utilised for war purposes.[13] In 1918, however, the Maharana expressed his inability to take part with other States in the scheme for raising a battalion of troops for G.O.I. the depots of which were to be located within their own States.[14]

H.M. the King Emperor awarded the title of G.C.V.O. to the Maharana on the 1st January, 1918, for his services in connection with the war.[15] Maharaj Kumar Bhopal Singh was awarded the title of K.C.I.E. on the 4th Nov. 1919. The Governor-General gave a private interview to the Maharaj Kumar and himself invested him with the K.C.I.E. insignia.[16]

3. Restriction on Poppy Cultivation in Mewar

In the beginning of 1913, the G.O.I. sent instructions to the Mewar *Durbar* to reduce considerably the poppy cultivation in the state as the export of opium from India to China was being curtailed. The Mewar *Durbar* issued public notification in the months of May and June asking the cultivators to suspend the cultivation of poppy. A warning was given to the people that those who would be found cultivating poppy would be punished.[17]

However, the cultivation of poppy in Mewar was not sufficiently reduced and the inflow of opium continued at the depot of Chittor. The prices quoted at the depot were much higher than those demanded by the merchants at other places.[18] Traders complained that the price-rise was mainly due to the enhanced excise duty imposed by the Mewar *Durbar*, who had increased the tax from Rs. 60 per chest in 1912 to Rs. 1250 per chest in 1914. The G.O.I. observed as to why it should contribute to the revenues of Mewar *Durbar* by paying the enhanced prices. It further observed that the Mewar *Durbar* had made little or no effort to restrict the cultivation of opium despite strong admonitions of the A.G.G. and, therefore, there were adequate grounds for the rejection of all the tenders from Chittorgarh, which would result in discouraging the cultivation and compel the traders not to demand high prices. The tenders were rejected and the traders were thereby put to great loss. In the month of March, 1914, the A.G.G. reported that he had taken steps to induce the Maharana to bring the poppy cultivation in his state under severe restrictions.[19]

4. Mica Mining Work Started in Mewar

In August, 1917, the Secretary of State, London asked the G.O.I. to take measures to enhance the output of Indian mica to the greatest possible extent which was being required for war purposes in Europe. Mewar was known to have a great store of mica in its territory, which lay hitherto untapped.[20] The G.O.I. requested the Udaipur *Durbar* to conduct prospecting operations in the tract of Mewar containing Mica. Messers Jones and Campbell conducted operations and found large and extensive promising deposits of mica in Mewar area, especially in the tract covering Nansa. Amli and Sorthi villages which they considered to be of the best quality in Rajputana and Central India. Having received the reports, the G.O.I. decided to take prompt steps to exploit the Udaipur field.[21]

Negotiations regarding the working of mica mines were conducted between the G.O.I. and Mewar *Durbar*. The latter was asked to lease the mica deposits to a private firm owned by one Dadabhoy. The Maharana was opposed to lease it to any private firm. He proposed that the G.O.I. wored it. In case the G.O.I. was unwilling to work it itself, the Maharana proposed that it would be done by the Mewar Government itself under the supervision of a qualified Indian engineer.[22]

The negotiations progressed tardily as the Maharana was found using his usual way of delay and procrastination. Looking at the urgency of the requirement of mica the Governor-General found it necessary to bring his personnel influence to bear on the Maharana. In February, 1918, he wrote a personal letter to the Maharana to expedite the proceedings and agree to the G.O.I.'s proposals. Mr. Hayden, the Director, Geological Survey, G.O.I. met the Maharana at his Kumbhalgarh camp on the 31st March and made the following alternative proposals for his consideration:

(1) The mines would be nominally worked by the Udaipur State, the British Government would either pay the whole cost, giving the Government representative a free hand, so long as his expenditure did not exceed a monthly sum to be agreed upon, or else to leave the question of expenditure to the Government, the *Durbar* contributing a fixed sum monthly.
(2) The Maharana should place the deposits at the disposal of the Government for the duration of war and should give all possible facilities in the matter of transport, labour, etc., and should also give the mica free of royalty.
(3) He should lease the property to some private person or company.[23]

The Maharana agreed to none of the proposals. The point at issue was that while the British Government was not willing to leave the management of the work of mines with the inefficient and tardy administration of the *Durbar*, the latter was opposed to allow any foreign agency working in Mewar. In April, Holland, the A.G.G. met the Maharana to convey the Viceroy's disappointment at the delay in complying with his request. The Maharana then agreed to grant the mining lease to a private company. The Mewar *Durbar* entered into an agreement with Messers Christian Ltd. of Bihar and Dadabhoy of Nagpur by which the latter jointly got the lease to work the mines in the tract covering Nansa, Amli and Sorthi villages for 5 years and they agreed to pay royalty at the rate of 7 per cent share of the net profit.[24]

5. Depreciation of the Value of British Rupee in Mewar

In the year 1918, the local Udaipur rupee began appreciating greatly in value in Mewar, in comparison to the British rupee. The intrinsic value of the local coin was said to be considerably less than that of the British coin and the usual rate of exchange placed the value of the local rupee at about 12 annas in British currency. In the famine days of 1899-1900 the value of Udaipuri rupee fell down so much that Rs. 175 of Udaipuri currency were exchanged for Rs. 100 of British currency. In 1918, however, the position got entirely reversed, 100 British rupees being taken as equivalent to 76/50 Udaipuri rupees. On the 6th October, 1918, the A.G.G. Mr. Manners Smith reported to the G.O.I. that though the cause of this affair was private hoarding and speculation, however, it appeared to be primarily due to the failure of the *Durbar* to keep a sufficient stock of their local currency in the market. He stated that in view of Imperial interests the depreciation of the British rupee in local purchasing power and fall of its prestige was highly undesirable.[25]

The A.G.G. addressed a letter to the *Durbar* to take immediate steps, lying in their power, to restore the previous position of the exchange of coins. In the meanwhile, he asked the *Durbar* to take such temporary measures as saved the British Government servants working in Agency office, Post and Telegraph offices, offices of the Political Superintendent and Assistant Political Superintendent, Hilly Tracts at Kherwara and at opium Agency office at Chittorgarh from the loss effected by the new exchange rate. The measure suggested by him in this connection was that the *Durbar* should allow the Government servants, on the certificate of the Resident, to exchange British rupees not exceeding the amount of Udaipur rupees.[26]

The Maharana attributed the cause of the fall in the value of the British rupee to the speculation (*satta*) by the traders in the forward values of the two currencies as well as to the manipulation of the exchange market by local traders in their own interests, as they did in the famine days of 1899-1900, when the local rupee depreciated in comparison to the British coin. He claimed that there was no deficiency of Udaipur rupees in the market, as he was distributing about 10 lakh local rupees per year in salaries while only 5 lakhs of British rupees were being distributed in that way in the State. The Maharana saw no cause of grievance on the part of the Government servants for this temporary change, as they had been previously benefited by the exchange when Udaipur coin had fallen in value.[27]

The Maharana agreed to exchange British rupees with local coin for the Agency servants only. However, the G.O.I. urged him to do it for all the servants in the service of G.O.I. working in the state. The *Durbar* expressed reluctance to agree to it as the British Government servants did not spend the entire amount of their salary in Mewar and it was apprehended that they might resort to making personal profit out of such a regulation. At last the *Durbar* agreed to exchange a graded proportion of their salaries for one year.[28]

The appreciation of Udaipur rupee, however, continued during 1919 and the beginning of 1920. The exchange rate between British and Udaipuri coins by then came to the ratio of 100 : 68.75.[29] On the 5th January, 1920, the A.G.G. wrote to the G.O.I. that it was high time that necessary measures were taken to check further depreciation of the Imperial coin in the state. The existing state of affairs in his opinion, was politically undesirable and practically inconvenient. The Maharana was again asked to take measures to restore the value and prestige of the Imperial coin. The Maharana was then induced to agree to fix the exchange rate at 112.80 Udaipuri rupees equal to 100 Imperial rupees by an executive order. This rate was decided on the basis of the relative amount of silver in both the coins. The Maharana, however, obtained the G.O.I.'s prior assurance that it would give him moral support in enforcing his executive order and would not attend the complaints, which might be made by the interested parties about the decision.[30]

6. Question of Police Reforms in Mewar

In 1914, the British Government realised the urgency of maintaining efficient and sufficient police force in the Native States of Rajputana in order to make adequate security arrangements in the area against anti-British activities of the revolutionaries. Most of the states maintained no regular network of trained police. In Mewar, at that time, the only part where a police force existed was the district comprising and surrounding the town of Udaipur. Even this force was inadequately paid and was, consequently, below the authorised strength and standard, and majority of the policemen was past their work.[31]

On the advice of the British Government, the *Durbar* obtained in 1914, the services of an officer of the U.P. Police named Babu Sardar Singh. However, little improvement took place as the *Durbar* did not give him the sufficient control over the Police Department and he eventually resigned his services. The same year the A.G.G. advised the Maharana to appoint a British Officer, Mr. Kaye to superintend the police force. In January, 1915, the Resident reported that the Maharana had persisted in turning a deaf ear to all his entreaties. The Maharana was of the view that no political conspirator had been found to be active in Mewar, and that he had issued order to the District Officers in Mewar to keep a strict watch over the movements of suspicious persons and arrest those who were found spreading 'seditious' propaganda. The Resident was of the opinion that the inefficiency of police arrangements in Mewar constituted a serious public danger.[32]

The G.O.I. did not press the Maharana further in that connection considering that the Mewar was not being visited by 'sedition mongers' and also because the Maharana was not willingly prepared to carry out the task. The Resident was instructed to remain alert about the movements of the political agitators in the area.[33]

Peasant Unrest

The upsurge of the Indian people witnessed in the first decade of the twentieth century in the form of '*Swadeshi*' movement, had its echo hear in the hilly tracts of Mewar, Malwa and Gujarat inhabited mostly by the Bhils. In 1905, an organisation called "*Sabhya Sabha*" was formed under the leadership of Swami Govind. This organisation worked for the boycotting of foreign goods, for the growth of national industries, for administrative reforms in the area and for the revival of the Panchayat system in the villages. The movement was crushed by 1908 by the States of Mewar, Sirohi and Dungarpur.[34]

In 1913, a peasant agitation started in the *jagir* of Bijolia, in the eastern corner of Mewar under the leadership of Sadhu Sitaramdas. The cultivators raised their voice against certain taxes and imposts, levied by the *jagirdar* of Bijolia. In addition to the land revenue, there were, the cultivators alleged, as many as

80 different *"lagats"* levied on them.³⁵ It was said that the voluntary services and presents which the cultivators offered to their Chiefs and officials during the days of turmoil and hardship had become permanent privileges of the *jagirdar*. The cultivators had to pay several taxes at the time of harvest, festivals, marriages, birthdays, installations of the Chief, and many other social and ceremonial functions. In failing to do it, the peasants were subjected to severe harassment and repression. There could be no appeal against the *jagirdar's* decisions and actions to the Mewar *Durbar*. Any body found trying to file an appeal against his Chiefs was inhumanly tortured. There were other grievances also. Revenue settlement had not been carried out in the *jagir* areas and excessive demands were made by the Chiefs. The latter spent nothing towards the development of the agriculture. Their main grievance was against the forced labour (*begar*) which was taken from the people belonging to rural labour classes on several occasions, as at the time of hunting, marriages, visits of state officials, etc. They were paid nothing for their work and even had to take their own food with them, when rendering free and forced labour.³⁶

In 1913, the cultivators of Bijolia suspended cultivation of the land for one year and refused to pay the revenue. Next year the estate was placed under the *Durbar* management, as the Chief died that year and his successor, Kesari Singh was a minor. Amar Singh Ranawat, a distant relative of the family was appointed as the Munsarim of the *jagir*. Amar Singh could not take his charge, as he also held the post of the Superintendent of Police at Udaipur.³⁷ The Nayab Munsarim, Dungar Singh Bhati was, therefore, entrusted to look after its management. The *Durbar* management pacified the cultivators by accepting some of their demands provisionally until the Chief of the *jagir* came of age. The Maharana expressed dissatisfaction at the settlement as in his view the settlement must have been on permanent basis and several more demands of the cultivators accepted.³⁸

The peasant unrest gradually spread to other *jagir* areas in Mewar. Several progressive *jagirdars* as of Putholi and Ochhari and several Mewar Government officials also sympathised with the anti-feudal cause of the cultivators. Those were the days when movement for social reforms was gaining ground in some of the towns of the state and societies such as *Mahila Mandal*,

Vidya pracharuni Sabha, etc. were springing up. Such reformist activities were being directly influenced by what was going on in the British India on the one hand and they had covert or overt links with the upsurge growing in the peasantry on the other. Under such circumstances the peasant movement in Mewar area of Bijolia, Begun and other adjoining *jagirs* grew in momentum being more broad-based and united and better led.[39]

The cultivators of Bijolia were then being led by Sadhu Sitaramdas, Fateh Karan and others. The movement took a new turn when Bijay Singh Pathik arrived on the scene. He was Bhup Singh of the revolutionary party and has adopted pseudonym of Bijay Singh Pathik to conceal his identity after his flight from the detention at Tadgarh. He moved from one place to another in disguise and was received enthusiastically at every place by people and even Chiefs and officials. Maharana Fateh Singh is believed to have developed sympathy for him and it is for this reason that he was not arrested by the Mewar Government for several years. Pathik stayed at Kankroli, Bhana, Jahajpur and Ochhari. Everywhere he established youth organisations and social and educational societies. In 1915, Sadhu Sitaramdas of Bijolia met him at Chittor and invited him to Bijolia, the "Andamans of Mewar," where he could work more safely. By the end of the year he reached there and in order to maintain secrecy, he stayed with the Naib Munsarim Dungar Singh Bhati, himself, the highest *Durbar* official in the estate at that time.[40]

Bijay Singh stayed for about seven months at Bijolia. He started a school and a library there and got a state-grant of forty rupees per month for the same. Thereafter he started a youth organisation called *"Sevadal"*, which gave physical training to the youth. In 1916, a Kisan Panch Board was established in the presence of about 1000 cultivators at the village of Berisalnivas and Sadhu Sitaramdas was elected its president. The Board drafted their demands and submitted them before the estate management.[41]

In 1916, the 'war-Loan' at the rate of fourteen rupees per plough was levied on the cultivators in Mewar. The cultivators of the Bijolia estate refused to pay the amount. The officials resorted to repressive measures and arrested Sadhu Sitaramdas, Ramnarain Chaudhary, Premchand Bhil, Manik Lal Verma and others. By then the identity of Pathik as the chief organiser of the movement came to the knowledge of the British Government. The Maharana was induced to issue orders for his arrest. Coming to know of the above orders, Pathik left Bijolia and entered the territory of Kota, from where he continued directing the movement. Severe repression was let loose against the cultivators. Mass arrests were made, men and women were beaten and land, cattle and other property of the peasants were confiscated. The cultivators, however, did not yield. They suspended the cultivation once again and refused to pay the revenue.[42]

The movement continued for about five years. For three years the cultivators did not till the land at all. The repression by the state and the stiff resistance of the people got an all India publicity owing to the efforts of Pathik, Arjun Lal Sethi and other political workers. Bal Gangadhar Tilak, Mahatma Gandhi, Madan Mohan Malviya, Ganesh Shankar Vidyarthi and other national leaders supported the cause of the peasants. Mahatma Gandhi sent his private Secretary, Mahadeo Desai to Bijolia to obtain complete information about the happenings there. Mahatma Gandhi afterwards wrote to the Maharana requesting him to redress the grievances of the peasants.[43]

In 1920, owing to the efforts of Pathik, Arjunlal Sethi, Kesari Singh Barhat and others, *Rajasthan Seva Sangh* was established at Wardha. Bijay Singh Pathik was elected its President and its offices were, soon after, shifted to Ajmer. A paper called "*Rajasthan Kesari*" was published from Wardha in the beginning. Afterwards Pathik brought out "*Navin Rajasthan*" from Ajmer. The workers of Rajasthan Seva Sangh spread their activities in various parts of Rajasthan. They launched the Gandhian programme of spinning and weaving, wearing the *Khadi* cloth, removing untouchability and similar other activities of social reform. Its workers in Mewar took up the cause of the oppressed peasants against the *jagirdars* and officials at various places, as at Begun, Parsoli, Amargarh, Basee, Kapasan and Chittor, as a result of which the peasant movement spread over a large territory of the state in 1921-23 on the lines of Bijolia agitation.[44]

The cultivators of Bijolia during their struggle consolidated their unity and organisation under their *Kisan Panchayat*. As they were non-cooperating with the *jagir* officials in all respects and were being compelled to protect their life and property themselves, they began to run almost a parallel Government through their *Panchayat*. They organised a core of volunteers, who wore belts of and badges of the *Panchayat* and guarded every village. *Panchayat* heard all types of cases and decided them and the cultivators obeyed its orders and paid fines and necessary taxes to it. The *Panchayat* decided that no cultivator would have any direct dealing with the *jagir* management and asked the latter to deal all cases of the individuals through it. Such *Panchayats* were organised at other places as well where the workers of *Rajasthan Seva Sangh* took up the cause of the cultivators. The British Government got alarmed at those happenings. It declared that the "Bolsheviks" had entered into Mewar and the hilly areas, and were creating dissatisfaction among the people, organising them into "Soviets" and provoking them to revolt on the pattern of the Russian revolution. It called upon Mewar and other Native States to take most severe measures to crush the Bolshevik movement which was declared to be subversive of all human values and traditions and aimed at everthrowing the existing set-up.[45]

The cultivators' movement continued to grow in momentum in Mewar. During the religious congregation at the holy place, Matri Kundia in 1921, the cultivators about a lakh in number swore not to pay the land revenue until their grievances were redressed. In addition to the demand of abolishing all 'lagats' and 'Beth-Begar', they put forward the demands that the revenue settlement in the state lands should be carried out again as the twenty year period fixed by Wingate had long expired, that the cess collected for education and public health along with the revenue should be only half an anna and should be utilised for opening more schools and hospitals in the state, that the taxes and duties levied on the sale of cattle and on the grazing of cattle in the pastures, etc. should be annulled.[46]

The British Government continuously pressed Maharana Fateh Singh to use all his means to crush the agitation of the cultivators and prevent it from spreading to other areas. The suppressive measures adopted by the Mewar *Durbar* proved ineffective. The British Government was entirely dissatisfied with the measures as they were restricted and not as severe as it desired. Fateh Singh was led to believe that the Bijolia movement was against the oppression of the cultivators by the *jagirdars*, that the leaders of the movement were against the western education and culture and that they were against the interference of the political Agents in the internal affairs of the State. Consequently, harsh measures were generally avoided in dealing with the agitators.[47] Bijay Singh was not arrested, cultivators continued holding meetings and bringing out processions and the unrest gripped more and more areas. The British Government saw a potential danger to its security in the peasant agitation spreading like an infection. The Political Department grew hectic and a careful plan to remove Maharana Fateh Singh from power was hatched. Maharaj Kumar Bhupal Singh, the only and paralytic son of Maharana Fateh Singh was prevailed over by the British conspirators to play into their hands against his own father. The latter excited Bhupal Singh's craving for power who was 37 years old in 1921.[48]

In May, 1921, the British Government received alarming reports from the Resident in Mewar about the serious state of affairs there. He stated that conditions in Mewar were worse than they were in 1905, in which year the Maharana promised to carry out certain measures of reform suggested by the G.O.I.[49] The Minister in the State had practically no authority. The three irrigation works promised by the Maharana in 1905 had not been carried out and the Irrigation Department had become almost defunct in want of a capable officer. The management of Court of Wards in various estates during the minorities of their chiefs had been notoriously inefficient and arbitrary and it was significant, the Resident noted, that in 3 out of 5 estates under the *Durbar* management the agrarian unrest had broken out. The Maharaj Kumar was being entirely debarred from participation in public affairs. The *Mahadraj Sabha* remained as inoperative as it was before 1905. The Education and Health Departments were in a very miserable condition, no new schools and hospitals were being opened and education and health cess was accumulating in treasury amounting to about 6 lakhs. The same was the condition of the other departments, as Police, Judiciary and Revenue. The Resident further noted that crying need of the people was to introduce a new settlement of revenue in all the parts of Mewar, including *jagir* area. The *Durbar's* failure to take proper measures to deal with the currency problem, Wilkinson observed, had created obstruction for the trade and suffering for the people. The practice of taking "Beth-Begar" and "Rasad" by

Durbar officials and *jagirdars* from the rural people was being so much abused that people in rural areas, specially the Bhils and Jats are rising against them. The relations between the Maharana and his chiefs were in the most unhappy state. The Maharana has further embittered the feelings of his *sardars* by issuing an order making it an offence for them to leave Mewar territory without his permission. Several hundred cases relating to boundary disputes were lying unattended.[50]

The Resident further reported, "Mewar is becoming a hot-bed of lawlessness. Seditionist emissaries are teaching the people that all men are equal. The land belongs to the peasants and not to the state or landlords. It is significant that people are being urged to use the vernacular equivalent of the word 'comrade' instead of customary honorific styles of address. His Highness is said to have been threatened to meet the fate of the Czar." In the end Wilkinson observed that the movement was mainly anti-Maharana, but it might soon become anti-British and might spread to the adjoining British areas. Therefore, it was, in his opinion, highly desirable to take away ruling powers from the Maharana and entrust them to Maharaj Kumar Bhupal Singh.[51]

Sir Robert Holland, the A.G.G., while forwarding the Resident's views to the G.O.I., remarked that the Maharana had become too old and that he was attempting to concentrate too much work in his own hands as a result of which the administration had suffered.[52]

Delegation of Ruling Powers to the Maharaj Kumar

The Governor-General, having received reports about the state of affairs in Mewar approved of the proposal that the Maharana should give up his active participation in the administration of the State. He observed that the greatest failure of his power had synchronized with a period of unprecedented political ferment. There were, in his opinion, features in the situation which were of grave import not only to Mewar but to Indian States in general and to the British India. The Governor-General stated that time had came when it was desirable that he should abdicate in his son's favour. In view of his advanced age, such a step would not excite undue attention of the people and would be represented as due to that cause.[53]

Meanwhile the wheel of events moved fast in Mewar. Just

after their pledge at Matri Kundia the peasants from all parts of Mewar thronged in thousands to Udaipur to place their grievances before the Maharana. The Bhil leader Motilal Tejawat drafted a petition of their demands *"Mewar Pukar"*. The people were in so defiant a mood that they detained the Mewar police officer Amar Singh Ranawat for a few hours when the latter tried to arrest their ring leaders. Most of their demands were accepted by the Maharana leaving a few, about which the leaders (*Panch*) declared that as they (*Panch*) were not lower in position to the *Durbar*, they accepted the rest of the demands." The peasants then dispersed in a jubilant mood.[54]

The Udaipur assembly of the cultivators and the "Unity movement of Mewar and Hilly area," as they called it, had tremendous political repercussions. News reached far and wide that the people had gained victory by their unity and strength. A thrilling wave of democratic awakening swept over Rajputana, Gujarat and Madhya Pradesh. Entire Bhil area comprising the hilly tracts of the above regions, celebrated victory on a vast scale. The British Government was entirely shaken and got apprehensive that the people everywhere would soon adopt the Bijolia way of establishing *Panchayat* Governments thereby paralysing the administration of the British Government and the Native States if the events were allowed to take their own course. Brutal repressive measures were atonce let loose in all States where the cultivators raised their heads. In Mewar, the British Government precipitated its action to oust Maharana Fateh Singh from power so as to enable itself to take complete control of the situation in its own hands.[55]

While the political Department was proceeding with its preparation to attain its object, another event of defiance of law on the part of the cultivators took place in Mewar. On the 8th July, 1921, a body of Bhil cultivators forcibly drove the cattle to graze on the reserved State lands at Nahar Magra near Udaipur. The district officer and his men, who tried to prevent them from acting against *Durbar* orders were surrounded and attacked by the crowd compelling them to flee to Udaipur.[56] The Maharana requested the Resident in Mewar to despatch a company of Mewar Bhil Corps stationed at the Residency to disperse the rioters, stating that his own troops were not reliable.[57] The Maharana's request was not complied with. It was believed that the Maharana was thereby attempting to involve the British Government in suppressing his subjects, as Mewar Bhil Corps were under the latter's management.[58]

Sir Robert Holland, the A.G.G. arrived at Udaipur on the 12th July, four days after the above happening. In his interview with the Maharana he gave him to understand that it was the desire of the Governor-General that he should abdicate in favour of his son. The A.G.G. placed before him the observations of the G.O.I. about defects and abuses prevalent in the administration of Mewar resulting into open criticism and resentment against them by the people of the State. The widespread discontent was being exploited by the agitators, he said. The A.G.G. took opportunity to remind the Maharana that though the G.O.I. constantly present upon him the need for reform but he never showed any readiness to benefit by the advice offered.[59]

The Maharana was bewildered at this proposal and pointed out that nothing which had taken place, warranted such a step. He expressed his willingness to make changes in the administration and asked the A.G.G. to suggest them. He stated that in the Native States the Ruling Princes kept the whole power of administration in their own hands. Regarding the agitation in the cultivators he stated that the agitators were coming in Mewar from the British India to instigate the people and that it had originated outside Mewar. At the end the Maharana argued that any measures amounting to this abdication would impair his prestige among his own people, when they knew that he was keeping sound health.[60] The Maharana expressed his willingness, however, to delegate some authority to the Maharaj Kumar or to high officials of the State but it was indispensable that ultimate control should remain vested in his own hands.[61]

For four days, Sir Robert Holland held discussions with the Maharana, persuading him to comply with the G.O.I.'s wishes. When much pressure was brought to bear on him the Maharana requested that a period of one month be given to allow him to fully consider over the Governor-General's request. On the 17th July, Sir Holland addressed a letter to the Maharana stating that he was sending a telegram to the G.O.I. at four o'clock in the afternoon that day conveying His Highness's reluctance to comply with Governor-General's wishes, unless he received from him any further message modifying the terms of reply. In the same letter he drew the Maharana's attention to the resolution of the Foreign and Political Department of the G.O.I. dated the 29th October, 1920 and cautioned him that in all probability the procedure laid down in the said Resolution of instituting a commission of enquiry might be resorted to though the G.O.I. desired to avoid by all possible means to take measures which might cause unnecessary pain to the Maharana.[62]

In his report to the G.O.I., despatched on the same day Sir Robert Holland claimed that the Maharana had offered him a bribe of two lakhs through a banker. The Maharana, he stated, would never undertake reforms. He was a past-master in procrastination and evasion of advice. He suggested that in case he declined to abdicate, a commission of enquiry should be imposed on him.

At last Maharana Fateh Singh gave in. He realised that times had run against him and he was left alone. A compromise was arrived at, by which an attempt was made to maintain apparently the Maharana's authority and status in public view. On the 21st July, 1921, Maharana Fateh Singh delegated his ruling powers to the Maharaj Kumar. The terms of the delegation of ruling powers were:

1. Maharana Fateh Singh would retain all honours, titles, etc., and remain on the *gadee*.
2. Civil and Criminal cases would be decided by Council of Ijlas Kamil with the Maharana at its head and the Maharaj Kumar attending it.
3. A Commission to enquire into the affairs of the Chiefs of the State would be appointed by the Maharana and the Maharaj Kumar would conduct its functioning.
4. The amount, which was to be fixed for Maharana's personal expenses would not be interfered with and his personal treasury would remain in his own charge.
5. The Maharaj Kumar would not be entitled to confer *jagirs*.
6. The rest of all the powers of the State Government were delegated to the Maharaj Kumar.[63]

The A.G.G., after conclusion of the above settlement, reported to the G.O.I., "I have accepted the Maharana's proposals as modified by discussion. Delegation now appears to me complete for all practical purposes and the Maharaj Kumar, whom I have consulted, is satisfied."[64] The official announcement of the delegation of powers was made on the 28th July by the G.O.I. It sent official communique to the press stating that the Maharana of Udaipur, owing to advancing years, had delegated wide powers to his son.[65]

British Supermacy Restored in the Internal Affairs

The delegation of powers restored British supremacy in the internal affairs of the State. Sir Robert Holland, the A.G.G. and Mr. Wilkinson, the Resident, themselves, proceeded to Bijolia to settle the affair. They entered into negotiations with the leaders of the cultivators. Ram Narain Chaudhari and Maniklal Verma represented the cultivators during the negotiations. The settlement, arrived at, fulfilled most of the demands of the cultivators. The practice of taking forced labour (*Begar*) and most of the '*lagats*' were abolished. Cases launched against the cultivators during the movement were withdrawn and land revenue of the years, during which the land was not cultivated, was exempted. Concessions were made to the demands of the cultivators relating to the forests, pastures, etc., and the *Kisan Panchayat* were recognised.[66]

Though the demands of Bijolia were accepted, the same treatment was not meted out to the cultivators of other places. In the estate of Begun when the Chief of the estate came to a settlement with the leaders of the cultivators, it was disapproved of, calling it a "Bolshevik Settlement".[67] Troops were despatched to Begun under the command of Mr. Trench, the Revenue Officer in Mewar, recently appointed by the Maharaj Kumar. On the 13th July, 1923, troops besieged the village of Govindpura, where the peasants had assembled. Trench ordered to set fire to the village and then resorted to firing at the villagers. Two of them were killed and several of them were wounded. About 500 of them were arrested, who were severely beaten and driven to Begun. It was alleged that during the attack, the troops entered the houses of cultivators and molested their women. The movement was entirely crushed.[68] Bijay Singh Pathik was arrested on the 10th September, 1923 at the village of Ganeshpura and was tried at Udaipur by a three men tribunal before which he gave a long statement of his case. He was sentenced to five years imprisonment by the tribunal, which was reduced to one and a half years by the *Mahadraj Sabha* on appeal.

The same brutality was perpetrated on the Bhils of Bhomat and Sirohi who rose as one man under the leadership of Motilal Tejawat in 1922. In a large area the administration of Sirohi and Mewar States ceased to function and the *Bhil Panchayats* began dealing with all the administrative affairs. A large force under an English official attacked two villages of Sirohi, burnt all the houses and fired indiscriminately at the fleeing Bhils, killing about 1800 men, women and children.[69]

Maharana Fateh Singh could never forget the injustice done to him by the British Government. A wedge was mischievously created between him and his son and then he was coerced to abdicate his powers which was termed as "veiled deposition" by the public opinion in India. He made several efforts to get justice from the Imperial Government at London, but in vain. He died on the 24th May, 1930.[70]

Personality of Fateh Singh

Fateh Singh was the last glow of the fading Sisodia dynasty of Mewar. Though he lost his struggle against the foreign intervention in his State, he nobly maintained the dignity of his race and glory of his ancestors for about thirty-five years. His bold and dignified attitude, his high character and grand personality not only earned fame and respect from the highest English officials of the British Government, but got him a leading position among the rulers of the Native States and a wide support of the people of India for his actions. Several times did he boldly refuse to do the bidding of the British Government, but the latter could never dare to take any severe action against him, though they had disgraced and deposed many a ruler in India on the smallest pretext from time to time.

Fateh Singh had a high sense of morality and character. Unlike his predecessors, he abhored drinking and indulging in licence. He had only one wife and avoided all the luxuries of the court. He had regular habits from morning till evening. He was also a deeply religious and superstitious ruler and used to devote some hours daily to prayer. He led a simple but dignified life.[71] Never for a moment did he lose his faith in high status and kept his position high under all stresses and strains. "Great traditions, greatly maintained" was a true representation of his position, and he was rightly described as the "true embodiment of ancient Rajput chivalry."[72]

Fateh Singh had a striking personality and dignified manners. Even Curzon, who was no respector of persons, fell under his charm and spontaneously characterised him as a conscientious and hardworking ruler, who lived simple and exemplary life.[73] Sir Robert Holland, the A.G.G., who played prominent role in the veiled deposition of Fateh Singh, said of him, "His Highness's strength and personality are so striking that who knows him or has even once come into contact with him can not but feel a deep veneration for him." Martindale, the A.G.G. said of him, "His charm of manners and address, his hospitality and perfect courtesy are known beyond the borders of Rajputana. As a private gentleman of unblemished life and character, he is beyond reproach.[74]

His greatest hobby was hunting. He was an excellent shot. Despite his advanced age, he maintained his energy and endurance, which he displayed during *'Shikar.'*[75] He was a hard working ruler and took regular and keen interest in the State affairs. The delay in deciding matters, which was a continuous complaint against him was not so much due to his indifference and lack of interest but mainly due to his illiteracy, inexperience and slowness in coming to a decision.[76]

Fateh Singh was very much jealous of his dignity and authority.[77] He had developed a suspicious nature and, therefore, he believed in nobody and concentrated the whole work of the administration in his own hands.[78] Consequently, inefficiency prevailed in all the departments and several complaints were made against him, which would have otherwise been avoided.[79] His deep conservatism and stubborn resistance to change brought him into conflict with the forces of progress, which had begun to develop rapidly at the beginning of this century. Consequently he had to face attacks, in his later period, from two sides, the Indian Government and the politically conscious sections of his people.

Despite his conservative outlook in political matters, he was a social reformer. He took interest in the activities of *"Walter Krit Rajput Hitkarini Sabha"* (organisation created by Col. Walter for welfare of the Rajputs), which agitated for abolishing social evils, prevalent in Rajputs, e.g., polygamy, child marriage, extravagance during marriages or mournings, custom of giving "Tika"(dowry) in the marriage and keeping concubines, etc. His keen efforts helped a great deal in the success of the endeavour.[80] In order to save the Rajput nobles from economic ruin, he issued orders in 1917, prohibiting them from mortgaging their villages to the money-lending usurers, who sometimes misappropriated all the income of the estate.[81]

Many a British Political officer called him a miser but it was not true. He was thrifty by nature and was, therefore, against extravagance. Being a man of rigid principles, he spent on what he thought right. He spent about 50 lakhs on several irrigation projects including Fateh Sagar lake. He constructed buildings of Lansdowne Hospital, Walter Female Hospital and Victoria Hall Museum. He constructed several inns at various places in the State and a building of Minto Durbar Hall at Udaipur. He spent several lakhs in completing the construction of Sajjangarh and Shivnivas palace at Udaipur and in repairing old mansions at Chittorgarh and Kumbhalgarh.[82]

NOTES AND REFERENCES

1. *Hamara Rajasthan* by Prithvi Singh Mehta, p. 304.
2. *Ibid.*
3. The *jagir* of Kesari Singh Barhat was seized by the Shahpura ruler and his family members including ladies were stranded. Kesari Singh's son Pratap Singh died in Barreli jail in 1916 succumbing to the tortures inflicted on him by the British authorities.
4. F.D., *Sec.*, June 1908, No. 39.
5. F.D., *Sec.*, Feb. 1909, No. 547.
6. *Ibid.*
7. *Ibid.*
8. F.D., *Int.*, May 1888, No. 110-111.
9. F.D., *Int.*, May 1915, No. 323.
10. F.D., *Int.*, Aug. 1915, No. 301-305.
11. F.D., *Int.*, Aug. 1916, No. 267-268.
12. F.D., *Int.*, May 1916, No. 32.
13. F.D., *Int.*, Oct. 1918, No. 315-322.
14. F.D., *Int.*, Aug. 1918, No. 15.
15. F.D., *Sec.*, Nov. 1913, No. 15.
16. F.D., *Int.*, Nov. 1911, No. 60.
17. F.D., *Sec.*, July 1915, No. 24-27.

18. F.D., Sec., May 1913, No. 161.
19. Ibid.
20. F.D., Int., August, 1918, No. 16-44.
21. Ibid.
22. Ibid.
23. Ibid.
24. Ibid.
25. F.D., Int., Aug. 1919, No. 160-161.
26. Ibid.
27. Ibid.
28. Ibid.
29. F.D., Int., March 1920, No. 7.
30. Ibid.
31. F.D., Sec., May 1917, No. 104.
32. Ibid.
33. Ibid.
34. *Poorva Adhunik Rajasthan* by Raghubir Singh, p. 320.
35. *Jub Janta Jagi Thi* by Jagdish Prasad Deepak, p. 8.
36. Vijay Singh Pathik's statement, pp. 79-88.
37. Rajputana Agency Records, 1921, No. 69, List 1.
38. An interview with Dungar Singh Bhati.
39. Ibid.
40. Ibid.
41. Ibid.
42. *Jab Janta Jagi Thi* by Jagdish Prasad Deepak, p. 43.
43. *Vijay Singh Pathik* by Jagdish Prasad Deepak, p. 6.
44. *Rajputana Agency Records*, 1921, No. 69, List 1.
45. 'R.R. Holland', a letter to Fateh Singh, Feb. 4, 1920 (Bakshi Khana Udaipur).
46. *Rajputana Agency Records*, 1921, List 1.
47. *Hamara Rajasthan* by Prithvi Singh Mehta, pp. 332, 355.
48. *Chiefs and Leading Families in Rajputana* by C.S. Bayley, p. 28. Bhupal Singh was born on 22nd February, 1884.
49. *Rajputana Agency Records*, 1921, No. 69, List 1.
50. Ibid.
51. Ibid.
52. Ibid.
53. Ibid.
54. Memoirs of Motilal Tejawat.
55. Ibid.
56. *Scraps of Paper* by A.P. Nicholson, p. 245.
57. Rajputana Agency Records, 1921, No. 69, List 1.
58. *Scraps of Paper* by A.P. Nicholson, p. 245.

59. Robert Holland's letter to Maharana Fateh Singh, dated July 17, 1921.
60. *Scraps of Paper* by A.P. Nicholson, p. 245.
61. *Ibid.*
62. Robert Holland's letter to Maharana Fateh Singh, dated July 17, 1921.
63. *Rajputana Agency Records*, 1921, No. 69, List 1.
64. *Ibid.*
65. *Scraps of Paper* by A.P. Nicholson, p. 251.
66. *Jab Janta Jagi Thi* by Jagdeesh Prasad Deepak, pp. 39-44.
67. Bijay Singh Pathik's statement, p. 94.
68. *Ibid.*, pp. 99-100.
69. *Hamara Rajasthan* by Prithvi Singh Mehta, p. 358.
70. Ruling Princes, Chiefs and Leading Personages of Rajputana and Ajmer, p. 166.
71. The Earl of Reading, the Viceroy and Governor-General of India in his speech at the Udaipur banquet in Nov. 1923 lauded the Maharana's well ordered and abstemious life, observing that his was a shining example, in that respect, for the nobles and the people of his State. (*Speeches by the Earl of Reading*, Vol. II, p. 82).
72. Udaipur, 1885-1921, p. 7. Maud Diver observes; Sir Fateh Singh was the embodiment of Rajput royalty with his height, his fine features and his cleft beard. In full Darbar, surrounded by his nobles, he might have stepped straight out of the twelfth century... A life of austerity and restraint so preserved his vigour and energy that he could stickpig and shoot tigers up to late middle age. Stoutly he refused to let 'fire carriage" (railway train) enter his sacred city." (*Royal India*, p. 31).
73. Ruling Princes and Chiefs of India by Walter Lawrence. Lawrence writes: "He had the most perfect manners in the world, gracious and inscrutable alike to all. It was interesting to watch the effect of his wonderful manners on diverse persons. It was a privilege merely to sit with him."
74. F.D., *Int.*, Feb. 1904, No. 51-56. Udaipur 1921-26, p. 7.
75. He was so fond of hunting that the senior officers of the Mewar Government also accompanied his expeditions or were called there to take his orders. Jaisamand used to be generally the Capital during hunting expeditions. A.G.G., Residents and other senior British Officers were invited to join him there and they enjoyed his company. Most of the political and administrative matters, particularly relating to the British Government were settled in that sportful atmosphere. ("The Speeches of Sir Robert Holland", p. 17).

76. Fifty years in the service of India by G.E.C. Wakefield, p. 92. The author, who served the Udaipur Government as the Boundary Settlement Officer for about 6 years (1903-1908), observes: "The Maharana was one of the finest characters I have ever known, the soul of truth and honour, but very slow to decide because of his overwhelming fear of deciding wrongly. The Maharana used to advise him not to be in a hurry to settle cases, saying, 'If you leave files alone they often settle cases themselves."
77. *Ibid*. When Lord Curzon's observations, that in modern days Kings were the servants of the people etc., were conveyed to the Maharana, the latter reacted strongly and said that he could not understand anybody having such insane belief.
78. *Ibid*. "He had two Joint Prime Ministers, 'the Twins' as we called them, because he could not trust one." According to a tradition whenever he received a communication from the British Government, he got half of it read by one minister and the other half by the second minister. Sir Cloude Hill, one of the Political Agents in Mewar with whom Maharana Fateh Singh developed intimacy and feeling of confidence, observes: "The difficulties which have surrounded His Highness throughout his long reign have been due more to his unwillingness to concede any dignity... and to long delays in coming to a decision... 'Wasting' was one of the chief sources of grievance against the Maharana." (India-Step mother.)
79. Though Maharana Fateh Singh came to develop a suspicious nature, yet when he happened to trust anybody he reposed full confidence in him. Sir Claude Hill, in his memoirs, relates some very interesting anecdotes showing how the Maharana worked. He kept papers of all important cases with himself. One day the Maharana arrived at the Residency to consult Sir Hill on some matters. The H.H. on such occasions took one or two slips of paper with scribbled memoranda on them. One would be concealed in the folds of his headdress and another tucked into his waist-band. On the roof sitting on the chairs the slips were folded flat.
80. India's Princes: A souvenir (1903), p. 55.
81. *Udaipur Rajya Ka Itihas* by G.H. Ojha, Part II, p. 850.
82. *Ibid.*, p. 856.

15

The Assessment

The virtual deposition of Maharana Fateh Singh of Udaipur in the form of forced abdication of his powers caused great alarm among his fellow Native Rulers and people in general.[1] The measure was challenged on political and constitutional grounds. It was stated that the Treaty of Friendship and Alliance concluded in 1818 A.D. between the British Government and the Maharana, though on the basis of subordinate cooperation, clearly provided that the Maharana would always be the absolute ruler of his country and that the British jurisdiction shall not be introduced into his principality. The provision of subordinate cooperation did not mean vassalage.[2]

The measure of depriving him of his ruling powers was also at variance with the policy declared in Chapter X of the Report on Indian Constitutional Reforms, published in 1918. The report laid down the principle, "that in a composite society like India's and in times when ideas are changing rapidly, personal devotion survive as the active principle of the government, has been more clearly seen to have an abiding value." The Report admitted the fact that the Rulers were perturbed by the feeling that their sovereignty and independence had not been fully maintained, and apprehended that their individual rights and privileges might be swept away. In demanding his abdication, the Maharana stated, there was a good ground for such an apprehension, and no State could feel secure from intervention.[3]

The greatest confusion prevailed in the political circles over the fact that no ground other than the Maharana's advancing age and failing of his physical powers, was given for his abdication. Everybody knew that it was a lame excuse, as the Maharana was as healthy and energetic as ever.[4] Again, there was no precedent of compelling a Ruler to abdicate on account of his old age.[5] As regards the concentration of all the powers of the administration in his own hands, it was argued on the Maharana's behalf that it was an internal matter for his discretion, and that he had already consented to and was taking measures to decentralise the work of the government.[6] Another reason put forward by the Political Department was that there was an agrarian agitation in 1921 in Mewar, which took the form of something like an outbreak.[7] The Maharana, in this connection stated that the agitation had its origin in British India and the agitators were coming into Mewar from outside, over whom he could have little control. He also stated that the said agitation was not limited to Mewar only, it was prevailing in other Native States and in the British territory as well.[8]

The Maharana's supplications were of no avail. The reply which he received from the G.O.I. was that "the sure fact, that the whole of the administrative arrangements have been concentrated in your Highness's hands, has already rendered your task impossible of achievement." In the same communication, however, it recognised that "it was fully aware of the Maharana's labours on behalf of his people throughout many years and of his concern for justice, and of His Highness having performed the duties of his high office with unselfish and unremitting zeal".[9] The Maharana was not accused publicly of his stubborn resistance to reforms in Mewar, about which the British Agents made much ado in the political circles, as the Udaipur State was not the only State in Rajputana which was regarded as backward. Subsequent developments in Mewar after the change, bear out the real intentions of the British Government and its illogicity and pretentiousness. The change of power did not bring about the decentralisation of the administrative arrangements for which much fuss was created. Another strange aspect of the whole transaction was that whereas all the executive functions of the State were transferred to the Maharaj Kumar, administration of justice was still left in the Maharana's hands, while the greatest indictment by the British Agents against Fateh Singh was his "usual delay in dispensing justice."[10]

As has been stated heretofore, Maharana Fateh Singh always resented and resisted active interference and arbitrary advice and dictation on the part of the Residents and was opposed to all such reforms and changes as were contrary to his medieval concepts, or damaged his dignity and harmed his personal privileges and prerogatives as a ruler and the interests of his State.[11] We have already accounted how the Maharana resisted stubbornly the domineering attitude of the Residents with a large measure of success. The haughty and unscrupulous political officers of the British Government had been desiring and counselling his removal from power from the very early years of his rule.[12] The Udaipur case, however, disclosed two new aspects of the British policy towards the Native States. Firstly, the British Government was now fully aware of the odium that attached to the public punishment of the Native Rulers, and, therefore, wanted to avoid such a measure, and secondly, in consequence thereof, a policy of meddling on minor pretexts and forcing veiled depositions in the States was developed.[13]

We have waded through a crowded period of more than sixty years, in which the British influence continued to grow in Mewar despite resistance and it became a massive and all-pervading reality in 1921. Since the assumption of direct sovereignty in India in 1858 by the British Crown, a theory was adumberated that the British Crown had succeeded to the rights of the Mughal Emperors of India in addition to those acquired by the Treaties, Engagements and position of supremacy in the country.[14] *The Paramount Power, thereby, came to regard all the Native States of India as its feudatories and began to assert certain "feudal" rights, which involved the right to settle succession, constitute regency, permit adoption, grant titles, assume wardship and decree deposition etc.*[15] This theory was mainly responsible for doing away with all the independent powers the Native Rulers claimed to enjoy in accordance with the terms of the Treaties and for bringing under one level all the Native States of India irrespective of Treaty obligations. *A new note was struck in the policy of interference, when the British Government started claiming "its moral responsibility as the Paramount Power" to see that there* was minimum of good government in the States, Lord Mayo declared at Ajmer, in 1870, "If we support you in your power, we expect in return good Government and demand that everywhere through the length and breadth of Rajputana, justice and order shall prevail, that every man's property shall be secure....... that you shall make roads and undertake the construction of those works of irrigation which will improve the conditions of the people and swell the revenues of your States, that you shall encourage education and provide for the relief of the sick."[16] This policy resulted in the practice of veiled intervention by the loaned officers of the British Government, viz. the nominated 'Dewans' and strict control through the Political Agents. The attempt was to aggrandise not the territories but the power of the Central Government, and to make the Indian States a part of the Indian Polity.[17]

The history of relations between the Udaipur State and the British Government narrated heretofore amply shows that the former was reduced, irrespective of Treaty obligations, to the status of a feudatory in all respects during the post-Revolt period. The ruler was granted an Adoption Sanad in 1861. After this the adoptions in the Family were always approved by the G.O.I. Whenever a new Ruler succeeded, his succession was regarded final only after it had been confirmed by the G.O.I. Whenever succession disputes arose at Udaipur, as in 1874, and 1884, it was the word of the British Government that decided it finally. During the minorities of Shambhu Singh and Sajjan Singh it assumed the functions of the guardian of the minors and appointed Regency Council to administer the State. In 1863, when the Regency Council failed to function, the Political Agent assumed all the powers of the State Government until the Ruler became major. Even after the Ruler's investiture with full powers of government, certain temporary restrictions were put upon him as was done in the cases of Sajjan Singh and Fateh Singh. The orders of previous Rulers were reversed during Regency governments presided over by the British Agents as happened in the Deogarh succession fee case during Shambhu Singh's minority. When the Ruler became major and desired to stick to his predecessor's orders, he was not permitted to do so. Titles and honours were granted to the Rulers of Mewar, though they never accepted them with pleasure. The *durbars* were held from time to time by the British Government to display its supremacy making it compulsory for all the Native Rulers to attend them. The Rulers of Mewar were, despite their opposition, compelled to attend the same. We have seen how Maharana Fateh Singh resisted all such actions as reduced his status to a feudatory and even went to the extent of defiance during the Delhi *Durbars* of 1903 and 1911.

The Political Agents of the British Government behaved usually as masters and dictators. "The whisper of the Residency was the thunder of the State", and there was no matter on which the Political Agent or the Resident did not feel justified in giving advice. Commenting on the affairs, Prince of Wales wrote to Queen Victoria from India, in 1875, "what struck me most forcibly was the rude and rough manner with which the English Political officers treat them (the Native Rulers). It is indeed much to be deplored and the system is, I am sure, quite wrong." The history of Mewar provides several instances of the Political Agents' high handed and dictatorial behaviour. They interfered with the personal life of the Rulers and intimidated them, as was done during Shambhu Singh's minority. They appointed teachers of their own choice for them. They got removed from Udaipur, at their will, such favourites and counsellors of the Ruler, as they did not like. Several times they gave protection to those officials of the State, whom the Ruler found guilty of misappropriation of State money or of any other fault. They are found taking action on the representations of the State nobles and officers against the decisions of the Maharana and asking explanation from him. *The Rulers were required to visit the Residency for consultations, and the Political Agents considered most loyal and friendly the Ruler who did their bidding without any protest. Thus they reduced the Ruler to a mere protege.* Maharana Fateh Singh resisted this attitude and tried to assert his internal independence much to the irritation and resentment of the Residents. Consequently, the latter usually made exaggerated complaints to the Supreme Government and hatched conspiracy against him.

The Treaty rights of Mewar were infringed and internal independence of the State was violated in several other ways as well. The British Government imposed such agreement on the State as harmed its interests and dignity, e.g., agreements regarding railways, salt, opium, extraditions, etc. In the same way the extension of British postal and telegraph services, creation of the Imperial Service Troops, introduction of the British jurisdiction in the cantonments and Residency, introduction of the British currency in the State and several other measures, on the part of the British Government, further reduced the independent status of Mewar. There were a large number of British subjects in the State over whom the Ruler had no control.

Mewar, by the end of the second decade of the twentieth century, was still a backward state, despite several reforms introduced during the last sixty years. The administration was carried on by the Maharana himself assisted by two ministers and their staff, who conjointly formed the executive department, the *Mahakama Khas*.[18] (During 1918-19 Pandit Sukhdeo Prasad and Mehta Jagannath Singh were acting as the ministers).[19] Subordinate to the *Mahakama Khas* were a number of departments, with a separate officer as the head of each, e.g., the Revenue Department under Hakim Mal, the Treasury under a *Daroga*, the Customs under a Superintendent, the Public Works under a State Engineer, the Irrigation under an Engineer, and so on.[20]

For administrative purposes the *Khalsa* lands of the State were divided into eleven '*Zilas*' and six '*paraganas*'.[21] An official called 'Hakim' had charge of each of these seventeen divisions or districts. *The Bhomat area of Kherwara and Kotra was included in this arrangement, but in practice the British Political Superintendent and Commandant of the Mewar Bhil Corps at Kherwara exercised almost independent civil and military control in the area and state matters were seldom referred to the Maharana.* There were in Mewar 24 *jagirdars* of the first class and 32 nobles of the second class and several other fief-holders,[22] who had internal administrative arrangement of their own, which was, in most cases, totally corrupt and despotic. The *Kalambandi* of 1879 had given powers to the *Durbar* to hear, directly, the cases of heinous nature, taking place in the estates.[23]

Notwithstanding the above arrangements, the government of the State was still carried on in the old way of personal rule. The orders emanated from and decisions were taken by the Ruler himself. His ministers were merely his secretaries, responsible to him and working for him in the *Mahakama Khas*. He nominated several members to *Mahadraj Sabha*, the highest judicial council of the state, to assist him in judicial matters. But the members had no powers and, generally, the Council did not function at all. The beginning had yet not been made towards the establishment of the representative institutions in the State, such as elected municipal boards, etc. Some rules relating to the administrative arrangements in the State had been enacted, e.g., Administrative Rules of 1872-73, Rules for the Administration of Mewar, No. 1 (1880), Stamps and Registration Rules of 1873-74, etc., thereby certain codes and regulations, in force in British India, were taken as the basis of decisions, but the proceedings in civil and criminal courts were, generally, guided by ancient Hindu law and local customs. At lower level the *Hakims* and *Naib Hakims* had judicial powers along with their executive functions. The position in this regard had changed little from what it was in 1880. Theoretically, the Maharana had the powers of the appellate authority over the *jagir* area, but actually very few cases were referred to him.[24]

Reforms, introduced in the State from time to time, brought Mewar gradually out of isolation and laid basis for modernisation of the State. *Railways had been introduced in the State and a large number of big and small roads had been constructed.* There were about 140 miles of metalled road and 300 miles of country highways in Mewar. But there were very few roads in the hilly area of the State. There were about 40 British post offices and four telegraph offices, in addition to the local post offices of the State.[25]

Industry had made no progress in Mewar. At Udaipur, ivory and wooden bangles, cotton cloth printed in gold and silver and swords and daggers were manufactured. Bhilwara was noted for its articles of tin. There were soap factories at Udaipur and Bheendar and a paper factory at Gosunda. There were State controlled ginning factories at Bhilwara, Kapasan and Gulabpura. The lead and zinc mines of Jawar were lying idle. The work in mica mines had just started in a part of Mewar. The principal exports of the State included wool, cotton, opium, cooking utensils and sheep and goats, while salt, sugar, tobacco, metals and piece goods were imported.[26]

More than sixty per cent of the people were engaged in agriculture and the methods of cultivation continued to be of primitive character.[27] Revenue settlement had been introduced in the *Khalsa* area between 1884 and 1894 for a term of twenty years, but it was not renewed after the expiry of the term. *The conditions of the cultivators in the hilly part of the Khalsa area and in the jagir area of the State were very poor and miserable. It was particularly in those parts that people died in a large number, whenever a famine or an epidemic occurred.* The class of nobles had greatly degenerated and was entirely irresponsible and despotic. The chief function of this class during medieval times was fighting. As it was no longer required and as they disliked enrolling themselves in the State army, they gradually lost their martial character, indulged in factional quarrels and became addicted to wine and women. The British Government, notwithstanding its efforts to introduce some changes in the State administration under the direct control of the Ruler, remained averse to any changes in the *jagir* area. Consequently, people smarted and chafed under an exploiting, ignorant and arbitrary management of the worst character.

The State maintained a military force of 6015 men of all ranks, namely, 2549 regulars and 3466 irregulars. The regulars comprised 1750 infantry, 560 cavalry and 239 gunners. There were Imperial Service Troops numbering 129 of whom 86 were sent out on Imperial service during the First World War.[28] There were about 543 police men for city and the Girwa area.[29] In other parts of the State there was no regular police force.

The Revenues collected in 1918-19 was about Rs. 52 lakhs and expenditure was about Rs. 43 lakhs. The revenues were derived from land, customs and transit duties, railways, Salt Agreement, tribute from *jagirdars* and other miscellaneous sources. Mewar Government paid 2 lakhs of Imperial rupees to the British Government as tribute.[30] About twenty per cent of the revenues was spent on the Maharana's personal and palace expenses.[31] Progress in the spheres of education for boys and children and health services placed haltingly in the State. By 1920, in addition to 10 schools maintained by the Missionary societies, there were three Secondary Schools and one High School at Udaipur and two Anglo-vernacular Middle Schools at Bhilwara and Chittor. Total yearly expenditure incurred on education by the State was about Rs. 36,000, about half of which was realised by a special cess from the cultivators.[32] Besides these schools there were a few traditional indigenous institutions as well, viz., *maktabs* and *pathshalas*. There were about 16 hospitals and dispensaries in the State including a Central Jail Hospital. They were placed under the Supervision of the Residency Surgeon at Udaipur. Total yearly expenditure incurred on the Medical Department was about Rs. 49,000.[34] The State spent, ranging from 3 lakhs to 5 lakhs yearly, on public works and irrigation. There were forty-one Imperial post offices and four telegraph offices. The indigenous postal system known as Brahmini Dak continued working for State and private correspondence and at the places not served by the imperial system.[35] Thus by 1920 the State of Mewar was still a very backward country notwithstanding a few reforms and renovations. However, under the impact of mass awakening in the country and political agitation, the demand for reforms grew with momentum in Mewar manifesting itself in the unrest and uprising in the agriculturists. The close of the period of this study marks the beginning of the end of the lingering medieval order in the State heralding the new epoch of democratic urge and mass upsurge.

Notes and References

1. *Royal India* by Moud Diver, p. 33.
2. Relations of Indian States with the G.O.I. by K.M. Panikkar, pp. 68-70. The King Emperor, George V in his proclamation of 1919 had declared: "I take the occasion again to assure the Princes of India of my determination ever to maintain unimpaired the privileges, rights and dignities of the Princes of India. The Princes may rest assured that this pledge remains inviolate and inviolable."
   Indian States and British Paramountsy by S. Sankar. Arguments put forward on behalf of the Maharana against the British action laid stress on certain practices and prerogatives signifying internal independence of the Maharana as the coins minted at Udaipur had the words "Dost London", Udaipur still retained its own currency, postal stamps and internal postal system and the Maharana never bowed before the Imperial problem (as in 1903).
3. Expressing concern over the action, the Standing Committee of the Chamber of Princes in its memorandum to the Butler Committee observed: "the Government of India proceeded, in July 1921, to take peremptory measures which resulted in the signal and public humiliation of His Highness (of Udaipur). This action involved repudiation of treaty rights and departure from the lines of policy, definitely prescribed for the regulation of the affairs between the

Government of India and the Indian States............" (*Relations of Indian States with the G.O.I.* by K.M. Panikkar, pp. 68-70).
4. *Scraps of Paper* by A.P. Nicholson, pp. 245-250.
   Col. Patterson, the A.G.G. for Rajputana and Lord Reading the Governor-General for India testify to this fact. Speaking at Udaipur banquet on 8th Jan. 1926. Col. Patterson said, "Your Highness still retains the vigour which was so remarkable a quarter of the century ago and that far from being obliged to give up your shikar expeditions, you are still able without undue fatigue to yourself to wear out in a day's sport the hardiest of your nobles." (Udaipur, 1926, p. 9).
   Lord Reading, speaking at the State banquet at Udaipur on 11th Nov., 1923, said, "I am gratified to find that the years which have elapsed since I last saw your Highness have not robbed you of your due measure of health and activity at your Highness's time of life." (*Ibid.*, p. 4).
5. The Political History of British India under Crown abounds with numerous examples of gross interference in the internal affairs of the Native States, going to the extent of the curtailment of the governing powers of the Rulers and even the deposition of the Ruling Chiefs on flimsy pretexts. To quote some precedents, the ruler of Kashmir was compelled "to resign active participation in the government of the State in 1899 on the pretext of disorder in the State. The same year witnessed the Resident taking over the charge of administration from the Ruler of Indore on the grounds of maladministration. In 1896, Maharaja Rana Zalim Singh II of Jhalawar was deposed on the grounds of "maladministration, misconduct and violation of his obligations to the British Government." As early as 1868 Maharaja Takhta Singh of Jodhpur was subjected to unjust pressure to hand over the charge of the government to a ministry appointed by the British Government.
6. *Scraps of Paper* by A.P. Nicholson, pp. 245-250.
7. *Relations of Indian States with the G.O.I.* by K.M. Panikkar, p. 68.
8. *Scraps of Paper* by A.P. Nicholson, p. 251.
9. *Ibid.*
10. *Scraps of Paper* by A.P. Nicholson, p. 251.
11. For some years before 1899 the Resident at Udaipur (Col. Ramsay) used to take action on the representations of the feudal Lords of Mewar and asked for explanation from the Udaipur Darbar. With the arrival of Col. Yate in 1900 as the Resident, a change in that attitude is visible but that did not last long. (*Indian States and British Paramountsy* by S. Sankar).
12. F.D., *Int.*, Feb. 1904, No. 51-56.

13. *Relations of Indian States with the G.O.I.* by K.M. Panikkar, pp. 69-70.
14. *Indian States and British India* by Gurumukh Nihal Singh.
15. *Relations of Indian States with the G.O.I.* by K.M. Panikkar, pp. 39-40.
16. *Ibid.*, p. 36. This sort of interference on moral and humanitarian grounds was resorted to under the influence of Gladstone, the Liberal Party leader, whose solicitude to force upon Independent Turkey internal reforms and humanitarian measures is well-known.
17. *Ibid.*, p. 37.
18. *Indian States* by Somerset Playne, pp. 19-20.
19. F.D., *Int.*, Jan. 1920, No. 272.
20. *A Gazetteer of the Udaipur State* by K.D. Erskine, p. 63.
21. *India States* by Somerset Playne, pp. 19-20.
22. *Ibid.*
23. *A Gazetteer of the Udaipur State* by K.D. Erskine, p. 66.
24. *Ibid.* p. 65.
25. *Indian States* by Somerset Playne, pp. 19-20.
26. *Ibid. A gazetteer of the Udaipur State* by K.D. Erskine, pp. 55-56.
27. *Indian States* by Somerset Playne, pp. 19-20.
28. *Indian States* by Somerset Playne, pp. 19-20.
29. F.D., *Int.*, Jan. 1920, No. 272.
30. *Ibid.*
31. *Gazetteer of the Udaipur State* by K.D. Erskine, p. 69.
32. *Indian States* by Somerset Playne, pp. 19-20.
33. *The Ruling Chiefs, Nobles and Zamindars of India* by A. Vadivelu, p. 73.
34. F.D., *Int.*, Jan. 1920, No. 272.
35. *The Ruling Chiefs, Nobles and Zamindars of India* by A. Vadivelu, p. 73.

Index

Accession:
    of Rana Sambhu Singh, 192
    Fateh Singh, 299
Achaldas Khichi ri-Vachanika, 21
Acharpradeep, 93
Acharya, 92
Action against Sohan Singh, 251
Administrative and Economic Aspects, 118
Administrative Changes, 285
Adoption Sanads, 190
Agreement Regarding Railway Line, 267
Ahilyan Shri Durbar Rajya Mewar, 205
Ahmad, Nizamuddin, 52, 59
Antecedents, 1
Anti-British Stir in Rajputana, 348
Appointments of the Council of Regency, 194
Arnapurna Mandir, 10
Arrangements for Maharana's Education, 254
Attack of Neemuch, 172
Attempt to Commit Sati by the Palace Ladies, 248

Bagada, Mahmud, 56
Banera Chief's Effort to be Independent of Mewar, 283
Banjara and Gadolia, 269
Banmata, 45
Bapota, 138
Barhat, 135

Bari Sadri, 40
Beginning of Reforms, 214
    Re-appointment of Kothari Singh, 214
    Maharana and the Chiefs, 215
    Reconciliation with the Salumbar Chief, 216
    Succession Case of Amet Reopened, 217
    Reopaheli-Lamba Case, 219
    Deogarh Chief's Succession Fee Case, 220
    Maharana Assets his Suzerain Right, 221
    Trial of Mehta Ajeet Singh, 223
    Extradition Treaty, 1868, 225
    Bhil Disturbances in the Hilly Tract, 227
    Illegal Detention of the British Prisoners, 228
    Maharana's Severe Measures against Sati, 229
    Cases of Witch-hunting, 230
    Ajmer Durbar of 1870, 232
    Establishment of Opium Scales at Udaipur, 234
    Administrative Reforms, 236
    Administrative of Justice, 236
    Revenue Settlement, 237
    Changes in District Administration, 240
    Maharana Awarded with the Title of G.C.S.I., 241

Maharana's Serious Illness an Arrest of Mehta, 242
Personalty of Shambhu Singh, 243
Bhandari, Khemraj, 276
Bhats, Charans, Purohits, 135
Bhil, 29
Bhil Disturbances in Hilly District, 274
Bhil ka Gaon, 164
Bhonk of Persian Chronicles, 77
Bhopa, 230
Bhumia, 99, 134
Bhumija, 106
Bombay Cavalry, 161
Bombay Civil Service, 265
British Government:
  Approved Eden's Policy, 200
  Presses for Reforms, 324
British Reverses at Auwa and Kota, 167
British Supermacy Restorted in the Internal Affairs, 368
Bux, Sheikh Mohammed, 168

Cannaught Bandh, 315
Case of Mewar Portion of Merwara, 278
Case of the Spurious son of Sakat Singh, 303
Capt. Hardy, 161
Chacha and Mera, 13
Chahamanas of Ajmer, 2
Chakhra Charan, 8
Chakari, 144
Chalukyas of Gujarat, 2
Chamar, Morchal, 89, 234
Chand, Mehta Gokul, 252
Chandi-Shatak, 87
Chanwar, 342
Chaprasis, 165
Charans, 71

Chauhan, Khichi, 29
Chauhan, Prithvi Raj, 3
Chaumukha, 107
Chetavani ra Chungatia, 340
Chhaganlal, Kothari, 261
Chhatoond, 144, 238
Chhogamal, Seth Jawaharmal, 309
Chhoti Sadri, 164, 265
Chishti, Shaikh Muin-ud-din, 51
Chobiasa, Dayalal, 278
Chudasama, Mandalik, 66
Chunda, Kunwar, 15
Chundawat, Raghavadeva, 39
Col. Bradford, 300
Col. Breokes, 232
Col. Eden, 198
Col. Holmes, 173
Col. Miles, 301
Colvin, Sir Elliot, 326
Col. Wyllie, 329
Completion of Revenue Settlement, 302
Construction of Railway Line from Chittor to Udaipur, 314
Court of Directors, 148
Cultural Achievements:
  Literary Activity, 85
  Works of other Scholars, 88
  Scholars Associated with Courts, 89
  Contribution of the Jains, 92
  Tapagachha Group, 92

Dandani, Shams Khan, 20, 57
Das, Joshi, Narayan, 306
Dass, Kaviraj Shyamal, 8
Delegation of Ruling Powers to the Maharaj Kumar, 364
Delhi Durbar of 1903, 340
Deora Dungar, 79
Devi, Saubhagya, 37

Devi, Shringar, 75
Dharma, 33
Dharma Shastra, 337
Dhonsa, 197
Direct Interference in the Internal Affairs, 198
Disagreement between the Resident and the A.G.G., 311
Dismissal of:
    Kothari Kesari Singh, 200
    Regency Council, 202
    of Mehta Pannalal, 312
Durbar, 157

East India Company, 140, 153
Eklinga Mahatmya, 64, 85
English Raj, 205
Expulsion of Maharana's Favourites, 258

Fakers, 175
Famine Relief Measures, 321
Faruqi, Raja Ali Khan, 10
Fiscal Organisation, 122
Fiuzdari, Diwani, 208

Gazetteer of Rajputana, 34
General Michel, 177
Geological Survey, 355
Ghuri, Sultan Muhammad, 34
Girdawar, 278
Girwa Hakim, 304
Gitagovinda, 89
Gosain of Nathwara, 255
Governor-General Disapprove's Col. Herbets Dealings, 259
Grasia, 134
Gujarati, Qutbuddin, 60
Gulf of Cambay, 141
Gurvavali, 93

Hamir's Occupation of Chittor, 7

Hanumanagopura, 102
Harbhamji in Udaipur Service, 321
Hiranya, 122
History Department, 289
Holland, Sir Robert, 364, 366
H.R.H. Prince of Wales Visit, 343
Hume, A.C., 272

Ijlas Mamuli, 286
Imperial Assemblage of 1911, 343
Imperial Interest and Mewar:
    Imperial Service Troops Raised in Mewar, 352
    Maharana's Cooperation in the Great War, 352
    Restriction on Poppy Cultivation in Mewar, 353
    Mica Mining Work Started in Mewar, 354
    Depreciation of the Value of British, 356
    Question of Police Reforms in Mewar, 357
Imperial Service Troops, 380
Indian Railway Act, 314

Jagir, 157
Jambuswamirasa, 94
Jauhar, 5
Jawas Succession Case, 337
Jaya Stambha, 33

Kadia Prashasti, 90
Kala Gora ka Maidan, 183
Kalambandi, 328
Kalambandi with the Chiefs, 281
Kalanidhi, 112
Kamdar, Badriji, 175
Kamraj-Ratisar, 86
Kanthal, 46
Karan, Khem, 72
Kalyan Khan Rasa, 57

Index ✦ 389

Kesari Hind, 260
Khalji, Alauddin, 4
Khan, Ali, 52
Khan, Bahar, 35
Khan, Dilawar, 19
Khan, Fidan, 77
Khan, Firoz, 20, 55
Khan, Ghazi, 49
Khan, Ikhtiyar, 76
Khan, Khizr, 6
Khan, Mujahid, 58
Khan, Rahmat Ali, 182
Khan, Shams, 57, 64
Khan, Umar, 31
Khan, Zafar, 14
Khareeta, 178
Khas Ruqquas, 262
Khidmati, 49
Khillat, 234
Khillat to Maharana, 180
Khyats of Mewar, 19
Kiledar, 30
Kine-killing, 204
Kirtistambha, 36, 64
Kishan Panchayat, 361
Kulya Mandapa, 110
Kumbhalgarh Prashasti, 81
Kyamkhan Rasa, 20
Kyamkhani of Jhunjhunu, 72

Lake, Fateh Sagar, 312
Lakha's Marriage with Rathor Rao Chauhan's Daughter, 15
Lal, Kothari Chhagan, 148
Lal, K.S., 6
Lawrence, George, 156, 202
Lord Curzon, 340
Lord Lake, 143
Lord Lytton, 260
Lord Ripon, 290
Lt. Col. Gordon, 339

Lt. Col. Hutchinson, 229
Lt. Col. Mavtelli, 310
Lt. Col. Walter, 269
Lt. Col. Wright, 250
Lylle, Alfred, 138

Mahadraj Sabha, 285, 320, 363
Mahajana Sabha, 124
Mahakama Khas, 237, 260, 335
Maha Mahopadyaya, 289
Maharana Asserts his Sovereignty, 327
Maharana Attends Delhi Durbar of 1877, 260
Maharana Kshetrasimha, 1364-1382 A.D., 10
Maharana Kumbha, 18, 74
Maharana Lakshasimha, 1382-1397, 13
Maharana Mokul, 17
Maharana Supprots the Cause of the British, 158
Maharana's Attendants and Relations Expelled, 198
Maharana Invested with Ruling Powers, 259
Maharana Refuses to have a Dewan, 319
Maharana's Congratulation, 178
Maharana's Counsel to other Rajput Rulers, 176
Maharana's Efforts to Gain Control of the Administration, 305
Maharao Lakha of Sirohi, 80
Mahila Mandal, 359
Mahmud Ghazni, 3
Major Burton, 158
Major Mackenzie, 227
Major Pinhey, 324
Mal, Pancholee Kuber, 170
Malcolm, Sir John, 191
Mandap, 109
Mandapika, 123, 125

Mandu Kalpusutra, 97
Manjaniks, 54
Mansur-ul-Mulk, 48
Matrikas, 107
Matri Kundia, 266
Max, Karl, 150
Measures to Suppress the Sati Custom, 197
Mehta Ajeet Singh's Case, 202
Mehta, Rai Pannalal, 313
Mewar:
    Source of Trouble for the British Government, 350
Mewar and the British, 139
Mewar Bhil Corps at Kherwara, 231, 251, 277, 338
Mewar Feudalism, 131
Mewar Pukar, 365
Mewar Raj, 37
Mewar-Shahpura Border, 223
Mewari, Lali, 17
Moond Catti, 219
Moostagirs, 239
Mughal Emperor Babar, 142
Mukhya-mantri, 120
Murder of Mokul, 22
Mutinies at Nasirabad and Neemuch, 160

Nagar Seth, 207
Naik, Gomla, 202
Naik, Kripa, 202
Navin Rajasthan, 361
Naubat Khana, 39
Nawab of Tonk, 181
Nawlakha Oswal Shanpal, 114
Nazarana, 232
Nimbahera taken back from the Maharana, 180
Nixon, Lt. Col. J.P., 224
Nrityaratna Kosha, 87

Occupation of Nimbahera by Mewar Troops, 170
Ojha, G.S., 13
Oppressing of the Bhils in the Hilly Tract, 263

Pai-Kotra, 27
Painting, 94
    Architecture, 98
    Forts, 98
    Kumbhalgarh, 100
    Achalgarh, 101
    Chittorgarh, 102
    Temple, 105
    Ranpur Jain Temple, 107
    Ekalingji, 108
    Kumbhaswami Temple, 109
    Shrinagar Chauri, 110
    Sculpture, 111
    Music, 112
    Religion, 113
    Vaishnavism, 114
    Jainism, 114
Panchakula, 125
Panchayats, 126
Parwana, 254
Pathyaratna Kosha, 86
Patwee, 233
Peasant Unrest, 358
Personality of Fateh Singh, 369
Personality of Sajjan Singh, 290
Political Agent's Government, 1863-1865, 204
Political Unrest:
    Fateh Singh's Abdication, 348
Pradhan, 319
Postponement of the Railway Project, 307
Prasadmandan, 91, 106
Progress of Reforms, 315
Province, N.W., 265

Punishment of Begun Chief, 208
Purohit, 195-96
Pursuit of the Neemuch Mutineers, 164

Queen's Proclamation, 177
Queen Victoria, 251
Queen Victoria's Jubilee Celebrations, 301
Question of Maintaining Imperia Service Troops, 307

Rajadhiraj, 221
Rajadhiraj of Shahpura, 332
Rajaniti Shastra, 85
Rajasthan Seva Sangh, 362
Rajballabhamandana, 122
Rajput Chivalry Displayed at Kesunda, 163
Raj Vinod Mahakavya, 68
Rakhwali, 145
Rana Raj Singh of Mewar, 256
Ranmal of Eklingji, 11
Rao Chunda of Mandor, 16
Rao, Lachhman, 201
Rao of Setrawa, 71
Rao, Pandit Yadav, 163
Rao, Sahasmal, 30
Rasik-priya, 87
Rathor, Narbad, 130
Ratnasimha, 5
Rawat Ranjeet Singh of Asind, 336
Recalcitrant Chiefs of Mewar, 181
Reforms by the Political Agent, 206
Regency Council in Mewar, 1874, 202, 334
Regency Council's Government, 1874-1876, 252
Rehman, Maulvi Abdul, 253
Relation with Malwa:
    Loss of Gagraun, 47
    Loss of Ajmer, 50
    Loss of Mandalgarh, 52
Relations with Gujarat-Nagor, 54
Relations with Rajput Chiefs:
    Settlement with Jodha Rathor, 70
    Heads of Bundi, 75
    Deora Chauhan's of Sirohi and Abu, 78
    Other Rajput Chiefs, 81
Relations with the Rathors of Mandor, 21
Re-organisation to the State Council, 261
Residence Surgeon at Udaipur, 383
Resistance Calms Down, 210
Resistance to the British, 190
Rising of 1857 and Mewar, 153
Rukamgarh-ka-Chhapar, 174
Rupamandan, 105, 129
Ruqqa, 159

Sabha, 119
Sabhya Sabha, 358
Sachiva, 120
Saith, W.H., 265
Sahasmal, Maharao, 78
Sahiliyon-ki-Bari, 208
Sajjan Kirti Sudhakar, 289
Salt Agreement, 271
Salumbar Chief Threat to the Maharana, 166
Samanta, 132
Samastara-javali-Samalankrita, 4
Sangheshwar, 115
Saraswati, Dayanand, 291
Sati, 149
Sati Affair on the Death of Maharana Swaroop Singh, 193
Sawagpadikaman Sutta Chunni, 96
Sayyid Sultan, 51
Seelay, Sir J.R., 153

Setback for the Interference, 320
Sethi, Arjun Lal, 361
Seth's Affairs, 309
Settlement Operations and Stir in the Peasants, 264
Sevadal, 360
Shah, Ahmad, 27
Shah Firuz, 176
Sainya-durga, 99
Salila-durga, 99
Shah, Ami, 11
Shah, Hoshang, 31
Shah, Sultan Tughlaq, 6
Shahzada, 35
Shambhu Paltan, 241
Shambhu Ratna Pathshala, 206, 240
Shail Kantar Sambhandhini Sabha, 264
Shihab Hakim, 41
Shikhara, 109, 370
Showers, Capt. C.L., 157
Shreshthi, 107
Simha, Hada Lal, 11
Singh, Aman, 275
Singh, Amar, 142
Singh, Baba Gyan, 330
Singh, Banera Raj Govind, 330
Singh, Bar, 13
Singh, Bhopal, 216
Singh, Chatra, 218
Singh, Kesari, 158
Singh, Khushal, 182
Singh, Kothari Balwant, 310
Singh, Kunwar Raghunath, 339
Singh, Maha, 180
Singh, Maharaj Gaj, 253
Singh, Maharaj Shardul, 192
Singh, Maharaj Sohan, 249
Singh, Maharana Fateh, 287, 298, 325
Singh, Maharana Raj, 283
Singh, Maharana Sajjan, 248, 259, 378

Singh, Maharawal Samant, 136
Singh, Mehta Ajeet, 204
Singh, Mehta Bhopal, 323
Singh, Mehta Sher, 162, 195
Singh, Rana Swaroop, 148
Singh, Rao Jodh, 224
Singh, Rawat Pratap, 276
Singh, Sahiwala Arjun, 305, 319
Singh, Sawai, 171
Singh, Shambhu, 181, 268
Singh, Sheonath, 218
Singh, Zalim, 216
Sisodia-Rathor, 37
Situation in Mewar, 157
Slavery, Traffic in Women and Cases of Infanticide, 270
Sleeman, Sir Willion, 190
Smith, Jacob, 325
Smith, Major Dunlop, 322
Smith, Manners, 356
Smriti, 126
Som Saubhagya Kavya, 97
Stir in Udaipur Troops at Neemuch, 166
Strike and Disturbance in Udaipur City, 207
Succession Dispute of Bohera Jagir, 249, 284
Sultan of Malwa, 31
Sunder, Muni, 93
Swaroop Shahi Rupee, 149

Talwar Bandai, 196, 217, 220
Tamboli, Gwala, 129
Tantia Tope in Mewar, 173
Tarka Shastra, 85
Temporary Restrictions Placed upon the Maharana's Powers, 300
Thakur of Bandnore Sentenced, 199
Throne comes to Kumbha:
    Age of Kumbhaat his Accession, 27

So-called Battle of Sarangpur, 32
Internal Troubles in Mewar, 36
Tika, 8
Title of C.I.E. Conferred on Bakhta Singh, 283
Title of G.C.S.I. Conferred on the Maharana, 289
Tope, Tantia, 173
Towards a New Awakening, 184
Treaty of 1869, 227
Tughlaq, Firuzshah, 14

Udaipur-ri-Khyat, 9
Udaipur Troops Rescue British Refugees at Dungla, 162
Unrest in Udaipur, 205
Upadeshtarangini, 93

Vadyaratna Kosha, 86
Vaishonav Shrine of Nathdwara, 342
Van Mata, 5
Vanshprakash, 9
Various Measures of Reforms, 287
Vastumandan, 91
Vastushastra, 105
Vayaganama, 120
Verma, Shyamji Krishna, 329, 333

Viceroy's Visit to Udiapur, 255
Victoria's Diamond Jubilee Celebration, 321
Vidya Pracharani Sabha, 360
Vigat, 73
Vir Bharat Sabha, 349
Vir Vinod, 33
Vishaya, 121
Vishikha, 103
Vishnu, 104
Visits of the Duke of Cannaught and Prince Albert, 301
Visits of various Viceroys to Udaipur, 341
Vrindavati, 81

Wakfield, G.W., 325
Walter Krit Rajput Hitkarini Sabha, 370
Wingate and Thompson Retire from Udaipur, 312
Withdrawal of Prohibitory order on Export of Cotton, 326

Yadavas of Devagiri. 3

Zanana, 168